APPLIED

PSYCHOLOGY

Problems in Living and Work

B. von **HALLER GILMER**

PROFESSOR OF PSYCHOLOGY
CARNEGIE INSTITUTE OF TECHNOLOGY

McGraw-Hill Book Company
*New York, St. Louis, San Francisco,
Dallas, London, Toronto, Sydney*

1 2 3 4 5 6 7 8 9 10 (MP) 7 4 3 2 1 0 6 9 8 7

DEDICATED TO

Ellen, Nan, Tom, Yip,
Fritz, Ken, and Ted

Preface

◆ ◆ ◆

How can the vast amount of information which psychology has be of interest to you? This text is designed to help answer this question.

There are many excellent books in the general field of psychology, in the specialized areas of child and adolescent psychology, and in the areas of social adjustment and work. There are several good textbooks on applied psychology. Why write another? The answer is threefold. First, there is no one text of applied psychology covering the wide band of practical problems from childhood through the many aspects of adjustment and work. Most texts concentrate on child psychology, on adolescent psychology, on adjustment, or on industrial psychology. This is the first text to bring all this material together in one book. Second, books on applied psychology usually have been written for advanced levels. This is a book for the beginning student. Third, most texts cover much detail of technique and methodology. They often present the material with the assumption that each reader plans to specialize in psychology. This book is written for the person who wants general principles and practical answers to problems of daily living and work.

This text is written with emphasis on problems we face in raising children and in understanding teen-age behavior. It also deals with problems of middle age and of retirement and with stress situations in which there are no winners, only survivors. Much attention is given to the adjustment of the college-age student, with special discussion of how he or she can best prepare for career decisions. The text includes some material on work in industry. This material is taken in part from the author's textbook, "Industrial Psychology." A final chapter is devoted to psychology in the military, giving students a view of this wide area of applied psychology that may relate to many of them, directly or indirectly.

Psychology has become so specialized that the experimentalist has difficulty understanding the technical language of the clinician and that of the other branches of the science and the profession, and vice versa.

v

This book treats all of psychology at the same nontechnical level. Since it is written for the first- or second-year college-student level, subjects are discussed in everyday terms, with new concepts and words introduced only when needed. In this way the text is well adapted for continuing education programs of various types.

All references have been put in the back of the book, with no citations in the body of the text. Most references can be identified by title. Some extend beyond the scope of the text for those who may wish to expand their technical reading. Suggested readings for possible follow-up are given at the end of each chapter.

A summary is given for each chapter, beginning with Chapter 2. This summary is followed by Suggestions for Thinking and Discussion, designed to stimulate the individual to extend his thinking beyond the text in areas of personal reference. The suggestions may also serve as starting points for class discussions. The problem-solving approach has been stressed, rather than technical description.

More and more we are becoming a nation of people who have problems. The science and the profession of psychology are concerned with these problems at two levels. First, we are interested in these problems as scientists in coming to understand the nature of human behavior. Second, as applied professional psychologists we are interested in providing people with information which we hope may lead to solutions of many of these problems. May the reader note the word "many." May he also note that this leaves other problems to which we have no suggested solutions.

Let us take a look at the general kinds of problems we shall discuss in the five parts of this book. This overall view will provide a chance to think of behavior as a whole before we turn to specific problems. The book proceeds from the general bases of psychology through the more specific parts to follow.

PART I

Basic to understanding all problems of human behavior are the "why" questions of motivation. Rarely, if ever, do we make a choice for one reason only. Most of what we do, of what we think, and of what we feel has several causes. For example, behind many defensive types of behavior is a personal history of failure to satisfy needs and wants.

We may think of behavior as going in one of three directions. First, we may attack our problems in ways that *lead to solutions*. Most normal people do solve many of their problems in ways that lead to effective adjustments. Second, there are some situations that involve *no-solution problems.* In the extreme, these are the problems we classify as nonadjustive. Third come those problems somewhere between effective solution and no solution. These are the problems to which we make partial or substitute adjustments. Such partial adjustment is called *defensive behavior* and includes such common reactions as trying to withdraw as a defense or to blame another person for our behavior by projecting our difficulty onto him. And possibly most of us want to be accepted for what we should like to be rather than for what we really are.

Understanding problems begins with how we *perceive* the world around us. "Things are not always what they seem." This is a common saying that has much evidence to back it up. How can we be sure, then, that we really see what we look at, and hear what we listen to? How can we be sure what things stimulate us?

"We learn by what we do" is another common expression backed by much research. How do we learn? How do we improve our learning? How can we become more efficient in our study? These are a few of the questions which will be answered in the introductory chapters.

PART II

Most of us are interested in how things grow. Around the college age we are particularly interested in finding out how we as individuals developed into the persons we are. Also of interest to us is the question "What can be expected of the future?" In the chapters of this part of the text, we trace the development of human behavior from birth to old age through both description and suggestions for handling hundreds of such practical problems as "how to deal with that six-year-old bundle of energy"; "why teen-agers fly off in so many directions"; "why middle-aged parents are so conservative"; and "how we can predict what personality we will have in old age." We shall describe the problems of people of varied ages living together in families, in groups, and in communities. The problems of growth and development are many and varied. Interestingly, the problems of childhood, of adolescence, of early youth, of middle age, and the declining years can be helpfully described in such a way as to give us a preview of what to expect at any given age.

PART III

The three chapters of this section of the book deal, for the most part, with the everyday problems of the college student. We begin with a chapter on individual and social adjustments. Covered here are such problems as why we all have feelings of inferiority and what we can do about them. The "psychological center" of the college campus is described in terms of counseling and guidance, with research data to support the conclusion that counseling is becoming more important than ever in career planning. *The days are over for drifting into success.* Technological change is creating a job world of uncertainty. We must prepare ourselves "to go all the way," we must learn how to run and control the engine of change, and we must learn to be comfortable with ourselves at the same time.

PART IV

The world of work is projected along four horizons—the nature of work, the climates for work, leadership, and job satisfactions. The content of the four chapters dealing with work covers four levels: those of the worker, the supervisor, the executive, and the men and machines as a system. Based on several thousand researches, our discussion covers much of the content of industrial psychology in answering questions about accidents and safety, the nature of good supervision, and the requirements of the executive. We include checklists of supervisory skill and personality descriptions of people who succeed and of those who fail. One of our failures in evaluation is that we tend to rate an individual for his personal appeal rather than for his behavior.

PART V

The first four parts of the text center on the problems of the individual in his or her daily living in the home, the school, the community, and at work. This final section describes the applications of psychology in the other professions and in military settings. It is here that much of the wide range of human behavior is covered in one overall context through the applications of experimental, social, counseling, and clinical psychology to a wide array of problems.

May we suggest that you scan the text, chapter by chapter. It has been written in a sequential order, from basic principles to development, to college, to work, and to the professions. After such a scanning, you may wish to make your own sequence for study. Throughout the book we have included true instances of everyday behavior. From time to time the reader may be able to identify with these problems.

There is a world of data about human behavior useful in helping to solve, or to at least understand, daily problems in living and work. Perhaps in some measure this book may help each reader to see himself occasionally as a hero in his own private drama.

B. von Haller Gilmer

Contents

PART I

BASES OF APPLIED PSYCHOLOGY

CHAPTER 1

The
Nature and Scope
of Applied Psychology

❖❖❖❖❖❖❖❖❖

Living in the twentieth century is an exciting and sometimes a bewildering experience for most of us. And it requires no great stretch of the imagination to explain why. Extraordinary technological achievements are changing our world with alarming regularity. This is the age of moonflight and artificial satellites; of computers and teaching machines; of miracle drugs and insecticides. The rapid march of technology, although bringing to us many benefits, is also creating problems heretofore never encountered. And some of us possibly do not charge quite so hard after bumping our heads repeatedly on the same old problems. In large measure, the reason is people.

THOSE HUMAN PROBLEMS

Many contemporary problems arise from man's difficulty in learning to live in a rapidly changing world. One of the most critical changes is that, from a psychological standpoint, the world is shrinking. Modern forms of communication and transportation put everyone in close contact with his fellowmen. Men can no longer solve the problems of getting along with one another by isolating themselves in time and space. Technology has broken the time and space barriers. Although physical distances between people are decreasing in some respects, "psychological distances" are becoming greater.

That modern man is having difficulties despite the benefits from technology is apparent from a quick glance at today's news. The headlines characteristically read: "Thousands of workers on strike," "Race riots in two cities," "Juvenile delinquency on the increase," "Workers fear threat of automation," "Hospitals for the mentally sick overcrowded." All these headlines bear mute testimony to the fact that our society is in conflict. And, significantly, practically all our problems are human problems. Where shall we turn in order to solve the human problems that threaten our well-being and in some instances our actual survival?

The answer to the question concerning sources of information about human problems is obvious if we reflect on how one goes about solving problems in any specialized field. A man who is having difficulty in designing and planning his house turns to an architect for help. A man with a legal problem seeks out the aid of a lawyer. For problems in measurement and the relations among quantities we turn to the mathematician. The best source of information in any problem area is the specialist who has studied and understands the facts and principles in his particular field. Logically, then, in our efforts to deal satisfactorily with problems having to do with the behavior of people, we should turn to specialists in this field—psychologists and other behavioral scientists who have made the understanding of human behavior their goal.

WHAT IS APPLIED PSYCHOLOGY?

Applied psychology is not fundamentally different from scientific psychology, although such a distinction is popularly made. A scientist who works in applied fields is first a scientist and only secondarily an applied scientist. A large chemical company like DuPont does not hire applied chemists; it hires chemists—men and women who are trained in the basic science. These scientists then apply their knowledge and skills in chemistry to practical problems underlying the production and utilization of commercial products. In psychology the case is no different. The applied psychologist is first and foremost a psychologist. He is trained in the science of psychology and uses his psychological know-how to solve practical human problems at home, in school, in government, and in industry. In short, applied psychology is the use of scientific principles in dealing with problems of everyday living. In a very real sense, an applied psychologist is a professional practitioner. He may be a teacher, a counselor, a clinician, or a general industrial psychologist.

THE SCIENTIFIC METHOD

To the average person "scientific method" is a foreboding term that brings forth visions of complex mathematical formulas, elaborate laboratory equipment, professional words, and techniques that are beyond the understanding of everyday mortals. Actually, *the basic ingredients of scientific methodology are not hard to comprehend*. The method is the cornerstone of all science, and an appreciation of what it means is necessary for an understanding of psychology and its applications. By the scientific method the psychologist, like all scientists, discovers the facts and principles that are applicable to the solution of practical problems. Let us look at some examples of getting such information.

OBSERVATION EXAMPLE

The basic characteristic of the scientific method is that it gathers all relevant information by means of observation. The scientist puts aside personal opinions regarding the relationships among the phenomena of nature and, instead, seeks out these relationships by observing them under specifiable conditions.

An example of the way in which the scientist observes is shown in a study of the effects of the cradling board on the age of walking among Hopi Indian children. The investigator had lived among the Hopi Indians in northern Arizona and was interested in studying their culture and behavior. He observed that Hopi children started to walk at a later age than the average non-Indian American child. Since it was a practice among many Hopis to strap their children when they were very young to a cradling board, it seemed obvious that the late walking was due to the restriction of activity by the cradling board. Here is a logical opinion, but it is not a conclusion based on scientific observation. Observations are made, to be sure, but they are unscientific because they are incomplete, being restricted to Hopi children who have been subjected to cradling-board practices.

The psychologist who made the study of the Hopis realized that in order to arrive at an accurate conclusion, observations would have to be made of walking behavior among Hopi children who had never been subjected to cradling—on a *control* group, so to speak. He did find a considerable number among the Hopi tribes who did not practice cradling and, interestingly enough, these children started walking at the same age as the cradled children. So it is now clear that, despite the logic of the initial observations, cradling does not affect the age at which Hopi children first start to walk. What is responsible for the late walking in Hopi children remains to be settled by further study, but the cradling board as a cause has been eliminated by scientific observation.

A   T E S T   E X A M P L E

Let us now take a look at the scientific method as used by a psychologist whose findings have immediate practical application. The problem is to develop a test for selecting lathe operators. The first thing the test designer does is to observe the behavior of lathe operators to determine the knowledge they need to have, the necessary manipulations and mechanical skills, etc. From these observations the test designer compiles a series of questions or makes up actual sample work tasks that he believes will permit discrimination among good, fair, and poor operators. Does he then have a good test? Not necessarily. His opinions and beliefs, although based on preliminary observations, are not enough. He checks out his observations by testing the test. To do this he must observe his test in action. So he administers it to a large group of lathe operators. If it actually permits discrimination of the good from the bad, then and only then is it a good test—a test which is valid.

E X A M P L E   O F   E F F E C T S   O N   P R O D U C T I O N

Another example of the scientific method is provided by a businessman trying to decide whether to install a music system in the workplace. He has been told that music is beneficial, and he receives glowing reports to this effect from companies who sell these services. The businessman seeks the advice of a psychologist. What would the psychologist do? To begin with, he would decide what is meant by "beneficial." If it means an increase in production, then a measurable criterion of production would be selected. Next, the productive output of two comparable groups of workers would be observed, one group being exposed to music and the other group not. Only if there was a significant difference in output in favor of the exposed group would there be any justification for attributing beneficial effects to the music.

E X A M P L E   O F   C O O R D I N A T E D   R E S E A R C H

One of the researches on human behavior that has involved many different professional specialists is the study of sleep. The scientists include psychologists, psychiatrists, chemists, biologists, physiologists, and mathematicians. Since the reader himself is interested in this important daily routine, we shall use the study of sleep as an example of *interdisciplinary* research. After all, a person spends one-third of his life sleeping.

Neither the problems connected with sleep nor the research on it are new. What is new, however, is that we are now finding some answers to problems that we once only speculated on. By using machines to measure such bodily functions as breathing and heartbeat we now can obtain permanent records of what goes on during sleep. Through measures of eye movements we can study dreams. Particularly important are the records obtained by the *electroencephalograph*. This machine measures *brain waves,* recorded as a tracing called an *electroencephalogram,* or EEG.

Many of us think of sleep as a blanket of darkness, painted with a few dreams, in which we are "out like a light." Nothing could be further from the truth. Let us look at what we know about sleep and its four stages.

In stage 1 the pattern of brain waves is small and irregular, and they change rapidly. The sleeper in this stage may be drifting with idle thoughts and dreams. If he is not awakened by some disturbance, which may be a small one, sleep soon gets deeper.

The brain waves change again as the sleeper passes into stage 2. The EEG begins to show quick bursts of electrical activity, and the eyes move from side to side. In this stage the sleeper can be easily awakened, often insisting that he was awake all along. He may actually have been asleep for as long as ten minutes.

Stage 3 is characterized by slow brain waves. Breathing has evened out. Muscles have become relaxed, and the heart rate slows down. Body temperature declines, and blood pressure drops.

About one-half hour after "dropping off to sleep" the deep level of stage 4 is reached. The brain waves are large and slow and breathing is even. Temperature and blood pressure are still falling. It is of special interest that there is little or no evidence of dreaming in this stage.

Contrary to some popular views the deep sleep of stage 4 lasts for only about twenty minutes. The sleeper gradually returns to the lighter sleep levels. By the time the person has been asleep for about one and one-half hours the brain waves resemble those of waking. Around 3 to 5 A.M. body temperature reaches a low point and then starts to rise.

What about dreams? Although we may dream off and on most of the night, for a total of about one and one-half hours, the only dream that we remember is usually our last one. And again, contrary to some popular opinion that dreams last only for seconds, dreams may last as long as forty minutes, but they evaporate very quickly. They may be affected by fatigue, illness, or emotional upset. Dream content may be influenced by stimuli of the moment. For example, running water may bring on dreams of a waterfall, or the thirsty person may dream of drinking. Yes, there is evidence that we can dream in color. Dreams which occur during the early part of sleep are usually close to our present situations. Dreams which occur later often deal with earlier aspects of our life. Research has finally led to the conclusion that everybody dreams.

Are there individual differences in sleep patterns? Yes, indeed. People who sleep poorly give physiological measurements more like those when they are awake than do people who sleep soundly. Laboratory studies confirm our experiences that a disturbed frame of mind interferes with good sleep. Even creative excitement can get us wound up to the point where sleep is interfered with. Most people need about eight hours of sleep; the range in the general population, however, covers a period of four to fourteen hours. When have you had the right amount of sleep? One simple answer is, "When you feel rested after you have been up for a while."

Researchers conclude that sleeping pills do not induce normal sleep. They advise that only a doctor can determine what drug should be given to the insomniac. The same sedative that may soothe the normal person may cause the depressed individual to fail to sleep by driving him into deeper despair. On the other hand, a drug that provides rest for the depressed person may keep the normal person awake.

Although we may think of sleep as part of a twenty-four-hour clock, its patterns can be changed. Military studies show that army recruits who need eight hours of sleep at home can manage with six or less under certain military conditions. But a person who cuts his sleep to four hours or less for several nights may get his system out of control. The college student, for example, who does without sleep, studying for exams, may break his sleep pattern enough to change certain kinds of behavior. He may go without sleep one night. The next day his attention may wander a little or he may feel like lying down, but nonetheless he may actually function normally in taking exams. Staying up night after night, however, causes irritability, and judgment becomes impaired. Although we can to a degree "catch up" on sleep, researchers say we cannot "store" it up. One practical thing worth remembering centers around *motivation* and not getting enough sleep. Loss of sleep, like other effects of fatigue, does not appreciably change a person's capacity to perform. What happens is that the *willingness,* or *drive to perform,* is cut down. All the person wants to do is to lie down and sleep.

One interesting thing about studying applied psychology is that the problems we discuss often relate closely to our everyday behavior. Experiments sometimes confirm our beliefs—and sometimes they do not. Sometimes science itself fails to confirm its former beliefs.

You will note that in the preceding examples the questions (Does cradling have an effect upon age of walking? Is the test valid or useful in the selection of lathe operators? Does music affect production? What is the nature of sleep?) are answered by gathering evidence in a systematic fashion, i.e., by collecting relevant facts that bear upon the question.

The scientific method is nothing more nor less than fact finding through observation, and a verification of conclusions based on the facts tested under controlled conditions. The final conclusions are held to be true only as long as the available facts support them. As you proceed with the study of applied psychology you will find a great number of psychological generalizations drawn from systematically conducted observations that are applicable to the solution of practical problems.

QUACKERY

More than any other science, psychology has been beset by pretenders such as mind readers, astrologers, phrenologists, palmists, and other self-styled users of psychology. Many gullible persons turn to these quacks for advice, which, of course, is of questionable value or worthless.

How does the astrologer carry out his predictions? He asks you first the month of your birth. Suppose it is August. The astrologist has surveyed the heavens and observed that a constellation of stars in the shape of a lion is clear or visible or in the ascendant during August. The lion is the king of beasts; so, says the astrologist, children born under this sign have kinglike traits of dominance and power. And the astrologist will "prove" it by pointing out that G. B. Shaw, Henry Ford, and Herbert Hoover were born in August. These are observations to be sure, but obviously they are selected and biased observations. They are not scientific observations because they do not include the characteristics of people who were not born during August.

Phrenologists claim that it is possible to determine a person's intellectual powers and personality traits by examining the shape and size of the skull and the protuberances, or bumps, on the surface of the skull. A person with a large skull and a protuberance on the front of the cranium is alleged to have great intellectual powers and unusual literary talent. And of course this is so, for one need only recall the great Daniel Webster, who had a massive head and a cranial bump in exactly the right spot! Of course, the eminent intellectuals with small skulls and bumps in the wrong places are disregarded.

Psychology is a fertile field for quacks because when people are involved it is difficult to be scientific about one's observations. Preconceived notions, prejudices, and attitudes contaminate our conclusions. The quack takes advantage of the common human tendency to believe only what one wants to believe. Everyone likes to think of himself as the possessor of outstanding intellectual abilities and character traits, and the quack is quick to demonstrate that what is wanted is indeed present.

People from all walks of life, including many persons in high places, spend millions of dollars yearly on worthless gadgets, so-called psychological analyses and cures that accomplish nothing, tests which have no validity, and patent medicines without any curative properties. Worse yet, they may find some real problem ignored which the professional would discover.

APPLIED PSYCHOLOGY AND COMMON SENSE

Let the layman ask the astronomer how far it is from the earth to the planet Mars and he will accept the answer without question. Let him ask the chemist or the botanist or the physicist questions in these scientific fields, and the answers are similarly accepted. But the story with psychologists is sometimes different.

Psychologists are less likely to be viewed as authorities in their field than are other scientists. The reason is that most people feel that they themselves know quite a bit about psychology. After all, they argue, everyone has been observing people all his life and from these observations has learned to be a practical psychologist. "You don't have to study psychology in the laboratory or in school; you learn it from everyday experience," is a typical layman's comment. Or, "Psychology is nothing more than common sense." People who make and believe such statements are willing to admit that there are psychological quacks and that one should be on guard lest he be "taken in" by them. But quacks ply their trade intentionally. They are fakers and they know it. If one uses common sense, the argument goes, he will not fall prey to quacks and can readily work out solutions to problems of human behavior.

The commonsense observer is of course not a quack, but sometimes unintentionally resorts to the same kind of thinking that causes many persons to become victims of quacks. Specifically, he makes the grave mistake of drawing conclusions from isolated instances or incomplete evidence. Observe this type of error in the following case. A student dreamed that he would make an A grade on an examination that he was to take the next day. Sure enough, when his paper was returned to him it was marked "A." Proof paramount that dreams come true. Of course, isolated instances of this kind establish no causal connection between dreams and realities. Many times the student had dreams that did not come true, but these negative instances are neglected or forgotten.

We must guard against the belief that fat men are genial just because we know a few genial fat men. We have failed to observe a representative sample of fat men or have neglected the fat men who are surly. We hear of a genius who goes insane and erroneously conclude that genius causes insanity. But what about the many geniuses who do not go insane?

The neglect of negative instances, i.e., instances which do not support the positive observation, is the pitfall of the amateur psychologist.

Let us now restate our position. Commonsense psychology may be substantiated by scientific research, but often the commonsense approach oversimplifies the problems. Let us illustrate this by the following example.

SIMPLE QUESTIONS THAT BECOME INVOLVED

Out of commonsense observations do come some practical questions and good answers at times. But often research finds that the original question is not so simple as stated. Let us look at the question, "Who makes a good leader?" There are some commonsense answers to this question, to be sure, but possibly they do not spell out all we should like to know about leadership in its many aspects. To date, there are over 2,500 articles in the professional journals and in books on the study of leadership. From these studies come many conclusions: some persons have no qualities of leadership, some make good leaders in one situation but not in another, etc. In later chapters we shall make more comments on generalizations about leadership, but for now let us ask one more question: "Leadership for what?"

There is a difference between being in a leadership position as an athletic coach and serving as a committee chairman in a community project. There may be a different set of requirements for success as a leadership counselor to the girl scouts as compared with the requirements for success as a production supervisor. The man who holds leadership position because of wealth or power may be a flop in leading a combat platoon. Leading a bridge club differs a bit from directing the behavior of a teen-age gang. Leadership in education often involves long-term results and differs from leadership in an advertising agency, where the executive has to get creative ideas from his people in short order. The person who may succeed as a leader of a college revolt may fail in some constructive project of building class morale.

Maybe one factor that makes the study of applied psychology so interesting to some of us is that it supports the feeling we have at times that human behavior is complex, however simple we may try to make it.

WHAT DO APPLIED PSYCHOLOGISTS DO?

Let us take an overall look at a sample of the kinds of work of the applied psychologist. This overview will be broad in scope. Detailed treatment of various aspects will follow in later chapters.

ASSESSMENT AND EVALUATION

How to select a person for the kind of job for which he is best fitted is a perennial question in industry, school, and government. Inefficient work performance, failure in school, and a wide variety of maladjustments can be traced to the fact that a person is not temperamentally, educationally, or intellectually suited for his job. These problems can be eliminated to a marked degree through the proper assessment and evaluation of an individual's capabilities, skills, and personality.

Psychologists have made outstanding contributions in assessment and evaluation through the use of methods, techniques, and instruments designed for the purpose of measuring, understanding, or predicting performance. Included in this repertoire are intelligence tests, tests of special aptitudes, interest inventories, personality tests, rating scales, interviews, personal histories, and direct observation.

MANAGEMENT AND ADMINISTRATION

Within recent years psychologists have become actively concerned in the study of management and administrative skills and the nature of organizations. Many management and administrative problems can be traced to the structure of an organization—its size, shape, and complexity. For example, the pyramidal shape of most organizations creates critical personnel problems among those at the lower levels in the hierarchy because they are encouraged to climb to the top and yet there is less and less room as they move up. Another example stemming from organizational complexity is in the realm of communications, where inefficiency occurs because of misinformation or lack of information among the organization's members.

The contributions of the applied psychologist in the area of organizational dynamics have included remodeling of the organizational structure, changes in the organizational atmosphere, or climate, and improved techniques for selecting and developing managers and executives. Psychologists themselves as managers and executives are found in business, government agencies, hospitals, and educational institutions.

HUMAN ENGINEERING

This new and rapidly expanding field of applied psychology has to do with the design of equipment and the tasks of the individuals who operate the equipment. The human-engineering approach may be illustrated by a study in which instruments of five different shapes were used to determine which type of display could be read most accurately. An analysis of reading errors showed a clear superiority of the open-window design in reading accuracy where the pointer remains fixed and the dial scale moves. The horizontal and vertical designs were particularly inaccurate where the pointer moves along the dial scale, which remains fixed.

The task of the human engineer is, in a broad sense, that of developing effective equipment and work procedures through the utilization of scientific knowledge about human behavior. Human engineering is really a product of World War II, when psychologists and engineers worked together on the design of airplane cockpits, weaponry controls, and instrument displays. Human engineers continue to be active in the military field and, of course, in the whole manned orbital space-flight program. Also they are assisting in the design of equipment in everyday civilian use—automobiles, lawn mowers, stoves, lathes, washing machines, and railroad locomotives, to mention just a few.

THE MANAGEMENT OF LEARNING

Learning is an everyday occurrence, familiar to most of us. It is as common as sleeping and eating. The psychology of training or teaching is nothing more nor less than the applied psychology of learning. In view of the persuasiveness of learning in all human activity, it is not surprising that a great deal of the work of the applied psychologist is focused on the management of the learning process.

Some practical questions on the management of learning for which applied psychology has or can supply answers include: What is the best way to study? What is good teaching? Does material learned in one course transfer to other courses and to problems of everyday living? Why are some subjects more interesting than others? Can a person be trained to be a leader? How should an industrial training program be organized?

The answers to the above questions are contained in the facts and principles of learning, many of which suggest outright practical applications; in some instances special adjustments are also required to fit special conditions.

COUNSELING AND GUIDANCE

The function of counseling and guidance is to help essentially normal people in the solution of their personal problems. Counseling and guidance psychologists work in secondary schools, colleges, governmental agencies, in industry, and in private practice. They administer and interpret tests of intelligence, aptitudes, and personality, and they conduct interviews in order to obtain information which will enable them to give the kind of guidance and counsel that is needed. If the maladjustment does not appear to be serious, the counselor frequently engages in psychotherapy.

The different types of psychological counseling fall roughly into four groups, on the basis of the kinds of problem dealt with. *Educational* counselors help students decide what curriculum to pursue, what specific courses to take, how to study, and how to handle other academic problems. *Marital* counselors are concerned with the reasons for incompatibilities between husband and wife, and with ways and means of facilitating interpersonal adjustments in the family. *Vocational* counselors analyze the individual's intellectual potential, special aptitudes, and interests; on the basis of these analyses, they guide the individual in selecting an occupation for which he is best suited. *Personal* counselors deal with personal problems of adjustment that are primarily emotional in character.

SOCIAL PROBLEMS

Psychologists are frequently called upon to render aid in solving such varied problems as crime and delinquency, irresponsible driving, and prejudice. Through research, the underlying causes of such attitudes and types of behavior have been determined and strategies for their elimination have been proposed.

The social problem of law enforcement has even brought psychology into the courtroom. For example, an understanding of psychology proves useful in formulating ways to elicit accurate information from witnesses. Psychology tells us that when attention is directed toward the witness himself as an observer he tends to be cautious and more accurate than when attention is not directed toward him. Therefore, "Did you see a briefcase on the desk?" is more likely to bring forth a correct answer than "Was there a briefcase on the desk?"

From the foregoing broad overview it is clear that psychology is applied in many and varied contemporary human activities. Psychology as a science had its origins in the biological and social sciences. As the science developed it became apparent that many of its proponents had discovered wide areas of practical application in such fields as education, engineering, medicine, law, advertising, and business.

One television personality, after interviewing some 14,000 people, concluded that each person has a story to tell: "Some are better than others, but each individual feels his or her story is the most important. The fulfillment of experience is the sharing of that experience with others." The psychology classroom provides such an opportunity.

SOME QUESTIONS IN APPLIED PSYCHOLOGY

Let us take a look at the content of this book by beginning with some sample questions.

Why did you come to college? Why do you sometimes avoid facing an unpleasant task? What are the psychological differences between wanting food and wanting prestige? These are questions about *human wants and needs*.

Do women dislike the same things about a job as do men? Which person is the most content with his pay? Why do some people struggle so hard for status and others do not? These questions concern *individual differences*.

Why do some people see a painting as beautiful that someone else calls ugly? Why is a job boring to one person and interesting to another? Why do some people get upset when you turn off the radio in the middle of a song? Why are so many people interested in only their own little world? These are questions in *perception,* in how we come to know the world.

What do you do first when you face a new situation? How do you account for the fact that a good learner selects right responses and eliminates wrong ones? Why is it so difficult to break bad habits? These are important questions in understanding *human learning*.

How can you get more out of study? Should you set up a study schedule? With an assignment before you, how should you treat it so that it will be meaningful? Why do you sometimes get answers at one time "out of the blue," only to fail the next time? Involved in these questions are principles of *learning how to study.*

Can we predict when the child will have temper tantrums? Does practice hasten the child's walking? When can we expect the child to start talking in sentences? What is the peak age for nightmares in children? These are but a few of the questions related to *early childhood development.*

Are all teen-agers basically rebels? When does "psychological weaning" start to take place? Do adolescents have the same worries and fears as adults? Why does "togetherness" consume an average of three-fourths of the adolescent's leisure time? From the world of teen-agers come unique problems in *social, emotional,* and *intellectual development.*

There are 20,000 ways to make a living; how easy is it to choose one? Why is middle age called "a point of no return"? We are aging from the moment we are born; how can we go all the way? Why does old age come gracefully for some and in anger for others? These questions are typical of the problems found in *maturing people.*

Where do *you* fit in as an individual? Why do people come together in groups? Why are some men more "family-oriented" than others? Why are some communities conservative and others radical? These questions relate the individual to people as they come together in tens, hundreds, and thousands, and as they are studied in terms of *groups.*

Why do we say that feelings of inferiority are normal? Where does anxiety come from? Are we born with a set of personality traits? How can we lessen worry? What are the stages of effective adjustment? These questions deal with the *processes of adjustment.*

Who am I? Where am I going? What will the costs be in getting there? What other questions should I ask myself? These are personal-identity questions which bring students to seek out one of the most rapidly growing units on the college campus—the *counseling center.* Fortunately, most students realize that confusion seems to be a part of the process of coming in touch with reality.

Do you want to work with "people" or with "things"? Why is that first job so important? What do you have to do to get promoted on the job? What do you have to offer an employer? How are jobs changing? Many such questions are involved in *career decision making.*

What are the differences between work and play? What are the common characteristics of work? Why do we get tired? How can we cut down on accidents? These are the types of questions which describe the *nature of work.*

What are the effects of noise, lighting, temperature, and music on work output? Why do some people like a given psychological work climate that others dislike? What kind of work climate would you choose? How is personality related to job satisfaction? These questions are related to the new researches on *organizational climates.*

What are your chances of becoming a supervisor? Do you have the characteristics of successful leaders? What is the nature of on-the-job counseling? What do executives actually do? These questions are related to problems in *leadership.*

How do personal attitudes affect what we do on the job? What does the worker want from his job? What does the manager want from his job? How can you prepare yourself for liking your job? Some two thousand research studies have been made on *job satisfaction and morale* which will be summarized.

How is psychology applied in advertising and selling? What are the human factors in engineering? What do studies show about "lie detectors"? Why do some people who have been told they have cancer not report for treatment? These are the types of questions related to such professions as *marketing, engineering, law,* and *medicine.*

How do military organizations use psychologists? What are the psychological problems of adjusting to military living? How do people react to combat and to disaster? What is the nature of brainwashing? How do we use psychological warfare? These are questions involved in applying psychology to *military settings.*

We believe you will enjoy studying applied psychology and hope you will profit from doing so. Sometimes we spend such an undue amount of time on minor annoyances that we wait too long to deal with the more basic problems. In this volume we shall try to lay emphasis on the fundamental questions and generalizations, and relate psychology to new problems. Just as yesterday's innovations proved to be moments in history, so today even the computer is to the new student a thing of the past.

Summary

Man has always had interest in human behavior, but today some new concerns have been added. These involve problems brought on by rapidly advancing science and technology. Both change itself and the problems it entails are here to stay. Psychology, in some measure, provides us with understandings about human behavior which enable us to sit a bit looser with the changes of time. For each of us it is important to learn that pressures from without, and conflicts from within, sometimes can be stimulating as well as frustrating.

Applied psychology uses scientific methods and principles in dealing with a wide variety of problems of everyday living, ranging from observations of the growth of walking in children to coordinated researches on the nature of sleep. Psychology is concerned with helping rid the public of quacks who take money under false pretenses. Through scientific study psychology has shown that the "commonsense" approach is not always a sufficient guide to a reliable knowledge of human behavior.

Applied psychologists work in a wide range of fields. They work in management and administration on problems of organizational climates and leadership. Through human engineering they study the design of equipment and the psychological aspects of space flight. Psychologists deal with the improvement of learning and education, of counseling and guidance, and with a variety of social problems.

Applied psychology studies human wants and needs; it is concerned with individual differences and how we come to know the world through perception. It helps us to get more out of study. Of much concern to psychology are the problems of development from childhood and adolescence through youth and middle age, to the age of retirement.

The applied psychologist concentrates on the individual as he moves through education into the world of work. Here he is concerned with providing understandings for making career decisions and getting satisfaction out of work.

Applied psychology works with other professions—marketing, law, engineering, education, and the military. It lays emphasis on fundamental questions and generalizations.

CHAPTER 2

Human Wants and Motivation

People want many things. We want food, a place to sleep, money and the feeling that we belong as a member of a group. We also ask why we want these and many more things. We ask why did we come to college? Why do I prefer doing one job rather than another? Why do most people work harder when they feel they are overpaid? Why do we sometimes avoid facing an unpleasant task?

Such terms as "wants," "desires," and "needs" describe the motivations that distinguish between the *positive* forces which impel us to work *toward* certain ends. Such terms as "fears" and "aversions" refer to *negative* forces which repel a person *away from* certain objects or conditions. Yet the two types of forces are similar in one respect—they both initiate and sustain behavior, and this we call *motivation*. "Wishing" and "wanting" describe the positive driving forces in us which direct our behavior toward "approach objects"; such an object would be the food sought by a hungry person. A situation or object that a person tries to avoid or escape from is called an "avoidance object"; an example would be a party that one does not wish to attend.

A BASIC DIAGRAM OF BEHAVIOR

There are three broad statements that we may make about human behavior. First, behavior is *caused*. Second, behavior is *motivated*.

Third, behavior is *goal-directed*. These interacting forces are represented in Figure 2-1.

In this closed-circuit model, attaining a goal eliminates the cause of the behavior, which in turn eliminates the motive, which consequently eliminates the behavior. When one's stomach is empty, the emptiness stimulates a feeling of hunger, and this feeling stimulates action in the direction of food. When obtained, the food fills the stomach, causing cessation of hunger impulses, and this in turn terminates the behavior in search of food. The description seems simple, but at this point the psychologist emphasizes that the closed-circuit conception has a limitation of which we should be aware. Whereas one can consume enough food to stop hunger and food seeking temporarily, it does not follow

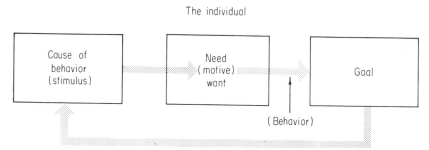

FIG. 2-1   Following the arrows of this closed-circuit model of behavior, we can see how obtaining a *goal* eliminates the *cause* of the behavior, which in turn eliminates the *motive,* which consequently eliminates the *behavior.*

that one can consume a given quantity of prestige, for example, and feel satiated. This is important to remember if we are to understand the drives of people in school, in the home, and in industry.

Often human behavior does fit in with the system just described. Behavior may be an effort to eliminate tensions by seeking goals that neutralize the causes of tensions. For instance, a man thinks that he has a need for a new car. The more he considers the proposition, the more his tension increases. He explores the market and finds the car that will meet his needs. The more he thinks about a new car, the more he is influenced by advertising, and the more a desire to obtain one builds up in him. Finally, when arrangements are made to buy the car, the tension is resolved.

Understanding something of the general nature of human wants sets the stage for dealing with many of the problems to be described later in chapters dealing with development work and social and personal adjustments.

HOW PEOPLE DIFFER IN WANTS

Behind the many ways people differ in their wants or needs three things are important—what each person *expects,* how persons differ in *ambition,* and how they differ in the *roles* they play.

GOAL EXPECTANCY

A job considered good by the son of a day worker might be thought of as poor by the son of a vice-president. Job satisfaction has a relation to job expectancy. The young man who comes from a working-class family may regard the job of a toolmaker or bricklayer as very satisfactory. This class of job would probably be considered inferior by the young man from a higher social status. Thus, job status and social status go hand in hand wherever some degree of permanence is involved. The president may brag that his college son is spending the summer with a drag crew in the steel mill. The worker may also brag about his son having a similar job. However, the needs being satisfied in the two cases are likely to be quite different.

When we think in terms of needs being satisfied, we must think in terms of goal expectancy. A young man whose family or personal ambitions has set high goals for him may be dissatisfied with the same job his neighbor likes.

The level of aspiration of any given person in relation to his feelings of accomplishment determines, in large measure, his attitudes. The son of the worker who aspires to work his way up from the bottom, who pictures himself becoming a part of management, may play just such a role until he experiences failure and rebuff time after time. Being thus thwarted, he may turn his attention to union activities. If he is encouraged with success here he may well go on to become a leader and a strong union man. Some of the outstanding union leaders today, men with proved leadership and executive ability, have become union rather than management men because in the union they found the recognition they had been seeking.

DIFFERENCES IN AMBITION

Although we know how social status, age, and education determine, in part, an individual's ambitions and job satisfactions, it is important to remember that the drives of various persons differ regardless of the influence of these factors. Many persons seem quite adjusted to their job situation, though it be of comparatively low status and low financial return. It is hard for the highly motivated person to realize that some people are not so ambitious as he. In one industrial situation, psychologists were employed to study the attitudes of people who had several times been passed over in promotions. Some were indignant because they had not received recognition, but a surprising number seemed content to remain at their particular level. One man, who gave evidence of having more ability than he had used, was asked why he was content with his medium-status job. He pointed out that he valued other things in life more highly than job success. "I know what you are thinking," he said during the interview. "I don't have hypertension, I don't have an ulcer, I'm a failure!" If we stand still there is less chance for us to stub our toe—but also less chance of getting somewhere.

DIFFERENT ROLES

Needs vary not only from one person to another; sometimes they vary from group to group. A study made during World War II offers us a good example. In an industrial plant, blue-green lighting had been installed after research had indicated that it would reduce eyestrain. Careful records of production were kept. After the blue-green lighting had been installed the output of male workers increased. There were many comments from the men about less eyestrain. They were very happy with the new lighting. But with women employees the story was quite different. Output fell off, absenteeism hit its highest peak. Their production was greatly reduced. Why? Because the women felt that the new type of lighting made them look ghastly; and, in fact, it did. In this particular instance, an environmental situation which motivated one group of people in one way had just the opposite effect on another group with different specific needs.

DIFFERENCES BETWEEN WOMEN AND MEN AT WORK

Do women like their jobs? Do they have the same job dissatisfactions as those expressed by men? Do they have much interest in unions? Do they make good managers? Questions like these are important not only to personnel people but also to college students who are trying to decide what kind of job to prepare for or what particular job offer should be accepted.

DIFFERING ATTITUDES

Of several questionnaire-type studies comparing men and women in job satisfaction, some indicate that women are more satisfied than men; others show the reverse; and still others show no differences.

Qualitatively, women seem to express themselves more freely, either by written comments or in interviews, about such matters as cleanliness of working conditions, pleasantness of social relationships on the job, and treatment by supervisors. Women verbalize loyalty more than men. However, they show less interest in pay, benefit programs, and opportunities for advancement. The author had the opportunity recently to make a good comparison between the attitudes of men and women working together on the same types of jobs in a company employing about equal numbers of each sex. In response to a question of what they liked least about their jobs, two-thirds of the men mentioned low pay, but very few women mentioned money, even though their rate of pay was below that of the men. On an item concerning cafeteria conditions, 600 women made a specific complaint which only two men mentioned. Noticeable differences between men and women in their questionnaire responses were found in areas involving supervision and cleanliness in working conditions; the women were more sensitive than men. On questions involving a proposed installation of automatic labor-saving machines, the men expressed fear of losing their jobs, but the women were apparently not interested in the problem.

PROBLEMS OF ADJUSTMENT

The employed woman who has to divide her energies between the working world and her traditional role as a woman faces adjustment problems peculiar to her sex. The married woman has both home and job responsibilities somewhat different from those of her male counterpart. The social and psychological pressures on the single woman complicate her attitudes toward marriage, toward her job, and toward her associates. A major consideration of the young single woman in selecting a job may well be the opportunities which it offers her to meet eligible men of marriageable age.

MARRIED WOMEN WORKERS

Women differ from men in their original attitudes toward work. Most young women today take a job until marriage or a few years after. The married women are more likely to leave the labor force during the years when their small children require care. Many return to jobs when their children are partly grown and no longer need constant attention. Because of this cycle, the largest proportion are in the labor force between the ages of twenty to twenty-four. The proportion declines in the age range from twenty-five to thirty-four, and increases again around thirty-five.

Statistical surveys show that an increasing number of married women are going into industry. Part-time work is more likely to be sought by women than by men, since women frequently need to combine a paid job with household cares. Data show that 60 percent of all part-time workers are women. Most of them are married and over thirty-five years of age. They usually do the same type of work as full-time employees. Apparently part-time work has resulted from the normal needs of management and is not merely a by-product of full employment. Women work part time because of a need to increase or supplement the family income, or to have outside interests. Management uses them during busy periods, for relief schedules, or for temporary peak loads.

HIGHER-LEVEL POSITIONS

Apparently it takes a long time to establish a tradition favorable to women within the higher-level positions in industry. In the home offices of insurance companies, women hold only about 20 percent of the supervisory positions; and in banks, the figure is even lower. Both industries employ large proportions of women. Two-thirds of all insurance company employees are women. They constitute about one-half of the number of employees in banks. Only in department stores does one find an even distribution among women and men in the so-called "higher-level" positions. Here women make up about two-thirds of all employees.

Women officers in industry are no more than 4 percent of the total. Only a handful hold board directorships. In production operations in manufacturing, few women are found above the level of forewoman. Aside from prejudice, lack of education and training has been cited as one of the principal reasons why women do not advance. One writer summed the problem up well by pointing out that the young woman does not take specialized training because she fears it will be wasted in a hostile market. She has little chance for advancement because she lacks the training. This circular dilemma must surely be avoided if our economy is to continue along its predicted course. The women in middle-management brackets with no more than a high school education are usually older than those in the general labor market, and more of them are single. Women in personnel work, training, publishing, job testing, social service, science, and engineering are usually college graduates.

The opportunities for women at the administrative level are increasing in such positions as research analysts in banks and insurance companies, in merchandising, public relations, advertising, and personnel work. However, very few women in any field occupy the top executive jobs. One business magazine estimated that not over 5,000 women could be found among the 250,000 "real executives." A market analysis of women holding positions of responsibility in industry and commerce indicated that the way women *behave* on the job, rather than the way they *perform* the technical operations of their position, is a chief determinant of their acceptance as administrators. Apparently there is a widespread belief that women are "too emotional" or "too personal" to hold down supervisory jobs or executive positions. Most evidence, however, that seems to point in this direction is more subjective than objective.

WORKING FOR MONEY

The one thing people have in common in terms of motivation is pay. How does my pay compare to his? With whom do different groups compare their pay? Below a certain level pay may cause dissatisfaction, but above some satisfactory level, additional pay seems to add relatively little to satisfaction.

PAY AS AN INCENTIVE

If a person is promoted for successful performance and he sees it simply as a result of a tight labor market in his specialty, what becomes of the spur?

Studies have found that people who are made to feel *overpaid* for a job will work harder than control subjects who earned the same pay but were made to feel fairly paid. And just the opposite is also true. People who feel they are *underpaid* for a job will not work so hard as they do when they feel they are being paid fairly.

What do managers think about their pay? Who is the most content with his pay? One thing of critical importance for the leader centers around how his pay compares with his subordinates. The supervisor must feel that he makes more than his men or he will be dissatisfied. Higher-level managers make pay comparisons with their counterparts in other companies. Technicians compare their rate of pay with those similar in skill. The teacher compares his pay with other salaries in the community.

SOME GENERALIZATIONS ABOUT PAY

Researchers have come up with eight generalizations about pay.
1 Most people feel that their pay is inadequate.
2 Outside pay comparisons play important roles in determining how well a person is satisfied with his pay.

3   Pay satisfaction for a manager is related to the level of his job in the organization. Higher-paid managers give less attention to pay (maybe they have enough!), to the point where an increase in pay does not add to satisfaction.

4   Satisfaction with present pay (which may be low, as for the beginning salesman) may be good when there is an anticipation of adequate income in the future. The medical intern provides an example.

5   Higher-paid people give less attention to pay than do lower-paid people.

6   Increases in pay do not always spur more effort.

7   Lack of adequate pay brings on dissatisfaction, but increases in pay do not necessarily mean increased satisfaction.

8   Strong feelings of being underpaid bring on feelings of anguish and frustration.

One writer put it this way: "The greatest pleasure that money can give us is to make it unnecessary to think about money."

THE STRUGGLE TO GET AHEAD

What makes people want to move up? Certainly *upward mobility* is related to progress, at both the individual and the group level, but at what price? Some psychiatrists have voiced the opinion that the struggle for upward mobility is one of the big contributing causes of mental illness in the United States.

There are two aspects of mobility. The *situation* the person finds himself in is important. The person is given opportunity to move ahead by the offer of a job, or he finds himself trapped in a situation where he has to work his way out and up. The situational conditions favoring or hindering upward mobility are many. As a rule, they are easy to spot. It is more difficult, however, to get at the second aspect involved in mobility: *personal motivation*.

LEVELS OF ASPIRATION

Before we go on with the subject of mobility, however, let us consider some experimental studies on levels of aspiration. Here, in a simpler setting, we can find some useful facts for our consideration. Investigators have discussed the many facets of the subject. They pose the following simple problem: A person has scored 6 in shooting at a target with ring 10 at the center. He decides the next time to try for 8. He attains 5, is much disappointed, and decides to try the next time to reach 6 once more.

Within such a sequence there are four main points, as illustrated in Figure 2-2. Here in our level-of-aspiration situation, the subject begins a typical sequence of events. His last performance ("has scored 6") has set his level of aspiration for the next performance ("try for 8"). The new performance was below what he tried for ("attains 5"); hence, there is a "goal discrepancy." The difference between the goal level and that of the new performance is the "attainment discrepancy."

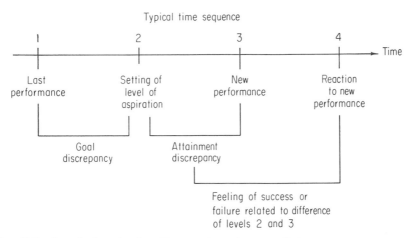

FIG. 2-2 Level of aspiration. Four main points are distinguished in a typical sequence of events in a level-of-aspiration situation: (1) last performance, (2) setting of level of aspiration for the next performance, (3) new performance, and (4) psychological reaction to the new performance. The difference between the level of the last performance and that of the new goal is called "goal discrepancy." The difference between the goal level and that of the new performance is called "attainment discrepancy." This difference is one of the bases of the reaction at (4). (*From Lewin, K., Dembo, T., Festinger, L., & Sears, P. S. Levels of aspiration. In Hunt, J. McV. (Ed.) Personality and behavior disorders. New York: Ronald, 1944. Vol. I, pp. 333–378.*)

This difference is one of the bases of the reaction at point 4 in the figure.

In our example the subject is really trying to hit center. This is his ideal goal. Knowing that this is too difficult for him, at least at the present, he sets his goal at 8, his "action level." It is the level of the action goal which is usually taken as the criterion for the level of aspiration for an individual at a given time. It has been found that nearly all individuals of Western culture, when first exposed to a level-of-aspiration situation, give initially a level of aspiration which is above the previous performance, and under most conditions tend to keep the goal discrepancy positive.

Being a realist about it, the individual will place his expectation somewhere within the boundary zone of his ability. Three facts we know from experiments:

1 People tend to seek a relatively high level of aspiration.
2 There is a tendency for the level of aspiration to go up only to certain limits.
3 There is a tendency for the person in his level of aspiration to stay out of an area that is too difficult or too easy.

The judgment of the probability of success or failure on a given level is determined by past experiences, certain realistic situations, and, in addition, by wishes and fears. A recent failure will tend to lower the level of aspiration, and the level will decrease more after resounding failure than after a near success. Success and failure also have their cumulative effects. Experiments show that the feeling of success or of failure does not depend on the absolute level of achievement. What may mean success for one person may mean failure for another; and even for the same person, the same achievement will lead sometimes to feelings of failure and sometimes to feelings of success.

FACTORS IN MOBILITY

Let us now return to the question of individual motivation and upward mobility. In his studies of community life, one researcher points out that the primary factor for upward mobility is a high achievement level. What is expected of a person in relation to his age level sets a standard. Traditionally, there are two basic areas for achievement. The first involves *obtaining an education,* and the second, finding a *place in the occupational hierarchy.* "Success in one or both of these areas is almost a basis for achievement in other aspects of living. It is an expression of the ambition drive of an individual." Achievement level is, of course, dependent upon *individual ability,* a sort of "special talent" for science, athletics, art, and so forth.

A third factor in mobility concerns an individual's *social techniques.* This means behaving in ways that fit the situation. The ability to perceive the situation and react appropriately to it are important in upward mobility.

A fourth factor that emerged from studies concerns the person's *ambitions* for getting ahead. This has been called "status anxiety." A person may place too high a value on status symbols, or seek recognition from those in superior positions, or strive for roles which may bring prestige. The person who overreacts in trying for status lowers his chances for upward mobility.

A fifth factor in evaluating potential mobility involves what has been called *situational responses*—an awareness of how other people evaluate us. We are all familiar with the words to describe the man with this asset, who "knows what to do," "has a pleasant personality," "always says the right things."

CLUB STATUS SYMBOLS

In any community one can find the club status symbols that go with upward mobility—country club, hospital charities, Daughters of the American Revolution, Rotary. Of the upper-class families in an average small community of a few thousand, three-fourths belong to at least two of these clubs, and half belonged to three or all four. In the Lions, Masons, and Eastern Star, the majority of the members came from the upper and lower middle classes. For the lower lower class in such a community "there isn't much."

Associations are very important for upward mobility. For some persons "the old school tie" has its importance. Membership in women's clubs, the PTA, and the Red Cross provides associations at another level. Individuals at the top of the social ladder are ready to identify with their own social status; those at the bottom derive little ego satisfaction from such identification. At the bottom of the socioeconomic hierarchy there is less feeling of belongingness. Maybe belongingness is *the* basic need underlying the struggles for upward mobility.

STUDY OF A HIGH-STATUS COMMUNITY

Lest one conclude that the struggle is over when high socioeconomic status has been attained, he should take a look at what is involved in staying up there. The sociological study of a high-status suburban community of 17,000 persons has been described in Seeley's book *Crestwood Heights* (see Bibliography for Chapter 9 at the end of the book). Here is pictured the community of material abundance, the "dream community where many aspire to live, but only a few can," populated to a large extent by those who have achieved rapid personal mobility. Here is described a community where the child, who in more static social situations might be permitted to take certain aspects of the common life for granted, is made to "appreciate" the close connection between effort and achievement; it is a community where one cannot take anything for granted.

The person who aspires to the Heights in his upward mobility must be prepared to follow the highly developed pattern of movement from one job to another, from one place of residence to another, from one city to another, from one class position to another. The man and woman of Crestwood Heights have few bonds that cannot be broken at the promise of a promotion. They have been prepared for this from the cradle, if they were born into this society.

Mobility must be matched by opportunity for training, for employment, and for advancement. To the man bent upon an executive career, training includes both the necessary technical skills and the social graces, plus the strong desire to manage. The executive or professional man of the Heights must be ready to abandon cherished usages and techniques as new ones arise. He must be willing to acquire new conceptions of life and organization, and to revise constantly in later life his procedures within his chosen field.

The authors of the book make the point that the differences between the careers of the person who has risen by his own effort and the person who has been born and brought up in Crestwood Heights have a relation to the flexibility which is so essential to the executive in a rapidly changing society. The person who is "born into a good start" is more likely to accept current techniques and practices than is the individual who is struggling upward. Psychologically, in work or in play, the key to survival in the Heights is *competition*. Success in making the Heights or staying there may well depend upon how well the person is prepared for competition at this high level, particularly in the more subtle phases of the status struggle.

REACTIONS TO FRUSTRATION

Attempts to obtain satisfaction of needs and desires frequently meet with obstacles, regardless of one's status or job. Many times these blockages are only temporary and are overcome easily. At other times, however, attempts to attain a goal are blocked time and time again, with the result that there is an accumulation of tension within the individual. Educational settings tend to spawn frustrations. The work environment in our highly competitive American industrial system is in itself particularly frustration-inducing for workers and managers alike. The examples given below, all taken from industrial settings, illustrate several kinds of reactions to frustration that normal persons show.

ELEMENTARY AGGRESSION

Elementary aggression as shown by the adult looks somewhat like the behavior of a naughty child. In an Eastern city, a union local called a strike which shut down all truck deliveries to and from the five largest department stores. As the strike, which involved hundreds of drivers, went into its second year, such childlike behavior was engaged in as throwing paint bombs into the homes of the store supervisors and breaking plate glass windows in the stores by throwing steel balls at them from moving automobiles.

DISPLACED AGGRESSION

Displaced aggression reactions are shown in indirect and subtle ways; they are so named because the behavior is directed against some object or person other than the real source of the frustration. The frustrated worker, for example, who is angry at the boss may rant and rave at his family. He cannot tell off the boss for fear of losing his job; so his wife and children become the innocent victims of his displaced aggression. The following example illustrates this kind of behavior.

A middle-aged woman employee was transferred from her regular operation of assembling parts in a metals fabrication plant to a new operation in the same department. The new job consisted of a repetitive type of task, machining springs for toy motors. After a day the woman became adept at the job and was able to produce about 250 pieces an hour, and after another day at the job, 350. The amount of production asked by the gang boss was 500 units per hour. The worker reported that she could not reach this requirement. The boss insisted that she could raise her production if she wanted to and that she was holding back purposely because she wanted her old job back. She was reported to the foreman as being one of several workers who balked at meeting production requirements. The foreman spoke to her harshly, telling her, in effect, to produce or else.

The woman became upset and was hardly able to do any work for the remainder of the day. She did not say anything to the foreman. During the next three days her work improved slightly in quantity but decreased in quality. It was also discovered later that she had been the one responsible for stopping up the toilet in the ladies' rest room on three successive days following the instance. On each occasion she had placed a whole orange in the commode. Certainly this was displaced aggression!

ORGANIZED AGGRESSION

Organized aggression may come about through well-laid planning, as is often found in prolonged labor-management conflict. But often closer to the real feelings of people is the aggression that becomes organized more informally. An example of this type of reaction to frustration is found in writings about the famous Western Electric researches. In the study of a wage-incentive scheme, it became apparent that the majority of a group of workers, regardless of other differences, shared some common feelings. If an individual turned out too much work he became a "rate buster"; too little work labeled him a "chiseler." The person who would say anything to injure a fellow member of the group was a "squealer." It was also accepted practice that no member of the work group should act officiously.

The wage-incentive scheme was planned to encourage output by setting pay rates on the basis of group earnings. The experts who devised the scheme assumed that the group would bring pressure to bear upon the slower workers to make them work harder and so increase the earnings of the group. Actually what happened was practically the reverse. The workers put pressure not only on the slower workers but upon the faster ones as well. Pressure was applied in various ways. One informally organized aggression was "binging," as the men called it. If one of the workers did something which the group did not consider proper, a fellow worker had the right to bing him. This consisted of a quick, stiff blow on the upper arm. The worker who was struck got the idea and did not strike back. The punishment was, therefore, psychological, not physical. Why was such behavior engaged in? For one thing, the industrial worker has his own ways of doing his job, his own traditions of skill, and his own satisfactions from achieving goals set according to his own standards—this, of course, within certain practical limits. The worker hates to be "told" or to be "planned for" by experts. In a sense he rejects authority, particularly when customs of work are challenged by innovations put in without his approval. The resulting frustration brings out aggression. The aggression frequently becomes organized when the majority of the group feel the same way about the source of the frustration.

WORK AS ESCAPE

Another kind of reaction to frustration, frequently found with the harassed executive, consists of attempts to escape through excessive work, more or less routine in nature. Such was the case with a former executive vice-president of a large corporation, whom we shall call Mr. Gregory.

Mr. Gregory was in his early fifties. He was a graduate of an engineering school and had worked his way up in the company over a period of some thirty years. He had held the position of executive vice-president for four years. To all outside appearances he was a highly successful executive; in the office before eight, he was the last to leave in the evening, carrying a loaded briefcase. It gradually became apparent to Gregory's superiors that he was working harder and harder and accomplishing less and less. There seemed to be no family or outside problems causing his difficulty. During a routine clinical examination held periodically for top executives, the following facts appeared. Gregory had been successful as an engineer, and he had made notable progress as the vice-president of manufacturing. In fact, his success in the latter position led to his appointment as executive vice-president. About two years after this promotion, the corporation expanded and the job became too big for Gregory, though he did not realize it at the time. He began to postpone more and more decisions and to become harder to see. He spent his time primarily on details of a clerical nature, working evenings and sometimes on week ends. When pressed for decisions, particularly from the lower echelons, he made it known that he was too busy, not verbally but by actually being busy.

Here is a type of reaction to a frustration caused by inability to cope with the important parts of a job; the reaction is to seek escape by concentrating on the unimportant things.

EXCUSES FOR FAILURE

One of the most common ways of reacting to frustration caused by failure to reach a goal is indulging in *rationalization*. The person tries for a way out by coming up with a plausible excuse for failure; he tries to justify his behavior. This is illustrated by the industrial clerk whom we shall call Harold.

Upon graduation from high school, Harold was employed by the ABC Company as a general clerical worker in the office. During the ensuing five years he made satisfactory progress, and at the end of that time he was transferred into the accounting department. Shortly after beginning work in the accounting department, he married. Within the next few years Harold's family responsibilities increased until his salary was not sufficient to sustain the standard of living to which he and his wife had become accustomed and which they desired to maintain. Harold requested an increase in salary from his superior in the firm, and he was told that he was receiving all that the job was worth. The head of the accounting department told Harold that the only way in which he could hope to receive an increase in salary was to qualify himself for a higher-rated job. He advised Harold to enroll in an accounting course in a local night school.

Harold had not participated in any formal educational training since graduating from high school, where his work had been of only average quality. He enrolled for courses in accounting, but within a few months he began to experience difficulty with his schoolwork. His conduct in the office and at home became noticeably different. At the office he discoursed loudly and long to his fellow workers on the unnecessary attempts by accountants to make their work unduly hard for students and the unnecessary difficulty of standard accounting practices. At home, Harold's behavior showed a change. Whereas he had formerly taken considerable interest in his home and enjoyed playing with his children, he became surly toward his family.

As time wore on Harold's behavior changed from rationalization to *withdrawal* through daydreaming. Instead of working on his lessons for night school he began spending more and more time hanging around the local beer parlor, drinking mildly, and making various plans to get a job in which he would make a great deal more money. No effort was ever made to carry through these plans.

PILING UP FRUSTRATION

Let us use one final example to show how frustration after frustration may accumulate to such an extent that a person will become aggressive in violent ways that may even lead to the loss of his job.

The XYZ Electrical Manufacturing Company decided to have a time-and-motion study made. Joe M. worked on the assembly line in one of the company plants. He was a hard worker and took pride in his speed on the job. Since he had skill and was fast, he received one of the largest pay checks in the department. One morning Joe got up late and, while rushing around to leave for work, had a severe argument with his wife. When he arrived at work, he found a man standing a few feet away from his table. No words were exchanged between them, but as Joe worked he saw that this man was checking his movements with a stopwatch. Joe found that he was slowing down, and as he attempted to work fast he began to drop some of the tiny parts making up the assembly. As time passed, Joe became more and more angry. Finally he lost control of himself and shoved the motion-study man to the floor.

One may at first interpret the aggression shown by Joe as resentment of this particular time-and-motion-study man. In the hearing that followed, however, it became clear that Joe had been frustrated all morning. It began with his getting up late and having words with his wife; the frustration was added to by Joe's having had a difficult time finding a parking space; and it was climaxed by the checking of the time-and-motion-study man. Any one instance in itself would probably not have induced the aggression, but the accumulation of pent-up tensions finally reached the explosion point.

FATIGUE SYNDROME

This maladjustment, sometimes referred to as "neurasthenia," is another adjustment frequently used by the anxious person to shrink his problem to a level where he can cope with it. Prolonged tension and the aches and pains that accompany it may be very fatiguing. They may interfere with sleep and leave the individual yearning for rest in the daytime. Resting during the day in turn increases the chance that the person will not sleep well at night. He becomes discouraged and perhaps apathetic, restricting his activities to those involving the least possible exertion. This way of living may further block the satisfaction of the motive that produced the conflict and anxiety in the first place and thus may tend to perpetuate the pattern. Decrease in productivity adds to the complications.

Individuals with fatigue complaints usually talk freely about their troubles and frequently demand attention and sympathy. They arouse the anger of their fellow workers by their complaining and their frequent absences.

A public relations man for a well-known corporation began appearing at the office in a more or less haggard or distraught condition. He claimed to his associates that he was not sleeping well at night. It was obvious that he was less alert during the daytime than he had been previously. Several times during the day he would sit back in his chair to rest or he would even go to the lounge for a short nap. When he also complained about slight nausea and lack of appetite, others in the company encouraged him to get medical and then psychiatric assistance. While undergoing psychotherapy, he reviewed his enthusiastic approach to the public relations field some twenty years earlier. He had felt that he had all the qualifications to move quickly toward one of the top public relations posts in the nation. To reach this goal, he had traveled extensively and worked long hours both in the office and at home. He had known all along that he was sacrificing family welfare for his own vocational aspirations. It was only when he passed his fiftieth birthday that he became dimly aware that he was never going to be the great man in his field that he had dreamed of becoming. This dimly sensed realization was apparently responsible for the insomnia. Both the insomnia and the anxiety over not reaching a top position were responsible for the generalized fatigue reaction.

SOME COMMON DEFENSIVE REACTIONS

"If one waits patiently everything will turn out all right." This statement may sometimes be true, but usually problems are not solved so easily, much as we should like to think they are. This kind of statement is typical of the person who depends too much on someone else or who rationalizes his behavior and shows other common defensive reactions. Such reactions tell us about a lot of the "whys" of behavior. Some people even create myths to rationalize their own inadequacies.

DEPENDENCY

Statistics show that dependency is used more often than is its opposite, self-reliance. Dependency shows up several ways in what people don't do. Chief among these failures is unwillingness to make decisions to exert extra effort. Dependency is sometimes characteristic of the person who is satisfied with the *status quo* and is willing to "let George do it"—even though George will get all the credit.

PROJECTION

One may try to cover up some weakness through projection. One may attribute to others motivations, however unworthy, which he recognizes in himself. The dishonest person judges others to be similarly dishonest. Another example is found in the greedy person who attributes greediness to others. Not only is a projection a poor judgment; it is also a false belief.

IDENTIFICATION

In identification we are doing the reverse of projection. A person may claim as his own the admirable traits of others. It is common in school for the student to identify with a favorite teacher, or for the high school quarterback to identify with the pro. Identification may be good or bad for the person, depending both on his personal goals and on those of the person with whom he identifies. The individual who identifies well does more than feel or express admiration for another; he tends to copy the other person's actions and even his attitudes.

COMPENSATION

Compensation is common in most people, for most of us feel inadequate in so many ways. When achievement of an original goal is blocked, one may substitute a second goal and satisfy it instead. For example, the small person may develop a deep, husky voice as compensation. A student who has high ability in mechanical skills but who is weak in speaking and writing may compensate by becoming outstanding in tuning a motor.

OVERCOMPENSATION

Frustration sometimes leads to overcompensation. Failure in a business deal may make a man attempt to regain his self-respect by bragging about earlier accomplishments. Whereas compensation may lead to an effective adjustment, overcompensation may bring out obnoxious behavior.

REACTION FORMATION

In reaction formation we find the person, successful or otherwise, who attempts to conceal motives by publicly displaying attitudes that are their direct opposites. A feeling of hostility toward another may be expressed by excessive thoughtfulness where the other is concerned. We may well suspect the presence of this defense mechanism whenever "righteous indignation" occurs out of all proportion to the circumstances.

STARTING RUMOR

One very common defensive type of behavior involves starting rumors, and sometimes spreading them. Rumors may be started for political ends to defeat an opponent, or they may be unintentionally inspired. In this latter case the rumor serves a competitive need to enhance one's own ego.

Rumors tend to flow best horizontally. They spread more widely when they are ambiguous. Knowledgeable people are less likely to transmit rumors, particularly in crisis situations. Studies show that errors in relaying rumors are in the direction of what one expects to hear rather than of what one actually hears. This is typical behavior related to need satisfaction.

TOWARD SATISFYING NEEDS

The tendencies to *like to be with people,* to *seek approval,* and to *desire sympathy* are derived from positive motives. An infant is helpless and has to receive all his satisfactions from the ministrations of other persons. By the age of four months the child will smile on seeing the mother, before any food or other bodily attention has been given. This indicates that the process of conditioning has begun. Since kind words and praise are given simultaneously with care and petting, they become positive stimuli and the individual then seeks them. Let us illustrate how we may study need satisfaction at the adult level through the *psychology of participation.* A second example will illustrate how in a work situation the needs for *recognition* and the feeling of belongingness may become established.

STUDIES IN PARTICIPATION

During the meat conservation program in World War II, the government decided to try to convince housewives that they should use cheaper cuts of meat and thus stretch the supply. What was the best way to get them to change their old habits of buying choice cuts? Two kinds of test groups of housewives were organized: lecture groups and discussion groups.

The first test groups were exposed to lectures by competent speakers, who used excellent visual-aid charts and slides showing the various cuts of meat. The lecturers presented statistics to show that the family could get good nourishment from cheap cuts and save money at the same time. However, follow-up checks showed that, although the housewives listened attentively, they were not motivated to buy the cheaper cuts of meat.

For the second test groups, a different approach was used. There were no formal lectures. The group of housewives listened briefly to a leader who presented the facts and then let the women argue about prices, budgets, and health. Each member of the group had ample opportunity to express her opinion. The problem now belonged to the participants, not to some bureau in Washington. When the buying habits of this second group were checked and compared with those of the first group, it was found that the discussion group responded much more favorably.

FEELINGS OF RECOGNITION

We know that men want recognition. They want to feel that they belong. In one large industry with which the author is acquainted, the safety director told him that when the familiar "tell and repeat," "tell and repeat," was reinforced by giving more recognition to the workers—by having them submit suggestions on safety and serve on small safety committees—accidents declined more. He concluded by saying that although the safety problem was still of concern, he felt that the reduction in accidents was due partially to the fact that the safety program now *belonged* to the men. A need was being satisfied, at least in part.

NEED SATISFACTIONS ON THE JOB

Let us look for the moment at how a supervisor may apply effective human relations skills in a practical way. Let us assume that a plant worker comes to his foreman with a problem. He is obviously upset. If the foreman is well trained in the principles of human relations he will try to get the man to see his own problem.

First, the supervisor will *act as a sounding board* for the man's frustrations. This means that he must get the man to talk about what is bothering him, to reveal his real feelings. It is wise for him to avoid making any suggestions to the man in this stage, because it is known that the frustrated person regards any suggestions as an attack on him and this leads him to some form of defensive behavior. The result is merely further frustration on his part. The effective supervisor will act only as a listener in this first stage of working with the man. He will encourage him to get his frustrations off his chest.

Second, the good supervisor will try to *help the employee locate the cause of the trouble.* He will try to discover whether the problem is restricted to the man or whether it is more general. If it is the man's alone, he will encourage him to talk about what he thinks is the cause of the difficulty; the supervisor will try to get *him* to locate the problem, to state it.

Third, the supervisor will try to *get the worker himself involved in finding a solution to his problem.* The employee is more likely to modify his behavior or his attitude if *he* decides to do something about the problem than if he is told what to do. He will be asked to tell what he thinks the facts are, what he thinks should be done. The effective supervisor will encourage the worker to give several possible solutions and then to choose the best one to try first. This makes the employee consider the consequences of his suggestions. Thus by listening and by asking questions the supervisor helps the man to be less emotional and more ready to work the problem out along rational lines.

We may now ask what needs in the man have been satisfied in this situation. First of all, he has *received recognition;* the supervisor

has listened to his problem. Second, *frustrations have been relieved.*
Tension has been reduced, and the worker feels more secure in the
situation. Finally, the worker's *ego has been boosted;* he has gained
the feeling of belonging. His thinking was asked for, and the supervisor
considered it seriously.

College settings offer excellent opportunities for sharing problems.
For the person who wants to become a good listener, these settings
are a fine social laboratory.

NEED SATISFACTION AND LEARNING

Two things are well known about the success or failure of students
and persons working on jobs. First, in a person's attempts to achieve
his goals, repeated *frustration* results in decreasing motivation. Second,
repeated *success in overcoming barriers* tends to raise the level of aspiration. It is also important to remember that the aura of success
has some tendency to wear off with the passage of time.

When levels of aspiration and levels of ability are not too far
apart, occasional failure may become an asset to the individual in helping him learn to face these ordinary frustrating situations. In Chapter 4
we shall discuss the basic principles of learning and how they may
be applied to everyday situations.

Summary

Many of us wish to feel needed, not just wanted. It is basic to an
understanding of this and other aspects of behavior to realize that behavior is caused, it is motivated, and it is goal-directed. It is also important to understand how persons differ in their wants, their ambitions,
and the various roles they play. There are differences between men
and women not only in a biological sense but in attitudes as well.
Recognition of such differences is important in the study of human
motivation.

For most people pay is related to motivation, but many other
factors are also related to the complexity of our drives to get ahead.
We tend to seek relatively high levels of aspiration, but only up to
certain limits. There is a tendency for each of us in setting his level
of aspiration to stay out of an area that is too difficult or too easy.
And it takes a measure of time and experience for us to realize that
the curriculum of success is not made up entirely of required courses.

Getting ahead involves several factors of upward mobility—education, occupational place, individual ability, social techniques, ambition,
and the responses we make in different situations. Status and status

symbols are important in our wants, but the basic need for each of us is to feel we belong, whether or not we live and work in a high socioeconomic setting.

We can come to understand human needs by observing the ways we react to frustration through elementary, displaced, and organized aggression. Other reactions include working as a means of escape, making excuses for failure, piling up frustration, and even showing fatigue in certain ways.

We reveal our needs through our defensive reactions—dependency, projection, identification, compensation, overcompensation, reaction formation, and even spreading rumors.

The tendencies to like to be with people, to seek approval, and to desire sympathy are derived motives involved in satisfying needs. We also learn about need satisfaction through studies of participation and recognition and by understanding the three steps of good listening—acting as a sounding board, helping to locate the person's problem, and guiding solution.

Suggestions for Thinking and Discussion

1 Make a list of *your* wants or needs and compare them with those of several other persons. Which ones do you share? Which ones are individual to you?

2 After you have listed your needs, put them into a "need hierarchy" of first, second, third, etc. Do you find this difficult to do?

3 There are differences between men and women at work. If your class is co-ed, what are some differences between the sexes in role playing and goals?

4 Where does "pay" fit into *your* need hierarchy?

5 List the factors that now have an influence on *your* aspirations. How do these compare with the factors that influence the aspirations of some of your classmates?

6 List the ways in which *you* typically react to frustration. Which of these can you best control?

Suggestions for Further Reading

Bartoshuk, A. K. *Motivation.* Dubuque, Iowa: Wm. C. Brown, 1966. An experimentally oriented small volume written as a part of a self-selection put-together text.

Gardner, J. W. *Excellence.* New York: Harper & Row, 1961. A stimulating book related to the challenge of excellence in all our endeavors.

Garrison, R. H. *The adventure of learning in college.* New York: Harper, 1959. A paperback of practical suggestions, primarily for the freshman. It follows a sequence from emotional confusion to purpose; from intellectual chaos to order in learning about need satisfaction.

Rethlingshafer, D. *Motivation as related to personality.* New York: McGraw-Hill, 1963. Current thinking on human motivation.

Shaffer, L. F., & Shoben, E. J., Jr. *Psychology of adjustment,* Boston: Houghton Mifflin, 1956. Contains chapter which expands on reactions to frustration and defensive behaviors.

CHAPTER 3

How We Know
the World

❖ ❖ ❖ ❖ ❖ ❖ ❖ ❖ ❖

In this chapter we shall continue our examination of the major psychological principles which underlie all of man's behavior. Practical problems in psychology can be solved only if the proper tools, in the form of pertinent principles, are understood and hence available for application. Knowing about the world is an exceedingly complex business; it is not nearly so simple as it appears at first glance. Thus, many persons mistakenly assume that we simply see or hear what is "out there" and that is all there is to it. Actually, the world as we see it is not necessarily the world as it is.

Things are sometimes not what they seem. Look at the forms shown in Figure 3-1. In the upper figure the two horizontal lines are to be compared in length. In the second part the open space between the first and second circles is to be compared with the space including the second and third circles. In the third part the lengths of the two middle lines are to be compared. When you make these comparisons, what you see is undoubtedly different from what is out there, for measurement shows that all six lengths are equal!

For another example of the difference between things as they are and things as we see them, consider the following demonstration on induced movement. On a wall in a dark room an illuminated outline of a rectangle with a dot inside it is mounted as shown in Figure 3-2. The dot and the rectangle can be moved independently. If the dot remains fixed and the rectangle is moved toward the left, what is actually seen is the rectangle at rest and the dot moving to the right. This demonstration of induced movement may remind you of the moon appearing to move swiftly behind the clouds. Actually, of course, the clouds, which appear to be stationary, are moving, and the "moving" moon is at rest.

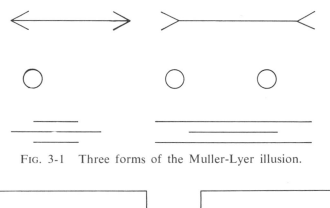

FIG. 3-1   Three forms of the Muller-Lyer illusion.

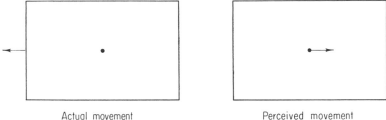

Actual movement   Perceived movement

FIG. 3-2   If the dot is not moved and the rectangle is moved toward the left as shown in the left drawing (actual movement), the subject will see the rectangle at rest with the dot appearing to move (perceived movement) as shown in the figure to the right.

That there are differences between objects, events, and people in the physical world and our observations of them is well known. If you would understand the world you must be aware of this basic fact. A painting is often seen in a variety of ways by different persons. The same painting will be judged beautiful by some observers; by others, ugly. Some students see the classroom as an exciting place in which to discover and learn; others see the same place as dull and uninteresting. To you, your dog may be friendly and playful; to the mailman, he may be threatening. A job is boring to one person and interesting to another.

PERCEPTION

The point to be kept in mind is that getting to know the world is a matter of interpreting, or giving meaning to, what is presented to the senses. This interpretive process is called *perception.* Percepts are different from the stimuli which act upon the senses. The stimuli come from objects in the world, but the stimuli are *not* the objects. When you see a river in the valley, what occurs is not that the body of water strikes your eyes but merely that light reflected from the surface of the water strikes your eyes. You perceive that the surface of the water is ruffled by a bridge when the light shimmers. You perceive a streamlined airplane when the whine of the jets grows louder and louder. Now an airplane is not a whining noise, any more than a river is a bright spot of light. If we are to know about man's behavior and eventually deal with the problems that confront him, we must examine critically the ways by which he gives meaning to, or interprets, the world about him.

THE SENSES

The first stage in the process of getting to know or perceive the world is the stimulation of one or more of the sense organs. These organs provide us with the following senses: vision, hearing, smell, the cutaneous senses (heat, cold, pain, pressure), the muscle sense, and the sense of balance.

All the senses act in basically the same way. Some form of physical energy such as sound, heat, pressure, or light activates the receptor cells in the eye, ear, nose, or other sense organ, and the messages in the form of nerve impulses are carried along nerves to the brain. The stimulus energy acting upon the sense organs comes from objects in the world about us: TV sets, light bulbs, houses, automobiles, people, books, and so on.

THE EYE

The structure of our sense organs has to do with the kinds of experience we have. For example, in the eye, the light detector called the *retina* consists of two kinds of anatomical structures: the *rods* and *cones.* The cones do the seeing in bright light, the rods at night. There are millions of rods and cones in the retina of each eye. The cones are most densely packed in the center of the retina. For this reason you must look directly at an object in order to see it best in daylight. The cones also see colors.

The rods of the retina are most closely packed in the periphery or outside edge of the retina. The center of the retina does not contain any rods at all. The rods are completely color-blind. And they do not provide us with sharp vision for detail, as do the cones. Thus, we cannot read or detect the markings on a map or sign with the rods alone. But the rods do provide us with night vision, and this is a great convenience, of course, since the cones, which are very sensitive to bright light, are blind at night. So sensitive are the rods to faint light that a match can be seen 10 miles away on a completely black night. The same mechanism permits us to see the planets and stars.

THE EAR

The world of sound is determined to a considerable degree by the structure of the hearing sense organs, just as the world of sight is determined by the anatomical and physiological characteristics of the eye and its parts. The most important part of one's hearing equipment consists of the hair cells of a membrane lying in the snail-shaped cochlea of the ear. Sound waves are picked up by the eardrum and transmitted by three bones of the middle ear into the inner ear. Here the hair cells become activated and start an impulse to the auditory nerve.

That the structure of the ear determines the experience of sound is illustrated by the fact that there are actually many sounds that the human ear does not detect at all. Generally, the best ears cannot hear sounds with frequencies below twenty waves per second, and on the other end of the scale, people seldom hear tones above 20,000 waves per second—just about the pitch of a cricket's chirp. Your dog can hear sounds much higher in pitch than you can! Indeed there are "silent" whistles made for dogs, whistles which dogs hear but you cannot.

TASTE

Often we come to know aspects of the world through a cooperative kind of activity on the part of several sense organs. A good example is the complex experience we have in eating. In the tongue there are nerve endings for taste—four kinds of receptors, in fact, which respond simply to sour, sweet, salt, and bitter. In the upper parts of the nasal cavity are nerve endings which provide information about the fragrant, spicy, putrid, and burnt qualities of food and other objects. These senses work in combination when food is eaten, and the information obtained about the food is affected if any one of the senses is not functioning properly. Thus food "tastes" flat when you have a bad cold because the nose is out of use and you get only combinations of the four simple tastes.

Perhaps you are thinking that to point out differences among the sense organs is an elaboration of the obvious. But the obvious things about man are frequently neglected in our attempts to explain his behavior. Our brief excursion into the structure of the sense organs and the way they act emphasizes the starting point or first stage in the complex process of getting to know the world. Without the sense organs and nerves and the activity within these structures, perception cannot take place. The absence of functioning eyes and ears in the blind and deaf automatically eliminates all visual and auditory perception from the experience of these people. If they have been blind and deaf from birth, the world can have meaning for them only through the other senses.

We shall have numerous occasions later in this book to use the basic principles of perception in dealing with psychology applied to life and work. Even at this early point the importance of functioning sense organs is apparent in connection with the practical problems of architectural design, television and radio advertising, camouflage, and accident prevention. This conclusion has been reached through a comparison of the accident experience of workers whose visual skills were superior with the experience of those workers having inferior vision. The findings show that employees whose vision is adequate for the job have fewer accidents than do employees with less-adequate vision.

PERCEPTUAL ORGANIZATION

Perceiving is under way when stimuli activate the sense organs. But at that point the perceptual story is not nearly complete. When we ask about the nature of what is perceived, we observe at the very outset the distinguishing feature of *organization*. The sensory information from the eyes, ears, nose, and skin is arranged in an orderly and meaningful manner. The problem of perception is also semantic in nature; even simple words become involved. Besides a certain color's being "blue" in English and "bleu" in French, it is just another shade of what we call "gray" to the color-blind person.

FIGURE AND GROUND

One of the most elemental organizing principles in perception is the tendency to pattern stimuli in terms of a *figure-ground* relationship. Not all parts of a stimulating situation reach one's awareness with equal clarity. That which we focus on at any given moment with any of the sense organs is the *figure*. That which is experienced at the same time but is out of focus is known as the *ground*. At this very moment your perceptions are organized in terms of figure and ground as you read this page. The printed words represent figure and the white pages are ground. In every perceptual act the figure-ground principle is operating when a selected part of the stimulating situation is perceived as standing out from the background: roses stand out against the green leaves of the bush, peach blossoms against the leaves and branches of the tree, mountains stand out against the sky, soloists against the background of the chorus, the melody lines of a trumpet against a background of harmonies. The factors that determine what will be figure appear to be distinctiveness of shape and contour, familiarity, novelty, grouping, and meaningfulness. In short, the things that make "sense" and are important to the perceiver stand out as figure, and the unimportant and less meaningful things form the ground.

CAMOUFLAGE

Sometimes we want to make a deliberate confusion of figure and ground. The aim of camouflaging is to destroy the enemy's perception of the figure—to conceal things that are familiar, meaningful, and important. Thus sharp contours which make an airplane hangar stand out as figure are removed by the use of roof netting; a soldier's uniform is made to blend with the jungle; a field gun located on the edge of the jungle is painted to resemble trees. In the protective coloration of birds, animals, and insects, we see many examples of camouflage in nature.

WHEN THINGS ARE SIMILAR

The organized nature of perception is strikingly apparent in the tendency to group stimuli in certain ways. According to one grouping principle, stimuli that are more *similar* to one another will have a greater tendency to be grouped. In Figure 3-3a the rows are perceived as horizontal, owing to grouping by similarity. Similarity may, of course, manifest itself through a variety of characteristics—shape, size, color, expression, or any other distinguishable property of the stimulus. And the similarity must always be envisaged in a psychological sense, i.e., as perceived by the observer. To you, the similarity between a kangaroo and an opossum may simply be that both are animals; to a zoologist the similarity may be that both are marsupials.

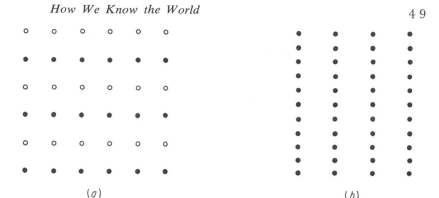

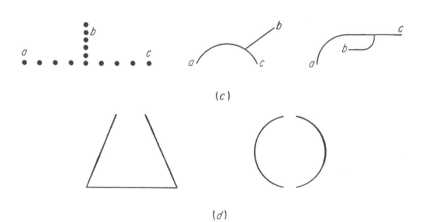

Fig. 3-3 Some stimulus organizational principles. In *a* the rows appear to be put together horizontally, rather than vertically, because of the complete *similarity* between elements. In *b* the dots are seen in vertical columns because the vertical columns are in closer *proximity* than the horizontal columns. In *c* the dots or the lines *continue* (*ac*), leaving the dots or lines of *b* going off alone. In *d* the figure at the left looks more like an enclosed triangle than a set of three lines. The figure to the right looks more like a broken circle than a pair of arcs.

PROXIMITY

Another grouping principle has to do with how *near* in time or space stimuli are to each other. Stimuli that are in closer proximity have a greater tendency to be grouped. In Figure 3-3*b* the dots are seen in vertical columns because the dots are nearer to one another in the vertical arrays than they are in the horizontal direction. Grouping on the basis of nearness or proximity in time is apparent when, in a series of light flashes, the flashes occurring close together in time tend to be grouped.

Stimuli are also organized according to the *continuity* principle, which states that there is a tendency for elements to go with others so as to permit the continuation of a line, curve, or movement in the direction already established. The dots or lines in Figure 3-3c group themselves as *ac/b* rather than as *ab/c*, for it seems that with the *a* segment, the *c* segment is more continuous than the *b* segment. Because of the continuity principle, two crossing lines are perceived as two crossing lines instead of as four lines. The tops of the buildings in New York are perceived as a skyline, instead of as isolated units, because of the continuity principle.

A final grouping principle that shapes one's perceptions is called *closure*. This refers to the tendency to complete or close figures with missing parts. In Figure 3-3d the observer tends to treat the configuration to the left, not as a set of three lines forming two angles, but as an enclosed triangle. Similarly, in the other figure the perceiver is more likely to see a broken circle than a pair of arcs. There is a need, it seems, for one to complete a configuration. The closure tendency operates in other sensory areas, too. In hearing, for example, there is a strong tendency to bring about closure by completing the rhythm.

You now see not only that perception is a process of sense-organ activation but also that the messages from the sense organs, are arranged or ordered so that the world as we come to know it is organized. But there is more to perception. Still to be reckoned with are a variety of personal factors such as prior experience, mental sets, needs, and emotion, and the ways in which they influence one's perception of the world.

The apparent size of people can be influenced by placing them in rooms of distorted shape. This is illustrated in Figure 3-4. Here we see three students of about the same height in a distorted room. They appear to be of three different heights.

Perception is certainly not a simple process. We see things in relation to our own needs, past experience, and feelings. In one experiment, a woman observed in a window the face of her husband to whom she had been married for twenty-five years. When compared with the face of another man in a nearby window her husband's face seemed to her to remain unchanged as he moved around. The other man appeared to grow or shrink as he moved to and fro.

FIG. 3-4 Three students of the same size in a distorted room. The man on the left is actually nearly twice as far from the camera as the one on the right, but the distorted perspective of the room conceals this fact. The floor of this room slopes upward to the right of the viewer. The rear wall recedes from right to left. A clue as to the construction of the floor may be noted by the way in which the men's shoes contact the floor. (*From Wittreich, W. J. Visual perception and personality. Scientific Amer., 1959, 200, 58. Reproduced by permission. Photograph by William Vandivert in the psychology laboratories of Princeton University.*)

Suspecting that there might be some special emotional relationship between this woman and her husband, the investigator repeated this experiment with other married couples. A stranger acted as the "control" in each experiment.

Most of the individuals saw their partner grow and shrink in the usual manner, and to the same apparent degree as the control stranger. However, six viewers reported that their partners altered less than the stranger or did not change at all. These couples turned out to be only recently married.

The experiment was continued because this phenomenon related apparently to marriage but not necessarily to how long the couples had been married. At the present time there is no complete explanation for the findings in this study.

In another study, involving the use of distorted lenses, some interesting observations were made. When an enlisted man looked through the lenses, his immediate superior, an officer, appeared less distorted than enlisted men in the room. Later twenty-four navy recruits viewed two different men through the lenses. One man wore the insignia of the recruits' immediate petty-officer superiors. The other man wore the insignia and canvas leggings of a recruit. The results showed that twenty-two of the twenty-four subjects *required lenses of higher distortion power* to perceive the "officer" as distorted. Measurements showed that the increase in lens power averaged about 50 percent.

Is some emotional anxiety involved in these phenomena? Is some feeling of identification playing a part? We do not have good answers to these types of questions. Even children who view themselves in a mirror through distorted lenses report different kinds of distortion at different ages. Girls, who are typically more anxious about their appearance than boys, *consistently* report less distortion than boys of the same age. Both children *and* adults report that their own mirror image is distorted in different ways from that of another person. One's own image changes mainly in detail. The other person's image appears to change in overall size and shape.

There is little doubt that in daily living we perceive the same things in different ways, and at different times. Some people characteristically view their world for only a moment in time; other people relate to the past. Perhaps one student put a great deal of understanding in this statement, "When I was nineteen my dad didn't know anything. When I was twenty-one I was surprised to see how much he had learned in two years."

PAST EXPERIENCE

The part played by prior experience as a perceptual determinant is nicely demonstrated when a person localizes sounds. When you hear a sound you try to localize it in some place "out there." We are so used to doing this that anything which interferes with this habitual coordination upsets our localizing ability. Such an upset was experimentally studied by a psychologist who had people wear a device called a "pseudophone." The pseudophone consists of a pair of ear trumpets so arranged that each receiving trumpet carries sound to the opposite side of the head. Wearing this instrument was at first disturbing, since there was a reversal of sounds, right and left. If the person was spoken to at the dinner table by someone at his right, he would turn to the left in answering. On the street the wearer of the pseudophone would often bump into people, because upon hearing their approach, he would move in the wrong direction. In time the subjects learned to get used to the new locations and made appropriate responses. The whole experiment is an interesting example of the effect of past experience on perception.

INTERPRETATIONS

Suppose that a man wearing a white shirt is standing in bright light holding a piece of coal. By appropriate physical measurements it could be easily shown that the amount of light reflected from the shirt is many times greater than that reflected from the coal. Now if the man goes into a shadowed area or a dimly illuminated cellar and physical measurements are again made, the amount of light reflected from shirt and coal would be proportionately the same. But a comparative measure of the total amount of reflected light in sunlight and shadow would show that actually more light is coming from the coal in the sunlight than from the shirt in the cellar. Yet under all conditions of illumination, the coal looks black and the shirt looks white. We have learned these color properties from past experience, and this experience determines our perceptions, despite the physics of the situation. This discrepancy between perception and physics also occurs when, from past experience, you know the color of a dress or the upholstering of a piece of furniture. These familiar objects "keep their color," regardless of the conditions of illumination.

The ability to see objects in depth or at a distance provides a number of illustrations of the effect of past experience on perception. From experience we know that objects near us are seen in clearer detail than far-away objects; hence vagueness in detail means depth or distance from the observer. If you live in an industrial section of the country where there are smoke and fog, try sometime to guess distances in a part of the country where the atmosphere is clear; you will find that your estimates are quite inaccurate. From experience we know the approximate size of a man and also that a man looks smaller the farther away he is from the observer; hence, knowing the size of objects, we perceive them at various distances from us, depending on how big they appear.

The way one is reared in a particular culture often shows how one's past experience influences his perception. For example, a loud belch from the mouth of a dinner guest in some places of the Orient is perceived as a compliment by his host. It goes without saying that an American without knowledge of Oriental customs would perceive this behavior quite differently. Another example is the case of a group of African visitors in London who perceived the London bobbies as especially friendly because they raised their right hand, palm forward, to approaching traffic. Instead of perceiving this behavior as a signal for stopping traffic, the Africans perceived it in terms of what this gesture meant in their own country.

To ignore a person's past experience is to ignore a major determinant of perception. The world is perceived in terms of experience formerly associated with it. Keep this in mind and you will stop making the commonly unwarranted assumption that everyone perceives the world in the same way.

THE ROLE OF SET IN PERCEPTION

Set is the term applied to the tendency for a person to pay attention to certain features of a situation. The sprinter is set when he is waiting for the race to begin at the crack of the starter's gun. A tie salesman is set to notice his customer's neckwear; a shoe salesman, his shoes. Some sets are habitual; others are determined by the immediate aspects of a situation, including instructions as to what we are to observe. Right now you are set to learn about the role of set as a perceptual determinant.

Consider the following facts, keeping in mind that you will later be questioned about them. At the first floor of a building an elevator starts with six occupants; it stops at the second floor where two people get off and four get on; four persons get on and one gets off at the sixth floor; on the eighth floor, two people get off and three get on. How many stops did the elevator make? Many people cannot give the right answer, because, instead of counting stops, they were counting the number of persons getting on and off at each stop.

INFLUENCE BY SET

Here is a laboratory experiment which demonstrates the effect of set on perception. In Figure 3-5 the object in the center is exposed very briefly. After the exposure, the subjects of the experiment are asked to make a reproduction of what they have seen. When the subjects are told ahead of time that the exposed figure will be like a pair of eyeglasses they perceive glasses, as indicated by reproductions such as those on the left. When other subjects are shown the same figure under the same conditions but are told to expect a dumbbell, they draw reproductions like that on the right.

Another experiment on set and perception was carried out by briefly exposing to groups of subjects a series of words, some in their normal printed form and some reversed. Without definite instructions as to what to expect, the subjects were slower to recognize the reversed words than those presented in their normal way. When, however, they were told beforehand that some of the words would be reversed, this induced set caused a great increase in their accuracy of perception.

Everyday living is replete with examples of set as an important determinant of what one perceives. After hearing the words "ham and" you are set to hear "eggs." You are set to hear "beans" if you hear

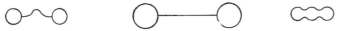

FIG. 3-5   The phenomenon of *set*. When subjects are told that they will be shown something that looks like a pair of eyeglasses and are very briefly shown the figure in the center, they make a drawing like the one on the left. When other subjects are told that they will see a dumbbell, they make drawings similar to the one on the right. In each case they are set to see a particular object.

"pork and" first. And you will be likely to hear "beans" even if the word actually spoken is "greens." Some persons say that they cannot sleep because their hearts pound in their ears or because of the ticking of a bedside clock. Most of us are scarcely aware of this pounding and ticking. The insomniac, however, is looking for explanations for his sleeplessness and so is set for many types of stimulation which are disregarded by most people. Everyone will hear the ticking clock and beating heart if he sets himself to listen for them. The doctor generally hears the telephone ring in the night, but not the baby's crying. His wife, however, will sleep through the ringing telephone but waken to the stirring and crying of the baby.

THE INFLUENCE OF NEEDS

Perceptions are to a large degree determined by needs and desires. In other words, we see what we want to see. Like the mirrors at amusement parks, we distort the world; the distortion is in relation to our needs and desires. In the last chapter you saw the importance of needs in governing man's behavior. Perceptual behavior is no exception to the all-pervasive influence of needs.

The influence of need in shaping perception has frequently been studied in the experimental laboratory. An example is a study in which subjects in various stages of hunger were asked to report what they saw in ambiguous white and black drawings flashed before them for very short periods of time. The results of the experiment showed that as hunger increased up to a certain point, the subjects saw more and more of the ambiguous figures as articles of food. Thus the hungry subjects "saw" more steaks, salads, and ham sandwiches than subjects who had just eaten.

For an everyday example of the effects of needs on perception, consider two men looking through a store window at a display of automobile accessories. One man needs a tire, and the other, some antifreeze. Both men are exposed to the same objects in the window display. The first will notice the brand, tread, and price of the tires and pretty largely neglect the other objects. The second will be able to tell you all about the antifreeze preparations and will have little information about anything else. What was clearly perceived by each of these men was determined by his particular need. If you need to buy a car you will see structural characteristics, colors, and styling of automobiles that are missed completely by a person who has no interest in buying a new car.

EMOTIONS AND PERCEPTION

A person's emotional state—whether he is angry, happy, sad, or excited—has a lot to do with his perceptions. A strong emotion like fear can make a person perceive danger on all sides. People have been known to shoot bushes, trees, and fence posts when they anticipated danger. Such common expressions as "blind rage," "love is blind," and "paralyzing fear" describe the influence which emotion may have on a person's perception of a specific situation and his reaction to it.

INFLUENCE WITHOUT AWARENESS

In a study on emotion and perception, children at a summer camp judged the characteristics of faces in photographs before and after playing a "scary" game of "murder." The amount of maliciousness or evil seen by the children in the faces was much greater after the game than before. The emotional state aroused by the game caused the youngsters to perceive the faces differently than before.

Emotional states may even operate at a level so primitive that they influence perception before the individual is aware of the stimulus. This is indicated by an experiment in which subjects studied a list of nonsense syllables. Certain of these syllables were always accompanied by an electric shock on the subject's hand. Shock normally induces an electrical skin response which can be accurately recorded with suitable apparatus. After a number of pairings of syllable and shock it was possible to omit the shock and get the electrical skin response by presenting only the syllable. Now the experimenter presented the syllables in an exposure device for extremely short periods of time. The subjects gave the electrical skin response *before* they recognized the syllable. For syllables that were not accompanied originally by shock, the effect was not nearly so pronounced. It would seem that the shock syllables came to be threatening syllables, and their general fearful character was perceived before the detailed make-up of the syllables themselves.

ATTENTION

At this point in your reading about perception, it should be clear that in getting to know the world one selects or filters out stimuli from the sense organs and organizes them in a meaningful way. We use certain stimuli and reject others or else relegate the other stimuli to minor roles. The fact that the perceiver picks out certain kinds of stimuli is another way of saying that he attends to only a few at a time. When you pay attention, you focus your attention on something. What, now, are the conditions which cause us to focus our perceptions on what is going on in the outside world? You should have some ready answers. One's past experience, sets, needs, and emotions play important roles. And so does the way the world is organized in terms of figure and ground, similarity, nearness, and other principles of stimulus organization. But certain additional causes of attention warrant specific mention, especially in view of their use in applied psychology.

FACTORS IN ATTENTION

The changing quality of a stimulating situation influences perceptual focusing. *Change attracts attention:* change from one color to another; change from present to absent; change from one intensity to another; change from moving to stationary; change from big to small. Your cat ignores the stationary ball of yarn but pounces on it when it moves. You scarcely notice the traffic noises on a busy street, but if the volume of traffic decreases, the "quiet" attracts your attention.

Repetitiveness is another determinant of attention. "Help, help, help!" will attract attention when a single "Help!" would pass unnoticed. Repeated taps on the shoulder attract attention more surely than a single signal. A weak stimulus frequently repeated may be more effective than a strong one presented only once. But there are limits to the effectiveness of repetition. If a stimulus is repeated many times, it ceases to hold attention, because of its monotony, or yields to some other stimulus that has the advantage of novelty and change.

Intensity, of course, is a powerful determiner of attention. When we are not perceptually focusing on anything in particular, we are likely to notice the loudest noise, a bright flash over a faint twinkle, the most pungent perfume. With visible objects, size has the same effect as intensity. Small details are less likely to catch the attention than large objects.

Some stimuli are more potent than others in attracting attention because of their *novelty* or unusual quality. Recall how attention-demanding is a dog who runs onto the football field during a game. A new suit or hat, the smell of smoke where usually there is none—all these are examples of attention arrest by unusual or novel stimuli.

Difference or *contrast,* somewhat like change, contributes to the focusing of perception. Anything that is different from its general surroundings stands out and catches the eye: a hole in the carpet, a smudge on a smooth wall, a dark spot in a bright landscape, a small pebble inside one's shoe.

Social suggestions may cause people to attend to a particular stimulus. You probably know the old stunt in which several students gazing intently at an ordinary notice on a bulletin board soon attract a crowd. And perhaps you have tried the prank of looking intently at the sky, moving your head slowly in a wide arc, and having other people do the same thing even when there is nothing of interest to see. People respond to social suggestion by paying close attention to something which other persons are apparently observing.

DISTRACTION

It is appropriate to discuss in this chapter the influence of distracting stimuli on behavior because distraction is simply changing the focus of perception or attending to something else. Everyone has had difficulty in directing his attention because of flashing lights, loud noises, odors, gossip, or other kinds of distracting stimuli.

When the stimulus causing the distraction acts upon the same sense organ that is concerned with attention, the effect is pronounced. Thus outside noises interfere greatly when one is talking over the telephone, but flashing lights may have little distracting effect.

Of course not all distraction comes from the outside. It is difficult to attend to what you are doing if you are worried, afraid, or excited.

In this connection it has been found that taxicab drivers who had family worries were more likely to have accidents than those who did not. The accidents occurred because the worried drivers were unable to meet the attention requirements of safe driving.

From a practical standpoint, the control of distraction is important because a person's efficiency may be reduced by stimuli that take attention away from his job. The accidents incurred by the taxi drivers is a case in point. In one study, the actual cost of distraction was determined in terms of the energy required to perform a unit of work. Typists worked under two conditions: some days surrounded by sound-proof walls; other days in the same place except that the partitions were removed, allowing the usual noises to prevail. The energy cost was measured by having the typists breathe into a bag so constructed as to capture the expired air. The air was then analyzed for the amount of carbon dioxide, and from this, oxygen consumption was determined. The amount of typing accomplished under the quiet and noisy conditions was the same, but the energy cost was much greater under the noisy condition.

ILLUSIONS

When something goes wrong in either the physical or the mental world, the underlying reasons for the mishap may be more easily seen than when everything is running smoothly. For this reason we can learn something regarding the process of perception from a study of illusions. An illusion is a surprising error of perception. We experience illusions when a stimulus is so misleading that we fall into a trap and get a false meaning from the signs received by our sense organs.

You can easily demonstrate one of the most ancient of illusions by shutting your eyes, crossing two fingers, and running a pencil between the fingers, as shown in Figure 3-6. Your perception will be such that you are aware of two pencils being run over your fingers instead of one. This occurs because, in the past, when adjoining fingers were stimulated on their outside edges, the stimuli always came from two objects, not from one. In other words, this illusion is due to habit and familiarity derived from prior experience. You should be reminded at this point of our earlier discussion about the important role played by past experience in shaping all our perceptions.

Familiarity and habit give rise to what is known as the proofreader's illusion. In learning to read we learn to respond to larger and larger patterns—words, sentences, paragraphs. Once these habits are established they tend to be aroused by a variety of particular stimuli that have been a part of the whole stimulus pattern. This means that a word will be perceived as such when not all the parts are actually stimulating. But the reader, set for the meanings, responds to a few cues and reads on, not noticing the printer's errors. If the word as printed has enough resemblance to the right word, it arouses the same response. In the effort to print books perfectly, proofreaders are employed whose job is to look specifically for printer's errors. This means that the proofreader must ignore the tendency to perceive whole units and must concentrate on the elements. But so deeply ingrained is the old habit that even the professional falls into the trap of the proofreader's illusion and makes errors.

An illusion familiar to everyone is experienced at the movies. Actually, not pictures in motion but extended series of still pictures are projected on the screen. The seen or apparent motion must be

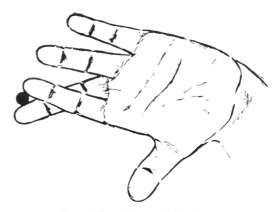

Fig. 3-6   A tactual illusion.

in the viewer; in other words it must be the product of perception. You can readily demonstrate apparent motion by holding your forefinger about 3 inches in front of your nose and looking at it while blinking first one eye and then the other. To the left eye, the finger appears to one side and to the right eye, more to the other side. When you blink by closing one eye and simultaneously opening the other, the finger seems to move across your field of vision. Apparent or illusory movement is an illustration of the general tendency to perceive wholes or patterns. In trying to combine successive stationary objects into a perceptual whole, the observer creates a sense of movement between the actually stimulated points.

A variety of common visual illusions is shown in Figure 3-7. In the Poggendorf illusion the continuity of a line is interrupted by strips of narrow width laid across it at an angle. You can easily see what effect is given to the character of the line. In the Zollner figure, lines as indicators of direction are made misleading by the introduction of cross-hatching; the lines were originally drawn parallel. An interesting error occurs in the ring segments illusion: the two arcs are drawn with lines of the same length, but the misleading effect of the spatial separation of one from the other is clearly apparent.

Illusions are extreme instances of the difference between what *is* "out there" and what we perceive to be "out there." Illusions dramatically illustrate that perception can play tricks on us. The point to be remembered is that illusory experiences are simply illustrations of the main theme of this chapter: that the world as people see it is not necessarily the world as it really is. We must be concerned with what people see in addition to what we show them; with what they

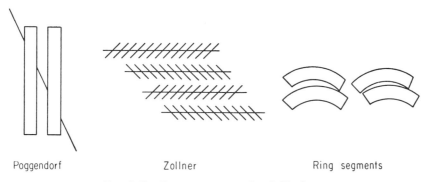

Poggendorf   Zollner   Ring segments

Fig. 3-7   Some common visual illusions.

hear besides what we say to them. Whether we feel hot or cold depends largely on us, not on the thermometer.

PERCEPTUAL FACTORS IN ADVERTISING

Nowhere are the applications of the basic principles of perception brought to our attention more forcefully than in advertising. Printed advertisements, regardless of media, involve visual perceptual processes exclusively. Radio advertising, in contrast, depends on auditory perception, and television involves visual and auditory perception combined. Let us illustrate with some studies showing how advertising and selling are related to some of the principles of perception which we described in this chapter.

Two investigators measured the relevance of illustration to copy in thirty-nine advertisements appearing in *House Beautiful, House and Garden,* and *The Saturday Evening Post.* The pictures were cut from the copy and mounted on a white-cardboard background. The college student subjects were asked to indicate whether they had or had not seen each of the pictures before. They were asked what product was featured in the picture and what caught their attention. The product judged correct most often was the conspicuous, and in most cases the centermost, object: judged correctly next most often was the trademark. The product and its trademark stood out and were remembered best when there were fewer distracting objects in the picture. Plain and unambiguous representation of the product was characteristic. Further, these pictures contained within their borders printed words which tersely informed the reader of the desirable features of the product. The human subjects of the illustrations reflected happiness and contentment in their faces. The investigators concluded that not only must an advertisement be perceived, its message must be understood. Word choice and sentence structure are key variables in understanding. (Note how this is featured in the advertisements you remember.)

In a *spot-advertising* study, a packaged-drugs firm was interested in determining the effectiveness of its spots. Key words were taken from sample advertisements, and subjects were asked to free-associate with each. The final question posed was, "What product or service does this remind you of?" For example, when male and female subjects were asked to free-associate to the word "membrane," 42 percent responded with "form of skin or tissue." Also a mixed *emotional* attitude was found; 57 percent of the subjects expressed like and 42 percent dislike. The most frequent response to the phrase "shrinks swollen nasal membranes" was "colds." Further, the word had a high brand-associative value for the company.

The research indicated that very favorable feelings existed toward such words and phrases as "penetrating ingredient," "stimulates," and "gives you a lift." Such words as "antiseptic" and "medicates" aroused favorable responses, whereas unfavorable reactions were elicited by "bacteria," "congestion," and "inflamed." The researchers noted that when negative emotions are involved, the advertisement should provide a way out. The results of studies of radio spot ads are in effect similar. The "voice" of the announcer means much with regard to what feelings will be aroused.

Selling also relates to perception. Several years ago when the dairy companies first introduced bottled fruit juice on their milk routes, one firm set up an excellent sales presentation. The route man was instructed to ring the bell and to hand the housewife a bottle of the juice as she opened the door. Then he was to say, "Pardon me, please hold this for me." Imagine the impact of *feeling* the cold bottle, *seeing* the contents, and *hearing* the sales story!

A POINT OF VIEW

Just as engineering is dependent on the physical sciences to provide facts and principles for making things that work, so it is that applied psychology depends on basic data from the behavioral sciences. Although the emphasis in this book is *applied,* the reader will note that on occasion we shall describe fundamental researches also. Basic research really goes hand-in-hand with developmental applications, and often we shall make no attempt to draw distinctions between the "pure" and the "applied." When answers to good questions are demanded, we need both. Nowhere is this better illustrated than in the area of learning, particularly for the new college student who seeks to "learn how to learn." The following two chapters deal with the facts and theories of learning, and their applications, ranging from reward reinforcement to efficient study techniques.

Summary

We do not always "see" what we look at nor "hear" what we listen to. And it is possible to make "unreal" things look "real." Getting to know the world is a matter of interpreting, or giving meaning to what is presented to the senses. This interpretive process is called *perception.* The fundamentals of perception are basic to dealing with many applied problems, ranging from accident prevention to the use of camouflage.

The several organizing principles in perception include figure-ground relationships, similarity of stimuli, and the principle which has to do with how near in time and space stimuli are to each other. Stimuli also get organized according to the continuity principle and in terms of closure.

How we interpret the world we perceive through the senses depends on past experience and on what we expect to see, hear, or feel. Experience in a cultural setting is related to how we interpret a perception. Not everyone perceives the world in the same way.

There is a tendency for a person to pay attention to certain features of a situation. Thus it is that we get a set to notice a person's dress, or from a variety of noises in the night, we hear only the crying of the baby.

People's perceptions are also determined by their wants and needs. The hungry person may perceive the hot dog vendor at the ball game as a welcome sight. Someone else may see him as a nuisance. And our emotional state influences what we perceive. Such states may operate at a level so primitive that they influence perception before the individual is aware of the stimulus.

Factors involved in attracting attention include change, repetitiveness, intensity, novelty, difference, and suggestions. These are important in advertising and other situations involving the influencing of people.

It is important also in understanding perception to view the influences of distracting stimuli and the disturbances that may be caused by illusions. Such factors make it difficult for observers to identify objects accurately; they sometimes cause us to see or hear things that are not really there.

Suggestions for Thinking and Discussion

1 Go out of your room. Make a list of (*a*) the things on your desk; (*b*) any pictures on the wall; (*c*) the furniture in the room. After making the list, check it for accuracy. Did you leave out anything? Did you put in anything that was not actually there?

2 Close your eyes. Have someone snap his finger in front of you, behind you, at your side, and over your head. How accurately could you "locate" the sound?

3 People have a tendency to see problems "within their own point of view." Get several people of different ages to describe "college athletics and academic standards." What differences do you find in how people *perceive* the problem?

4 Repeat the word "man" aloud several dozen times. Does it temporarily lose "meaning"?

5 How do *your* needs influence *your* perceptions?

6 What is meant when we say, "There is no real movement in a motion picture"?

Suggestions for Further Reading

Dember, W. *Psychology of perception*. New York: Holt, 1960. An overall picture of perception from measurement to curiosity.

Geldard, F. A. *The human senses*. New York: Wiley, 1953. A description of all the human senses.

Hochberg, J. E. *Perception*. Englewood Cliffs, N.J.: Prentice-Hall, 1964. A paperback introduction to perception which extends the content of this chapter.

Solomon, P., et al. *Sensory deprivation*. Cambridge, Mass.: Harvard, 1961. How perceptual disturbances occur when an individual experiences markedly reduced stimulation for a relatively long period of time.

Vernon, M. D. *The psychology of perception*. Baltimore: Penguin Books, 1962. Another brief review of the field of perception.

CHAPTER 4

Changing Behavior Through Learning

❖ ❖ ❖ ❖ ❖ ❖ ❖ ❖ ❖

The account in the last chapter of how we get to know the world has shown how man becomes immediately aware of his environment. We have seen that to understand this becoming-awareness called "perceiving" it is necessary to take into account not only the nature of the sense organs which receive the stimulation, but also the perceiver's prior experience, "sets," emotions, needs, and other reaction tendencies. When we do this we know why, at a particular moment, the individual has a certain kind of perceptual experience. Now we face the question of how sets, emotional states, and related tendencies happen to be present at a given time in a given individual. Furthermore, we want to discover how one handles a new situation outside the realm of his past experience. For answers to these implied questions we turn to the topic of learning.

Learning is a universal human experience. A child learns to feed himself, to talk, to play, and in general to regulate his behavior toward people and things. He learns what is taught in school. He learns the social habits and customs of the community in which he lives. Later in life he learns how to do a job and how to meet the responsibilities of family life. Playing tennis, driving an automobile, getting along with one's wife, handling the boss—all these kinds of behavior are possible because people are able to learn. An examination of learning leads to the simple but important conclusion that its chief feature is a *modification* or *change* in behavior that *lasts* for some period of time. And it is helpful to remember that the learning process requires patience.

CHARACTERISTICS OF LEARNING

Let us now examine an everyday learning situation in some detail in order to see exactly what happens when we learn. Consider the case of a person learning to drive an automobile. Despite his desire to drive, he does not have the necessary skill, so he sets out to change his behavior. At first his efforts are only partially successful. He starts with a violent jerk or stalls the engine. Once he is under way, steering becomes a problem as he cuts the corners too sharply or is unable to stay on the right side of the road. Abrupt stopping may occur because of inappropriate braking action. The driver displays many responses— some right and some wrong. Those which he perceives as wrong are gradually eliminated in favor of the responses which are right in that they lead him toward the goal of driving the car in the proper way. He repeats the right responses over and over again and they become smoother, more precise, and better timed. Eventually, driving an automobile is added to his repertoire of behavior. And in one way, at least, the individual is a *different* person from his former self. He is now an automobile driver, whereas before he was not.

THE LEARNING GOAL

Certain elements common to most learning situations are present in the learning-to-drive-a-car task. In the first place there is a *goal*. This means that the learner wants something. He has a need or desire to learn. If such an urge is not present he will never get under way. Before a man can be taught to operate a lathe he must want to learn to be a lathe operator. You won't learn about psychology or tennis or calculus or typing unless you want to acquire this knowledge or learn these skills. Why a person would want to drive an automobile is perhaps obvious, but in this analysis the reason is of no consequence. The point to be remembered is that he did have the desire.

Often we fail to appreciate the importance of the learner's goal in teaching or training because the goal as the teacher perceives it may be different from the learner's perception of the goal. If the teacher's goal is to get the student to learn as much as possible about the subject matter in the available length of time, he may be disappointed when the student's performance falls far below the teacher's expectations. The reason for the mediocre performance may lie in the student's goal. Perhaps his goal was to learn just enough to get by or just enough to make a C grade. There will be a difference in what is learned in an industrial training program if the trainer's goal is to get the employee to learn to produce the maximum number of units of a given quality in a given time and the employee's goal is to produce just enough to keep the foreman off his back and the time-study man from cutting his rate.

RESPONSES ARE NECESSARY

After the individual has a desire or need to learn, so that there is a clear-cut goal in his own mind, what else is necessary if learning is to take place? The old adage that "we learn by doing" provides the answer. Thus, the second factor common to all learning is some kind of activity, or *response*. The learner himself must do something— make responses. This activity may be overt, e.g., arm, leg, or hand activity in playing tennis, or it may be inside the person, so to speak, as when he manipulates ideas in solving a problem. Trying to teach a person anything by giving him a verbal description of what you want him to do, or demonstrating to him how the task should be done, or showing him by means of a moving picture the nature of the skilled performance, is of little use unless it leads to active doing by the learner himself. The person who learned to drive the automobile not only had the desire to learn but he did something about it by resorting to many responses—arm, leg, finger, reading, judging responses—all of which were a part of his natural equipment.

Of course, the necessary responses for attaining a goal must be *potentially available* to the would-be learner. A feebleminded person cannot get through school because the intellectual responses necessary for schoolwork are not available to him. The very young child cannot learn to write until his nervous and muscular system are sufficiently developed to enable him to make the fine coordinations necessary for handwriting. The responses necessary for learning a new task may also be limited by *previous learning*. Learning may be slow or impossible in an advanced course in mathematics if a prerequisite is a basic course in algebra and the learner has never taken such a course. In the automobile driving situation the necessary responses are available to most people. In some cases, however, poor coordination, slow reaction speed, faulty vision, or some physical or mental defect may make it impossible to learn to drive.

REINFORCEMENT

How now do we account for the fact that the learner with a goal, and making many responses, *selects* certain of these responses—the right ones—and eliminates the wrong ones? This question brings us to the third basic characteristic of learning: *reinforcement*. The learner selects from all the responses he is making those that are reinforced. The responses that are not reinforced are eliminated or not learned.

You can easily understand the nature of reinforcement if you keep in mind that the person trying to learn is, in a sense, out of balance with his environment. He sets out to restore himself to a balanced state by learning some adjustive act. The consequences of any act—reduction of pain, avoidance of distress or punishment, recognition, success, reward, pleasure—which lead the learner toward his goal are reinforcing. The satisfaction which accompanies a successful outcome reinforces the success-getting response, so the learner tends to repeat such responses. The unreinforced responses, since they are not successful in leading to the goal, are weakened. Our automobile driver resorted to many responses, some of which he eventually discovered were successful; others were unsuccessful. The former were repeated over and over again, each time receiving added reinforcement; the latter were not repeated because of lack of reinforcement, and hence were not learned.

The effect of knowing how one is doing—whether his responses are right or wrong—provides the clearest and simplest illustration of reinforcement as a learning principle. In learning situations like playing tennis, bowling, casting for trout, or typewriting, the correct or successful response is usually apparent to the learner. When one makes a strike in bowling, the visual cues from the falling pins tell him immediately that the way he rolled the ball was the right way, and the ensuing reinforcement causes him to try to roll the ball the same way the next time. But suppose the learner has no way of knowing whether his response is correct. In a situation like this, reinforcement cannot occur, or is minimized, and hence learning should at least be retarded.

THE LACK OF REINFORCEMENT

A striking illustration of how the lack of reinforcement impedes learning progress is a wartime study in which men were being trained to track airplanes with a tracking apparatus. Two groups of equal tracking ability, as determined by previous performance, were observed. One group was given knowledge of results in the form of a buzzer which was sounded by the trainer whenever the trainee was off the tracking point by more than 2 miles. In other words, reinforcement was present in the form of feedback to the learner as to the correct and incorrect tracking responses. The other training group received no information at all and hence no reinforcement. After only sixty-eight minutes of practice, the group trained with the buzzer was found to be off target only 32 percent of the time, whereas the group trained without the buzzer was off 58 percent of the time. Reinforcement really works!

CLASSES OF REINFORCERS

Because of earlier discussions of perceptual principles you should not be surprised to know that the effect of reinforcement will depend on the *perception* of the individual who is learning. An outcome that is reinforcing to one person may not be reinforcing to another. What one person regards as a rewarding experience may be regarded as a neutral or even as a punishing experience by another. However, in general, one can count on an almost universal acceptance of certain classes of reinforcers such as money, food, status recognition, and companionship.

WE MAY NOT KNOW

Reinforcement often occurs automatically, without the learner's being aware of the effect at the moment. Suppose that you have been playing mediocre golf for a couple of years and decide to improve your game with the help of a professional instructor. The instructor watches you play and criticizes your habit of gripping the club like a baseball bat. He says, "That is no way to hold a golf club. How on earth did you pick up that habit?" You will probably reply to the effect that when you first took up golf you simply picked up the club and tried to hit the ball. But why did you learn to grip the club in the wrong way? The wrong way must have been reinforced, otherwise it would not have been learned. The important point is that you did not perceive it to be the wrong way. Very likely you gave little thought to the grip but concentrated on hitting the ball. The reinforcement that was responsible for your bad habit was probably the natural or comfortable feel of the baseball grip. You failed to grip the club the proper way because, to the novice, this way feels awkward and strained. Much human learning occurs and persists under conditions of reinforcement which were never specifically identified by the learner, or if once identified, were later forgotten.

We shall have a great deal to say about the operation of the basic factors of learning and their applications in coming chapters of this book. You will be in a sound position to appreciate the ensuing discussions if you keep in mind that a learner must have a *goal,* that he must make *responses,* and that these responses must be *reinforced.*

And do not forget that the responses which the learner makes are limited by his *abilities,* his *prior experience,* and his *perception of the learning situation.*

MOTIVATION AND LEARNING

Needs, wants, desires, interests, ambitions, and similar terms may all be subsumed under the more general term *motive,* as indicated in Chapter 2. Most students of human behavior agree that the human being is a goal-directed organism. This is another way of saying that man is motivated. You have no doubt used the word "motive" many times and think of it as something that moves a person to some kind of action. This is a conventional dictionary definition and, as a start, is acceptable from a psychological standpoint. A little reflection on your part about the conditions or bodily states or objects or events that arouse man to act in certain ways will bring to mind the need for food, the desire for recognition, the need for companionships, and the need for an education. The interesting psychological question is: how does man come to have these many and varied motives? The practical answer to this question is that he is born with some of them and acquires others. We do not learn to be hungry or thirsty or to need sleep. We come into the world endowed with these needs. But we do learn to want or need a new TV set, a new car, a trip abroad, or an education. Here, then, is a basic classification of man's motives: inborn or primary motives and learned or secondary motives.

PRIMARY AND SECONDARY MOTIVES

Man's first needs embrace the primary motives. These must be satisfied if he is to survive. But one can live without satisfying his learned motives. On the other hand, if they are not satisfied, life may not seem to be worth living. For most of us to be happy, certain learned needs, e.g., the need for new clothes, for entertainment, for education, and so on, must be satisfied. Some persons literally destroy themselves trying to satisfy learned motives. For example, a man's acquired desire for wealth and power may be so strong that he neglects his primary needs for food, sleep, and exercise, with the result that he ruins his health and dies.

With motives classified in two broad categories, let us now examine the relationship between the two kinds of motives and the learning process. We have mentioned hunger, thirst, and the need for sleep and designated them as unlearned. But the ways in which they are satisfied make it necessary to bring *learning* into the picture. You do not learn to be hungry, but you do learn to go to a restaurant or dining room or other food source to satisfy your hunger. The man who wants to go to Delmonico's for dinner is exhibiting two kinds of motivated behavior: the desire to eat, the primary motive, and the desire to go to a specific eating place, the learned motive. We do not learn the primary sex drive, but we do learn how to satisfy it. The primary motives, even though unlearned, energize or arouse the individual to learn ways of satisfying them.

Learned motives, although based on primary motives, may become motivating forces *in their own right.* By this we mean that a learned motive may call forth a specific kind of activity in the *absence of the primary motive* on which it was originally based. For example, a soldier learns to shoot a rifle in order to save his life. Handling the rifle skillfully is learned at first because of the primary need for self-preservation. But skilled rifle shooting, in and of itself, without any need to protect oneself, may become a motive that prompts the soldier to spend many hours on a rifle range long after the war is over. Now there is a motive in the form of a desire to use the rifle not to kill the enemy but to demonstrate to oneself and others how good one is at rifle shooting. What was once a means to an end has become an end in itself.

After a motive is learned, it may serve to induce still further learning. The rifle shooter may find it necessary to seek out certain influential people who can get him membership in a shooting club so that he can use the club's rifle range. Finding out who the influential persons are and persuading them to sponsor an outsider is quite a different kind of behavior from shooting at a rifle range. The learned desire for a college education induces some young men to learn to become steelworkers so that they can earn enough money to pay tuition. Learning to work in a steel mill is an altogether different kind of behavior from that which will be displayed in the classroom. Notice how the goal becomes complicated in a situation like this. To become a steelworker is not the ultimate goal. Working in a steel plant is a means for attaining the ultimate goal of a college education. Learned motives may give rise to a wide variety of behavior, just as do unlearned motives.

HABITS

The story of how we learn would not be complete without an analysis of habits. When a way of behaving is so well learned as to be *highly automatic,* it is given the term *habit.* Much of our day-to-day living consists of habits: speaking habits, eating habits, dressing habits, habits of punctuality, of geniality, of shyness, smoking habits, and hundreds of other routine ways of behaving. All learning involves some degree of habit formation. Indeed, one of the ways to envisage the learned behavior of an individual is in terms of the accumulation of habits of varying degrees of strength. In discussing habits we do not need to introduce any new principles, since habits are simply well-learned acts.

FORCE OF HABIT

A good way to appreciate the characteristics of a habit is to inquire into the meaning of the phrase, "force of habit." Why do we so often behave through force of habit when some other way would be more beneficial? The reason is that once we have learned to act in a certain way and that way has become automatic, requiring little attention, it provides us with the most comfortable way, the easiest response. It has proved satisfying or reinforcing in the past. Why try a new pattern when the old has worked for so long? There may be better ways, but can one be sure? The worker's reluctance to use a new tool, the businessman's hesitancy about installing a new time-saving method, the parents' tendency to raise their children in the old-fashioned way—all these are illustrations of adherence to habitual acts which have worked in the past and which are preferred to some new ways, the learning of which would require time and effort. In short, habits dominate much of our behavior because we are strongly motivated to behave now and in the future as we have behaved in the past.

BAD HABITS

Why is it so difficult to break bad habits? If one feels that a habit is bad it must have undesirable effects which would not be reinforcing, and reinforcement is necessary in order for learning to occur and persist in the form of a habit. The catch arises from the failure to recognize the *complex nature* of most habits. Take, for example, the habit of smoking cigarettes. What started it in the first place? Probably a number of factors, including curiosity about the taste, the desire to feel grown-up and sophisticated, and the desire to be socially acceptable. Therefore, although the smoker may no longer enjoy the taste of a cigarette or may feel that cigarettes are bad for his health, he continues to smoke because other components of the smoking habit are reinforced. When a bad habit is broken, some strong countermotivation must be present to overcome all the reinforcing effects which originally led to the establishment of the habit. If, for example, a smoker is convinced that continued smoking will cause lung cancer, thought of this consequence will override all the positive reinforcing conditions which accompanied the act of smoking, and the habit will be broken.

HABIT HIERARCHIES

What is usually called a habit is often a combination of related habit sequences referred to by psychologists as "habit hierarchies." In typing, for example, one first learns to strike the correct keys. These responses are called "letter habits." When letter habits approach the point of acceptable proficiency, word habits are developed. Letters like T, H, E arouse a single word response instead of perceptibly separate letter responses. The typist perceives the word "THE," and the separate responses take care of themselves. Word habits are built upon letter habits, so to speak. After a while, phrase habits appear. Common phrases like "Very truly yours" are typed without the operator's paying any attention to the separate letters or separate words. This analysis of habit formation may lead you to conclude that different levels of habit are learned and organized one after the other, with, for example, letters learned first, then words, then phrases. This appears not to be true. The entire habit of typing has a psychological unity, consisting of separate elements which blend with one another as the final habit develops. Modern methods of teaching reading in the elementary school recognize that the learning of a complex skill consists of the simultaneous development of simpler and more complex habits. No longer does the child learn first all his letters one by one, then isolated words like "man," "cat," "girl," etc., then short phrases; rather, from the first he practices reading as a total, meaningful process.

A CASE STUDY

With the material on learning, motivation, and habits freshly in mind, let us postpone further elaboration of these topics and take a look at a case study, the understanding of which calls for practical application of what we have so far studied.

The case involves five supervisors employed during World War II in the Methods Engineering Department of the Sundale Paper Company. During the early days of the war the five supervisors applied for officers' commissions in the Armed Forces. All but one, Bill Miller, were commissioned. Bill was turned down because of a diabetic condition which, however, never interfered with his work. The four men who left were replaced with temporary employees of very limited experience and little or no familiarity with

Sundale's practices and procedures. In effect, Bill, who before this had been merely one of the supervisors, now became Chief of the Methods Engineering Department with greatly increased responsibilities. He had some misgivings about his new job but decided to give it all he had in order to help the company and do his bit in the war effort on the home front. He made a good start and continued to make progress in his overall supervisory work. He was pleased with himself, and the company was pleased with him. Throughout the war years Bill did an excellent job.

This state of affairs continued until about four months after the end of the war, at which time the four former supervisors returned to take up their old duties. In effect, the wartime job ended and Bill once more shared responsibilities with his former partners. Shortly after the return to prewar operation Bill became dissatisfied with his job. Indeed he became somewhat of a problem child in the department because of his refusal to cooperate. Finally, Bill appeared before the works manager and announced that he was quitting his job at Sundale and taking a new job with a competing company at no increase in salary but where, in Bill's words, "his ability would be recognized."

In terms of the principles of motivation, learning, and habit formation, what is the basis for Bill's decision to change jobs? The works manager felt that Bill was very unreasonable because it had been thoroughly understood by all parties that the wartime assignment was of an emergency and temporary character, and that there would be a return to the status quo when the war ended. The works manager repeatedly stated that he could not understand what had come over Bill. Before and during the war he was hard-working and cooperative and suddenly there was a complete reversal in his behavior.

In analyzing this case it should be clear to anyone with psychological know-how that Bill before the war and Bill after the war were in some ways different persons. Bill's behavior patterns had changed because of something he had learned. Recall the conditions necessary for learning; it will be apparent that all of them prevailed during Bill's wartime job. He was willing to take the job and the company wanted him to do so. In other words there was a need or desire to undertake the supervisory task. Not only was there motivation to learn, but there was response making—active participation by Bill. He set to work. He tried out various responses which he perceived as necessary in supervising people. And he selected and continued to perform those that were successful, i.e., the responses were reinforced. The evidence for reinforcement is that everybody concerned, including Bill, felt that he did a good job. We need not mention here the specific responses that Bill made. The point to be remembered is that they were made. Behavior that is repeatedly reinforced is learned. Since it was practiced over many months it became highly habitual. Bill had learned in no uncertain terms that he alone could handle a supervisory position that he did not have before the war. He is now a changed man. He now has a desire to be the kind of supervisor that he learned to be. He now has a full-fledged learned or secondary motive as a part of his behavioral repertoire. With this analysis it should be clear why he decided to quit his job. The return to his old status required him to give up a job which he was motivated to do and which he could do with facility.

The lesson from this study is that we should expect different behavior from a person if he is placed in a situation where new motives and new skills are added to his behavioral make-up. An individual who has with all honesty and good intention made predictions about what he will do in the future will behave as he claims if his perceptions remain the same. But his perceptions will change if his behavior is modified through learning. This is precisely what happened to Bill and what caused him to quit his job.

LEARNING CURVES

Let us now return to further analysis of learning phenomena by inquiring into the nature and significance of curves of learning. The precise changes in performance that occur when a person learns can be quantified and presented in the form of a learning curve. Learning curves provide useful information, telling us not only that behavior has changed, but also to what degree it has changed and whether the change has been smooth or irregular.

Figure 4-1 shows some of the ways in which changes in behavior resulting from learning can be depicted by means of learning curves. One common type of learning curve (graph A) shows that production, as measured by the number of work units produced, perhaps refrigerator doors, or food mixers, or automobile wheels manufactured or utility bills processed, increases on successive stages of practice until it levels off. The learning shown in this curve was that of learning to be efficient production workers. What practical information does the learning curve provide? Suppose that graph A was made by averaging the daily production of a large group of trainees. The graph would answer a number of important questions about the progress the trainees were making. Thus the graph tells that on the first day the average learner would produce about twenty units and that after eight days he should be

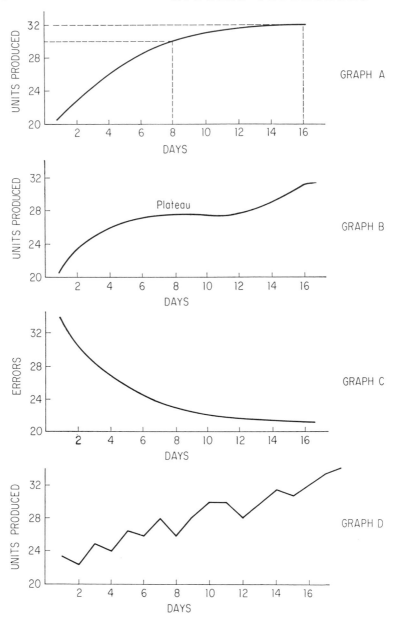

FIG. 4-1 *A*. A common type of hypothetical learning curve. Output increases until production levels off as practice has its effects. *B*. The plateau where learning is temporarily halted. *C*. Another way of showing learning through decrease in number of errors or in waste. *D*. A graph that is rather typical of learning most anything, characterized by ups and downs which show that the progress of learning is not smooth. The important thing is that overall the trend is upward.

producing about thirty units. After sixteen days he should have reached a peak efficiency of thirty-two units. Considerably more progress would be expected during the first days of practice than during later days. Indeed, between the eighth and sixteenth days, an increase of only two units could be expected, whereas between the first day and the eighth day there is an increase of ten units. If thirty-two units represents standard production, one would be justified in assuming that further practice would not bring about any increase in the production rate. Under the prevailing conditions the worker has reached his final plateau.

THE LEARNING PLATEAU

The occurrence of a plateau does not mean that the learner is necessarily at the limit of his learning efficiency. Motivation may be increased by increasing incentive pay, for example. Or the worker may be given a new method of work or a job shortcut of which he was previously unaware. If such a change in conditions occurs, it might lead to further increases in production after the leveling off that was previously considered to be the maximum.

In some cases plateaus seem to be a necessary part of the learning process in that a period of consolidation of previously learned elements is necessary before overall learning can occur. In learning to receive telegraphic code one shows improvement while he is learning the individual letters, but having learned them he must practice some time without further apparent improvement, while he masters word and phrase or sentence units. The situation just described is represented in graph B. Most often plateaus occur in prolonged learning processes such as learning a foreign language, learning to read, to operate a complicated machine, to play golf, to typewrite.

Where plateaus appear normally in learning it is important for a teacher or trainer to know of their existence. The ordinary learner does not realize what is going on as he learns and is likely to be discouraged and let down when he hits a plateau. The teacher or trainer can counteract this by explaining that the plateau is temporary and that with continued application it will pass. The knowledge that the plateau is a characteristic not of himself but of the learning process is often enough to prevent the learner from giving up. In one industrial concern, workers are given a card showing a typical learning curve for their job, with the plateau plainly marked. With the aid of the card the foreman in charge of training shows the workers who hit the plateau that if they stick to their jobs they should expect to meet the standard rate even though they seem to be stalled for the time being.

LEARNING IS SELDOM SMOOTH

Another way of showing learning is pictured in graph C. This curve shows that with continued practice the time needed to do a single job decreases. Or it shows that fewer errors are made or that less material is scrapped as skill develops.

Curve D shows what the learning curve of an individual is likely to be. An individual's learning progress is seldom smooth, but the progressive upward trend is unmistakable.

TRANSFER OF LEARNING

So far we have been examining learning as it occurs in a specific situation. But man moves from one place to another in his everyday life. He learns in school and then moves to a job outside of school. The soldier learns in the training camp and then moves on to the field of actual war operations. The child learns in the home and then moves to the homes of his friends. Does the learning that occurs in one place transfer to another? Most of us are inclined to answer this question in the affirmative. The right answer is that there is indeed transfer of learning but only under certain conditions.

SIMILARITY OF STIMULI

Let us analyze an instance in which transfer of learning is known to take place in order to clarify and specify the necessary conditions. Consider once more the case of the person who learned to drive an automobile, and let us say that he learned to drive a Ford. If now he moves to a Chevrolet, will he be able to drive it? Of course he will. He will have little or no difficulty transferring his driving skill from one make of car to another. There may be minor differences between the two cars; the dashboards may not be exactly alike, or the windshield may be a little higher on one than on the other. But in general, the stimulus conditions of the two cars are similar. If one studies Latin, the learning of Spanish is made faster because of transfer. Again, the reason transfer occurs is that some of the stimuli in learning Latin are similar to the stimuli encountered in learning Spanish. In general, the degree of transfer will increase the more similar the stimuli are in the two situations.

SIMILARITY OF RESPONSE

Transfer is determined not only by similarity of stimuli. It also depends on similarity of response. In the car-driving situation there are similarities not only in stimulus but also in response. In both cases, the driver uses his right foot to accelerate, his left hand to release the emergency brake, his hands to steer, and so on. In summary, then, we may say that transfer will be maximized to the extent that there is similarity of stimuli and response in two situations.

Do not neglect to keep in mind that similarity exists for the learner only if he perceives the similarity. This would certainly be the case in driving automobiles. But in intellectual tasks the similarity may not be so obvious. To the expert mathematician it may be perceptually clear that a principle of the calculus is applicable to two different problems. To point this out to the student is important, but in the long run it will do little good unless the student himself perceives the transferability of the principle.

NEGATIVE TRANSFER

Transfer of learning is not just a matter of considerable benefit, slight benefit, or no benefit at all. In some cases there is negative transfer. This occurs when something previously learned hinders learning in a new situation. A simple illustration is provided by the story told by a famous psychologist many years ago involving a change in the place where he carried his watch. He observed that if he changed his watch from the left vest pocket, where it was usually carried, to the right trouser pocket, he generally made a number of false movements when he wished to know the time. He eventually corrected these movements, but after the watch was returned to its original place, false movements again occurred. Old habits kept interfering or transferring to new situations, because opposite or competing responses were involved.

Negative transfer may have serious consequences. A pertinent example comes from a study of airplane accidents conducted during World War II. In one incident a pilot was undershooting the field in attempting to land. He perceived his mistake and attempted to make a correction by pulling back on the throttle and pushing forward the stick. The plane nosed into the ground because the throttle and stick responses were just the reverse from what they should have been. When questioned later the pilot reported that he was accustomed to flying planes in which he operated the stick with his left hand and the throttle with his right. In the plane in which he had the accident the positions of the controls were different so that he used his left hand on the throttle and his right hand on the stick. The old habits interfered and resulted in a near fatality. The key principle to keep in mind regarding negative transfer is that situations requiring dissimilarity of responses, i.e., opposite or competing responses, account for negative transfer.

PUNISHMENT IN LEARNING

An old question that is pertinent to learning principles and their application has to do with the role of punishment in learning. Everyday observation would indicate that people learn things through punishment or threat of punishment. The young child who pulls the dishes from the table learns to leave them alone if the act is followed by punishment. If one is tinkering with an electrically activated device and receives a shock, he quickly learns to stay away from that part of the circuit that caused the shock. Nothing in these examples contradicts what has been said about reinforcement as an essential condition for learning. The child who pulls at the dishes and is punished may continue to be attracted by the dishes, but the situation is now associated with punishment or the fear of punishment and so he learns the response of not reaching. In not reaching, his fear of punishment is reduced or eliminated, and this relief is rewarding or reinforcing. In other words, *punishment is not reinforcing, but the avoidance of punishment is.* The use of punishment is generally not advocated as a reinforcer in view of the findings from experimental studies that the wrong or erratic or undesirable response that is punished is actually suppressed and may appear again if the source of punishment is not present. Furthermore if the punishment comes from another person—a teacher, a boss, a parent—the learner may develop strong negative attitudes toward the punishing individual so that the effectiveness of that individual is lost in situations where he does not resort to punishment.

What about learning situations where one actually performs a sequence of acts and learns them even though the act is always accompanied by punishment or unpleasantness? Soldiers, for example, learn different kinds of military maneuvers under extremely unpleasant conditions. What can possibly be reinforcing in such situations? Any soldier can tell you if you ask him. He learns these unpleasant tasks because not to learn them may mean future guard duty or KP duty, or even his life on the battlefield. The realization that not to learn may be embarrassing or uncomfortable or disastrous sets up tension or anxiety states that are relieved by learning. Thus it frequently happens that punishment or unpleasantness may facilitate learning if what is being learned will enable the individual to avoid less-pleasant or less-punishing circumstances.

ORGANIZING WHAT IS TO BE LEARNED

The application of learning principles to the problem of changing one's behavior in the home or school and on a job calls for a consideration of how material to be learned should be organized. Suppose one is setting up a training program for apprentices in a workshop and their task is to learn how to operate a lathe. How should practice be organized throughout the day so as to yield the fastest and most efficient learning? Should the apprentice be given a continuous session until be becomes proficient, or should practice be spaced throughout the day? A logical approach to this problem would seem to indicate that if the practice sessions are too far apart, what the trainee learned on the first part would be forgotten by the time he got to the second. On the other hand, if the practice sessions are too close together or if there is a single continuous session, the employee's learning would be slowed down because of fatigue and boredom.

SPACED PRACTICE

There is considerable evidence to show that spaced or distributed practice is preferable to concentrated or massed practice. For example, in a typical experiment students read a passage of over four thousand words, either four times at one sitting or once a day for four days. Then they were given an examination on this material. It was found that the distributed method gave better results than the concentrated readings. In general, the results of experiments on massed versus distributed practice in learning manual skills and memorizing verbal material are fairly uniform in showing that distributed practice is superior to massed practice. Further research is necessary, however, before a sweeping generalization is in order. The need for caution is indicated by observing the learning of material that is relatively short. Thus if the material to be learned is a five- or six-step list of instructions for starting a machine, it is wise to mass the practice (read the list over and over without pausing) rather than to distribute it.

Just what the ideal way to distribute learning time should be depends on the nature and difficulty of the material to be learned. Distributed practice is best when the learning situation is such that continuous practice causes fatigue; when motivation wanes (the learner may work more intensely if he knows that a rest is soon to come); when the task is so complex that responses interfere with each other.

AN OLD PROBLEM

A question closely allied to the spacing of time in learning concerns learning by *parts* or *wholes*. Should the student deal with separate, or detached, pieces of an assignment, or should the material be dealt with as a whole? If a salesman wants to memorize his sales talk, should he learn one paragraph, then the next paragraph, and then another until the talk is learned, or should he read the entire talk over and over again? Studies of this problem indicate that the best first approach to most learning tasks is to deal with the task as a whole. When this has been done, the more difficult elements in the total task may be attacked by the part method. This makes good sense in terms of the principle of reinforcement. A total appraisal enables the learner to see the relationship among the parts, and this is more satisfying than trying to learn something that makes little sense. Concentrating on difficult items later saves time and effort on the easy items and allows the learner to see the difficult items in tneir proper meaning context.

LEARNING AND REMEMBERING

One of the most interesting topics that is related to the analysis of learning is *remembering*. How much of what we learn do we remember? Why is it so hard to remember certain common things? Why do we forget? What can be done to prevent forgetting? Answers to most of these questions will become apparent as you proceed through the next few pages.

In taking up the topic of remembering we are not leaving the field of learning for the study of a new psychological process. Remembering is simply one way of viewing learning. It is the mark or criterion of learning. It is a present knowledge of some fact or event that has occurred before. If your behavior now shows the effects of previous learning, you have remembered. Indeed, the only acceptable evidence that one has learned anything is a demonstration that he has remembered or retained the effects of some prior mental or physical activity.

Sometimes the term "remembering" is applied to the maintenance of learned acts over relatively long periods of time—weeks, months, or years. The term is equally applicable to a performance that is maintained for as short a period as ten seconds. If you learn a man's name, can give it one minute later, and then forget it, you have remembered for one minute. Some previously learned acts are remembered for a few minutes, some for months, others for years. What are the conditions that make it possible for us to maintain learned responses for varying intervals of time? Let us seek an answer by examining the nature of *forgetting*.

FORGETTING

If you were to ask a person what caused forgetting, you might get the offhand reply, "I guess it happens because of the passage of time. As time passes I seem to remember less and less." And everyday obser-

vation seems to support this belief. Do you not remember more of
Monday's lesson on Tuesday than on Friday? Very likely you do, but
not primarily because of the difference in time. Many experiments have
demonstrated that it is not just the passage of time that determines
how much we forget, but also *what happens during that time.* One
of the most striking demonstrations of this comes from a famous experiment on the ability to remember after a period of sleep and a comparable period of waking. In this experiment two students learned lists

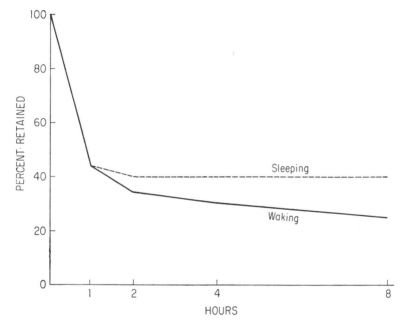

Fig. 4-2 A graph showing that we forget less when asleep than when
awake, because there is not so much interference with what has been
learned. (*After Van Ormer, E. B. Retention during sleeping and waking.
Arch. Psychol. N.Y., 1932, No. 137.*)

of nonsense syllables like BAF, LUM, and SEV at about 11 P.M.,
and soon thereafter went to sleep. After intervals of one, two, four,
or eight hours, their retention was tested. For controlled comparison,
the same students learned similar material at 9 A.M., and retention
was measured after one to eight hours of normal waking activity. The
results are shown in Figure 4-2. The curve of remembering during
sleep shows superiority, or less forgetting, at all but the one-hour interval. Interestingly enough, there is practically no forgetting during the
period between the second and eighth hours of sleep. Since comparable
subjects, learning comparable material, showed differences in forgetting

over the same period of time, the justifiable conclusion could be that forgetting was caused by the interfering effects of other activity, not by the mere passage of time. That some forgetting did occur even when the students were sleeping is no basis for discarding the idea that activity rather than time itself causes forgetting. Although one is not learning when he is asleep, dreaming and other bodily activities might interfere with the recall of what was originally learned.

WHAT HAPPENS BETWEEN LEARNING AND TESTS FOR RETENTION?

Experiments on what the psychologists call *retroactive inhibition* provide further evidence for the view that forgetting is due to what happens between original learning and tests for retention. Retroactive inhibition is the term applied to the influence of other material on previously learned material. A simple demonstration of retroactive inhibition that is often conducted in psychology classes is set up in the form indicated in the following table.

Order of Procedure	Experimental Group	Control Group
First:	Learns material A	Learns material A
Second:	Learns material B	Rests or engages in conversation
Third:	Recalls material A	Recalls material A

As the table indicates, two equivalent groups cf subjects learn the same kind of material, perhaps nonsense syllables or words. One group (experimental) then learns another list of nonsense syllables or words. The control group rests or engages in conversation or some activity not related to the learning material while the experimental group is learning the nonsense syllables or words. Finally, both groups are called together and tested on how well they can remember what they originally learned. Invariably, under these conditions, the retention score for the experimental group is much lower than that for the control group. A wide variety of experiments shows that the degree of forgetting resulting from retroactive inhibition varies directly with the meaningful similarity of materials designated in the table as A and B. A highly similar intervening task, like learning a second list of nonsense syllables right after the learning of an original list, causes much interference; a very different type of intervening task has less effect.

The demonstration of less forgetting during sleep than during waking hours, supplemented by the results of many experiments on retroactive inhibition, points to the conclusion that forgetting is a matter not so much of a fading away or weakening of learned activities as of the interference or obliteration of previously learned responses by recently learned ones.

OVERLEARNING AND RETENTION

You will recall from earlier discussion that practice makes perfect if the practiced response is repeatedly reinforced. Repetition under the proper conditions leads to degrees of overlearning, depending on the amount of practice. It follows, then, that the degree of overlearning determines how fast and how much the individual will forget; i.e., *overlearning should aid in remembering.* This has been amply demonstrated in numerous experiments. In one study the subjects learned lists of nouns with different amounts of repetition beyond that required for the first perfect recall. A list was considered just learned (with no overlearning) when the subject could go through it once without error. A criterion of 50 percent overlearning was determined by having the subjects repeat the list of nouns half again as many times as they did in the no-overlearning situation. That is, if twelve repetitions were required to meet the no-overlearning criterion, then eighteen repetitions were used for the 50 percent overlearning criterion. One hundred percent overlearning was induced by having the subjects repeat the lists of nouns with 0, 50, and 100 percent overlearning; remembering tests at intervals of one, two, four, seven, fourteen, and twenty-eight days gave the results shown in Figure 4-3. These data were gathered in 1929. In Figure 4-4 we see a study reported in 1962 with more preciseness of control. This and other recent studies support the view that for efficiency in recall one should study material until he has learned it and then continue studying awhile longer. This is just as true of text material as for words. The data indicate that retention is increased, or forgetting is reduced, by overlearning. Other experiments show that much greater retention will take place when the degree of overlearning is greater than that in the experiment just described. There are limits, however, to this process; betterment does not continue to be proportional to the amount of extra practice. Diminishing returns show themselves sooner or later.

Overlearning is beneficial in the business of making satisfactory adjustments in everyday living. You can certainly recall times when

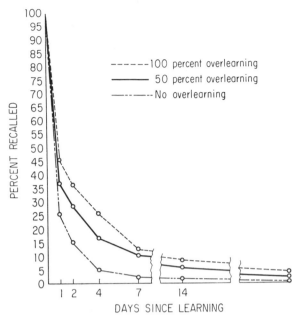

FIG. 4-3 We remember better when there is overlearning, as shown originally in this early study. Other studies emphasize the same principle. (*From Krueger, W. C. F. The effect of overlearning on retention. J. exp. Psychol., 1929, 12, 74.*)

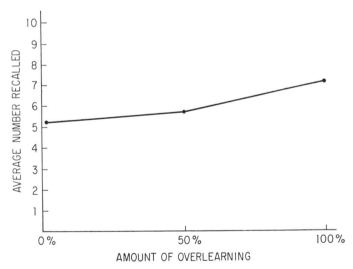

FIG. 4-4 Another demonstration that overlearning increases recall. In this experiment the subjects learned both frequently and infrequently used words. Overlearning by 100 percent is better than by 50 percent in helping the subject retain what he has learned. (*Data from Postman, L. Retention as a function of degree of overlearning. Science, 1962, 135, 666–667.*)

you have been frustrated because of your inability to remember a name, an address, or what you had studied in yesterday's lesson. The obvious way to avoid such predicaments in the future is to resort to overlearning. Overlearning is, in effect, habit formation. When you overlearn something you are increasing its habit strength. Well-learned acts are, of course, less likely to be affected by other activities than are acts learned less well.

REPRESSION

Clinical psychologists and psychiatrists in their case analyses often find that certain kinds of experience, even though well learned, are difficult to remember. Such findings would seem to contradict what has been said about the effect of overlearning on retention. A case in point is a study of the legal testimony given by two young girls who had been placed by their parents in a house of prostitution. When the girls' dire plight became known to the police authorities and the girls were called in for questioning, they gave highly detailed information sufficient to incriminate their parents. However, some months later, when the girls were again questioned, they were unable to remember much of the factual detail that they had previously reported, even including the more lurid parts of their experiences in the house of prostitution. Even when some of their earlier testimony was summarized for them, they denied that such things could have happened. And there was every reason to believe that they were sincere in their denials. In a case like this, where experiences are intense and vivid, it would seem logical to assume that they would be well remembered. Apparently, some psychological process is at work that causes the individual to "forget" such experiences.

LEARNING TO FORGET

The tendency to forget the painful or unpleasant is called *repression*. The person who represses develops the habit of not recalling those experiences that are distasteful. All of us, at one time or another, engage in a mild form of repression when we refuse to talk or think about some unpleasant experience that has occurred in the past. In extreme cases, where one has undergone some terrible emotionalizing experience, he may even inhibit the recall of this past life. This condition is called *amnesia*.

How can repression be accounted for in terms of learning principles? A reasonable answer is in terms of *learning to forget*. The response of remembering acts is a stimulus. Every time this stimulus appears, the result or effect is distasteful. The reward or reinforcement comes from avoiding the stimulus, and so the person practices this avoidance response, with the result that he learns to forget the stimulating situation that made him unhappy.

SELECTION AND ORGANIZATION IN REMEMBERING

You have already had a hint in the discussion of repression that remembering is a selective and organizing process. This should not be surprising, since perception and learning have been shown to have these characteristics.

REMEMBERING UNFINISHED TASKS

An experiment on the influence of failure to complete an assigned task illustrates how certain responses are selected for retention. Subjects were asked to do a group of twenty tasks such as stringing beads, modeling animals, naming twelve cities beginning with K, and solving puzzles and arithmetic problems. Most of these tasks required three to five minutes for completion. In half of the tasks, the experimenter permitted the job to be finished; in the other half the subjects were interrupted and required to go to a new task. As soon as the series of problems was completed, retention was tested.

The results of the experiment were striking. It was found that the *incompleted tasks were remembered about twice as frequently as* the completed ones, and this was true even though the subjects had actually spent more time on the completed tasks. The experimenter concluded that the recall value of the unfinished tasks was higher because there still existed an unreleased tension or anxiety with respect to the unfinished tasks. Apparently, unfinished business tends to linger in one's memory because there is a desire to complete a job once it is started.

Many examples from one's everyday experience illustrate the selecting of incomplete tasks for retention. Take, for example, a man who has to deliver an important speech. He will compile material and remember it well when he delivers the speech. But several days later he will have forgotten much of it. The task as he perceived it was delivering a speech, and until this was done the man was anxious because the goal had not been attained. He was motivated to remember those experiences that would eventually be reinforced. He forgot the material after the speech because there was no longer any need to remember. You practice the same kind of selective remembering when you gather information solely for the purpose of passing an examination.

Under such motivation you almost always forget most of the material shortly after the examination is over.

DETAILS ARE RAPIDLY FORGOTTEN

Another demonstration of the selective and organizing nature of remembering takes place when we forget certain details but remember the general idea of an experience that has occurred in the past. Suppose that I am asked if I remember a vacation cruise which I made twenty years ago. Of course, I say—it was the most interesting and exciting vacation that I ever had and I remember it vividly. Actually I am unable to remember most of the details of the trip. I do remember the ship, the time of the year that the trip was taken, the various ports of call, and that I had a fine time. If you ask me for details I provide them but not really from memory. My remembering of the details is hazy, and so I reconstruct them in accordance with what I think they were. Thus if you ask me to describe the street in Kingston, Jamaica, which runs from the ship's wharf to the post office, I would describe it as a very narrow street, because I remember that many of Kingston's streets are narrow. Actually I do not remember enough of this particular street to be sure that it is narrow. The point of all this is that in remembering we recall organized patterns of events that have been learned in the past. We select certain key experiences and organize them into a meaningful scheme. When forced to fill in details we tend to reconstruct items that are in harmony with the overall pattern, and often these items are false.

The tendency to remember a general plan, order, or arrangement and to fill in this plan with logical but false details has been studied by many psychologists. One investigator had English university students read a story taken from the folklore of a culture that was foreign to them. The story dealt with ghosts, war parties, seal hunting, and canoes. After reading the story twice the subjects were asked to reproduce it in writing as accurately as possible. The reproductions, although maintaining the general trend of the story, showed a considerable number of errors in detail, all of which, however, made good sense and in no way destroyed the story's theme. Thus the more familiar word "boat" replaced the original "canoe," and instead of "hunting seals" the subjects used the word "fishing." There is no doubt that in telling our favorite stories we sometimes change some of the details a bit. As has been said: "The story wouldn't be as interesting if it contained only what really happened." Some of us make a habit of telling a good story!

Forgetting details and remembering the overall scheme sometimes gets us into trouble, but for the most part it is a highly adaptive ten-

dency in one's total life adjustments. We are exposed to so many different experiences that it is impossible to remember all of them. So we
select and organize related experiences, and these take the form of
a meaningful frame of reference on which to base adjustive acts that
call for remembering.

MEASURING RETENTION

There are a number of ways for measuring how well we remember.
One way is by recalling previously learned material. Look at the digits
3, 6, 9, 2, 8, 1. Now cover them up and try to repeat them. If you
can do this you have *recalled* these numbers. Suppose you go to a
party and are introduced to a dozen people. If you can give the names
of all these people the next day, you have recalled these names perfectly.
If you can repeat only six of them, your recall score is 50 percent.
Essay examinations are illustrations of the recall method of measuring
retention. Recall is one index of remembering, but not the only
one. Strictly speaking, recall and remembering should not be used
synonymously, because it is possible to obtain evidence of remembering
even though the recall score is zero. In order to do this it is necessary
to resort to more sensitive ways of measuring retention—by recognition,
for example.

RECOGNITION EASIER THAN RECALL

The chief difference between recognition and recall is that in the
former, the stimulus is present for your perception, whereas in the
latter it is not. The difference is shown in connection with the average
person's vocabulary. The number of words that an individual can recognize in reading is much greater than the number he can set down
and write out, even if he has plenty of time. Multiple-choice examinations test retention through recognition, i.e., following the question is
a number of alternative answers, only one of which is correct. The
correct answer is before you; all you need to do is to recognize it.
Recognition is easier than recall because identification and familiarity
rather than exact reproductions are called for. We often recognize
names, dates, and objects when we see them in print or pictures, or
hear them mentioned or described. We recognize tunes when they are
sung or whistled which, for the life of us, could not be recalled.

EXISTENCE OF TRACES OF LEARNING

Even though you cannot recall or recognize, there is still the possibility of obtaining evidence that you have retained some previous learn-

ing. This can be demonstrated through *relearning,* the third index or method of measuring retention. You might, for example, completely fail a recall or recognition test on some school subject. If, however, you study the lesson a second time, relearning it to the point of being able to pass a test, and if it takes less time to learn the lesson the second time than it did the first, then you have retained the effects of the first learning. Traces of the original learning were present, even though they could not be detected through recall or recognition.

Summary

Learning is a universal human experience. Its chief feature is a modification or change in behavior which lasts for some period of time. Learning involves working toward some goal, and it involves some kind of activity or response: "We learn by doing." The learner selects from all the responses he is making those that are reinforced. The consequences of any act—recognition, reward, or avoidance of something unpleasant—which lead the learner toward his goal are reinforcing. Reinforcement often occurs automatically without the learner's being aware of the effect at the moment.

We learn to want a car or an education. Learned motives can and do become motivating forces in their own right. They give rise to a wide variety of behavior, just as do the unlearned motives, such as the desire for sleep.

When a way of behaving is so well learned as to be automatic we call it a habit; all learning involves some degree of habit formation. Habits dominate much of our behavior because we are motivated to behave now and in the future as we have behaved in the past.

Learning is not only the base for education; it is related to most of the problems we encounter in all applied psychology. The aspects of learning may be described in terms of curves of progress and lack of progress. We know much that is useful about both the positive and the negative aspects of transfer of learning.

The psychology of learning offers much to applied psychology in terms of organizing what is to be learned, whether it be such a skill as driving a golf ball or developing leadership abilities. Remembering and forgetting are described in terms of conditions which favor or hinder learning. Through studies of overlearning and retention we know how to increase habit strength. Overlearning is clearly beneficial in the business of making satisfactory adjustments in everyday living. The psychologist is also interested in how we learn to forget. Forgetting details and remembering the overall scheme sometimes gets us into trouble, but for the most part it is a highly adaptive tendency in one's total life adjustments.

Suggestions for Thinking and Discussion

1 Make a list of *your* good habits. What habits did you leave off the list? Why?
2 Make a list of the types of things that are reinforcing to *you*. How are these related to how you spend your time?
3 Assume that you desire to break some habit. List the learning principles that would be involved. Have you or any of your associates broken a habit? What did you or they do?
4 How can *you* organize your day to help make your learning more efficient?
5 What types of things do *you* forget most easily? What types of things do your associates say you remember best?
6 Describe some instance in which overlearning paid off for *you*.

Suggestions for Further Reading

Birney, R. G., & Teevan, R. C. (Eds.) *Reinforcement*. Princeton, N.J.: Van Nostrand, 1961. A paperback of readings on the practical aspects of reinforcement theory.

Bugelski, B. R. *The psychology of learning*. New York: Holt, 1956. A text that pulls together research on learning and its practical aspects.

Mednick, S. A. *Learning*. Englewood Cliffs, N.J.: Prentice-Hall, 1964. A paperback which extends the content of this chapter.

Skinner, B. F. *Science and human behavior*. New York: Macmillan, 1953. Learning in the laboratory and its implications for everyday behavior.

Weinland, J. D. *How to improve your memory*. New York: Barnes & Noble, 1957. A book on how to remember names and factual material.

CHAPTER 5

Efficiency in Study

One particular phase of applied psychology that is of major importance to all students, regardless of their special interests, is study efficiency. All too frequently students finish their schooling without having learned how to use their study time well. To complete one's assignment in a minimum amount of time with a high degree of success, permitting sufficient time for leisure reading, sports, relaxation, and various extra-curricular activities, is one important mark of a successful adjustment to college life.

That many students oversimplify the problem of how to study efficiently is shown in the frequently heard remark, "I didn't study hard enough." Statements like this imply that study efficiency is entirely a matter of putting forth extra effort. "Try harder next time and you will make out all right," is the pat solution. Certainly effort is important, but many students spend a great deal of time in study and accomplish much less than others who spend less time. The reason may well be that the effort of the time consumer is poorly directed. True, differences in ability may be a contributing factor, but on the other hand, there is ample evidence that a person of average ability who uses well not only his effort but also his time often surpasses in accomplishment a more capable but less efficient individual. Learning can be improved

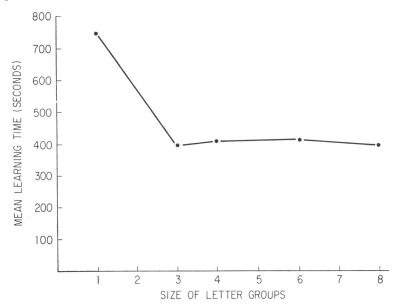

FIG. 5-1   The subjects in this learning experiment were asked to memorize random sequences of twenty-four letters of the alphabet. (The letters "e" and "i" were excluded, to reduce the possibility that real words would occur as part of the sequences.) There were five groups of fifteen subjects each. The letters were on three by five-inch index cards—one letter to a card, three, four, six, or eight letters to a card. Plotted in the figure are the mean (average) times that it took the subjects in each group to learn the entire list of twenty-four letters. Notice that any grouping—three, four, six, or eight—led to learning times that were much less than that for the one-letter-at-a-time condition. In fact, learning times were about halved. The investigators in this whole-part learning experiment concluded that efficient learning of arbitrary associations (the random sequences of letters) exceeding the short-term memory span depends on the learner's organizing the information into usable "chunks." (*Data from McLean, R. S., & Gregg, L. W. Free vs. induced chunking in serial list learning. Paper presented at the Midwestern Psychological Association, Chicago, Ill., May, 1965.*)

often by organizing the information into "chunks" that will cut down on learning time. Figure 5-1 shows an example of this fact in a memorizing task of simply learning letters. It takes about twice as long to learn letters one at a time as it does when they are presented in groups.

You should not make the mistake of assuming that study efficiency is a topic of importance for only the poor or average student. All students, regardless of their grades, can profit from an analysis of effective study principles and their application. Indeed, surveys show that

the study methods discussed in this chapter help good students as well
as poor ones. Significantly, the best students profited even more than
the poorer ones.

HOW GOOD A STUDENT ARE YOU?

Before reading further about the various conditions that you can
manipulate and control in the interest of increased study efficiency,
it will be helpful to subject yourself to an appraisal. The questions
in the following inventory have been found to permit differentiation
of the efficient from the inefficient among student learners. Read the
questions and answer each one "yes" or "no" as honestly and accurately
as you can.

1 Do you have several definite, strong reasons for going to college?
2 Do you have several good reasons for knowing the material in
each course you are studying?
3 Do you have difficulty in finding time for study?
4 Do you have a daily study plan or schedule of work?
5 Do you adjust your study time to the difficulty of a course?
6 Do you usually spend time trying to be as relaxed as possible
when you study?
7 Do you frequently strive to analyze your work and try to find out
just where you are weak?
8 Do you frequently use the facts learned in one course to help
you in the work of some other course?
9 In preparing for an examination do you try to memorize the text?
10 Do you often write the answer to a question, only to find that
it is the answer to some other question on the examination?
11 Do you take your notes in class just as rapidly as you can write?
12 Do you sit up late at night before an exam studying?
13 Do you usually skim over a chapter before reading it in detail?
14 When you find a word in the textbook which you do not know,
do you usually look it up in the dictionary?
15 Do you usually skip the graphs and tables in your textbook?
16 Do you stop at the end of each section of study material and
review in your own words what you have read?
17 Do you usually study every day in the same place?
18 At the end of an assignment, do you quiz yourself in a fashion
similar to that used in quizzes in class?
19 Do you read rapidly, always seeking the main ideas, and without
speaking the words to yourself or pausing over words?
20 Do you make frequent use of artificial memory aids?

At the end of this chapter you will find the answers which characterize the good student as compared with the poor one. Score your responses. Each disagreement with the key points to a bad habit or attitude which you should try to correct. Analyze your responses and make a summary of your weak points. Keep the summary before you as you read the remainder of this chapter. Doing this will make it apparent why a particular habit or attitude is undesirable.

MOTIVATION FOR STUDY

Despite an earlier statement that effort alone will not lead to efficient study, you should not minimize its importance. It is a basic requirement and one of the most difficult to cope with. Marshaling one's efforts presents a problem in motivation. From a previous chapter on learning, you will recall the importance of motivation in changing behavior. Learning will not take place unless there is an underlying reason or motive to learn. In dealing with techniques for efficient study we squarely face the learning problem. Indeed, the title of this chapter might well be, "Learning How to Study."

If you attack your assignments in a lackadaisical fashion, doing little more than sitting with your book open before you in the hope that something will eventually "sink in," you are not going to make much progress. If self-analysis reveals lack of motivation, you should try to determine the cause. What are your goals in life? Is there any relationship between these goals and what you are doing in school? Are you attending college simply because your parents want you to, or because your friends are in college? Are you studying subjects in which you are really interested? A careful consideration of such questions will usually lead to answers from which you can plan an intelligent attack on your motivational problem.

WHY COLLEGE?

Why go to college? One observer put it this way: "If a person has to ask this question, then he will most likely have difficulty understanding the answer."

When asked why they are going to college, many students reply to the effect that they want a good job, want to be distinguished citizens in their communities, and want to make good salaries. Surveys have shown that there is a significant relationship between these goals and college performance. On the average, those who make the best grades make the best incomes later on. The trend among employers is to offer the best jobs to those students who have made the best grades in school. Employers assume that the person who has learned to study efficiently, and thus to make good grades, will transfer his efficiency to the new job. Other measures of success besides salary are related to good grades. For example, men and women of sufficient distinction to be listed in *Who's Who* had, on the average, higher grades in college than those who are not listed.

It may appear that the main reason for learning to study is to make good grades. But grades are only incidental. Your ultimate aim in going to college should be to learn facts and principles that will help you to lead a well-adjusted life. Much of that learning will come from formal course study. Learning to study will lead to better understanding, make you more at home with books and ideas, and provide intense inner satisfaction from the learning process in school.

Students with motivational problems sometimes say that they cannot generate any curiosity about books and ideas having to do with the nature of man's culture, his discoveries, ideals, art, and music. Generating such curiosity is to a considerable extent a matter of talking and associating with others who already have some enthusiasm about these things. If you need stirring up, cultivate contacts with teachers, lecturers, writers, and good students, and you will most likely become infected with their enthusiasm, curiosity, and intellectual inquisitiveness. Wisdom is related to motivation. Wisdom comes from the awareness of timing, recognition of change, and knowledge of one's own limitations as well as strong points.

SETTING UP A STUDY SCHEDULE

Although motivation is a prime requisite for effective study, there are those who, despite a strong interest in schoolwork and a high degree of natural ability, find it difficult to perform well in their academic tasks. When teachers and counselors look into the causes of such academic failures, or near-failures, they often find an absence of an organized study routine. Efficient workers almost always have a set time and place for doing their work. If you think that you do not study enough, a schedule that outlines definite times for study will help. The student who protests scheduling his study time on the grounds that he will not have time for other activities is fooling himself. A schedule does not deprive one of time for nonstudy activities; it simply will see to it that each type of activity gets its fair share of time. It is interesting that busy students who have outside jobs and engage in many extracurricular activities often make better grades than those who are much less busy. If you ask such a student how he finds time for study, he will invariably tell you that he has learned to organize or schedule his time. Having so many things to do forces him to allot a certain amount of time for each activity. Regardless of how busy you are, planning is likely to improve your efficiency.

In preparing a schedule you should list all the activities of the day, whether class lecture, laboratory, students' activities, outside work, recreation, meals, or just plain loafing. In setting aside times for study, make them as specific as possible. Don't, for example, set aside two hours on Tuesday evening for studying; make it a time for studying a *specific subject*. Also, schedule a study period for a particular class as *close to the class period* as possible. The amount of time you give to a subject depends on individual circumstance. If you know that a subject is difficult for you, you will naturally schedule more time to study for it. These time allotments may, of course, change, depending on your experience with the schedule. You may find that preparation for an economics course requires more time than you had estimated, and that an English course requires less time. Make the change, but then stick to it until further experience tells how it is working out.

PHYSICAL SETTING

It is highly important that the student study in the right setting *for him*. Motivation and scheduling are *preparatory* to the act of study. If the act is to be effectively carried out it must take place in the proper environment. Reading should be done in diffused or indirect light. Green and blue lights should be avoided. Natural daylight of uniform intensity is easiest on the eyes. One's desk or table and chair should be so situated as to facilitate concentration. Sitting by a window that affords outside views is not a good practice because of possible distracting influences. Don't study in a lounging chair. Instead, use a hard, straight-backed chair and sit with the feet on the floor, shoulders squared, and book firmly grasped. These may be good suggestions for one person, but not for another. Some students prefer the comfort of lying down, with papers and books all around and a coke nearby. This may prove to be an efficient situation for study—but not for everyone! We must consider individual differences. What are your habits? How efficient are you?

In general, anything likely to produce excessive relaxation should be avoided during any kind of learning. There are numerous pieces of experimental evidence to substantiate this advice. For example, in one investigation, subjects exerted a mild muscular tension while learning. The tension was produced by gripping a hand dynamometer, an instrument designed to test the strength of grip. The subjects did not try to maintain their maximum grip. Instead, they merely exerted a continuous squeeze of moderate intensity. The results showed that those subjects who maintained a little muscular tension during learning were the most efficient in learning and in recalling what they had learned. Another experimenter found that mental work is done more efficiently during hunger contractions than at other times. These and related facts show that learning is facilitated by bodily tensions that are not too strong. Intense contractions of the muscles or intense hunger would serve as distractions to effective learning. The applicable conclusion for study is that one should maintain a firm body posture but not permit himself to become strained as he studies.

Many students report that on occasion they have sought out some isolated spot that was exceptionally quiet for studying an especially difficult assignment. Much to their surprise, they discovered that they did not accomplish nearly so much as they expected. The common experience of many is that work is done more rapidly and with less effort where there is some background of more or less regular noise. These observations are what one would expect in the light of what has been previously said about the effect of muscular tension on learning. Moderate intensities of noise produce some muscular tension, usually of such slight magnitude that it is not noticed. Nevertheless, these unnoticed tension states are likely to be responsible for added speed in learning.

MAKING AN ASSIGNMENT MEANINGFUL

Everyday experience and laboratory experiments in the psychology of learning and remembering attest that meaningful material is learned faster and remembered longer than meaningless matter. You can demonstrate this to yourself by adhering closely to the directions in the following exercise.

Read twice the following list of nonsense syllables and then close your book and write down as many of the syllables as you can. Then determine your recall score and record it.

KUB, WIB, RIX, POZ, GIG, LUP, MOR, VEB, BEX, DOV,

FEL, GEB, HIC, JOM, NEB, BOC, GOK, CEX, REB, TOC

Now read over twice the following list of related nouns and write them down in the proper order. Calculate your recall score and record it alongside the first.

TREE, GRASS, DOG, CAT, MAN, WOMAN, ELEPHANT, CIRCUS, HOUSE, TENT, BRICK, MORTAR, POLICE, JUDGE, PREACHER, CHURCH, LAWYER, DOCTOR, STUDENT, TEACHER

Now read the following sentence and record and calculate your recall score.

YOUNG HENRY WHOSE FATHER IS A BUSINESS EXECU-TIVE THINKS HE WOULD LIKE TO BE A POLICEMAN WHEN HE GROWS UP.

Compare your recall scores for the three types of material. A comparison of the findings will show the relative learnability of meaningful versus meaningless material.

Perhaps you are saying, "The results of the experiment are clear enough, but what application do they have to the study of an assignment in English or psychology?" Oddly enough, many students try to learn textbook assignments as so many meaningless statements. This they do when they memorize material and try to repeat it verbatim. This kind of learning may be retained for a short period, but it will never become a real part of one's mental equipment. It is much better to study for the purpose of getting ideas that make sense in themselves and are related to other ideas.

GETTING THE MEANING FOUR WAYS

With an assignment before you, how should you treat it so that it will be meaningful? The first thing to do is to *skim the assignment*. Read over the material rapidly before starting intensive study. This bird's-eye view will provide a general idea of what the assignment is about and will add greatly to the meaning of the parts to be examined later. As you skim through the material, pay attention to the section headings; they tell you how the material is put together and what the main subject of each section is going to be.

Another obvious, but usually neglected, practice that contributes to meaningful study is to *use a dictionary*. Don't pass over unfamiliar words. Whenever you encounter a new word or expression, look it up in the dictionary or mark it for later investigation. You thus clear up the meaning of an otherwise obscure word or passage and you add a new word to your vocabulary.

Meaningfulness is also enhanced if you *relate new facts to old problems*. When you meet a new fact, ask yourself how it affects your attitude on some issue or belief with regard to some proposition. For example, do the facts and principles of perception support the common belief that what we see, hear, and smell are entirely a matter of the structure of the eyes, ears, and nose? Do the facts and principles of learning support the old adage, "Practice makes perfect"? Does your study of habit formation give you an understanding of why habits are so hard to break? Talk these questions over with fellow students.

You can also make what you have studied more meaningful if you *summarize in your own words*. No amount of mechanical copying of text material will aid learning so much as a preparation in your own words. In summarizing, try to hit upon the essential material, neglecting the anecdotes and illustrations. They tend to stick of themselves. Emphasize the principles in preparing your summary.

RECITATION

Reciting to oneself after having read a section of material is a widely recommended study procedure, yet one that is very much neglected because it is time-consuming. One can easily fool himself into believing that what he has just read is understood and remembered, but generally this is not true. To make certain that one remembers and understands he should stop periodically and check himself out, so to speak, by trying to recall to himself what he has just read. In other words, he should *recite*. When this is done, errors and omissions should be carefully noted. Then a little later, recitation is once more in order. In preparing for examinations, recitation should be paramount in one's study procedure.

Experimental studies have shown that recitation is a great help in preventing forgetting and thus increasing remembering. Actually it is profitable to take time away from "studying" and spend it on recitation, for learning is better when part of the study time is spent on recitation than when all of it is given to reading. In one well-known experiment, when all the subjects devoted all their time to reading, recall of the facts in five short biographies averaged 16 percent after four hours. When 60 to 80 percent of the learning time was devoted to self-recitation, recall after four hours was nearly twice as great. Check by a fellow student helps.

The advantage of recitation over passive reading is that the student is forced to maintain *an active attitude*—to react and become involved in the subject matter rather than merely trying to absorb it. Recitation serves to keep his attention on the task. He cannot let his attention lapse by daydreaming if he is trying to recall something.

REVIEW

There is no doubt that frequent review is essential to efficient remembering. Experimental studies of forgetting show that the greatest loss in retention occurs right after learning. From this fact we may infer that the best time for review is immediately after studying. One experimenter found that when a class lecture was listened to by students but never reviewed, the class recalled only 25 percent of the content after eight weeks had elapsed. But when the lecture was immediately followed by a five-minute review test, the amount of recall after eight weeks was 50 percent better.

Reviewing immediately before an examination is also highly desirable. This review should be intensive, since the examination may cover an extensive amount of material, and it should emphasize recitation because, in effect, this is what is called for when one is examined. If you can recite well what you have learned from study just before an examination you need have no fears about the outcome of the test.

It also pays to have one or two reviews between the first review and that just before the examination. The more frequent the review the greater the degree of overlearning. You will recall from the chapter on learning that *forgetting is checked by overlearning*. Put this basic principle into practice when organizing your study technique.

TAKING LECTURE NOTES

Overall efficiency in study can be facilitated by taking notes in class. Good note taking is a skill that surprisingly few students have taken the time to acquire. Some instructors, by their poorly organized manner of presenting material before a class, make note taking difficult for the students, but by and large, the fault lies less with the instructor than with the student.

In taking notes keep in mind that your main task is to *organize* what the instructor is offering. Do this by trying to identify the main points. Don't be led astray by an interesting illustration and an amusing anecdote. Always keep in mind the point that the illustration or story is supposed to make. Condense the teacher's discussions into simple phrases or sentences. And to make them more meaningful to you, do the condensing in words of your own phrasing. A good note taker is *not* a stenographer, who merely records. He is a summarizer—one who *evaluates* material that will be useful to him in the future.

Even the best of note takers miss some salient points. They write down short phrases which seem meaningful at the time but do not make much sense later on. Therefore, notes should be reviewed after class. With the lecture freshly in mind, the missing items can usually be inserted and the meaningless ones deleted or corrected. If a review of your notes shows lack of organization, it will pay to rewrite them completely. The organization and review will stand you in good stead by furthering your understanding of your notes at some future time.

Taking notes in most courses can be greatly facilitated by using a system of abbreviations. If you use such a system, make it consistent. Many students, especially in the early months of college before abbreviations have become automatic, have found that a page set aside in the notebook for abbreviations is an aid to the mastery of the system. The use of a system of abbreviations is particularly desirable if the student is the kind who complains that he misses part of the lecture because he gets too wrapped up in note taking. In general, the use of abbreviations and other forms of condensation helps one to listen and write at the same time.

SOME MORE ON STUDYING

Let us add a few suggestions from several successful students.

1 *Study in the same manner as you will be expected to reproduce material.* Memorize more for objective exams and study broad ideas in outline form for essay exams. We shall expand on this in the following pages.

2 *Study the teacher.* Some teachers (often intentionally) will all but give away exam questions on pretest lectures and reviews. One professor may emphasize one subject that another will gloss over.

3 *Review notes with a classmate.* Often someone else will pick up points that you miss.

4 *Do not cut classes.* Even if you are not paying close attention in class, some things still get through that would have been missed if you were absent. The other person's notes are usually poor substitutes for your own; and one other point—some who teach feel badly that they cannot hold the interest of an audience enough even to get them to class. Physical attendance is easier to monitor than is psychological attendance.

5 *Do not overintellectualize in review.* Review should be just what the term implies. Too much thinking at this stage often leads to confusion.

6 *Do not fall behind in your work.* In some students this leads from a feeling of anxiety to that of panic.

7 *Help the other fellow study.* Explaining a point to someone else helps fix it in your mind.

8 *Underline the text.* This makes review easier, and textbook authors will love you!

PREPARING FOR AND TAKING EXAMINATIONS

If you are looking for some way to pass examinations other than by thorough mastery of the material to be covered in the examination you will be disappointed in what psychologists have to say about this subject. No one has yet come up with a magical shortcut or substitute for adequate preparation through study. Of course, mastery of the subject is on occasion not enough if the student is emotionally upset, fails to interpret questions properly, has his knowledge organized in such a way as to interfere with quick recall, or is overtired. If one follows the precepts of efficient study, he can avoid the factors which cause unsatisfactory test performance, despite adequate preparation, by getting enough rest, not engaging in a last-minute *hurried* review instead of a planned, systematic one, and adopting a relaxed, almost fatalistic attitude at examination time.

ESSAY AND OBJECTIVE EXAMINATIONS

The examinations given in most schools divide themselves roughly into two main classes, the *essay* and the *objective*. Although there are exceptions, these types are likely to have different purposes and you should therefore prepare for them and take them differently.

Essay examinations emphasize the ability to understand, organize, and *recall* information. The student has latitude in which to discuss and qualify his answers. Essay questions let the student show the depth and breadth of his knowledge. And they also demonstrate his ability to set down his thoughts in good English and to communicate his ideas to others. Keep these points in mind as you prepare for and take an essay examination. When you begin the examination, don't just start writing on the assumption that if you write enough the teacher can find the correct point somewhere in the hodgepodge. Take time to organize your thinking before you begin to write. Remember that the teacher will think better of a paper if the information in it is well organized and to the point, rather than full of rambling and irrelevant discussion. Survey the examination as a whole before you write, and estimate the amount of time you will spend on each question. Try to leave time at the end for rereading your answers so that you can correct mistakes or add missing points.

Remember that most teachers, most of the time, think of grading papers as a chore. You can help sell your answers through good organization. Also, keep in mind that your paper is compared with all the others in the class. Examinations are competitive. I believe it is fair to say that they are graded fairly, although subjectively. Outline answers, indent, and number points.

Objective examinations are usually *recognition* tests. The right answer is before you, as well as wrong answers. Your task is to pick out the right answer when you see it. Be on guard against careless reading of objective test items. All the answers usually have some degree of plausibility; otherwise they would serve no useful purpose as a testing device. Sometimes the correct answer may hang on such statements as "never" or "always" or "rarely," and you may miss the point if you do not read the questions carefully.

In objective-type examinations it is well to skip items temporarily on which the answer is uncertain, rather than to puzzle about them for an undue amount of time which might otherwise be spent on easier items. When you are finished with the easier items, go back to the harder ones. In objective examinations one question usually counts as much as another, so do not concentrate too much on difficult questions. Doing this will cause you to run out of time or make you rush through the remaining items and make needless mistakes. There is another good reason for perusing an objective examination and answering first those questions that you are sure about. To start with responses that you feel sure are right gives you confidence, facilitates your thinking, and helps you in seeing the relationship to other questions.

When your examination has been graded and returned, use the evaluation wisely for the future. Don't be content with a "Well, that's that" attitude. Learn from the results of the examination. Where should you have placed more emphasis in your study? Was your organization good? Do you have the proper technical vocabulary? What were the errors? Carefully work out the answers to these questions and profit from them in preparation for the next examination.

STEPS IN TAKING A MULTIPLE-CHOICE EXAM

First, one should pay attention to the instructions. Let us assume that the student is asked to choose the *best* answer of four or five possibilities. This means, of course, that perhaps two answers may be correct. Hence the student should not waste time arguing with himself that there may be more than one answer.

Second, the student taking a multiple-choice exam is in part like the accomplished poker player who is trying to get himself into a position where he is betting on a sure thing. In poker, one is in a stronger position if he knows pretty well what is in the other fellow's hand.

In the exam situation, *knowing the material* is a first step. There is no substitute for study. It is also unlikely that the student will be certain about *all* the answers. Our suggestions also assume that the student is not penalized for guessing.

What are the next steps? Let us summarize from a study:

1   *Go through the exam a first time and answer all the items of which you are fairly certain.* This helps get certain items out of the way without wasting time on single, difficult items. There is sometimes another advantage in doing this. Having gone through the exam once will suggest the answers to questions that might have been difficult had they been answered in serial order.

2   *Go through the exam a second time answering any other questions that now seem obvious.* There are usually a number of questions which were left unanswered from the first time through. It is in connection with these that the test-wise student knows what to do.

3   *Do not guess at this stage of the game. See what choices on any given question can be eliminated.* In a four-choice question, pure guess will give the student one chance in four of being correct. If one alternative can be eliminated as incorrect, the odds are reduced to one in three. If two can be eliminated, chances become fifty-fifty.

4   *Having eliminated some alternative, choose the answer which you first thought of as right.* Studies show that this procedure is better than pure guesswork.

5   *If you have no choice at all as to the right answer, take choice "2."* Again, from studies come this suggested rule of thumb based on how teachers make items. When the instructor makes up a multiple-choice item he usually has only a vague notion of what he wants to test. There is a tendency to make the first choice incorrect, the second choice the right answer, and the remaining ones anything that isn't too far afield. Of course, some instructors are conscious of this bit of behavior and correct for it. Remember, this suggestion is in the last-resort category!

6   *When finished, check your answers.* Clerical errors on exams are common for some people. Again, studies show that changing answers is in the direction of making them right. Yes, we are aware of the common misconception on this point. In a group of 100 papers (for example) it was discovered that two-thirds of the changes made in them resulted in the selection of a correct choice rather than a wrong one.

Besides studying *for the exam* and studying the *behavior of the instructor,* the above suggestions may help eliminate some of the anxiety one builds up about taking an exam.

Do we have any good suggestions for taking a true-false test? None except that one should study and look for give-away words such as "always," "never," etc. Remember, there is no substitute for learning the material in the first place, and for the time spent in overlearning.

MNEMONIC SYSTEMS AS AIDS IN STUDY

As a study technique, the use of artificial devices that aid in recall is popular with some students. You are no doubt familiar with "Thirty days hath September," for the number of days in the month; oysters are to be eaten only in the months that have an "r" in them; "Wash-Ad-Jef-Mad-Ad-Jack," for the presidents, and the like. Some of these crutches are good and some are bad. Certain arbitrary facts can be held together by means of a memory device until usage has fixed them firmly in mind. Thus the mathematics student can learn the value of π (pi) to the thirteenth decimal place by memorizing:

> How I wish I could remember
> Of circle round
> The exact relation
> Arkimedes found

and then counting the number of letters in each successive word: 3.1415826535895.

Memory crutches such as these are useful in dealing with material that does not lend itself to logical analysis and fails to fall into any meaningful order. They are to be resorted to when there are no generalizations possible from the facts to be remembered. The advantage of the broad generalization over the memory crutch is that the former operates in many situations whereas the latter functions only in highly specific situations.

If you find occasion to use an old memory crutch or invent a new one, take care that it is a genuine short-cut. If the device is more complex and harder to remember than the material itself, don't waste time on it. A humorous example of this is the system used to remember that Adams follows Washington as President of the United States. Here is the way you do it:

> Washington suggests washing,
> Washing suggests laundry,
> Laundry obviously suggests the Chinese
> And the Chinese certainly suggest missionaries,
> Missionaries suggest the Bible,
> And the Bible begins with Adam.

READING

All that has been said about efficient study is based on the assumption that the student has normal reading, writing, and arithmetical skills. However, many studies, surveys, and reports from those who counsel students show that high school and college students have deficiencies in these basic skills. Probably the most common deficiency is that having to do with reading ability. Some college students read no better than seventh-grade pupils and at least one-third of college freshmen read too slowly to do their most effective work.

READING IS COMPLEX BEHAVIOR

It is not surprising that reading deficiencies are so common because the reading act is exceedingly complex. This complexity creates numerous opportunities for error to occur. An examination of the behavior of the eyes during reading makes one wonder how reading is possible at all. If we stand directly behind one who is reading and carefully observe one of his eyeballs by reflection in a small mirror held just below it, we will see that the eye moves from left to right not with a steady sweep but with jerks and pauses, then swings back from the extreme right to the extreme left to start the next line of reading. Experimental studies have shown that during the actual movement of the eyes, perception of letters and words is impossible. How, then, can one ever learn to read? We now know that the eye's work as a receiver of information from the printed page is done during the *stops* or *fixation pauses*.

During fixation pauses the reader attends to the stimulus material not in a piecemeal fashion but as a pattern or whole. He does this because he has learned that it is not necessary to perceive every letter and every word in order to obtain the essential information from a page of print. All languages contain letters and sounds that are redundant, and the languages themselves are redundant, i.e., they contain more words than are necessary for conveying information. When you perceive the letter *q,* you know it will be followed by *u.* When you see *informati* you know it will be followed by *on.* When you see *ps ch l   y,* you fill in the missing letters easily. When you see

The land   the free   home   brave

you fill in the missing words without difficulty. In reading, certain cue letters or words are all that is necessary for ordinary comprehension.

SLOW AND FAST READERS

What, now, is the difference between slow and fast readers? Both, of course, take advantage of redundancy in language. But the fast reader does so to a greater extent than the slow reader. The faster reader pauses just often enough to get the sense of what he reads and thereby reduces the number of glances per line. The *poor reader spends too much time looking at words* that carry irrelevant or repeated information. To improve his reading speed, he should therefore decrease the number of pauses per line. And to accomplish this it is necessary to expand the number of words perceived in a single glance. The trick is to force oneself to take in more territory during the information-gathering process when the eyes are at rest.

Another common fault of poor readers is to make *regressive eye movements*. Such movements are back tracks, or returns, to a word or phrase which did not clearly register. These retreat movements usually defeat the reader's purpose, which is to gather information from the material before him. Regressive movements may impede the information-gathering process by interfering with the train of thought, so that ideas become jumbled and unrelated. If you are a backtracking reader, make every effort to break the habit.

Don't vocalize as you read. You have no doubt seen children whisper to themselves when they are beginning to read. As they gain reading skill, the whispering becomes inaudible, but their lips, tongue, and throat muscles still move as if they were talking. Some college students have not progressed beyond this stage. This kind of vocalizing lowers the rate of reading and acts as a distraction, preventing the reader from grasping the full significance of what is read. The purpose of reading is to perceive not words, in and of themselves, but significant cues, which are the raw material or vehicles of ideas. Phrases and sentences are the units which convey the ideas on the printed page, and they are the units which must be comprehended. Reading without vocal activity allows one to grasp the phrases, and hence the thought, quickly, in a minimum of time.

Efficient reading is, of course, impeded by a *deficient vocabulary*. You should not attempt to read with speed at all costs. Some students do this by skipping over new words, hoping to get their meaning from some later sentence or paragraph. Occasionally these deduced meanings are correct, but frequently they are not. The safe procedure is to get into the habit of checking definitions of all unfamiliar words. Underline new words when they are first encountered and look up their meaning in a good dictionary before leaving the assignment. After a dictionary has been consulted for the meaning of a word, return to the context in which the word was seen and reread it so that you can see how it fits into the total setting. This adds meaning to what you are reading and helps to establish the meaning of the word for future use.

Individual reading habits vary greatly. In general, those people who read widely, read well, the subject matter ranging from newspapers and magazines to technical material and pleasure reading. Availability of reading material is important and so is convenience. Most people will not go out of their way to read a conventional bulletin board, but they may habitually read single daily items placed in the office elevator.

STAGES OF CREATIVE THINKING

Efficiency in study is related to certain basic principles of learning, as we have been describing. *The development of good study habits is also related to how we think in a creative way.* We are sometimes slowed up in our attempts to write a theme in English, or to come up with the solution to a mechanical problem, by failure to understand the thinking process. Creativity is the act of giving shape to experience. Too much prefabricated thinking can prevent us from trying something new.

It is not uncommon to hear a student describe the experience of working on some problem all afternoon and into the evening without any apparent success. He finally retires for the night. Next morning the solution comes from "out of the blue." The first reaction is to feel that time has been wasted on misspent effort. But is this really true?

Although we tend to think of such people as Einstein and Edison when we talk about creativity, it must be emphasized that many persons of lesser capability *also use exactly the same processes.* The modest inventor who devises a new improvement for lawn mowers, and the domestic poet whose works are never published, use the same stages in thinking. *The differences between great thinkers and little thinkers are of degree, not of kind.*

There are four stages in creative thinking. First, we have the period of *preparation.* This is the stage during which facts are learned, skills acquired, and observations made. Second, comes the discouraging period of *incubation,* in which no progress seems to be made toward the goal. Third, the new creative product emerges during the period of *inspiration.* The fourth period is that of *verification,* during which one checks to find out whether the end product is any good. Let us look at each of these stages in more detail. We suggest that the reader think of some creative effort he has gone through as he reads the following descriptions.

PREPARATION

During preparation the thinker finds out all he can about his problem, both facts and concepts. He goes through some trial and error in groping for an answer. Preparation for an act of creative thought may be deliberate or nondeliberate. In a scientific discovery preparation is usually quite deliberate. The scientist studies everything related to his problem. Sometimes ideas seem to come together without deliberate preparation. Many writers say that they jot down observations, chance thoughts, and bits of fact or style corralled from their reading. One writer says, "I heard the expression 'It takes two to tango,' made a note of it, and later found use for the expression in writing a TV script." Such nondeliberate preparation is helpful, even though only one of every hundred or so notes is ever used.

INCUBATION

One of the most remarkable, and possibly encouraging, observations about creative thinking is that a period of seeming inactivity typically *precedes* a discovery or solution to a problem. This period has been called *incubation* because the thinker is literally "hatching something." Of course, it may be well for us to keep in mind that if one incubates long enough he may lay an egg.

Different persons behave differently during this incubation stage. One person may be restless and pace the floor, scribble a few lines, and then throw them away. Another may sit quietly during this hatching period. It is not untypical that a feeling of depression accompanies incubation. (But one must remember that it is quite possible to feel depressed without anything cooking.)

Incubation does not always occur in obvious form. It is not unusual to awaken from sleep with an inspiration or solution to a problem. In other instances, quite common in the college student, the individual may turn to another task, in the midst of which the answer to his previous problem will suddenly dawn on him. A period of relaxation may have the same effect. A vacation helps with larger types of problems. But it must be remembered that *preparation* is a necessary stage coming before incubation! The subject should also struggle to test and eliminate false facts and hypotheses.

INSPIRATION

The period of incubation often ends with an *inspiration* of a sudden solution to the problem. It is characterized by three things. First, it comes *suddenly*. Second, it is accompanied by an emotional feeling of *elation*. Third, the inspiration seems to come from the *outside*. Hence the expression "out of the blue." One author has called it the "Aha! phenomenon." You name it.

Inspiration is not an isolated stroke of genius, but a culmination of all the preceding labor. It has been aptly put, "Perspiration precedes inspiration." Some people, however, seem to suffer from creative inertia.

VERIFICATION

Inspiration is sometimes the final stage in creative thinking. This is true of most of our everyday problems—writing the theme, fixing the noisy engine, or coming up with a new menu. For the scientist, however, comes the stage of *verification*. This sometimes leads to revision of the hypothesis formed.

The labor of verification is necessary in the fine arts as well as in the sciences. The painter must transfer his inspiration to the canvas. The musician must work out his broad conception in terms of melodies and harmonies. Manuscripts of great authors show much crossing out and rewriting. The final stage of writing is not easy.

Efficiency in study somewhat automatically leads to efficiency in thinking. We need *both* facts and thought. There is no evidence that originality is ever contaminated by knowledge.

Answers to Questions on the Study Habit Inventory

The good student answers as follows: 1 Yes; 2 Yes; 3 No; 4 Yes; 5 Yes; 6 No; 7 Yes; 8 Yes; 9 No; 10 No; 11 No; 12 No; 13 Yes; 14 Yes; 15 No; 16 Yes; 17 Yes; 18 Yes; 19 Yes; 20 No.

Summary

Many students oversimplify the problem of how to study. All students can profit from an analysis of study principles and their application. Learning how to study begins with questions of motivation: Why am I attending college? What are my goals in life? What subjects do I have curiosity about?

Improving study begins with setting up a workable study schedule. Next comes a look at the physical setting for study. This includes appropriate lighting, having the right books and study materials at hand, and using a chair that is not so comfortable that it lounges one into sleep. And the study setting may be best if it is not totally quiet.

Make an assignment meaningful. Experiments attest that meaningful material is learned faster and remembered longer than meaningless matter. One can put meaning into the situation four ways: (1) skim the assignment before starting intensive study, thereby getting an overall picture of where you are going; (2) use a dictionary for all unfamiliar words; (3) relate new facts to old problems; (4) summarize what you have studied in your own words.

The above procedure should be followed by self-recitation. This is a check on what you know and how well you can express it. The advantage of recitation over passive reading is that one is forced to maintain an active attitude. One can well afford to spend over 60 percent of his learning time in self-recitation. Frequent review helps remembering, because of the well-established principle that forgetting is checked by overlearning.

Note taking is a skill that one should acquire early, and we have suggested ways for becoming efficient in it. Preparing for examinations and taking both essay and objective exams can be made into efficient habits. The student who learns early the procedures that classify him as "test-wise" has an asset that can be used throughout formal schooling. Steps are suggested for acquiring these skills. Suggestions are given in the chapter as to when mnemonic aids may and may not be helpful in remembering. The complexities involved in acquiring good reading skills are discussed.

Understanding creative thinking is most important for efficiency in study. It involves four stages—preparation, incubation, inspiration, and verification. Efficiency in study leads to efficiency in thinking. Thinking itself is a skill that has to be learned.

Suggestions for Thinking and Discussion

1   How many correct answers did you get on the twenty questions on page 95? How does this compare with your classmates?
2   Make a list of things *you* need to do to improve your study habits.
3   Set up a study schedule. Do other people believe it is reasonable?
4   In order to improve your study, what things in *your* physical environment would you list as being good? What things would you list as being bad?
5   Review some preparation you made for a quiz. What percentage of the learning time was devoted to *self-recitation?*
6   What do you do wrong in preparing for and taking an examination? What do you do right?

Suggestions for Further Reading

Brown, R. *Words and things.* New York: Free Press, 1958. A book on language, indirectly related to developing good habits of study.

Carroll, J. B. *Language and thought.* Englewood Cliffs, N.J.: Prentice-Hall, 1964. A paperback showing how language is related to thinking.

Humphrey, G. *Directed thinking*. New York: Dodd, Mead, 1948. An old standby on the practical aspects of thinking.

Morgan, C. T., & Deese, J. *How to study*. New York: McGraw-Hill, 1957. A paperback extending in detail the content of this chapter.

Wellington, C. B., & Wellington, Jean. *The underachiever: Challenge and guidelines*. Chicago: Rand McNally, 1965. A paperback which suggests programs for helping the student who is not living up to reasonable expectations.

PART II

VARIETIES
OF PROBLEMS
IN DAILY LIVING

CHAPTER 6

The Practical Aspects of Child Development

No subject area of human behavior relates basic science to practical everyday problems as frequently as does child psychology. Questions range widely from "Does the newborn infant have a personality all his own?" to "Should the child be spanked?" "How should sex play among children be handled?" "How can the parent help the child get rid of those 'naughty' words?" "What should be done about the timid child?" These and dozens of other questions will be dealt with in this chapter, with answers provided from literally thousands of formal studies of children and from many practical writings. For the parent, and for the teacher, knowing what to expect in the growing child is helpful in coping with most of these problems. For the student, much can be learned about human behavior by watching how children grow. Since most students eventually become parents, we shall talk about problems as parents face them.

WHAT TO EXPECT

For the newborn infant "my day" falls into a sleeping-feeding-tending sequence. Around eighteen weeks of age the baby can sit up with support, and by the end of the sixth month he is showing some motor coordination, beginning to be a little more sociable, and expressing various emotions such as fear, disgust, and anger. He is now ready for the playpen. (In the interest of readability we shall use "he" for both boys and girls in the descriptions to follow.)

Around the first birthday motor behavior has moved into the "Wave bye-bye" stage, and such vocalizations as "mama," "dada," and "nana" are coming out. Socially the child may still be a bit shy around strangers; some temper is showing up, which will become quite noticeable in another year as the child begins to display a little more independence.

A GREAT EXPLORER

The eighteen- to twenty-four-month-old is a great explorer. He gets into everything and is too big for a playpen. He is coming to understand his environment better, imitating the behavior of others. At this age the child piles blocks in a mass, later making a tower of three or four blocks. All this indicates that he is beginning to have constructive ideas, however simple they may seem to the adult. By the time the child is three years of age, ideas sometimes outrun conventional words. In asking to be weighed, the child may get on the scales and say "pound me."

THE NEGATIVE STAGE

The stage of the "city manager" arrives around two to three years of age when the child is beginning to show domineering ways, alternating between temper tantrums and showing affection; shifting from exuberance to shyness, from being eager for food to rejecting it. Such *negativism* is quite normal, yes, even though the routine includes "no-no-no" even to reasonable requests and a repertoire of biting, pulling, and hitting. Some children of this age ask for privacy on the toilet. Lingering in the bathroom can be expected.

The two-year-old has a listening vocabulary of several hundred words, which grows rapidly. "Tell me the story of so-and-so," you will hear him ask over and over again. He will detect even the slightest variations in his favorite stories. Emotional upsets are found commonly between the ages of two and three years.

BETTER ADJUSTED

It may be hard to believe, but the self-centered, negativistic child of three can grow into a child with some self-control, ready to accept suggestions and learn social conformity, and fortunately this happens within the brief span of about a year. By four years of age the child is beginning to show a sense of humor and is dramatizing events and happenings in an interesting manner. "Natural" baby talk is disappearing and will continue to drop out if not encouraged. By four years of age the child has become more cooperative and sociable in play with other children his own age. Taking turns in riding the tricycle is a concept much better understood. But before one concludes that now the child is really ready to settle down, just wait!

OFF AGAIN

As the child approaches his fifth birthday he becomes a bundle of energy, both physically and mentally. He races here and there. Imagination is becoming extensive in scope, ideas shifting rapidly from one thing to another. Socially, boys in particular are becoming more aggressive, boasting of their abilities, being bossy at times, and "hating" everything. However, they are not returning to the stage of negativism they went through two years earlier, even though it seems so at times. The four-to-five-year-old is quite a talker, exaggerator, show-off, creator of make-believe, and user of naughty words. Number concepts are beginning to appear, and the child is becoming a little more "other-directed." Although he plays more cooperatively with others, quarrels among children of this age can be expected. He will tell you he can count from 1 to 10, but, "I can't count down a missile."

By six the child has become better "housebroken," more manageable. He appears to be taking things a little easier, consolidating his gains made earlier. One may even detect some politeness on occasion! Although still talkative, he speaks with more thought behind what he says. Questions center around practical matters: "What's it for?" "How does it work?" Emotionally the child is becoming better adjusted, though he may pick up certain fears easily. Bad dreams and nightmares are not uncommon. By the fifth or sixth birthday sex differences begin to make their appearances, boys showing interest in tools and mechanical gadgets, while girls are interested in domestic things. The six-year-old is becoming clever in sizing up both situations and himself. After a week in school one boy put it this way: "I can't read, I can't write, and they won't let me talk."

Just after the child's sixth birthday he becomes temporarily rather trying. He is impulsive, compulsive, bossy, and full of indecision. The child in this age range will start some things that he doesn't finish, yet he may pursue other activities from one day to the next. As he approaches his seventh birthday, indecisive behavior of just a few months back begins to give way to more organization.

The child of seven is beginning to calm down somewhat. He is a little more reflective and does not branch out into so many new adventures. One can reason with him with a fair degree of success, and he even likes to please. Emotionally the seven-year-old has more control over his temper, but he also has up and down swings of mood. Nose picking, tattling, and alibiing seem to have gotten programmed into his behavior patterns. At seven the child is ready to take on more responsibilities.

By eight the child is "no longer a baby." He understands adults better and they understand him better. The child at this age likes to play different roles from time to time—from being a "woman hater" to utilizing the "wolf whistle." Boys and girls show much the same developmental trends in behavior. The eight-year-old is a good observer. He likes to attack problems that take some effort to bring about a solution. The use of tools, sewing, and drawing interest the child at this age, but preciseness of psychomotor control is still lacking. As one psychologist stated it, "The child's level of aspiration at this stage in development is higher than his level of skill."

Individual differences are quite marked in the age range from nine to ten. Each sex seems to show some contempt for the other sex, although when they get together kissing is not uncommon. Both sexes are becoming more self-sufficient. They have more staying power in sticking to a task and are more positive in their likes and dislikes. The ten-year-old gives an impression of being an adult in the making, but in spite of many grown-up ways, his development, both physically and psychologically, has a long way to go.

In some respects the best global picture of psychological development can be had by taking a look at problems related to physical habits, walking, talking, thinking, and the like. This we shall do in the following sections as we deal with some very practical questions.

EATING, SLEEPING, AND TOILET TRAINING

One might expect that such basic needs as eating, sleeping, and elimination get off to a good start in development. Unfortunately many children develop "feeding problems," and some develop undesirable sleeping and toilet habits. Both good and bad habits begin early. Where do they come from? Bad habits are acquired in the same way as good habits, for both come through learning.

EATING

One of the strongest of all drives is that of obtaining nourishment, but this in itself does not assure good habits of eating. Resorting to pressure methods of feeding may bring on difficulties. Most children, like some adults, have times when they eat little simply because they do not feel like eating. Studies have shown that parents' food dislikes are often reflected in the behavior of the child. One investigator found that among children who presented "feeding problems," 47 percent of the foods disliked or refused by a member of the family were also disliked by the child. Many foods are not liked by the young child on first trial—he must learn to like them. This learning may be en-hanced by giving new foods early in the meal when the child is hungry and giving them in small quantities at first. Give the baby only one new food at a time. If the mother takes a "This is good and you're going to like it" attitude, the child is more likely to think the food really is tasty.

One of the most difficult things for parents to recognize is that mealtime should not be the time when unpleasant subjects are discussed. Even too much conversation can distract the child and cause him to play with his food. But of all the "don't's" the most important one centers around not getting the child emotionally upset at mealtime. Both appetite and digestion can be disturbed by an emotional climate.

CHANGE IN EATING HABITS

One of the most noticeable changes in eating habits occurs around one year of age. During the first several months of life the infant seems always to be hungry at mealtime. About the time he begins walking, food becomes less important and he becomes more choosy about what and how much he eats. Allow the child some choice in what he eats during the second year, because this seems to be the time in his life when he is beginning to have some say-so for himself. Expect changes in taste from month to month.

On the average the baby can sit up well without slumping sometime after six months of age. This is a good time to start feeding him in his high chair. Not until the child is around a year to fifteen months old can he begin using a spoon. Using the fork comes somewhere around two to three years of age. As the child progresses from spoon to fork, table manners will improve. But even the child best trained in table manners will revert occasionally to some cruder form of eating.

SLEEPING

In many respects we can think of sleep as a habit. The child used to a quiet environment may have sleep disturbed by noise. But in most homes a noiseless environment is almost impossible. As long as the child feels safe he can soon learn to sleep well under any normal conditions. Taking the youngster on trips where he must sleep in a new bed each night, under different noise conditions, may be good experience for him.

The amount of sleep needed by children varies from individual to individual. But on the average the newborn infant sleeps about three-fourths of the time. By one year of age the average child is sleeping a little over half the time. Gradually the amount of sleep needed decreases. The average five-year-old sleeps about eleven hours. By eight years of age he will sleep ten hours or less.

Crying out, grinding teeth, and even walking in one's sleep are not usually regarded as abnormal. These types of behavior generally occur when the child is overtired, overexcited, or puzzled about some problem. Some suggestions for developing good sleep habits are:

Maintain some regularity at bedtime.

Avoid inducing sleep by rocking or walking.

Avoid excitement before bedtime.

Let the child take some harmless toys to bed with him.

Let the child sleep alone in bed, if possible.

Don't start being taken in by his many and varied tricks.

TOILET TRAINING

Toilet training should be delayed until the child has matured to the point at which he is beginning to have some ability to restrain his bowel movements and urination. Many writers say that ten months is early enough to start bowel training; bladder training may be started around fifteen to eighteen months. Training readiness is indicated when bowel movements begin to occur at about the same time each day and when the baby begins to strain. He is ready for bladder training when he begins paying attention to the puddle he has made on the floor or listening to his urination while waiting for a bowel movement on the toilet.

Encouragement in learning to use the toilet comes about in two ways. First, the apparent satisfaction that goes along with not messing up the diaper serves as an indirect influence in training. Second, the feeling of accomplishment that goes along with the learning serves as reinforcement. But just expect accidents in toilet habits as a matter of course—children often misjudge the time-distance relation back to the house!

WALKING AND OTHER MOTOR SKILLS

Crawling, creeping, walking, jumping, running, riding tricycles, using the hands and fingers in dressing and undressing, and other motor skills follow somewhat an average trend in development in all children. However, children often vary as to the ages when specific skills begin to be evidenced. Some children even reverse the order in which specific performances appear.

The development of locomotor behavior which leads to walking comes about gradually. At birth the infant cannot hold his chin up, but in about four weeks he can do this for brief periods of time. In the second month the chest can be raised, and at four months of age the infant can sit in an upright position if given support. The average baby can sit alone around the seventh month, and the development of this skill is followed by the ability to stand with help a few weeks later.

WALKING

Walking, with some aid, follows after the period of crawling and/or creeping. The baby usually can stand alone before he learns to walk by himself at about fifteen months of age. Of course some babies walk much earlier than this, and some later. As a general rule, the child who is advanced in his ability to creep before ten months, as compared with the average child, will walk before fifteen months. However, some babies become so efficient in their creeping that this in itself may delay walking. Some children never creep at all, some never even crawl around on their abdomens, but just sit around until they grow enough to stand alone and, later, to walk.

A number of factors, such as weight, illness, and motivation, may play a part in determining the age of walking. If the baby is carried around much of the time or has become very efficient in creeping, his desire to learn to walk may be delayed. Can the "age of walking" be hastened through training? The practical answer is "no." Many experiments lead to this answer, most of the studies having been made on twins, with one twin receiving training and the other being left alone. Walking is one skill the child will "grow into" through maturation. The same holds true for riding behavior. Most children can easily learn to ride a kiddy car around two years of age and a tricycle about six months later.

GRASPING

If you observe a child about six months of age trying to pick up a block, a peanut, or any other small object, you will most likely be impressed by the child's inability to use his fingers successfully; he grabs the object in an awkward sort of way with the palm of his hand. Through maturation the infant goes through stages of scooping the block in with the whole hand, followed by a crude manipulation of the fingers and thumb in grasping. It's not until the child is about one year of age that he can pick up the block with the thumb and two forefingers without resting the hand on the table. Such observations remind us that motor skills develop slowly and that we should not try to force the child to be precise in his movements while growth is still playing the major role in his development.

UNDRESSING AND DRESSING SKILLS

On the average, children begin to show an interest in learning to undress themselves at about eighteen months of age. At two years the child does a pretty good job of it—scattering clothes all over the place!

Dressing involves more motor coordination than does undressing, but certain parts of the process, such as slipping on shoes and holding an arm or leg for the clothing to be put on, start at about eighteen months of age. By two years of age the child can help put on his coat and pull up his pants, and by three he shows interest in buttoning clothing or tying shoes, but without much success. By the time the child is four he can do a pretty good job of dressing with only a little help. Between five and six years of age he begins to tie his shoelaces, which is, by the way, a very difficult motor skill to acquire.

EMOTIONAL BEHAVIOR

The newborn infant shows no definite emotional responses, but gradually through growth and learning, distinct forms of emotional expression appear. First comes excitement, noticed readily in the one-month-old child. By three months of age the child may be seen to exhibit delight as he smiles or distress when his movements are hindered. A few weeks later anger will appear as an emotion. Some mild unhappiness is usually noticed by the time the child is six months of age; some fears appear by twelve months. At two years of age the child has quite an impressive array of emotional responses: fear, anger, jealousy, distress, excitement, delight, joy, elation, affection.

FEAR

Fear is produced by such a large number of situations that we are likely to conclude that all fears are "native" or unlearned, but this is not the case. The child who is sent to bed with some threat may come to fear the dark. A child who observes a member of the family showing, or even talking about, fear of an animal, may become afraid of it without having directly been frightened by the animal himself.

Although the baby learns most of his fears, there are a few things he will naturally be afraid of. Babies are afraid of strange and unexpected situations and objects. Practically all babies are afraid of thunder, lightning, and sonic booms. Once they get used to these happenings, so that they are no longer strange and unexpected, the fear may cease to appear "naturally."

There are no simple and direct rules that all parents can follow in obtaining effective emotional control over the fear of their children, but several helpful suggestions can be made. First, one should keep reminding himself that *most fears are learned.* Removing certain stimuli will prevent some fears from becoming established. Preventing disturbing associations for the child insofar as possible goes a long way toward keeping fears at a minimum. Second, it is important that the child be made to *feel secure,* free from threats, too-frequent punishments (psychological as well as physical), and sudden unexpected situations. Third, *fear* will be *associated with injuries,* so give the child comfort when he is hurt. This kind of comfort will not lead to spoiling. Finally, *set the child a good example,* not an example in "bravery," but the example of not exhibiting or talking of fears. It is comforting to remember that most fears, all save the very severe ones, pass away with time.

ANGER

Anger in most children should not be taken too seriously. As the child grows older, outbursts of anger become fewer and longer. The most common causes of anger for the first couple of years include restrictions of movements, interference in play activities, and direct conflict with authority. With increasing age, anger responses become more specifically directed at the obstructing person or object, frequently taking the form of fighting.

Around two to three years of age temper tantrums are rather common ways of expressing anger, and closely associated with tantrums is the negativistic behavior we spoke of earlier. Negativism is a form of anger in which the child refuses to cooperate, often doing the opposite of what he is told. It is so typical that psychologists regard it as normal behavior. As the child gradually learns more and more effective habits in getting along with other people, anger responses diminish. But the child who is frequently given in to when he becomes angry is likely to resort to more fits of rage because they get him what he wants.

Studies show that among parents who are tolerant with their children fewer anger responses are found than among those children of critical parents who are unreasonably concerned as to whether they are "good" or "bad." By the time the child starts to school he usually learns one way or another that anger does not pay off too often. As with adults, children show anger more frequently when they are tired, in need of sleep, or overstimulated. If the general psychological climate is one in which one frustration piles upon another, anger may well erupt with the least provocation.

JEALOUSY

Most children show some jealousy, particularly when a new baby comes into the house. One can prevent the child's jealousy somewhat by telling him in advance about the new member of the family and getting him to feel that it is *his* baby brother or sister. Letting him help in little ways with the care of the baby and letting him show off the new arrival give him a feeling of participation in a family project. He is less likely to feel that his psychological territory has been invaded.

Reassurance to the older child that he is still loved pays better dividends in decreasing jealousy than do punishments, scoldings, and reasonings. The fewer comparisons one makes between jealous children the better. Not much "natural" jealousy comes from children over five or six years of age. Jealousy between brothers and sisters arises not so much from discrimination between them with regard to gifts and privileges as from unfairness in the general attitude of the parents toward them. The girl who claims that she didn't get as nice presents as her brother may be using this an an excuse to point out unfairness shown in more subtle ways. It is not uncommon for the child who feels insecure to set up a defense for his feelings by exhibiting jealousy against a brother or sister. It is also quite common to have a younger child jealous of an older one who has more possessions and is permitted to do more.

SEX PLAY

Practically all children handle their genitals at one time or another. Such behavior begins around six to eight months of age. Most children boys in particular, around three to six years of age will masturbate somewhat. Calling attention to the activity in a direct disciplinary sort of way may only make matters worse. Getting the child interested in something else, a toy or some other activity, may lessen the problem. Children sometimes masturbate because they need to urinate, because their clothing may be irritating them, or just out of boredom and lack of anything else to do. Nervousness is not caused by masturbation, but sometimes children masturbate because they are nervous.

SEX QUESTIONS

Giving children honest answers to their sex questions, although lessening to some extent the behind-the-barn type of sex experimentation, does not mean they will not engage in some sex play among themselves.

Child psychologists offer a few suggestions that may be helpful in handling sex play among children.

1   Don't let children play alone in a closed room for long periods at a time without casually dropping by to see what they are doing.
2   When interest in what they are doing begins to lag, have some other interesting things for them to try.
3   Don't cause the child to feel that there is something mysterious about sex. Children who have their sex questions answered truthfully and within the bounds of their understanding are less likely to be secretive about sex.
4   As far as possible try not to let children get a sense of guilt about sex.

OTHER ANNOYANCES

Perhaps there is no other subject in child psychology on which there is so little agreement as there is on the question of what to do about *thumb- or finger-sucking*. Fortunately, however, most researchers agree that it is not a habit to worry about too much. Nearly every infant puts his thumb, or fingers, in his mouth. Since the child always has his thumb with him, it is natural that the thumb finds its way into the mouth. Preventing thumb-sucking from becoming a habit involves recognition that sucking behavior is natural and should be allowed to continue. Substitute something else for the infant to suck on and he may leave the thumb alone. If one can prevent thumb-sucking for the first year, the chances are it will not become a habit. Even if it gets started, most children are over the habit by four or five years of age, and usually before permanent teeth start to come through.

Nail-biting is an emotional type of response found more commonly in high-strung children. Scolding or punishing the child for biting his nails won't break the habit; in fact, it may only increase tension. It is necessary to get at the cause of tension and remove it before the habit can be broken.

Stuttering in children learning to talk is not uncommon. After all, speech is a very fine skill that has to come gradually and many little things can upset the smooth progress of acquiring it, especially when the child is in an emotionally charged environment. Let the child who stutters have plenty of time to say what he is attempting to say. It is wise not to interpret the child's repetition of the same words over and over again as stuttering. Most children who stutter for a time will outgrow it if their attention is not called to the stuttering. For a few the problem may be serious, requiring professional attention. Tension and anxiety are inseparable from true stuttering. Calling attention to the stuttering only increases the sense of inadequacy.

THE PLEASANT EMOTIONS

We read and hear so much about fears, angers, and other emotional problems, and have so many opportunities to see them dramatized that we tend to forget that there is another side to our emotional life. Very little is said about *joy, laughter,* and *happiness,* perhaps because these responses are rarely, if ever, problems. But there is a great deal that both parents and teachers can do, directly and indirectly, to help develop this side of the child's emotional life.

Enjoyment of good music, the other arts, science, work, literature, social contacts, and play—all comes about through learning. Good music should not be forced on the child. He should be given the opportunity to hear it. Releasing energy through enjoyment is one of the best ways to keep down emotional tensions that produce problems.

LANGUAGE AND UNDERSTANDING

In one sense we may say that language begins with the birth cry of the newborn and continues to develop with such sounds as "ma-ma" and "da-da," which are sometimes proudly interpreted to mean "mama" and "daddy." In the stricter sense, however, we may say that language begins when *meaning* becomes attached to words. In this sense the baby really doesn't speak his first word until he is about a year of age, often older. At first a single word may carry a number of meanings. For example, "milk," given with varying inflections and gestures, may mean, "I want milk," "There is milk," "I spilled my milk," or "Want more milk." After a time the baby passes from the single word to phrases, such as, "All gone." Finally, language develops to the stage at which ideas are conveyed by whole sentences.

VOCABULARY GROWTH

Here are some rough estimates of the growth of spoken vocabulary in the average child:

At 12 months	3 words
At 15 months	18 words
At 18 months	22 words
At 21 months	120 words
At 2 years	275 words
At 3 years	900 words
At 4 years	1,500 words
At 5 years	2,000 words
At 6 years	2,500 words

Increase in size of vocabulary is, of course, only one aspect of the child's language development. Ability to pronounce words clearly lags far behind vocabulary growth. Not only are new words added to vocabulary, but old words become used with fuller meaning. *Listening* vocabulary grows larger and faster than *speaking* vocabulary.

LEARNING TO TALK

Children learn a language largely through imitation. Speaking clearly and correctly to the child aids in learning good speech. Pushing the child into talking, even after he has some speaking vocabulary, may make him become stubbornly silent. When the child is given too much attention, when every need and whim are anticipated, talking may be delayed. Silence itself can indeed be reinforced. In cases of delayed speech, a careful study of rewards and punishments, in non-speech matters, almost always results in improvement in speech.

It is quite common for children seemingly to drop words from their vocabulary as new words are added. It isn't so much that they forget the words as it is that a change in the need for using certain words comes with increasing age. The preschool child (and exceptions are few) seems to take on those naughty words which to the adult may seem useless. When the child gets into the second or third grade of school bad language increases. Fortunately, he grows out of these habits as he grows out of bad manners, which he will pick up somewhere between six and eight years of age.

UNDERSTANDING

By the time a child is three years old his sensory perceptions are well organized. Some children can give good descriptions of what they perceive, feel, and understand. Experience with concrete situations is an essential aspect of the early development of understanding in the child. Such experiences are often used in describing related events. For example, when the "crazy bone" of a three-year-old was stimulated for the first time, the child described the tingling sensation as, "my fingers are singing." Apparently the child perceived a relationship between the nerve sensation, a new experience, and auditory perception, which had familiarity and therefore was meaningful. Another described the perception as feeling like ginger ale. When his foot went to sleep, one five-year-old said, "My foot is fizzing."

One of the most difficult conceptions for a child to grasp is that of *time*. Since time is a relatively abstract concept, this is to be expected. For the five-year-old a favorite TV program may have meaning in terms of "late afternoon" or "after dinner." The average child is seven to eight years of age before he can tell time on a clock to the quarter hour, and the conception of a month or a year comes even later.

THINKING

The thinking of children is not unlike the problem-solving process found in the adult. It is natural that children should confuse the real with the imaginative and should fail to see certain cause-and-effect relationships in the manner of the adult. A child may say, "Clouds are alive because they move," or he may have the idea that thinking is done with the mouth.

Much of the mental life of the pre-school-age child is based on make-believe activities which, as a mode of early adjustment, allow the child to carry on his thinking without much effort. In the growth of understanding, make-believe, fantasies, and other imaginative activities of the child play a significant role. Around four-to-five years of age imaginations reach a peak. These fantasies may serve the child as escape (just as they sometimes do for adults), or they may provide the bases of constructive ideas. Out of childhood make-believe come useful habits of thinking. Through them the child is also provided with a good means of emotional release. As far as the five-year-old is concerned, he is not telling a falsehood when he says that he was chased by a bear. If he turns out to be a liar, it will be for reasons other than early understanding through make-believe!

ABILITIES, INTERESTS, AND PLAY

General mental ability, mechanical ability, ability in music, and other psychological characteristics are found to conform to the same principle of distribution as do physical traits.

GENERAL MENTAL ABILITY

The I.Q. (intelligence quotient) score is a measure that allows us to compare any one child with all other children, regardless of chronological age. Various descriptive words are useful in making certain comparisons. Let us give one conventional table.

I.Q.	*Verbal Description*
140 and above	Gifted
130–139	Very superior
120–129	Superior
110–119	High average
90–109	*Average*
80–89	Low average
70–79	Inferior
60–69	Borderline
Below 60	Mentally defective

As an illustration of the nature of mental growth, let us take the development of the ability to generalize and recognize abstract ideas. The ages and accompanying descriptions are of the average child. At the age of three and one-half years the child can identify the *longer* of two sticks or the *larger* of two balls. (Length and size are abstract ideas, although for us adults these ideas are so simple we may forget that they are abstractions.) At four years the child can point to the longer of two lines drawn on paper, thus using the same concept in a more abstract setting. At four and one-half years he can select drawings of faces as *pretty* or *not pretty*. At five he can distinguish *heavy* and *light*. By six years of age the child can tell the *difference* between two objects such as wood and glass. Not, however, until the average child is seven years old can he describe the *similarity* of two objects such as a peach and a pear.

Many research studies have been made on the nature of mental growth. They give us answers to a number of practical questions. They indicate, for example, that superior children grow at a more rapid rate throughout the growing period of their mental development, continue to develop for a longer time, and reach a higher level at maturity. Children of high intelligence, in the main, excel in school achievement. They have a wider range of interests, do well in sports, read more books, and are better adjusted emotionally than the average. Long-range studies show that they are highly successful in later life. Of course, some individuals of superior intellect run into problems as children and others do as adults.

In contrast to the mentally bright children and those with average intelligence, we find the mentally handicapped children. Many slow children can be directed through proper home handling and schooling to make satisfactory adjustments to life. Since this is a problem requiring special attention, we offer no advice here.

SPECIAL ABILITIES

In addition to general mental ability, children often exhibit special abilities. Through aptitude tests we are able to measure potentials in the arts, mechanical skills, and other special talents. Interests are important in developing abilities.

One reason we find so many individual differences in interests is that we all have individual differences in abilities. Children change their interests for much the same reasons that adults do, although they change more often. Whereas we adults soon get set in our ways and make the following through on our interests habitual, children are bombarded with so many changes in their environment, so many new acquisitions of skills, and so many opportunities for trying out new activities that they consequently show many shifts in their interests.

PLAY

Many interests find opportunity for development through play. Whether it be playing with rattles, blocks, or dolls, pretending to be a cowboy or an astronaut, learning to jump rope, or making mud pies, playing is more than just fun, it is "work" for the child. Through the study of attention spans in children we know that play also satisfies needs. In Figure 6-1 we see a tendency for attention spans of children in play to increase with age. The increase, however, is not regular. Also, a toy that may be a good attention holder for a two-year-old may decline in its appeal as the child grows older. Some toys, of course, are beyond the age range of the child.

Every good toy should contribute to the mental, physical, and aesthetic development of the child. Toys should be selected for *child appeal* rather than parent appeal. Thus the three-year-old may play

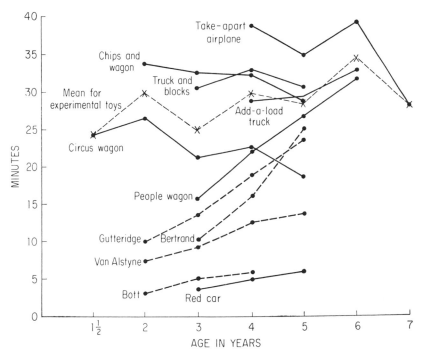

FIG. 6-1 Results of five studies dealing with how long children will concentrate in play with toys. The dashed curves show the results of the researches of four experimenters using toys available on the market. The solid lines show toys designed and redesigned to meet needs at different ages. Toys ranged from a very simple "red car" to a complicated "take-apart airplane." Some toys lose in interest with age ("chips and wagon"), while others gain in interest ("people wagon"). (*From Moyer, K. E., & Gilmer, B. v. H. Attention spans of children for experimentally designed toys. J. genet. Psychol., 1955, 87, 187–201.*)

with a given toy for a certain amount of time, the four-year-old for a longer period of time, and five-year-old for the highest period of time. If when the child is six years of age the toy has lost its appeal, then it is no longer satisfying a need. The closer a toy comes to satisfying the particular needs of the child, the higher will be the play value of the toy. The length of time children will concentrate in play depends on the use of the right toy for the right age.

SOCIAL DEVELOPMENT

A few years ago a study was made of the personnel records of seventy-six companies to find out why they had fired some four thousand of their white-collar workers. The reasons given, of course, varied somewhat from individual to individual; but when all the cases were combined, two main categories stood out: "lack of competence in their jobs" and "inability to get along with other people." Even more surprising was the relative number of persons fired for one or the other of these reasons. Those let go for lack of competence totaled around 11 percent, while the records showed that some 89 percent lost their jobs because of inability to get along with other people.

DEVELOPMENT OF SOCIAL RESPONSES

One study illustrates how individual social behavior may be acquired indirectly through the influences of the environmental situation. An experimental comparison was made between the social responses of children who were organized into "autocratic" and "democratic" clubs. As time went on, the children who were treated in a rather dictatorial way exhibited more aggressive domination in their relations with one another and showed less give-and-take than did those subjects who lived in the more democratic climate. Individual expressions of resistance, hostility, demands for attention, and competition were more than twice as frequent in the authoritarian group. The children in this autocratic group were less spontaneous and friendly in their relations with their adult leader than were those in the permissive club.

When a child joins a social group, he *takes into the situation* many attitudes and habits which he has learned at home. These may be such as to reinforce the habits acquired outside the home, or they may come in conflict with them.

The child, of course, becomes more social as he grows older and at the same time becomes more independent. He must learn a balance between these two, must learn to share his toys, yet at the same time not be taken advantage of. He must learn some reserve, yet avoid becoming timid. He must learn cooperation, yet be able to carry on an activity by himself. He must learn to respect the rights of others, yet not develop a submissive attitude. He must learn to resolve his own conflicts, yet avoid overaggressiveness. This is a tightrope hard to walk.

FRIENDS

One way in which parents can help the child to have friends is to give him a chance to be with other children around his own age.

Selfishness among young children comes naturally, cooperation comes gradually. There may be many reasons why a child fails to make friends. It may be that some of these questions are related to the problem: Is he a "mama's darling"? Have the parents prohibited his noisy friends from coming around? Was he pushed too hard into being sociable? Good teachers recognize that often an unpopular, sometimes lonely child has to be worked into a group activity where he can warm up to the situation, become more friendly himself. The lonely child has a hard time expressing why he is lonely. This is also true of some adults. One person put it this way: "I feel most alone when I am misunderstood."

By the age of two years children may begin to show preferences in friends among several children, and a year or so later strong attachments between two children may be noticed. Such attachments may last only a few days or weeks, or they may last for years. Some companionships may become so close among two or three children as to limit the widening of their social contacts.

Quarrels among children are frequent, and so are aggressiveness, teasing, bad manners, and impoliteness. These types of behavior, however, rarely have a long-term bad effect on social development. In contrast, prejudice instilled in the young may restrict opportunities later.

LEADERSHIP

Leadership differences may be noticed in children even at the preschool age. There are no set rules for helping the child develop leadership.

Several children who are leaders may differ markedly. One child may become a leader because he gets around, one may become a leader because he is constructively aggressive, while still another may be resourceful in ideas for play. Another may have the knack of running things behind the scenes while he makes the other fellows feel important. A child may be a leader in one situation and a follower in another. It is not always the child who makes the big splash that leads the group. Behind him or her may be the idea child, quiet and mild.

THE GROWTH OF PERSONALITY

When we think in terms of watching personality grow we may find it useful to break behavior down into reactions of dominance, indifference, submission, self-confidence, inferiority, sociability, and the like. The big job involves understanding the integration of habits, skills, interests, abilities, emotions, and perceptions into a whole concept we call personality. How does it grow?

TRAITS

The shy, timid child is heading more in the direction of becoming too self-centered than in the direction of sociability. It is doubtful if an introverted child can be transformed into an extrovert, and it would perhaps be undesirable to attempt such a transformation. However, children who seem to be headed toward withdrawal can be helped by being given more opportunities to be with other children of their own age, size, and abilities. The more studious type of child may be encouraged to get out and develop interests that will involve cooperation with others. The socially minded child may be encouraged to settle down more to schoolwork.

Children raised in a family in which the parents are aggressive, autocratic, and hard-headed may take on dominance instead of becoming submissive as one might expect. Submissive persons may have many creative qualities and they may be well-adjusted and easier to get along with than the upward-mobile person. Research on the past lives of people who have shown extreme tendencies of submission show that related causes may include physical defects, real or imagined; unfavorable comparisons with other persons; friction in the home; ridicule by others; lack of opportunities to learn; and rigid parental discipline. Among the causes of dominance, investigators have found such contributing factors as early assumption of responsibility; parental training; absence of discipline in the home; superior mental or physical ability; and some unusual skill, frequently in athletics.

SELF-CONFIDENCE

Another way to come to understand the nature of personality traits and how they grow is to pick a very desirable trait and see how it can be destroyed. For this we shall use self-confidence. How many of the dozen questions below would you say are involved? Here let us address the parents.

1 Are you babying the child rather than encouraging him to do things on his own?
2 Are you making his home climate tense rather than relaxed?
3 Are you giving out with more disapproval than praise?
4 Are you pushing the child beyond his abilities rather than realizing his limitations?
5 Are you aloof rather than friendly with the child?
6 Are you riding the child on his weaknesses rather than trying to correct them?
7 Are you holding up a superior child as an example rather than comparing the child to someone nearer his own abilities?

8   Are you demanding perfection rather than showing tolerance?
9   Are you providing the child with unnecessary worries rather than making him feel secure?
10   Are you setting an "I can't" example rather than exhibiting self-sufficiency yourself?
11   Are you overprotecting the child rather than teaching him responsibility?
12   Are you telling the child to withdraw from situations he should be made to face?

To illustrate a positive approach let us show how parents can help the child develop *self-confidence in problem solving.*
1   Be sure that the problems are within range of the child's abilities at any particular growth level.
2   It is well to let the child work on only one big problem at a time. Several coming all at once lead to frustration.
3   Be patient; solving problems takes a lot of trial and error. A part of this process involves learning what not to do.
4   Be cautious in judging the child's accomplishments in terms of adult standards. Expect him to regress in his ability to solve problems.
5   Don't get in the habit of solving problems for the child.
6   See that the child receives reinforcement when problems are solved.

It may be beneficial to remember that practical child psychology deals with essentially all the *kinds* of problems we face as adults. In biological development, time is on the side of the organism, but in psychological growth time seems to be always running out.

SOME SHORT ANSWER GUIDES

Books, many of them, have been written about practical child psychology in terms of answers to practical questions. The description already given in this chapter deals with the more general questions of interest to parents and teachers. Let us here add some others, bearing in mind that many pages can and have been written on each of them (see the suggestions for further reading at the end of this chapter). *When does the infant smile at me?*

There are two kinds of smiles, the "reflex" smile and the "social" smile. The first may be noticed at birth, the latter in about six weeks. *Should the child be cuddled?*

Yes, most parents naturally do not go to extremes in showing affection.
Does the newborn child have a personality all his own?

Yes, some are placid and serene, while others are more or less restless.

When does the child begin to learn?

He is all set to start learning at birth.

When does the child begin to make choices in eating?

Around the second year. When he loses interest in food take him out of his high chair and forget about feeding until the next meal.

Should the sleeping child be awakened to be played with?

No.

Should the baby be rocked or sung to sleep?

No harm can come of this other than it will become an expected habit.

Can the child be put to bed too hurriedly?

Yes, hurry and excitement delay onset of sleep.

Should he be put to bed with toys?

One favorite soft bear or doll—or blanket.

Is training necessary to get the child to stay dry at night?

As the child matures the bladder will gradually "train itself."

How may toilet training and other habits be affected by physical illness?

Temporary regressions are not uncommon even in the healthiest of children.

When should the baby be put into a playpen?

Around three or four months of age. When he learns to walk alone he will "want out."

Are mechanical baby walkers advisable?

No.

When is telling the child "no" necessary?

When he is good at walking and has developed some skill at using his hands, a few "no's" are necessary to prevent accidents.

Can the three-year-old be trusted not to run into the streets?

No.

Should we expect the child to be awkward while learning new motor skills?

Yes, be patient. Feelings of confidence and satisfaction go along with achieving something new.

When does handedness begin to show up?

Whether the infant is going to be right-handed or left-handed, or in some cases ambidextrous, cannot be determined for several months after birth. Some children do not settle down for four or five years.

Is the left-handed child really handicapped?

No, the southpaw soon becomes adjusted to the right-handed world.

Should you try to influence the child's handedness?

Let the child determine which hand he prefers. It takes time for dominance to show up, a time that varies from child to child.

Should children be taught rhythmic dancing?

Yes, it helps with the development of motor skill, self-confidence, and social poise.

Will the child slip back at times in the development of motor skills?

Backsliding in sports, art, language, and other skills can be expected.

How can the child learn not to fear lightning?

Sit with the child by the window while a storm is going on.

How can fear of the dentist be prevented?

Start casual visits to the dentist early, before any work needs to be done. Two to three years of age is not too early.

Can the child learn caution without fear?

The child should learn caution in crossing streets, approaching strange animals, and keeping away from open fires, not fear of these things. Safe experimentation makes him more, rather than less, cautious.

Should the child be spanked?

There is little agreement from authors on the "yes" or "no" of this. They do agree generally that children learn to behave well not through threats and punishment, but through respect.

How can parents help the child learn to talk?

He picks up words from us, so we must speak correctly and clearly.

What things may delay early talking?

Coaxing, lack of patience, anticipating his every wish, and too much attention.

Should "baby talk" be encouraged?

No, it may seem cute, but will soon become a social handicap for him.

Can children learn two languages at the same time?

Yes, there are some advantages in being able to understand and speak more than one language. Getting mixed up can be expected.

Do children project their feelings through make-believe?

This is quite common in preschool children. It provides some insight into the child's thinking and feeling.

Should the child be told the truth about Santa Claus?

Yes, after the make-believe stage is over. He usually gets wise about the seventh or eighth year.

Is it normal for the child to have a hard time paying attention?

Yes, averages show three-year-olds show sustained attention for *eight* seconds, five-year-olds for *seventeen,* and six-year-olds for *twenty-eight* seconds.

Why do children ask so many questions?

Out of curiosity, to establish social contact, to get attention, to show resistance, to learn the "what," the "why," and the "when."

When should the child be given an intelligence test?

Many authorities say to wait until the child is at least three years of age.

Who should give the child an intelligence test?

Only a competently trained person. Ask a counselor for advice.

How can parents help the child develop ability at problem solving?

1 Keep problems within the range of the child's abilities.
2 Let him work on one problem at a time.
3 Be patient. Problem solving involves trial and error.
4 Be cautious in judging accomplishments by adult standards.
5 Do not solve his problems for him too often.
6 Analyze *your* problem-solving habits.

What can we predict about interests?

Children change their interests for much the same reasons that adults do, but more often. Interests run along with the development of abilities.

What can be done when interest lags?

1 Show enthusiasm yourself.
2 Don't press the irritable or tired child.
3 Participation stimulates interest.
4 Give help in getting over snags.
5 Encourage "helping" you.

What should be done about laziness?

Most children (and adults) are lazy from time to time. If laziness seems a way of life then ask these questions:

1 Is he bored?
2 Is he daydreaming excessively?
3 Is he happy?
4 Is he being disciplined the wrong way?
5 Is he trying to cope with too many problems?
6 Is he in good physical condition?
7 Are you supplying motivation correctly?

Such questions often lead to a *cause* that may be corrected.

Should boys and girls be encouraged to play together?

This is something that takes care of itself—at all ages!

Should the child play alone?

Yes, at times. We must learn to live with ourselves as well as with others.

What are some arguments as to why the child should have a pet?

1 A dog or cat provides something alive that is more nearly the child's own size.
2 Helps teach responsibility.

3   Gets used to animals.
4   The child learns some caution, some give-and-take with a safe animal.
5   The child learns something about giving as well as receiving affection.
6   A well-trained dog can be a protection.
7   Children often become interested in nature through pets.
8   Provides companionship.

How can interest in good music be fostered?

By listening to it.

Should the child read comics?

Yes, the good ones help motivate reading.

How can interest in good music be fostered?

Babies show an interest in other babies within a few weeks after birth, but for the most part friendliness begins around the third year.

Should the child be teased?

"Kidded," yes; "teased," no.

Does the child sometimes regress in his manners?

Yes, children have their ups and downs, but eventually training takes over.

Does generosity come naturally?

Generosity must be learned gradually. Sometimes the child swings a bit far in giving things away, but he soon learns where sharing leaves off and give-and-take begins.

Is nursery school or kindergarten necessary for the child?

It is helpful for the child, yes, but not necessary for the child who has children his own age to be with. For the mother? Yes!

Are there individual differences in adjusting to school?

Yes, children vary greatly in this, and for many different reasons; the chief factor involved is their degree of independence.

Is the "only" child at a disadvantage?

Not really if there are other children in the neighborhood.

What about feelings of security in the adopted child?

All the principles of good child psychology relative to raising your "own" child apply to the adopted child. There is no special age at which the child should be told that he is adopted, but he should be told, preferably as soon as he is capable of understanding.

When the young child takes things, should this be interpreted as stealing?

Children two to three years old will take things that do not belong to them. This can hardly be called stealing. The idea of property rights is not very clear to the young child.

What should you do about stealing in the child who knows better?
   Again we suggest trying to get at the cause:

1   Is he lonesome?
2   Is he using the money to buy friendship?
3   Is he jealous?
4   Is he seeking revenge?
5   Is it a defense against insecurity?
6   Does he want special attention?
7   Is he getting some kind of approval—satisfaction from his gang?
8   Is there some kind of emotional frustration which is not coming to the surface?
9   Do *you* have "hotel towels" at home?

What are some basic summary principles in raising children?
   1   Give the child every chance at good health.
   2   Help the child learn to solve his own problems under proper guidance and discipline.
   3   Give the child a chance to become adjusted to one situation before thrusting him into the middle of another.
   4   Be constant enough in your behavior to let the child know what to expect from you.
   5   Stay emotionally well adjusted yourself.
   6   Keep the home situation as free from quarrels and conflicts as possible.
   7   Hold on to that sense of humor.
   8   Try to enjoy the child instead of thinking of him as a problem.
   9   Be friendly with the child.
   10   Have patience!

   And remember—often when you feel that it is the child who is the problem it may be well to consider that the problem might be elsewhere.

AN ORDERLY SEQUENCE

   Children follow an orderly sequence in development. Some are more rapid in motor development and slower in verbal development. The reverse is true in other children. Some are slower in all steps of development, and others develop rapidly step by step. There is a wide range of individual differences in growing up. No child is exactly like another. It is difficult to compare unlikes. Sequential development is the same, but growth does not necessarily proceed at the same rate at any given time. Understanding these generalizations is helpful in answering many practical questions.

RAISING BOYS AND GIRLS—A CULTURAL
DIFFERENCE

Our North American culture decrees that a girl can seek affection, but a boy is discouraged from doing so. If he seeks help he is a sissy. One college counselor put it this way, "The girls from the women's college come into the office with their problems, and sometimes cry. The boys come in and fight against revealing their feelings, and this slows down the problem-solving process."

In our culture girls may shed tears. This is even expected. They may let off steam in ways that are denied to boys. Father tells junior, "Don't cry," "Get up, be a man," "There is nothing to be afraid of." When little sister is afraid she is soothed. We hear the parent say, "She can ride as well as a boy," but rarely do we hear, "My boy can cook as well as a girl."

The press for masculinity often begins before it has any real meaning. Many fathers (not all) equate roughness and toughness with being a male. Often boys are called upon to prove their masculinity in athletics, even fighting, whether or not they are so inclined.

In their earlier years boys spend most of their time in a woman's world. In the home and in the school women set their standards ("Be nice, like your sister"). These standards sometimes conflict with those that prevail in the man's world; yet father says raising children is a mother's job.

Boys, as well as girls, need reassurance in the trials and tribulations of growing up. Girls get reassurance from Mother, but often boys do not get it from Father. A father should try to involve his son in some of his activities. Just having the son near him assures the boy of his father's affection. Problems in adolescents sometimes can be traced to early boyhood in which the child felt father rejection. In our culture living in a man's world does not come so readily for the boy as living in a woman's world does for the girl.

Summary

In large measure the study of applied psychology begins with the newborn infant. Since most children grow up in the same manner it is possible to describe "what to expect." This helps us get ready for those problems of negativism, aggressiveness, and frustration, as well as providing practical answers to the dozens of questions that arise about eating, sleeping, and toilet training.

From hundreds of studies of walking and other motor skills we learn what children of various ages can and cannot do. We learn that the age of walking cannot be hastened through training, and why the young child cannot pick up a pill with his fingers. Many practical answers can be given to questions concerning the emotional development of the child, and parents can be helped in handling such problems as reducing fears, controlling anger and jealousy, sex play, etc.

There are many data which provide clues for understanding vocabulary growth and the processes of learning to talk and to think. General mental ability, mechanical ability, ability in music, and other psychological characteristics are found to conform to the same principle of distribution as do physical traits.

Following social development in children provides us with understandings for dealing with some adult problems. Follow-up studies of children who were treated dictatorially showed that in later life they were aggressive and domineering in their relations with others. Individual expressions of resistance, hostility, and demands for attention were more than twice as frequent among them as among children who had experienced a more democratic climate.

When we think in terms of watching personality growth we find it useful to study reactions of dominance, indifference, submission, self-confidence, inferiority, sociability, and the like. Understanding the child helps in understanding the adult integration of habits, skills, interests, abilities, emotions, and perceptions into a whole personality.

In this chapter we have illustrated how such traits as self-confidence can be destroyed by unfavorable comparisons and pushing the child beyond his abilities. We described how to help the child develop self-confidence in problem solving.

Practical child psychology deals with the same kinds of problems we face as adults. Many of the keys to understanding the assets and liabilities of adolescents lie in knowing how behavior developed during childhood.

Suggestions for Thinking and Discussion

1   If there is opportunity, record some of the behavior characteristics of the three-year-old. What would be *your* theory as to why he is so negative?
2   Make a checklist of what to expect in the two-year-old, the four-year-old, and the six-year-old. What generalizations about growth would you make?
3   What evidence supports the conclusion that emotional growth and language development follow a general-to-specific sequence?
4   Give some examples of how social responses are learned.
5   Do you exhibit any personality traits which can be traced back to some influence in early childhood?
6   Give some examples of how early fears can be learned.

Suggestions for Further Reading

Dennis, W. (Ed.) *Readings in child psychology.* Englewood Cliffs, N.J.: Prentice-Hall, 1963. A collection of readings covering a wide range of papers from basic research to practical problems.

Gesell, A., & Ilg, Frances L. *Infant and child in the culture of today.* New York: Harper & Row, 1943. A classic in describing the norms of "what to expect" during the first five years.

———— & ———— *The child from five to ten.* New York: Harper & Row, 1946. Describes "what to expect" from ages five to ten. A sequel to the preceding reference.

Kagan, J., & Moss, H. A. *Birth to maturity: A study in psychological development.* New York: Wiley, 1962. The total picture of growth from childhood to maturity.

U.S. Government Printing Office. *Your child from one to six.* Washington: Children's Bureau Publication No. 30, 1956. Practical advice on raising children.

CHAPTER 7

Psychological Problems of Adolescence

❖❖❖❖❖❖❖❖❖❖❖❖

Adolescence is more than just childhood extended. It may be described negatively as the "un" stage—*unbalanced, unstable,* and *unpredictable.* It may also be described positively, as a time when a low threshold for boredom is counteracted by an even lower threshold for stimulation. Adolescence is a period of transition between childhood and adulthood, a time when a few bad decisions can lead to delinquency or a few lucky breaks can get the individual off to a good start in programming a future.

Adolescence extends from the time preceding sexual maturity to the age of independence. For boys, who mature slightly later than girls, we regard preadolescence as the period roughly from ten to thirteen years of age, early adolescence from thirteen to seventeen, and late adolescence from eighteen to twenty-one years. For girls, preadolescence comes between ten and eleven, early adolescence extends from twelve to sixteen, and late adolescence from seventeen to twenty-one years.

TEEN-AGE PROBLEMS

"I think of myself in relation to others, how I stand up by comparison. I may put on a show of self-confidence, but it's only a cover-up. Everywhere I face nothing but competition—from my classmates, my teachers, and my parents. I need help in this business of growing up—I'm just an adolescent with problems."

What are the problems of the adolescent? Before we turn to scientific studies, let us give a sample of what teen-agers say about themselves:

"I am concerned about physical attractiveness."

"I want to wear the right clothes."

"I dread making a decision."

"I am lost with time on my hands."

"I want to be different, but not too different."

"I am unhappy with my name."

These statements are typical. For example, of 334 eighteen-year-olds, 77 percent disliked their name because it made them shy or embarrassed. In discussing the process of going from dependence to independence one teen-ager gave this insight: "My problem is that I can't have it both ways."

MATURITY

For the teen-ager, maturity has the advantages of freedom—a chance to bring aspirations in line with ability—and more feeling of security. The disadvantages are that one is held accountable for his behavior, that he is alone in an unfriendly world, and that there is little guidance from others.

Intellectual maturity, growing strongly between sixteen and twenty-five years of age, is indicated by such behavior as making up one's own mind, taking responsibility, and learning the difference between compromise and butting one's head against the wall.

Social maturity is a sort of "psychological weaning," with no clear-cut ages defined. It is indicated by such behavior as self-reliance, absence of prejudice, and being able to amuse oneself. It also involves release from conformity to a succession of fads.

Emotional maturity also has no age boundaries. Some adults never get beyond adolescence. Among the indicators of growing up emotionally are the ability to adjust to stress, being selective in what to worry about, and discovering harmless ways of letting off steam.

Mature adult morality is stable. It does not vary with the environment and is indicated by tolerance, understanding, and adjustment to rules and laws. The teen-ager wants this kind of morality also, *but now*. Adolescent morals are lofty, often idealistic. The teen-ager wants to solve the world's problems overnight. He typically responds to problem situations by verbalizing, "It's not fair."

Academic maturity comes slowly. One finds both the "underachievers," whose performance falls below their potential, and the "overachievers," who exceed expectation. Many of the problems of dropouts center around failure to reach academic maturity—failure that can be overcome in the right climate. Basically, however, there is no "normal" age range for attaining academic maturity.

EMOTIONAL BEHAVIOR

Emotionally the adolescent is more of a problem to himself than to others. He faces new roles faster than he can adjust to old ones. It is important in understanding the development of human behavior to realize that most of these emotional problems are *normal* in the statistical sense.

There is a marked *sex difference* in both interests and problems in early adolescence. Girls, maturing more rapidly, have more problems than boys. They are more concerned with school, family, and social adjustments, and with personal appearance. Boys are more concerned with money problems and career planning. Both groups increasingly become concerned with emotional problems. Particular difficulty is experienced with the individual who was unsuccessful in dealing with his childhood problems. The older adolescent is concerned with problems related to getting into college, and once in, staying there.

NERVOUS HABITS

At puberty there is likely to be an increase in nail-biting. This nervous behavior decreases as the adolescent becomes more appearance conscious. Substitutes, such as finger tapping, hair twisting, or cigarette smoking, may come in. Girls may show excessive responses of giggling or overreacting to mild stimuli; such behavior usually lessens after puberty. Boys tend to display exaggerated behavior in such acts as "burning rubber off the tires."

The nervous habits of adolescent college students have been studied extensively. One may conclude that worries, swings in mood, and the more acceptable emotional feelings take over from earlier overt emotional expressions. A part of the heightened emotionality of the college freshman centers around breaking off not only old nervous habits such as nail-biting but habits of thought as well. Moods of exhilaration and depression alternate, varying with environmental influences (the big weekend versus examination periods).

Modern researchers indicate that increased emotionality, and the many individual habits which are displayed, during adolescence is attributable to social factors. Chief among these are unfavorable family relationships, restraints imposed by parents, situations in which the individual feels inadequate (e.g., dating) and where expectations of mature behavior exceed actual performance. For the college freshman, however, coming to understand and learning to cope with a new psychological climate is most difficult. Once he learns more about "the system," the adolescent's nervousness decreases considerably.

FEAR AND WORRY

One observer put it this way: "Adolescents have the same worries and fears as adults, only more so." Possibly one reason why we hear so much about teen-agers' fears of social relationships is that adolescents are more likely to talk about their feelings than they are to analyze the fear process itself.

Fears of social situations include fears such as meeting people, being alone, being in a crowd, reciting in class, making a speech, or, for the younger adolescent, being in situations with members of the other sex. An overamount of self-consciousness makes the teen-ager easily embarrassed if he is teased about someone of the opposite sex, or if he is observed in clothing not like that of the group. He overemphasizes status; such overemphasis may even lead to delinquency.

Shyness in adolescents reaches a peak around fifteen years of age. It is often prolonged and intensified if the individual is forced into situations in which he has to display a weakness. By the time the adolescent is in college he has acquired enough skill to make a good appearance, and hence fears decline. It is at this stage that the mental counterpart of fear, namely, worry, increases. Most worries center about anticipated situations, clustering around schoolwork, feelings of inferiority, and loss of prestige.

Worries in early adolescence relate a great deal to lack of understanding on the part of parents and the inability to communicate with them about problems of physical development, religion, money, and "what is expected." Worries become a little more "other-directed" as adolescents grow older. In Figure 7-1 we see represented how worries change with age in both boys and girls from the sixth grade through college. Women become more concerned with being popular socially and getting married. Men are more concerned about future career possibilities.

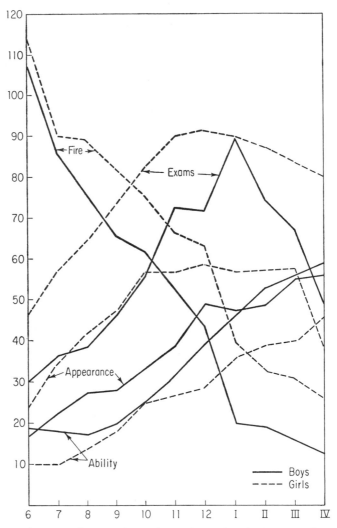

FIG. 7-1 Changes of worry in students from the sixth grade through four years of college. Childhood worries (fire) decrease rapidly in both boys and girls. Note how worry about exams begins to decrease after the first year of college. Worries about ability, however, continue to increase year by year. (*From Pressey, S. L., and Robinson, F. P. Psychology and the new education. New York: Harper & Row, 1944. Reproduced by permission of Harper & Row.*)

EMOTIONAL EXPRESSIONS

Normal adolescent emotions differ from those of childhood and of adults in some six ways:

1 Emotional responses are often intense and out of control. The adolescent gives way to feelings of the moment. He reacts out of proportion to stimuli evoking the behavior.

2 Responses shift rapidly from one extreme to the other; from joy, pride, and hope to despair and gloom, from self-confidence to self-distrust, from success to failure and the reverse.

3 There is a lack of control at times. Typically girls will weep or giggle, boys will grin and become silent.

4 Moods become drawn out in duration. When outward expressions are inhibited, moods take over. Emotional feelings seem to get bottled up inside, where they may smolder for days.

5 Oversentimentality is characteristic of teen-age emotions—for school, for family, and for groups.

6 Steam gets let off in the wrong places and at the wrong time.

ANGER

Adolescents, like many adults, become angry when mechanical things fail to work or in other impersonal situations. But the most effective stimuli in evoking anger are social—unfair treatment, unjust accusations, unwelcome advice. Among college students, high on the list comes *thwarted self-assertion*.

The most frequent response made by the angry adolescent is talking. Boys swear and lash back with sarcasm and ridicule. After such explosions the teen-ager often becomes sulky or engages in behavior annoying to the individual with whom he is angry (e.g., whistling under the breath). Adolescents may kick and throw things, and, in the case of girls, cry. Gradually language responses substitute for more direct acts. Studies show that college girls exhibit more frequent verbal responses to anger than do boys, who engage in more physical combat.

The frequency of anger responses in adolescents is quite individual. It is related to such factors as college climates, parental restrictions, and in particular the degree of realism present in dealing with problem solving. For many people annoyances take over in place of anger with maturity. *Jealousy* often grows out of anger, and *envy* may take over. This is particularly true with the adolescent girl. In both jealousy and envy, the typical adolescent reaction is verbal.

THE PLEASANT EMOTIONS

There are two reasons why more attention is given to the undesirable emotions of fear and anger and less to the more positive emotions of joy, pleasure, delight, and affection. First, fear and anger are usually exhibited in *specific* ways. One has a fear of failing an examination. One is angry about a regulation that he perceives to be unfair. On the other hand, pleasure, happiness, and the like are generalized feelings, difficult to pin down. Second, fear and anger often bring on a sequence of problems which must be dealt with. No doubt a part of the reason why adolescence seems to be the *un* age, a time of storm and stress, is that negative behavior is so easily observed. It often creates community problems. A part of the problem is that adolescents are expected to be disturbed.

For the teen-ager with abilities, with a sense of humor, living in a favorable home and school climate, the pleasant emotions may outweigh the negative behavior. Some of the disturbing emotions may even have in them a source of enjoyment, i.e., they provide excitement. They may even help provide certain required amounts of stress.

EMOTIONAL CONTROL

Achieving emotional control during adolescence can be most beneficial to adjustment in adult life. Application of the *problem-solving process* enables one better to objectify the cause-effect relations in behavior. This, in turn, enables the person to gain better control of the expressions of emotion. An individual who maintains an *appearance of calmness* in the face of stimuli that provoke fear or anger has taken the first step toward real calmness. Helpful also in the control of an emotion is *becoming adjusted to the stimulus* that produces it. Since emotion is a nonadjustive reaction, procedures that give a person more adjustive power over his environment will lessen emotional reactions. Though emotion inhibits clear thinking, fortunately it is also true that *clear thinking inhibits emotion* to some extent.

Many studies support the conclusion that counseling can help the adolescent objectify and think through his problems. Though guidance may not, in and of itself, solve the problem, it encourages problem-solving behavior. Sharing problems makes the adolescent more aware that he is not alone with his problems. Learning that many of the emotional problems are "normal" aids understanding. Guided group discussions are most beneficial in this respect.

SOCIAL BEHAVIOR

Many researches, ranging from studies of industrial work groups to those of retirement communities, emphasize the importance of providing people with opportunities for social interaction. Although most disturbing emotional problems of the adolescent come through social contact, no other individual needs people more.

CHANGES IN SOCIAL BEHAVIOR

Changes in social behavior and attitudes are more related to sexual maturation than to chronological age. It is to be expected that when boys reach sexual maturity they will break away from the old gang and begin to enter into activities with girls. They show more interest in personal appearance and in competitive sports in which they can "look good."

In early adolescence social experimentation centers around organizing activities, selecting leaders, and creating on a small scale a society modeled after that of adults. Lounging around and talking occupy much time. In late adolescence three social worlds become important—family, school, and friendship groups. For some, a fourth world may come into being—the work group. In attitudes, by the time the adolescent reaches college, there is a trend toward liberalism as the individual acquires more information and becomes less provincial in his thinking. For some students such broadening experiences may be emotionally disturbing.

CONFORMITY

In terms of conforming to group norms the adolescent goes the much-maligned "organization man" one better. He or she conforms not only to group dress and group behavior but also to group opinions. Although the adolescent is becoming liberal and somewhat idealistic in certain social attitudes, he is most conservative where his age mates are concerned. They want to be different and to conform at the same time. This leads to the formation of "in groups" that are different from the outsiders. The "gang wars," found in many of our large cities, combine the desire for togetherness with frustration and hatreds. Whereas one adolescent may find a certain amount of security and ego satisfaction in a school situation, another youth, usually underprivileged, finds gangs. Frustrated people often identify readily with violence.

In the gang, the adolescent can both be different and conform to gang conduct at the same time. It is important to remember, however, that numbers of adolescents are individualistic in many ways, despite their conforming behavior.

The desire to receive approval of the group sometimes leads the adolescent into trouble. With time, self-confidence increases and the urge for approval changes toward seeking recognition for effort expended. Until *he feels* accomplishment, reinforced by the recognition of others, the older adolescent may switch his attention-getting behavior from off-color jokes and clownishness to expressing radical points of view. It must be recognized that acceptance takes time.

SOCIAL PERCEPTIONS

Most children are lacking not only in social insight but also in self-insight. Hence, social perception is first noticed during adolescence. The perception of the status of others develops during the high school years. The perception of one's own status comes later. Freshmen college counselors report that one of the most bothersome problems at this age concerns the question, "Who am I?"

Perception of the class status to which one belongs is often confusing. The adolescent is born into a family that is a member of a socially ranked group. He is influenced both by his social position and by pressures from this group. Often he has to play socially approved roles not of his own choosing. The idealistic attitudes of the adolescent predispose him to disappointment, disillusionment, and even cynicism.

An individual's evaluation of himself is gradually determined by his perception of his *relative* position in two different kinds of groups. First, where does he stand in some group of which he is a member? Second, how would he rate himself in a group of which he is not a member but in which he aspires to membership? For example, the premedical student may evaluate his intelligence by comparing himself with his fellow college students. Here he has more evidence on which to base his judgment than when he compares himself with "great doctors," a group to which he aspires to belong.

Adolescents have some tendency to perceive themselves in comparison with "the ideal." Girls who try to rate their own physical attractiveness may feel badly when they use the calendar girl as a model. Boys often get feelings of inferiority when they fail to compete with adults. Gradually the adolescent learns to perceive himself in relation to many social groups. Older college students are found to be more cynical than younger ones. This may be, in part, because there is sometimes a thin line between cynicism and wisdom.

SOCIAL GROUPINGS

The group affiliations of late childhood gradually break up during the preadolescent period. The need for belonging to a group becomes more important during adolescence. The close parent-child relationship, which served as a source of security for the child, becomes strained during the transition to adolescence. The possibilities of groupings are many: kinships, chums, playmates, neighbors, classmates, schoolmates, and cliques.

Groups may be charted in three ways. First, groups are characterized by the rules of behavior accepted by a majority of the group. This *group norm* spells out the attitudes and actions expected of members. Second, in voluntary groups (such as a fraternity) *cohesiveness* is important. Here one sees the group's policing power over its members. The greater the cohesiveness of a group, the greater is the amount of conformity to its norms. A nonvoluntary group (for example, an Army reserve unit), i.e., one which persons are constrained to join, may have absolute power. Third, control over members involves a *monitoring system,* under which deviant behavior may be punished.

There are three characteristics of group membership: (1) the *rank status* in the group; (2) the degree to which the new member *values membership* in the group, membership being valued more highly when it is difficult to get into the group; (3) the influence of the *perceived legitimacy* of the group norm on the impact that norm will have upon a new member.

There are marked individual differences as to how people fit (or fail to fit) in a group. Figure 7-2 pictures the basic structure of adolescent groups, showing the *isolate* (*W* and *B*), the *pair* (*U-V*); the *chain* (*R-Ro-M*); and the *clique* (clusters). The leader is designated by *L*.

Many of the problems of the social behavior of adolescents can be understood by seeing where each person fits into a group. The clique has been studied extensively. In many respects investigation of cliques reveals the nature of adolescent social needs.

CLIQUES

The clique is usually a small, informal, and somewhat exclusive affiliation of individuals in a face-to-face group. It has a common set of values but no formal rules. Members of a clique satisfy their feelings for belongingness in ways that make them think and act alike. Sometimes loneliness helps to force the individual to conform to the behavior of his group. Cliques are made up of members of common standing in the community or class.

A clique may or may not be associated with a geographic location. Cliques are, however, made up of individuals who are brought together daily in some practical way (among adults, for example, we have car pools). Adolescents usually fall into school cliques, recreational cliques, and institutional cliques (scouts, church groups). Cliques begin to form around the fourteenth year. They start off by being comprised exclu-

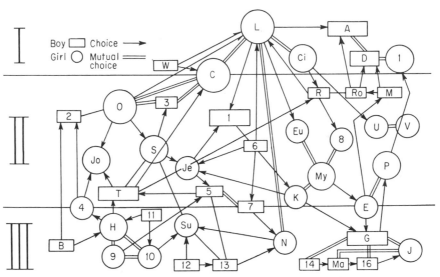

FIG. 7-2. Basic structure of an adolescent group. Note how the lines of communication flow toward leader L. A mutual *pair* (*U-V*), the *chain* (*R-Ro-M*), the *clique* (clusters), and *isolates* (*W* and *B*) may be seen. Three socioeconomic classes are shown. These adolescents lived in a town of 4,500 population, near a large city. (*From Cook, L. A. An experimental sociographic study of a stratified 10th grade class. Amer. sociol. Rev., 1945, 10, 250–261.*)

sively of boys or girls, developing later into mixed groups, with the sexes being equally represented.

The typical adolescent *crowd* is composed of several cliques that join together. Activities involving both sexes have more organizational complications than those which are on a single-sex basis. For example, cross-clique dating requires approval by members of the cliques to which the boy and girl belong. Girls' cliques are more closely knit than are boys', with more resistance to change. This makes it difficult for a new person coming into the school or neighborhood to gain acceptance.

Adolescent cliques come into existence informally, with individuals just getting together to do things. Congeniality based on interests or special aptitudes provides a basis for clique formation. Studies show that the cliques hold together well because their selection system makes sure that the individual will "fit." One researcher found that being together consumes from 64 to 99 percent of the young adolescent's leisure time.

Typically the clique tries to avoid supervision of its activities by adults, engaging in such pastimes as gossiping, dancing, dating, watching television, *and* eating. Influence of the clique on attitudes and behavior of the adolescent is enormous for both good and bad.

BENEFICIAL FEATURES OF CLIQUES

On the positive side the clique offers its members:
1 Opportunity for satisfying the need for belonging.
2 Opportunity for release of emotional tensions in a friendly climate.
3 Opportunity for development of social skills.
4 Opportunity for reinforcement of one's own personal importance.
5 A status power structure providing prestige in the eyes of his peers.
6 Incentive to behave in mature ways.
7 A source of protection in striving for independence.
8 Trial-and-error experiences in developing human relations skills.

UNDESIRABLE FEATURES OF CLIQUES

On the negative side the clique:
1 Restricts development of individuality of its members.
2 Tends to encourage hostility of members of "out groups."
3 Creates competition of "keeping up with the Joneses," or "down with the mob."
4 Creates conflict of allegiance between parental authority and clique mores.
5 Amplifies the development of class segregation.
6 Sometimes disrupts organizational harmony of school or campus.

INTERESTS AND ATTITUDES

One of the oldest continuous research programs in psychology has been the study of male and female interests. The researches begun by Strong in the 1920s, and expanded by a number of scientists, emphasize the importance of early interests and experiences in career development. Although interests change, and for many reasons, vocational decision making is nevertheless influenced by adolescent interests. Measures of the interests of high school and college students show that some one-third change between 15.5 and 16.5 years of age, one-third between 16.5 and 18.5 years, and one-third between 18.5 and 25 years.

Although interests are influenced by sex, age, physical development, and the climate of opportunity, it is useful to take an overall look at adolescent interest patterns, particularly since interests are so highly individual. We shall say more on this later in Chapter 11 on counseling and guidance.

SEX DIFFERENCES IN INTERESTS

In recreational activities girls show interest in less vigorous endeavors. Boys prefer competitive activity requiring psychomotor skill. They go in for organized sports. These sex differences lessen in late adolescence.

Girls are more verbal than boys. They spend more time on the telephone (though this observation will probably be doubted by some parents) and express themselves more in writing. Girls often keep a record of their social and emotional life in a diary; boys rarely do so. By the senior year of high school conversations among boys center around ball games, dates, television, records, and money. Girls give more attention to books, dates, and parties. One study of the college bull session found that men discussed an average of 3.4 topics as compared with 5.7 for women. Men tend to dwell longer on one topic than do women. College women talk most about dates, clothes, sororities, food, and dancing. Men talk about sex and about topics directly or indirectly related to careers.

There is some evidence to support the position that girls are discouraged from showing intellectual interests in our society. In spite of our increasing need for the better utilization of women's brainpower, our culture discourages women from more than casual interest in science, mathematics, and those activities involving decision-making processes. The role of the male centers around career, expressed by interest in money and success. The role of the female centers around domestic activities and marriage as a career. While girls have an interest in money as a means to an end, boys have a broader and more varied experience with money during childhood, which is amplified in managing financial affairs in adolescence. One research study concludes that as girls grow up, they discover that women are not supposed to excel intellectually. By the twelfth grade something in their growing concept of the "woman's role" prevents them from competing with men in our North American culture. Social pressures by her peers help mold the girl student into the stereotype of feminine charm—to be feminine they must quake at a column of figures. For the young girl in our culture the marriage-go-round is a primary goal.

INFLUENCES ON INTERESTS

Sex differences in interests and attitudes are both biologically and culturally determined. The adolescent boy in particular becomes concerned about voice modification when puberty changes cause his voice to crack. The change in tonal quality is far less pronounced in girls.

Our culture seems to demand that career choices be made early. Pressures to decide on one's life career are felt by the adolescent from all sides. Teachers often press him to decide. Counselors stress the importance of early career decision making, and parents want him to make up his mind so that they can proceed with their part in the developmental process. For the girl, pressure toward marriage plays a role in planning.

The author, who has studied career decision making in over one thousand college seniors of both sexes, concludes that women are concerned primarily about the dual role they must plan on of raising a family and making a living. Men are concerned primarily about two factors: knowing when all the alternatives have been covered for decision making, and knowing how best to relate abilities and interests to job climate and opportunities.

If it is any comfort to the reader who is finding difficulty in relating his or her abilities, interests, personality, and goals in a practical way, let us say that he is not by himself. Our investigations show that over half the seniors we have studied come up with doubts about what they really want to do. Vocational interests change frequently during adolescence. This may be good. It helps the person explore possibilities in something of a laboratory situation before having to make final choices. For those who would put pressures on the adolescent (and possibly for the better) to think about his or her career, one should be mindful that it is easier to try to exert influence than it is to make judgments and decisions.

DATING, COURTSHIP, AND MARRIAGE

One writer defines *dating* as "any kind of paired association of members of the opposite sexes without references to the intent to marry." On the other hand, *courtship* "involves obligations to carry through to marriage."

Dating not only gives the adolescent social experiences but literally aids in the processes of decision making in choosing a mate. Success in marriage depends on no single factor but is more closely related to personality than to anything else.

The age of beginning to have dates has been almost constantly lowered since the 1920s. Many boys and girls have their first dates before entering high school. Between the ages of sixteen and twenty years of age dating has become a major adolescent activity. Boys date slightly less than girls during the freshman year of high school. By the junior year the differences between the sexes in the amount of dating is slight. In the senior year girls date more than boys. They are now dating older boys in college or at work.

Dating begins as a form of clique behavior, frequently in combines of double dating. Early dating begins more out of social pressure than as an interest. Because of shyness and of not knowing quite what to do, early dates may well induce more fear and worry than pleasurable experience. In dating patterns, boys are more likely to cross "class boundaries" and date girls of a lower socioeconomic class. Girls, on the other hand, move up in dating boys of a higher class. Boys "can get by" better than girls in dating out-of-group people.

ADVANTAGES AND DISADVANTAGES

Dating as a form of social behavior has been viewed by cynic, critic, promoter, and researcher. Some contend that dating is a barrier to happiness in marriage and that on dates the girl must learn to protect herself against the boy's sexual advances. Some contend that it is a form of social behavior largely dominated by a quest for thrills, sometimes through deceit in the pretense of love and devotion. And some say that it is a built-in trap to promote marriage. Some ask the critics what alternatives might take the place of this widespread custom.

The advantages of dating have been listed as including educational aspects, that is, it helps in learning to adjust to members of the opposite sex and in gaining poise and ease in social situations. It is a process in which one learns to control behavior, evaluate personality types, and build up concepts of right and wrong. Dating is a means of mixing and having a good time socially, and it helps to define the roles of members of the two sexes.

BLIND DATES AND THE COMPUTER

"Just an evening wasted, I'll never go out on another blind date." Yes, *you* probably have said the same thing on some occasion.

Several mixer-weary Harvard students concluded that college students *do* know what kind of people they enjoy dating. They also agreed that blind dates are fine up to a point but that there must be a better way than the usual trial-and-error system. Why not use a computer? This was the beginning of Operation Match in 1965.

Operation Match began with the construction of questionnaires, which were sent to many college students. The data were analyzed statistically. During the first year some 200,000 college students across the country were matched, with a follow-up of a sample of 8,000 of them in a validation study. Through refinement of the questionnaire and programming, it has been found that much of the gamble can be taken out of the blind date by using the computer for matching couples on the basis of their preferences.

The student is asked to fill out a vital statistics and personality inventory on an answer sheet which comes with "the test." Thus, placed in the computer memory file are vital statistics of sex, race, religion, age, and interests. Also included are responses to questions about attitudes and how one reacts to specific situations. Data programmed into the computer include general and specific information about academic record, social standing, and even political affiliation. Physical appearance is added to the picture, as are self-evaluations of such qualities as "talkativeness" and "emotional responses." Not only does the male, for example, describe himself, but he records on an answer sheet what he wants his date to be like. Each client is sent a list of possible dates from which he or she can make choices. The matching is based on responses to items which have been found to be valid for "good matching."

Let us give a sample of a few of the items from Operation Match:[1]
(Sample A) *In answering, refer to table at right.*

My age is:	(1) 17
The ideal age for my date is:	(2) 18
Men: I would consider dating a girl as	(3) 19
young as (indicate minimum acceptable	(4) 20
age):	(5) 21
Women: I would consider dating a man as	(6) 22
old as (indicate maximum acceptable	(7) 23
age):	(8) 24 or 25
	(9) 26 or 27

(Sample B) *How important is it to you that your date share the interests you have indicated?*

       (1)   Unimportant
       (2)   Slightly important
       (3)   Moderately important
       (4)   Very important

[1] Reproduced here by permission of Compatibility Research, Inc., Cambridge, Mass.

(Sample C) *Do you think romantic love is necessary for successful marriage?*

Yes   No

1   2   3   4   5

(Sample D) *Your roommate gets you a blind date for a big dance. Good-looking, your roommate says. When you meet your date, you are sure it is your roommate who is blind—your date is friendly, but embarrassingly unattractive.*

You:

(1) suggest going to a movie instead

(2) monopolize your roommate's date, leaving your roommate only one noble alternative

(3) dance with your date, smiling weakly, but end the evening as early as possible

(4) act very friendly the whole time and run the risk of getting trapped into a second date

(Sample E) *Are you willing to date people from college areas adjacent to but outside your own area, if it significantly improves the quality of your matches?*

(1) Yes   (2) No

Reactions of students have been generally favorable to computerized date matching: "It got me out of a rut." "I met some other adventuresome people." Yes, sometimes the wrong number may get punched in. In a system of "1" for male and "2" for female, there have been reports of the mistake of "1-1" matching! Conclude the originators of Operation Match: "If you live in an area with several thousand college students, the number of possible matches for dating is several million. You yourself have a choice of several thousand dates, and be modest—that's too many to check out." In another study, of sex differences in dating aspirations and satisfaction with computer-selected partners, it was found that women have a higher aspiration for a dating partner than do men. Women register a high degree of satisfaction less frequently than men following the first date.

STAGES OF COURTSHIP

From a free-wheeling type of *dating*, a first stage of playing the field, boys and girls generally emerge into the second stage of *going steady*. This is a stage which provides a type of security, on the one hand, but restricts experiences on the other. The third stage involves *courtship*, in which there is an understanding to be married at some indefinite time in the future. Stage four is the period of *engagement*. At this time couples go together exclusively and make preparations for a wedding and establishment of a home. The final stage involves *marriage*.

MARRIAGE

The success or failure of a marriage psychologically is determined by the quality of adjustments husband and wife make to each other. The adjustive histories of childhood are important because the relationships in marriage have much in common with those experienced between a parent and a child. For example, the immature, dependent wife may expect the same kind of indulgence from her husband that she received from her father. The husband who had a rebelliously hostile attitude toward his parents may be overdominant with his spouse.

Researches show that young people who had good social adjustment before marriage had more successful marriages. Sexual compatibility is a significant factor in marital adjustment. Satisfactory sexual relations may be either a result or a contributing cause of generally successful marriage. Married couples who are relatively free from anxieties and hostilities are usually compatible in sex.

FACTORS IN SELECTING A MATE

Unhappiness in marriage is largely a matter of personal relationships between husbands and wives which result in conflict—being too critical, too emotional, too impatient. Happiness centers around common interests, common friendships, and common levels of aspiration.

Selecting a mate is a decision-making process involving *maturity* of judgment. Some signs of such maturity include:
1 Knowing the difference between romantic ideals and practical reality.
2 Few "typical" adolescent kinds of behavior.
3 Understanding realities of socioeconomic status.
4 Realistic goals.
5 Insight into human relations.
6 Freedom from "Momism."

Professor Clifford Adams of Pennsylvania State University has come up with some questions which may be helpful in guiding one's evaluation of whether he is in love or just infatuated by good looks and sex appeal:
1 Do you have a great number of things you like to do together? (Yes)
2 Do you feel you need to apologize for certain things about him? (No)

3   Do you suffer from a feeling of unrest when away from him? (Yes)

4   Do you have difficulty carrying on conversation together? (No)

5   Even when you quarrel do you enjoy being together? (Yes)

6   Would you be afraid to trust him for an evening to a most attractive person? (No)

7   Does he have the qualities you want in your children? (Yes)

8   Do your associates like him? (Yes)

9   Do your parents think you are in love? (Yes)

10   Do you approve generally of each other's friends? (Yes)

11   Do you ever doubt your love for him? (No)

12   Does trouble pull you closer together? (Yes)

From these and similar questions in studies he concludes that success in marriage means thinking through the many problems of personality adjustments. This involves not only study of the other person but also some self-analysis.

FOUR DIMENSIONS OF SELF

Strang, in her book *The Adolescent Views Himself,* pulls together the many answers to the question, "Who am I?" given in the words of the adolescent.

"I'm just an average, healthy American girl—I have many interests—I am smart, but I could do better in my schoolwork if I studied a little harder."

"My parents think I'm too slow even when I'm going as fast as I can. They think I'm too irresponsible—I guess they would like to trade me in for somebody like my cousin."

"Other people think I'm a stupid jerk—Some think I'm bright and some think I'm dull—I'm fairly quiet and a little shy."

"I would like to be a person that can look back through the years and feel satisfied with everything I have done."

We no doubt all get involved with three basic questions: "Who am I?" "Where am I going?" "What will it cost me to get there?" And we probably have difficulty in coming up with precise answers to these questions. Let us take a look at four dimensions of the self as viewed by adolescents. The college student may wish to extend the thinking here to apply to his or her own problems in a manner we shall describe in a later chapter.

THE BASIC SELF CONCEPT

This is the concept proper which is the individual's perception of his abilities and his status. This is the perception of the roles to be played in the outside world. This is the adolescent's concept of the kind of person he thinks he is. This concept is influenced by his physical self, his personal appearance, dress, and grooming; by his abilities and disposition, his values, beliefs, and aspirations.

The rapid changes that take place during adolescence in height, weight, body build, facial appearance, and voice bring about changes in the adolescent's body image. Such matters as not having clothes like the other youngsters and not having a home where one can entertain friends without feeling embarrassed decrease one's conception of his own importance. They bring on feelings of social incompetence. They make more difficult the problem of appraising true ability and worth.

The self concept is enhanced when there is intellectual ability to meet problems. The slow reader, for example, may find difficulty in learning, thus causing negative self concepts to operate in learning situations. Even for the person with intellectual abilities and good learning habits, the self concept still has its ups and downs.

THE TRANSITORY PERCEPTION OF SELF

The adolescent's self-image may at one time be compulsive, compensatory, and unrealistic and at other times insightful and practical. The self-perception which the individual holds at any given point in time may be determined by some "inner-directed" mood or by some "other-directed" influence. Many adolescents do not recognize the source of their self-perceptions or their transitory nature. They are optimistic or pessimistic, elated or depressed, satisfied or dissatisfied in an all-or-none sort of way. They are sometimes able to switch rapidly from one extreme to the other. Since there is some tendency for the adolescent to reflect more on his problems than on his accomplishments, the transitory perception of self is largely negative.

THE SOCIAL SELF

"To see yourself as others see you" may or may not be valid. At one time, when in an optimistic mood, the adolescent perceives that other people see him in good light. When depressed, he perceives that others depreciate him. When others think him stupid, or socially inept, there is a tendency for him to amplify his feelings of insecurity: "How could anyone like me?" More positive views on the part of others may enhance his perception of his social self somewhat, but they play a lesser role when he is down. "There are more ways to get feedback from a loused-up social situation than from doing things right." This perceptive college freshman may have something in this statement!

THE IDEAL SELF

The concept of the ideal self, the kind of person the adolescent hopes to be, involves questions of standards and comparisons. It involves relating levels of aspiration to levels of ability. It also involves opportunities for self-realization.

When the ideal self is set at an unrealistic level, frustration is increased. When it is set below one's level of ability, motivation may become lacking. The adolescent's level of aspiration tends to go up with success and down with failure. This up-down movement is more exaggerated than that usually found in adults. The ideal self of the adult has evolved slowly through experience. Lacking such experience, the adolescent depends a great deal on identification with someone else as the ideal—an older brother or sister, a parent, or a teacher. This ideal person may stimulate either emulation or resentment, sometimes both.

The concept of one's self is molded by reward and punishment, praise and blame, and by the feelings of accomplishment that come with solving a problem. During preadolescence both parents and peers influence the self concept. This situation changes gradually until the young person's self-evaluation is determined more by what his age mates think of him. Later, cliques and other organizations provide a climate of influence. *Finally the adolescent discovers that the self must be determined individually.* He has to learn the hard way that achieving identity is a long and arduous process. He learns that such identity comes through thinking, feeling, and decision making. It thrives on social interaction. And in the end, the question, "Who am I?" still remains.

THE POSITIVE SIDE

So much of the development of the adolescent is a sequence of meeting new problems before old ones are solved that it is easy to view this period of growth entirely negatively. But the positive side involves learning to react appropriately to stress, which is a normal counterpart of living.

One investigator did a series of experiments with laboratory rats. He kept one group immobilized for extensive periods of time and found that they struggled desperately to get free. They actually needed to engage in all the activities that *normally* provided them with their required quota of stress. When deprived of these problem situations, some of which were quite stressful, they became ill in their efforts to maintain health. Another group of rats, with the same hereditary background (litter mates), which were allowed to engage in stressful situations lived longer, healthier lives.

This researcher, from his many studies of stress on human beings as well as animals, concludes that the individual has to learn to react to stress. He points out that when an individual chooses his goals he should not attempt primarily to avoid stress, which is a natural part of life, but rather should watch his own individual stress level. Knowledge of this level comes through experience. Animals deprived of a wide variety of stress situations do not learn how to take care of themselves. Human beings who are overprotected likewise may fail to build in the ability to make appropriate responses to problems.

Facing too many problems too rapidly in an unfavorable environment may be unhealthy. With exceptions, of course, adolescence is a stage of development in our culture in which there is opportunity to discover oneself and gain independence in a semisympathetic environment. At least adolescence provides an interactional situation in which at each age group the individual problems have much in common. One may think positively of adolescence as a laboratory for experiences, for learning by trial and error, and for developing good problem-solving habits at the thinking level.

TRIAL AND ERROR

The first requirement of the problem-solving process is the existence of some *need,* motive, or urge to activity. Second, motivated behavior is subject to *thwarting* by circumstances that prevent immediate satisfaction of the need. Third, one must engage in *varied responses,* or "trial and error," until, fourth, some *solution* is hit upon which fulfills the original need and completes the sequence of activity.

What brings an end to the trial-and-error responses aroused by a need? The answer is *tension reduction.* A response that reduces the drive tension brings activity to a close because it removes the stimulus that maintained the behavior. When the adolescent is motivated by an emotional tension or by a social motive (usually related to emotion), any activity that reduces the emotional state is to him a successful response.

There are differences in the degree to which various responses will reduce tension. An unattractive college co-ed may experience conflict between her need for masculine attention and her fear of being rejected. Her anxiety will be reduced most effectively by actual success in attracting men. But suppose this solution fails to materialize? Tension can be reduced to some extent by her becoming a man-hater, by "going intellectual," by ambivalent behavior, by becoming emotionally attached to her peers with similar problems, or by some other solution.

The wide variety of problems present during adolescence brings out a wide variety of responses in trying for solutions. Fortunately, adolescence also allows for cognitive solutions to problems as well as the trial-and-error approach.

Adolescence provides opportunity to think problems through and try them out. Failure allows for seeking alternatives. At least the adolescent has one thing in his favor—he or she *is expected* to have problems. "It just happens that way, growing up," concludes an experienced counselor.

Summary

Adolescence is a period of transition between childhood and adulthood characterized by problems of intellectual, social, emotional, and academic growth.

Emotionally the adolescent is more of a problem to himself than to others. He faces new roles faster than he can adjust to old ones. Nervous habits, fear, worry, anger, and the other emotions seem to have their own teen-age versions. Studies support the conclusion that counseling can help the adolescent objectify and think through his problems. Sharing problems makes the adolescent aware that he is not alone with his difficulties.

Changes in social behavior and attitudes are more related to sexual maturation than to chronological age. By the time the adolescent reaches college there is a trend toward liberalism in his attitudes. He becomes less provincial in his thinking. Adolescents are individualists in many ways, despite their conforming behavior and their grouping into social cliques.

Sex differences in interests and attitudes are extensive during adolescence and change over the course of time. They are both biologically and culturally determined.

Behavior in dating, courtship, and preparation for marriage goes through stages which aid the adolescent in the many problems of development, ranging from gaining social perception and skills to the selection of a mate.

It is during adolescence that the individual meets the four dimensions of self. First comes basic self concept, involving the perception of abilities and status. Second comes self-perception as it is related to "inner direction" and "other direction." Third, the social self comes into prominence, and fourth, the ideal self is evaluated in terms of standards and comparisons.

The concept of one's self is molded by reward and punishment, praise and blame, and by the feelings of accomplishment that come with effective problem solving. The positive side of adolescence relates not only to gaining a self concept but also to learning about stress and living with it. It provides for cognitive solutions to problems as well as a trial-and-error approach.

Adolescence provides opportunity to think problems through and try out solutions. Failure allows for seeking alternatives in a climate in which the individual is expected to have problems.

Suggestions for Thinking and Discussion

1 Among your classmates can you identify any overachievers or underachievers?
2 Make a list of types of adolescent behavior which you would regard as normal. What standards would you use to pick out abnormal behavior?
3 Give an example from *your* experience of group pressure on you to conform.
4 What would you say pulls together the cliques you see on the campus?
5 What would you list as *your* biggest problems in dating?
6 Make a description of yourself. How does it check out with how some others see you?

Suggestions for Further Reading

Douvan, Elizabeth, & Adelson, J. *The adolescent experience.* New York: Wiley, 1966. A national survey of 3,000 American teen-agers.

Duvall, Evelyn M. *Facts of life and love for teenagers.* New York: Association Press, 1956. Seventeen chapters dealing with maturation, dating, loving and being loved, and preparation for marriage.

Ellis, H. (edited by J. Gawsworth). *Sex and marriage.* New York: Random House, 1952. A readable book for the scholarly reader.

Quay, H. C. (Ed.) *Juvenile delinquency: Research and theory.* Princeton, N.J.: Van Nostrand, 1965. A book of readings giving a critical review of a major social problem.

Van De Velde, T. H. *Ideal marriage: Its physiology and techniques.* New York: Random House, 1957. A source book for the sophisticated reader who wants to know the entire story from research to living.

CHAPTER 8

Youth, Middle Age, and Retirement

❖❖❖❖❖❖❖❖❖

Youth may be thought of as a time of practical decision making. *Middle age* has been described as the developmental stage, when we live with the consequences of our early decisions and planning. The age of *retirement* puts on the finishing touches. Each of these stages of development may possibly be differentiated better in terms of psychological and physiological age rather than chronological age. However, for practical purposes let us somewhat arbitrarily think of early youth as covering the twenties, and late youth the thirties. We may think of early middle age as covering the forties and late middle age the fifties, and reserve the sixties and on as involving preretirement to retirement.

Psychologically we may think of youth as a period involving some agonizing indecisiveness in career planning, whether the career is to be a vocation or marriage or both. In some respects it is a time when we look at what we want and then find out that we "can't have it both ways." Middle age is a time of realizing that one has reached "a point of no return." Old age has been described by one philosopher as "a triumph of hope over experience." The three ages of man have also been spoken of as youth, middle age, and "how well you are looking."

A POINT OF VIEW

In the preceding two chapters we have described the psychological development of the child and the adolescent. In taking development the rest of the way, possibly an unusual procedure for a book of this type, we have two reasons. First, one can get a better perspective of growth by going all the way. Second, many family groups and communities center around the interaction of persons of all ages. Some of the problems engendered can at least be understood with more perspective if we take an overall look at what to expect, even if the picture is a little out of focus.

YOUTH

Psychological needs change with age, and these changes affect our attitudes toward work, toward living, and toward understanding. Early youth is the stage in which the individual has one foot in adolescence and the other in maturity. It is a stage in which traditions are made within a few weeks and lost just as quickly.

WHEN CHANGE IS WELCOME

The youth is aware of change and welcomes it. Adolescence, with all its random trial and error toward adjustment, has given way to better-planned behavior (with some exceptions). The man just out of college, entering a career in technological development, salesmanship, or management, seizes every opportunity to get ahead, and he has the stamina to take the competition. The young woman often wants an opportunity to make a living on her own before settling down to family responsibilities. Both want and expect challenge, for herein lies the path to experience and to recognition. All this is in contrast to old age, in which for most people, change is unwelcome and often resisted. The dream of better days ahead is over, and the world is narrowing. Competition is shunned because few have the stamina to keep up the pace.

THE PROBLEMS OF YOUTH

The problems of youth are numerous and varied. However, in contrast with those of adolescence, the problems facing youth are better defined. The college student in his graduating year must decide whether to take a job or to continue his formal education. When he begins working he must somehow adjust his need to get started early with his desire to raise a family at a time when he can least afford it financially. Particularly for the young woman, the best years biologically for having children come at about the same time that both husband

and wife have to work in order to establish a home of their own. Youth sometimes learns how to spend money before learning how to make it.

On the job youth must look for an opportunity where anticipations can be realized and enthusiasms rewarded. He may not succeed at first. But youth has one big advantage; disappointments are soon overcome by hopes for a better future. Dissatisfaction with one job may be remedied by taking another. The opportunities for youth in our changing and expanding economy build up attitudes of both confidence and defiance—just the reverse of the kind found in the older person. A youth at the worker level, regardless of his limitations in education, is optimistic about the future. His physical strength and vitality to some degree make up for his lack of training and experience. Desires that are not readily fulfilled today are projected in terms of satisfaction in the future. The more sophisticated youth shares in this optimism, but with more of a sense of reality. Understanding the problem has some tendency to lessen that satisfying feeling of confidence in the future.

THE SEARCH FOR OPPORTUNITY

Moving upward is a problem which the sophisticated student plans for. Recent researches emphasize that upward mobility depends not only on training and aspiration but also on opportunity. Workers often feel that pull and luck are necessary for advancement. In contrast, for the aggressive type of individual, getting ahead is a part of the game in which education, formal or otherwise, is essential for the understanding of how opportunity can often be made. There is some tendency for people to advance occupationally during their careers, but for most people the advancement is not very far. The skilled industrial worker finds himself more of a commodity, the demands for which fluctuate with the economy and with technological change. Above the skilled level the individual is in many respects more on his own.

Do opportunity and income increase with age? Economists answer both "yes" and "no." In managerial jobs and in the professions earnings do increase with age. This is not true in the lowest-paid manual jobs. For such work, a man reaches his peak in his early twenties; after that he goes down hill.

CAREER PLANNING IN YOUTH

During early youth the individual finds that efficient career planning involves understanding a fourfold relationship in terms of psychological interactions. At this stage each person is interested in relations between *person and person,* between *person and group,* between *person and things,* and in problems of the *inner man* himself.

In early childhood career thinking involved a *fantasy* stage in which interests were transitory. For the most part they were unrelated to any potential capacities. Perhaps the fantasies involved wanting to be a fireman, doctor, teacher, or cowboy. Following this period, in early adolescence came the stage of *tentative choices.* Here there were some vague relations between interests and vocational preferences, but career planning was little more than daydreaming. In the late teens came a third stage of more *realistic planning* because do and don't types of choices were being forced on the person in terms of school curricula or work alternatives.

It must be recognized that not all people have choice in selecting their careers and jobs. Opportunity, economic responsibilities, and various other circumstances enter in measure. One man may have to quit school early because of a family problem. Another person may stay in school longer only because work opportunities may not be available. And data show that one reason why students in some types of technical training (e.g., computer programming) never finish their formal education is that their services may be in such demand that they cannot turn down an offer.

CHANGE

Technology is spreading irresistibly and bringing with it new problems. For some persons, automation expands the world of career choice; for others, it closes opportunity. Change, along with accommodation or resistance to it, is bringing about the retraining of the worker to give him new skills and is causing the manager to wonder how he can best use the computer in decision making. Unskilled jobs are becoming a smaller and smaller fraction of all jobs, making for some less than a bright future.

It may be well to remember that throughout a lifetime a person may have several careers. The man who is twenty years old may expect to make at least six job changes during the remainder of his working life and to retire earlier than his father did.

OCCUPATIONAL CHOICE

Making an occupational choice ranks second in importance only to the selection of a mate in marriage. How and where a person will spend even his nonworking hours is influenced by such choice. The

importance of giving considered attention to occupation centers around
the hard fact that in many respects the choice is irreversible. True,
some people change their occupations, sometimes for the better. However, for most people in our culture, the general area of vocational
choices are for a lifetime, although specific jobs may be changed several times, and a person may actually have several careers.

A LONG-TERM PROCESS

The choice of a vocation is not an event that happens suddenly,
but rather a *process extending over a period of time*. It is hoped that
applied psychology may play an important part in the process of thinking the problem through.

Studies show that college students who have chosen an occupation
but have not yet entered it change their attitudes toward the occupation
more favorably as time goes on. Students who have gone through highly
specialized training in order to be better prepared in their occupational
choice are less likely to change occupations later. People who have
a good conception of themselves and of occupations and know what
they are getting into are less likely to revoke their occupational choice
than those who have not made accurate appraisals.

FAMILY INFLUENCE

From many studies on the relationship between fathers' occupations and the occupational choices of their sons come several conclusions. First, college students' stated choices tend to coincide with the
occupations of their fathers more often than would be expected by
statistical chance. Second, the greater the income received by the father,
the more likely the student is to choose law, medicine, or some branch
of business, and the less likely he is to select one of the salaried professions. The more money currently earned by the father, the more the
student expects to be earning in the future. Third, sons tend to enter
and remain in occupations similar to those of their fathers. Fourth,
when occupations of fathers and sons are put together according to
level there is a regression toward the mean; i.e., sons whose fathers
are at very high levels (e.g., corporate vice-president) tend to enter
lower occupations than their fathers, and those whose fathers are at
lower levels (e.g., foreman) tend to enter higher occupations.

There are sex differences in occupational choices. Men follow their
fathers into the professions and business. Women select teaching, social
work, and the creative arts, much as their mothers before them. From
early years boys tend to identify with their fathers in becoming the

breadwinner in the family. Girls acquire the human relations interests of their mothers.

ABILITIES AND CHOICES

There is a rough correspondence between an individual's intelligence and the intellectual requirements of the occupation which he prefers. It is very difficult, of course, to get a fine measure showing the relationship between interest and actual ability. However, there is much evidence showing a relationship between interest and *perceived* ability. The activities which are most highly preferred are those in which the person believes himself to possess the greatest ability. This is certainly a type of finding useful to the student in trusting (to some extent!) his self-perception.

Many data from college board scores and graduate record examinations support the position that verbal and quantitative scores are related to choice of work. Students majoring in the physical sciences, for example, have higher quantitative scores, while those majoring in the social sciences and humanities have higher verbal than quantitative scores. There is a tendency for persons with abilities corresponding to an occupation to choose that occupation. One follow-up study of over two thousand high school students found that those who entered the mechanical, electric, and building trades had their highest scores on mechanical reasoning. Those who succeeded as clerks had superior knowledge of grammar and spelling. We shall discuss this more at length in a later chapter.

SELF CONCEPT AND OCCUPATIONAL CHOICE

One psychologist, who has been following thousands of students in their career development, has come up with a practical theory about vocational development. According to his theory, "The process of vocational development is essentially that of developing and implementing a self concept: It is a compromise process in which the self concept is a product of the interaction of inherited aptitudes, neural and endocrine makeup, opportunity to play various roles, and evaluations of the extent to which the results of role playing meet with the approval of superiors and fellows."

Many researchers have reported positive correlations between the extent to which a person is attracted to another person, or group, and the extent to which he describes that person, or group, as similar to himself. It may be that an individual tends to choose an occupation on the basis of his similarity to members of the occupation. Involved also may be the possibility that he tends to project his own characteristics on members of the occupation that he has chosen.

The belief that one possesses a skill is in many ways tantamount to a desire to use that skill.

MIDDLE AGE

The transition from youth to middle age is a gradual process. For some people who have prepared themselves "to go all the way" middle age is taken in stride. For others, middle age peaks in a crisis described by someone as "a time when what makes you tick needs winding." The middle-aged person is introspective. He is resigned and rebellious at the same time. Middle age attracts less attention than youth and inspires only little research. It is recognized, however, as a time when one thinks that decisions in the past have sometimes robbed one of choice in the present.

NEEDS IN MIDDLE AGE

Middle age for man is a time of determining whether or not he will be a success, as measured by the goals he set for himself in youth. In occupations such as engineering and science, in which long professional training is essential to productive activity and economic independence, men who have not yet been admitted to full standing may identify themselves as being young. A laborer, on the other hand, who may be the same chronological age as the newly licensed company lawyer may feel himself old at thirty-five. A steel worker or miner may feel he has reached his economic peak just at the age that the young businessman and accountant are ready for promotion and their best work. Needs in middle age center around self-evaluation—questions of status become important. In terms of behavior some people act in middle age as if they were living through a period of "emotional second adolescence." It is important for family harmony for younger people to realize that parents have problems of psychological adjustment also. Let us take an overall look at these problems.

MIDDLE-AGE REVOLT

Along with decreases in physical stamina and sexual activity, such signs as receding hairlines indicate the passing of youth, a stage soon to be followed in some people by what the psychoanalysts have termed "middle-age revolt." This usually comes earlier for the worker, later for the manager or professional man; but it comes to many in terms of lost dreams and failure to meet cutthroat competition. This revolt comes when the man cannot plead the inexperience of youth or the frailties of age. The middle-ager sometimes expresses guilt feelings of failure and blames himself for not having gone into the right job. He frequently wonders whether he married the right woman. Middle age begins when the phone rings on Saturday night and you hope it is a wrong number.

The man in middle age may see his weight climbing and his hair thinning. These easily observed changes disturb him. When youngsters call him "Sir," and the lone courtesy candle appears on his birthday cake, the middle-aged man is quite ready to magnify his problems. His ego suffers another blow when he moves into the bifocal stage and he finds that his insurance rates are going up. It is in this stage that the middle-aged man sometimes begins to take out his aggression against his family and his job. During this period of emotional second adolescence, the middle-aged worker may be difficult to deal with and the manager may be hard to work for. The professional man begins to take stock of where he stands as he quotes to his colleague the statement, "If you haven't made it by forty you won't." Or, as one *young* dean put it, "If the professor is over forty he is just collecting rent." These quips hurt the man in his middle-age revolt. Let us not forget, however, that there are many professors paying the rent!

STATUS

In middle age, status becomes of great importance. At this stage the man wishes to be looked up to by youth for advice and asked by the aged for help. Rules and procedures in the organization make status differences quite visible by making it clear who gives the orders, who wields the influence; and self-esteem gets into the picture. Whether one will attempt to persuade others depends in part on his estimate of his own competence. The higher one's status, the more control he has over what happens on the job. More status means more opportunity to participate in decisions.

Studies show a general tendency to overevaluate one's own job and to underevaluate the job of others. This often brings about confusion. The waitress may see herself as having more status than the short-order cook when she tells him what orders to fill. Not only does he resent taking orders from a female whom he regards as having lower status than his own, but he sees himself not as cook but as chef.

Status confusion also arises because a person with high status in one situation may be low in the pecking order somewhere else.

The superintendent of a small-town branch office who had the status of "Mr. Big" may find himself virtually without status when rotated to a staff headquarters position. The bookkeeper in the small operation may lose status when advanced to the position of one of many computer programmers, even though the latter job pays better.

People react differently to status symbols. One person who gets a job title change without additional authority, responsibility, and compensation may feel no status enhancement whatsoever. In fact he may resent being so treated. Another person may prefer a title change which makes his job sound more important; he may even prefer not to have additional authority and responsibility.

STATUS SYMBOLS

One large corporation changed job titles and then made a study of the effects on the people involved. It was found, for example, that changing a title from "staff engineer" to "plant engineering associate" enhanced the status of the man involved. Other changes in a positive direction included changing the title "clerk" to "confidential clerk," "motor vehicle inspector" to "motor vehicle supervisor," "general plant employment supervisor" to general plant personnel supervisor." When a title was changed from "draftsman" to "tracer" the study showed a loss rather than a gain in status. It was also found that even changing the name of the place where people worked was important. For example, employees preferred to say they worked "on the lower level" rather than "in the basement." Some workers prefer "incentive pay" to "piece rate." Even the word "company" often evokes a friendlier association than that of "corporation." However, some executives prefer to say that they work for a "corporation" because it sounds more prestigious. The bank teller thinks of higher status as being able to sit "on the platform." This symbol has its origin in the early days of banking, when executives actually sat on a higher level than did other employees.

The struggle for status and status symbols is not restricted to business. Consider large block letters on sweaters, fraternity pins on blouses, ornamental lodge pins, and colorful military ribbons. One physician says that among his patients pregnancy is a status symbol, particularly among middle-aged women. Sophisticated place and name dropping involves status, as does carrying the right newspaper.

We seek status because we wish to create an image. Possibly we search out symbols of status because we are looking for recognition. Says one social psychologist, "We seek status as individuals because we are getting lost in bigness—big high schools, big colleges, big businesses."

"ONEUPMANSHIP"

Juggling for the perquisites of rank and the acquisition of status symbols is characteristic of people with high rank as well as low. Certain needs of the executive are satisfied by attaining rank itself, but often this is not enough. The little privileges that go with an office may be more important to an executive than a raise in salary. One observer reports that a major crisis arose in a large company when it bought a new type of posture chair to test on a few of its executives. Those left out were so miserable that one man, to save face, bought a chair with his own money and smuggled it into the office. Another tells of a group of foremen who walked out on their job until management agreed to provide them with a separate table in the workers' dining room adorned with a tablecloth and other appointments symbolizing their superior status.

There are many subtle indications of status dominance. One may observe this by watching two foremen vie for the attention of the superintendent; the one who "gets told things first" may feel himself more in the know, and hence may feel that he is in a position of more prestige. One may wonder if some of the struggles to be near the top in the college class are motivated psychologically by the desire to "go one up on the competition," as well as to receive the more noticeable awards. It may even be good practice! The achievement-oriented individual may even try to get attention by playing up his many critical problems. He enjoys creating the impression that he is a person with a "high crisis quotient."

THE NEGATIVE AND THE POSITIVE

In terms of his problems the middle-aged man worries over the delinquencies of youth, the insecurities of old age, and the devastations of disease and war. He is concerned with the decay of democracy, with holding down his job, and with balancing budgets. One of the costs to the middle-aged person in terms of energy is exacted by his community responsibilities, in which he can contribute much in the way of skills and wisdom. However, for many people who have reached their limits on the job, community activities provide for lateral growth, which at least in part satisfies the drive to attain success.

Caught in the period between being "still young" and "already old" the middle-ager shoulders psychological burdens which he often keeps to himself. To talk too openly about them would possibly lower his status, even if he could get anyone to listen.

Guilt feelings of failure are typical of the middle-ager. He feels he has not advanced far enough in his job or profession. He is concerned that he has not made adequate economic provision for his family in the event that something happens to him. The man in middle age feels the doors of opportunity are closing fast. He is concerned about his status when he notes the high rate of divorces in his age group. In much the same way that the adolescent magnifies his problems, so does the person in middle age. And he sometimes reacts in a now-or-never gamble as he visualizes himself as the forgotten man.

But there is a *positive* side to middle age. Certain hazards of life have passed, and there is more tenure in office for those who planned ahead. These men are also in positions of dignity and power. They have more knowledge, skill, and wisdom than they had in youth. Anxieties are on the decrease. Now one can get more satisfaction from the "simple life." Marital companionship may be closer than ever if the woman can survive the biological changes and the man the psychological changes that take place during middle age.

CHANGES IN MIDDLE AGE

Physically, both men and women find their most difficult adjustment in middle age during the change of life. In women this period, with its loss of child-bearing capacity, is called *menopause*. The average age for cessation of the menstrual flow is around forty-five years. This age varies greatly with hereditary endowment and general health conditions. Early puberty usually means late menopause and vice versa.

The physical aspects of the male climacteric are quite different from those of menopause. It comes later, usually in the sixties or seventies, and occurs at a very slow rate. Psychologically, however, change comes around the forties in terms of the revolt we have spoken of.

SELF CONCEPT IN MIDDLE AGE

For some two decades the young adult has become used to himself. He knows much about his assets and his weaknesses, and he has learned to play various roles accordingly. But gradually, following the middle-age revolt, roles begin to change, and so does self concept. To replace the roles of parent, social affiliations widen. Citizenship activities expand. Homemaking and hobbies are intensified. The person who has played a narrow range of roles is less likely to expand interests. Shifting to new roles is more difficult for him than for the person who ranged widely in experiences during youth. It is particularly important for adjustment that one be able to shift emotional attachments as well as ego involvements. As one psychologist put it, "The individual must withdraw emotional capital from one role and invest it in another one."

Revision in self concept comes gradually. Changes relate more to physical than to intellectual abilities. Because the individual feels that there is a cultural demand to "stay young," he judges himself in terms of appearance, dress, and youthful activities. Women who find earlier roles ending, whose husbands (if successful) are emphasizing work and community activities, and whose children no longer need care express feelings of uselessness. Boredom is even at times added to the "three B's" of bridge, bonbons, and bourbon. The not-too-well-adjusted woman has the exaggerated idea that she is losing her sex appeal and that her husband may turn to other women. The unmarried career woman also undergoes change. Realizing that her career (particularly in glamour fields) is in danger from competition with younger women brings on stress. The realization that her chances of marriage are going fast enhances the problem.

Because men continue to work, they feel the effects of role change less than women. Competition at work does disturb the man who never felt himself too successful even in youth. Some men in their forties or fifties have symptoms similar to those of the female menopause. They complain of anxiety, depression, irritability, and fatigue. They are conscious of having to cut down on their intake of food and drink, and at a time when financially they can best afford some luxury. Some adopt the attitude that if you are over fifty you are entitled to indulge yourself.

CHANGES IN INTERESTS

The shift in the direction of cultural pursuits is characteristic of both men and women in middle age. There is a tendency to shift from interests that deplete the energy reserves to reading, art, and music. There is a shift from participative roles to observer roles.

Well-adjusted middle-aged men and women become more conservative about their clothes. The less-fortunate people are conscious of the lack of money. The man who has been comfortably well off in earlier years is less concerned about making money than when he was younger—assuming, of course, that there are no marked demands on him by children and relatives. The middle-aged woman, however, finds money of more concern, because it means security to her. In middle age there is a change in attitude toward the use of money. Studies show that college students consider extravagance less wrong than do middle-agers. (Note—you may have company!)

Some of the frictions between youth and parents relate to reactions to interests. One reason why solutions are hard to come by centers around *communication of feelings.* A comparison of college students with middle-aged business and professional men revealed that the older group responded more quickly to emotion-provoking stimuli. The older men were less calm and easygoing than the younger, but they were more reserved in expressing their feelings. Younger men had more frequent periods of excitement, restlessness, and "blueness" than did the middle-agers.

SUCCESS AND FAILURE

Some men enter middle life with a background of success revealed by various types of recognition. Other men enter the prime of life with a past history of failure. In either case there is no quarrel with the criteria of evaluation. But what of the man who feels himself a failure while others applaud his successes? What about the man who questions the standards for judging success and failure?

For most adults the early forties are a period of evaluation. The man examines his career to see how he rates according to goals established in youth; the woman looks at her career or marriage in terms of earlier alternatives.

In a culture such as ours, which both idealizes and rewards youth, some pressures act to prevent people from admitting to themselves that they are becoming older. Add to this the fact that our culture encourages youth to set aspirations beyond the bounds of realization. One can see how when evaluation comes, it comes with a jolt.

A person's criteria of success may be greatly different from those of his colleague. We cannot establish universal criteria. The generally accepted definitions of success seldom satisfy any one person. Sometimes a man's criteria for personal success do not satisfy society in its abstract, mass personality. A man may hold a position of authority, with responsibility and prestige; he may be making a good salary; yet in his own judgment, he may consider himself a failure. In contrast, the world at large may think a man a virtual failure, while he himself has reached a peace of mind which can fairly be called success. Through thoughtful career planning in youth, this middle-ager attempted to balance the levels of ability, of opportunity, and of aspirations within a critical set of limits to achieve success in work and in personal life. He gradually learned that repeated frustrations lowered his aspirations, and he also learned that repeated successes raised them. But when he sought to keep in balance his levels of ability and levels of aspiration he found he was walking a tightrope.

Many people who pass the middle-age test find their most psycho-logically rewarding years are ahead. There are others who age without growing up.

THE PSYCHOLOGY OF AGING

One of the problems that middle-agers face is caring for aged parents. One of the problems elderly people face is loss of independence and sometimes having to move in with children and in-laws. And some may have to play by new government rules in order to participate in Medicare programs. At best, getting old creates a new set of problems for both the individual and society. In the remainder of this chapter we shall discuss the psychological aspects of these problems. A house-hold made up of children, adolescents, youth, and old age certainly provides a laboratory setting for studying human relationships.

DECREASE IN PERFORMANCE

From a rapidly increasing amount of research come some gen-eralizations which add up to saying that aging is associated with a gradual decrease in the performance of most bodily organs. The speed of this change varies, however, from one organ system to another, even in the same individual. For example, muscle strength decreases 50 percent between the ages of thirty and ninety, while the speed of an impulse passing down a nerve fiber is reduced only 15 percent in this same time span. Responses in older subjects are harder to con-dition and easier to extinguish. For example, in a group of oldsters, average age seventy-two, the galvanic skin response was conditioned less readily and extinguished more rapidly than in college students of average age twenty. The electric shock was used as the unconditioned stimulus, and a 450-cps tone as the conditioned stimulus. Both these sensory mechanisms function less well with increasing age. On the motor side, habitual or very simple movements are not affected by age until late in life. Accurate or new movement patterns are less speedily per-formed, however, after the early thirties. Among production workers only a slight decrease in productivity occurs after age forty-five. The decrease does not become substantial until age sixty. As for office work-ers little, if any, decline occurs prior to age sixty, and the subsequent decline is minor.

Researchers looking for any suggestions of changes in mental func-tion resulting solely from age have found virtually no changes in the fifties that were inevitable. Some persons in their sixties and seventies show loss of memory, reasoning, and decision-making ability, *but many do not*. It may be that the brain does not become exhausted so much by overwork as by what happens during the process of working. The individual may become worn out from the emotional stress accompanying the effort. Of course, there may also be decline in the ability of the brain through disuse.

INDIVIDUAL DIFFERENCES IN AGING

Individual differences among older people are extensive. There are attitudinal sex differences which are significant. For example, a study was made of 590 men and 770 women, over the age range of twenty-one to sixty-five, on the need for affiliation, achievement, and power. Among men, need for achievement dropped with age but need for power rose. Among women, need for affiliation and need for power dropped.

The older person finds that he is sometimes in conflict with himself. He has a craving to straighten out the affairs of others and to express himself on every subject. After all, he does have experience and a store of wisdom. But he also is aware that on occasion he may be wrong. He knows a listener may get bored with his recital of endless detail. He wants to be thoughtful but not nosy, helpful but not bossy, and in the end he hopes to have some friends. Different older people react in various ways to this conflict.

With advancing age there is a tendency for behavior to return to an earlier pattern and a simpler level of function. This is one reason why it is advantageous to build up good habit patterns early in life. The idea that the single person, "alone in the world," will face an unhappy old age is contrary to experience. Not having had companionship over the years, he or she may be better adjusted to the declining years than a married person who loses the spouse. There are no traits found only in aged people. There is no "typical" description of old age, in spite of some overgeneralized stereotypes to the contrary. Literally thousands of studies of vision, hearing, muscular strength, reaction time, psychomotor coordination, and various job performances have shown great individual differences at every age. In general, *physical aging comes earlier than mental aging.* The reverse sometimes occurs, however, in those people whose personality is such that they believe they are growing old. Such people may say they are losing their memory, when in actuality they probably put little or no effort into learning something in the first place. Yes, psychological aging in some sense is a defensive mechanism, possibly useful at times.

Interest in money represents a highly individual type of behavior. Such interest, which may have waned some in middle age, generally is revived in old age for those who seek security or who wish to leave property to their children or grandchildren. However, some oldsters seem unconcerned about money above a subsistence level. A few like to accumulate or manage money as a game. Enjoying the manipulation of large sums of money may interest some, while others use its manipulation more symbolically. One former vice-president and treasurer of a large corporation living in retirement said he looked forward each month to a meeting of his local shuffleboard club. Much discussion of finances was always in order—what to do with a balance of $55 in the treasury!

The study of individual differences in older persons, among whom some are old at forty years and others are young at seventy, can teach us much about energy conservation. Experiments on animals have clearly shown that excessively stressful activities use up reserves of adaptability which cannot be replaced. One researcher has stated the concept thus: "Vitality is like a special kind of bank account which you can use up by withdrawals but cannot increase by deposits. The only control is the rate that withdrawals are made."

THE CREATIVE YEARS

Age is a factor in productivity. Championships in sports come early, often in the teens. The peaks of notable intellectual creativity come in the late thirties but fall off rapidly during and after middle age. Professional recognition and leadership status in business, education, medicine, law, and politics tend to come in later life. Figure 8-1

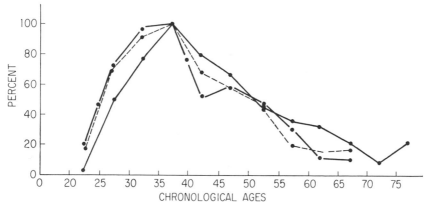

FIG. 8-1   A graph of the creative years of psychologists in three categories. The peak of productivity in research and writing comes around thirty-eight years of age. This curve is typical of the productivity of scientists in general. (*From Lehman, H. C. The psychologist's most creative years. Amer. Psychologist,* 1966, 21, 363–369.)

shows a summary of studies of the creative years of psychologists. These data are typical of all scientists. But before we too hastily conclude that the scientist is "through at forty," let us examine the kind of change that frequently takes place in a creative field. Interests change, the scientist becomes a leader of others doing technical work. In colleges, students take up more of the time of this man of experience, and administration problems become more demanding. Gradually our scientist moves from a do-it-yourself role into broadened professional activities.

COMPENSATION

There is much compensation for the slowing down of age. Less strength, vigor, and speed of reaction can be compensated for by increase in skill. For example, the older person may drive more cautiously, avoiding hazardous conditions. On the highway, as well as in industry, safety statistics are favorable to older people, partly because they take fewer risks. A study of the driving records of 15,000 persons in Iowa showed that men under thirty were involved in a large proportion of the total accidents. In a study of 9,000 steel workers it was shown that older people have a better safety record than younger workers. Important to the problem is the amount of risk-taking involved. In some circumstances when older people are put on "young workers' jobs" they have more accidents than might statistically be expected.

In terms of mental aging there is some decline in factors dealing with speed of computation and in certain perceptual situations. There is little or no decline in tests of information and vocabulary. Judgment and comprehension for many oldsters actually show an increase with age. Perhaps most important of all, *wisdom,* which increases markedly with growing years until possible senescence sets in, can compensate for many other losses. So many of the problems which youth faces are new. The elderly face many of these same problems, but with some familiarity, with the feeling, "I've been here before." The older one gets the less important arguments become.

Almost always there are some older people whose performance surpasses the performance of younger people. They compensate by placing more emphasis on accuracy and less on speed. Decision making may well profit someday by the memory and speed of the computer working hand in hand with some of the compassion and wisdom of age.

PRERETIREMENT—A CHANGING PATTERN

There are mixed trends in the thinking about earlier and earlier retirement. On the one hand, automation is pushing toward the earlier retirement of those people who are being replaced by machines and in those situations where there is need to spread jobs around. There are pressures to retire men early to give the new generation a chance. On the other hand, some people are just beginning to reach the peak of their skill, creativity, and wisdom as early retirement forces a change. Psychologically, there are, no doubt, some people whose personality favors a do-little kind of life; but the many studies of boredom and of how people spend their leisure indicate that having little or nothing to do may bring on problems.

Leisure time (free time after subtracting working time, sleeping, eating, and other essential activity) has increased from three hours in 1870, to five hours in 1910, and up to eight hours in 1960. It has been estimated that it will not be long before half of the twenty-four-hour day is leisure time. What do people do with this time? Most surveys show entertainment to be well in the lead. Upward of three-quarters of leisure time is so invested. To some, leisure time is a myth. It may better be thought of as time for creative expression. Planning for leisure may be psychologically the same in some respects as planning for retirement.

THE CRITERIA FOR RETIREMENT

"Aging, true physiological aging, is not determined by the time elapsed since birth, but by the total amount of wear and tear to which the body has been exposed. There is, indeed, a great difference between physiologic and chronological age." These words of Hans Selye, who has worked on the problems of aging and the stress of life for over three decades, give us a key to the problem of how long any given individual should continue to work. Measuring physiologic or psychological age is most difficult. Forces other than "the good of the individual" have set standards. After all, chronological age *is* easy to determine, and it does give us a universal standard.

The magic age of sixty-five for retirement came about originally as a base for social security legislation. It was lowered to sixty-three for women shortly after the Social Security Act was passed. One may question the logic of this type of differentiation. It could hardly have been made because women outlive men by some four years. Under various conditions and with some options one, of course, may, and in some instances must, retire before sixty-five or sixty-three. The trend, however, toward fixed retirement ages continues to increase. Most Americans never retire. They are either forced out of work or they die before retirement. Of those who retire, some 25 percent try to find new work. There is not a great deal of retirement moonlighting, particularly among those receiving social security.

PREPARATION FOR RETIREMENT

Most of those who work up to the last possible day, then facing the problem of no longer being employed, feel the retirement impact. Some organizations now have planned programs of preretirement counseling, seminars, and easing-up practices in which the person gradually gets used to doing less. Such job decompression programs are helpful for some people.

Social attitudes toward old age are generally unfavorable, causing some people to delay, even to resist, preparation for approaching old age, save for building up financial reserve in pensions. There is realization of the chance of having physical handicaps, but usually less attention is given to the psychological aspects of a feeling of uselessness, inactivity, loneliness, and boredom. One elderly woman in England reported that she was sorry when it was no longer necessary to cue up for buying groceries: "I had someone to talk to."

It is possible to predict in middle age, even sooner in some people, what kind of adjustment the person will make in old age. For those who have sought change, or at least showed only token resistance to it, and who have health, financial security, and companionship, old age can be a time of happiness. For some it is a time for enjoying the results of one's labors. It is a time of independence, when the person is no longer driven by ambition and regulated by work. It is a time to enjoy the prestige of wisdom, the loyalty and devotion of family. In a community where leisure is a status symbol of success, the elderly have priority. But, one may ask, what are the chances that these favorable factors will fall my way?

Individuals who are psychologically tough and resilient have learned patterns of adjustment that are useful in their declining years. They are, by and large, people who see themselves as active agents in their own progress, who are not willing to leave their future in the hands of others. These are the people who prepare for retirement psychologically as well as physically and economically. They are the individuals who see that preparation during middle age can lessen the impact of retirement. They are the people who understand that in some settings the older person can be hit by a "youthquake" and still survive.

RETIREMENT

Problems in retirement range widely; from boredom to bucking attitudes against age; from loss of relatives through death to the breaking up of friendship cliques; from loss of independence to deterioration in influence credit.

SELF CONCEPT

Several factors influence self concept in old age: (1) the history of one's habit structures; (2) acceptance or rejection of the cultural stereotype of aging; (3) feelings of success or failure in life; (4) the cultural climate in which one is spending most of his time. This cultural climate includes living arrangements, club affiliations, and the amount of independence one has in decision-making processes about his or her way of living. Finally, self concept is influenced by the criteria used for getting old. Some may use chronological age. Some evaluate themselves in terms of failing eyesight or hearing or a tendency to fatigue easily, and some use sexual potency as the indicator of their point of no return. For some getting old is indicated by an increase in the poverty of loneliness.

Studies show that subjective age is closely related to morale, rigidity, and fantasy behavior. It is also related to treatment by others and to the ability to get around. Among institutionalized people, negative attitudes seem to be the result of institutionalization rather than of age per se.

PERSONALITY DIFFERENCES

One man in his seventies described retirement in these words:

> I began planning for retirement when I was nearing sixty. My wife was involved in each decision made about it. Preparation involved three main problems—financial, physical, and mental. The most frequent question asked me after I retired was, "What do you do to keep busy?" Well, I never find the time to do all the things I want to. If you are married you find you are not retired. You have gone on a "Honeydew vacation"—"Honey do this, honey do that."

Another person put a description this way:

> My husband retired at sixty-two when his company merged. For the first few months it was wonderful, just like we were on an extended vacation. But then things became different for him. He gets tired of watching television and he can work around the house just so much. Although successful in the business world he has not succeeded in adjusting to retirement. As for me, a woman never retires anyway.

From many descriptions and studies of retirement one generalization stands out. People react to retirement according to individual patterns that may be more marked in maturity than they are in childhood, adolescence, youth, and middle age. Some retire and like it, some tolerate it, and some fight it. Aging may come gracefully or it may come in anger.

In a statistically analyzed study of male aging and personality at the University of California, five clusters of persons were found. Among the well-adjusted were the "mature" men who understood the developmental processes in a reasonable sort of way. They accepted themselves realistically and grew old without regret for the past. These men were relatively free from neurotic conflict, and they had little difficulty in spending their time in psychologically satisfying ways.

Next in order came the "rocking-chair type." These men welcomed freedom from responsibility. In some ways retirement gave them what they had wanted for a long time. Old age provided the opportunity to indulge in their passive needs. As one observer put it, "The rocking chair is a great institution. It is a way of sitting still and moving at the same time."

In the middle of the fivefold classification from well-adjusted to nonadjusted came the "armored" men. These individuals maintained a well-functioning system of defenses against anxiety by keeping busy. Always doing something keeps down worry and anxiety. No doubt this type of reaction in older persons is related to successes they had earlier in life.

Among the poorly adjusted came the fourth type, the "angry" men. These people were bitter over failures to achieve their life goals. They blamed other people for their disappointments, or they attributed defeat to the organizational climate.

Finally, the study factored out the "self-haters." These were the people who turned their resentments inward. They blamed themselves for their misfortunes. This unhappy group of retired people were depressed rather than angry.

Summary

Youth is a time of practical decision making. Middle age has been described as the developmental stage when we live with the consequences of our early decisions and planning. The age of retirement puts on the finishing touches.

The problems of youth are numerous and varied but better defined than those of adolescence. Youth is a time of searching for opportunity and preparing for a world exploding with technological change. Vocational decision making is demanded. People who have a good conception of themselves and of occupations and know what they are getting into are less likely to revoke their occupational choice than those who have not made accurate appraisals. There is a positive relationship between self concept and occupational choices.

The transition from youth to middle age is gradual. For some people middle age comes in harmoniously, for others it is marked by a crisis of revolt. In middle age, status becomes of great importance and there is a search for status symbols. Juggling for the perquisites of rank is characteristic of people with high rank as well as of those with low rank. Middle age has both a positive and a negative side; it is affected by both biological and psychological changes, which in turn are related to evaluations of success and failure. Thoughtful career planning in youth helps the well-adjusted middle-ager to balance the levels of ability, of opportunity, and of aspirations within a critical set of limits to achieve success in work and in personal life.

With advancing age there is a tendency for behavior to return to an earlier pattern and a simpler level of function. In general, physical aging comes earlier than mental aging. There is compensation for the slowing-down process. Speed of action and certain perceptual processes decline, but judgment and comprehension for many oldsters actually show an increase with age. Most important, wisdom, which increases markedly with growing years until possible senescence sets in, can compensate for many other losses.

One psychological problem concerns forced retirement and the utilization of leisure time. Some organizations have planned programs of preretirement counseling. One's habit structures, acceptance or rejection of cultural stereotypes of aging, feelings of success and failure, and the cultural climate influence the self concept in old age. Some retire and like it, some tolerate it, and some fight it. Aging may come gracefully or it may come in anger.

Suggestions for Thinking and Discussion

1 What are some of the ways in which psychological needs change with age?

2 What influences have so far been related to *your* thinking about occupational choices?

3 Ask someone in middle age (parents if this is possible, and wise!) what *their* biggest problems are. Chances are they may include you. Why?

4 What would be *your* criteria for judging success and failure?

5 In what ways can youth learn from the wisdom of some older people?

6 How can one learn to use leisure time for creative purposes?

Suggestions for Further Reading

Bergler, E. *The revolt of the middle-aged man.* New York: Wyn, 1954. A psychoanalyst looks at needs in middle age. One of the first and most descriptive books on the subject.

Birren, J. E. *The psychology of aging.* Englewood Cliffs, N.J.: Prentice-Hall, 1964. An overall view of the problems of aging.

May, R. *Man's search for himself.* New York: Norton, 1953. This book deals with one aspect of becoming aware of ourselves in an age of anxiety. Some interesting questions are discussed.

Stern, Edith M. *A full life after 65.* New York: Public Affairs Pamphlet No. 347, 1964. Some practical answers to practical questions on aging.

Walker, E. L., & Heyns, R. *An anatomy of conformity.* Englewood Cliffs, N.J.: Prentice-Hall, 1962. Relates to career planning and expectations in youth.

CHAPTER 9

Groups, Families, and Communities

When we think of the behavior of people in groups it is almost inevitable that we ask the question, "Where do *I* fit in as an individual?" In the preceding chapters we have covered the development of the individual. We have talked about how each of us is both influenced and constrained by other people. And we have indirectly raised questions about how people get pushed around. Psychologists have also been interested in the study of people not only by ones, but also by fives, tens, and hundreds, and thousands.

BEHAVIOR OF PEOPLE IN GROUPS

Nearly every individual is a member of several different groups, ranging from athletic teams and rec clubs to civic organizations and work groups. We have a *psychological group* when two or more persons get together to (1) influence the behavior of each of the others or (2) share something in common. It is important to recognize that every group, whether it be a football team, dance club, or some informal friendship gathering that sits around the lunch counter, has its own particular characteristics.

SATISFYING WANTS

A group comes into being *to help satisfy the wants of its members.* One may become a member of a group through biological chance. Thus the child is born into a family group. Or a person may actively seek membership in a group, e.g., marrying into a family or enlisting in the military service. For most people and most groups, the group serves two wants. First, for some people, those who seek leadership roles, the group serves the power want. For practically all members the group helps to satisfy the "belongingness" need. Often, of course, new wants are created when people function in groups; as, for example, when people join together in a civic enterprise to clean up the community.

GROUP GOALS

In the course of interacting with one another, members develop a group spirit. A common goal, or a common ideology, tends to lessen behavior differences in the group which are due to the different wants of the individual members. This lessening of differences comes about in two ways. First, a common ideology creates a situation in which a *core* of common wants is clearly spelled out by discussion. Second, a common method of *expressing different* wants comes into being. Hence we find developing group beliefs, such as the belief that group participation is essential to the democratic process of problem solving.

When we observe several people acting together, working together, or planning together we note that certain kinds of behavior may be present, or absent, that are not involved when people act individually. A common example is the "sit-in" or the riot. Motivational factors come into being in group behavior where the members of the group tend to *identify* themselves with the group. To identify oneself dramatically with an idea is not necessarily to serve it. There is a difference between joining a group as a personal catharsis and joining a group for the purpose of working for something in which the person strongly believes.

GROUP FORMATION

How do groups get started in the first place? There is much research evidence to support the conclusion that *spatial proximity* is important for the formation of groups. In a study of a housing community for married students, it was found that friendship groups were most often made up of next-door neighbors. The most popular couples were those who lived in apartments that opened onto stairways of the building. There one was more likely to meet people.

As time goes on spatial proximity becomes less important and *similarity in attitudes* takes over. Note how the cliques on the campus are made up of people who believe much the same things.

One group situation which combines both spatial proximity and attitudes with the added element of survival is the family group.

STUDIES OF FAMILIES

The structure of the family governs the influences brought to bear not only on the child but also on older members. And influence may be negative as well as positive, as evidenced sometimes by group discussions about family problems. In some people there is a separation anxiety when one is away from his family. Salesmen and scientists alike may perform less well when they are out of town. This is particularly true of the family-oriented man. One of the problems of adjustment the new military recruit has to face is that of being separated from his family. Children often become depressed when separated from their parents for hospitalization, for instance. And for college freshmen away from home, the period from September to Thanksgiving may be psychologically much longer than the entire spring semester.

The family sets the stage for strong emotional relationships. It also provides much opportunity for communication when the parents provide the model that the youngster must live up to. Home influences on personality development are great. Let us illustrate by comparing and contrasting the behavior of children and parents in deprived families with those in middle and upper socioeconomic family groups.

DEPRIVED FAMILIES

Many researches describe the mother in the so-called lower class as being closer to her baby in many ways than the mother in the middle and upper classes. Nursing continues longer, and weaning is far less abrupt than is usual in the middle-class home. Toilet training is delayed, infantile genital play is not inhibited. The child is permitted greater freedom in his explorations and is given more prompt and affectionate attention when he gets into difficulty. On the other hand, the lower-class parents are quick to anger. As the child grows up these parents resort to ridicule, shaming, whipping, and other forms of physical punishment. It is easy to see that growing up under both economic and psychological privation conditions one to belonging to protective groups and to exhibiting such "irrational" behavior (from the viewpoint of higher classes) as overeating when food is abundant or overheating the home when fuel is plentiful. When viewed from higher up in the hierarchy, these people are often considered shiftless and lacking in thrift and foresight. Their behavior in spending is as irrational as that of the person who has been under the strain of prolonged unemployment. Because they are generally deprived of "things," lower-class people have a strong urge to overbuy when they get money. These "have-not" frustrations tend to strengthen the drives for immediate gratification. Not only is there a desire to seize upon the pleasures of the moment, but these people tend to react with a greater freedom of emotional expression than is found among the middle class.

Children and adolescents from the lower class are less inhibited in their expression of sex and anger. Fights of a physical nature between husband and wife are frequent. Parents even teach their children to fight with fists and knives and to hit first. Dirty fighting appears to be one way of attaining considerable status both within the family and from one's peers. Interestingly enough, seeking protection from parents and fellow gang members is quite acceptable, in contrast to the middle-class emphasis on self-reliance. These behaviors are a part of the culture of poverty.

For many families unemployment is a way of life; for others it is psychologically different in some respects. Before proceeding with a further description of family groups, let us describe how economic variables enter the picture.

THE UNEMPLOYED GROUP

One way to appreciate, at least to some extent, the place of work in the lives of all of us is to get a view of the man who is out of work. Who is he? How does he feel? What can we learn from studying the behavior patterns of the unemployed, both as individuals and as members of a group?

PROLONGED UNEMPLOYMENT AND STATUS

What happens to the individual as a result of prolonged unemployment? A few studies were made of this problem during the Great Depression of the thirties in both the United States and England. From these studies, summarized below, we will get a descriptive picture of the changes which take place in the individual, as well as an insight into the nature of human needs and the place that work holds in the routine of modern living.

Unemployment, of course, affects individuals differently, but there is a general pattern in the way the unemployed feel and act. Two major factors govern both individual and general behavior among the unemployed: the cultural background of the person and the length of time he has been out of work.

A man from middle-class circumstances may find his ego deflated sooner and more deeply than will the laborer who has always lived on the borderline of poverty. The unemployed man from the poorer environment probably has more associates who are also out of work than does the person who lives in a better community. In this environment, contrast may not be so noticeable. But middle-class people live in a psychological environment where the incentive to independence and self-support prevails. When economic opportunity is lacking, not only does the individual feel it directly, but he feels the social sanctions that his neighbors apply. Although the man from the lower-class group may be worse off economically, the social pressures on him are less. One investigator summarized this status problem: "The unemployed were able to adjust to the loss of their jobs, the exhaustion of their savings accounts, even to the cashing in of their insurance policies, but they broke down on the day they asked for relief."

STAGES OF BEHAVIOR OF THE UNEMPLOYED

For most people the course of unemployment runs through three stages. First, there comes the *feeling of shock,* regardless of any forewarning that the loss of the job was imminent. In this stage, the individual reviews the sequence of events leading to his unemployment and rationalizes about the wisdom of having taken the job in the first place. He soon settles for the idea that he can use a much-needed vacation. This is followed by an appraisal of his abilities and the formation of plans to get another job.

The second stage includes the *active search for a job.* Most people begin looking for one better than the one they had, and then if unemployment continues, for a similar one. As time passes, they begin to look for work anywhere, doing almost anything. "During this period," one writer says, "the individual is rather unresigned. His spirit is unbroken, and although he is unhappy about his predicament, he is still hopeful of success."

The final stage in unemployment involves the *breaking down of the individual.* Failing to find a job, he becomes anxious and pessimistic and begins to lose hope.

Some people pass through these stages rapidly, particularly the person who has experienced more failure than success. Each stage lasts longer for the individual who has had more success than failure in the past.

EFFECTS OF PROLONGED UNEMPLOYMENT

There are several aspects of the psychological effects of prolonged unemployment:

1 There is a loss of the sense of security, both economical and psychological.

2 The worker comes to blame himself for his condition; then he takes an aggressive attitude toward the situation.

3 There is the problem of time. For the man who has a job the day's activities center around that job, because it takes the greatest share of his time. For the unemployed man, time hangs heavy.

4 Daily routines of the household become interrupted. Regular hours of getting up or going to bed, of eating or performing chores are disrupted. This adds to the feeling of being lost.

5 Early in unemployment, the individual attempts to conceal his status from others. He may even leave for his "job" at the regular time and return home at the usual time at night. He fills in this time by job seeking, watching movies, or just loafing around. One observer reports that in England during the Great Depression, the unemployed did not frequent the pubs during working hours, but rather at the closing time of the factories—when employed workers went in for their beer.

6 Irrational spending has been noted among the unemployed; they often spend their money on luxury items instead of on necessities; some even take up relatively expensive hobbies which rapidly deplete unemployment insurance funds or the relief check. This is one reason why relief is often given in goods or food stamps rather than in money.

7 Some unemployed attempt to retreat from their situation through fantasy and dreaming. Others escape through psychosomatic illness. Some seek illegal outlets; others become radicals. But in the main, most unemployed men remain good citizens. Suicide and drinking are apparently not common escapes.

8 The unemployed man becomes excessively depressed if his family, relatives, and friends change their attitude of sympathy and understanding to one of criticism of the former breadwinner.

9 One of the most interesting psychological changes that occurs with prolonged unemployment is the intensification of daily habits. For example, the person who has read extensively when employed reads even more when unemployed. The person who reads only

a little while holding a job will probably read even less when out of work. Those who were religious while employed become more religious during unemployment, whereas those people normally not very religious become even less so during unemployment.

10 The effects of prolonged unemployment of parents soon show up in the insecurities and anxieties of their children. This throwback to the parents reinforces all the other effects on the head of the family, lowering the morale as well as the authority of the father.

11 Personality changes related to unemployment show up eventually in irritability, new faults, a breakdown in morale, and loss of emotional stability. Prejudices may increase, and scapegoats are sometimes set up as a defense for the position the person finds himself in. Unemployment may well bring out into the open a person's previously concealed feelings of inferiority.

ASPIRATION AND UNEMPLOYMENT

Although the unemployed show types of behavior in common, the *degree* to which unemployment affects the individual depends on past experience and individual aspirations. The migrant worker without a home comes to expect less than the person who has seen better times. One study of over four thousand migrant families made in 1932 showed that 69 percent were on the move because of economic distress. Some were following the seasonal employment route; some were looking for a permanent home; all hoped for little more than a place where body and soul could be held together. In another study of some twenty-six thousand migrants, made in the prosperous year of 1954, the goal was essentially the same—economic survival. Ambitions for the children and hopes of becoming a part of some community were further goals, but little was expected. Aspirations of community status could not be verbalized too well by these people because most of them had never experienced it.

Somewhat in contrast to this group who had little to lose psychologically is a group of established families in New York City who had more to lose. A psychiatric study of the latter revealed that most of these people had been established in jobs, carried life insurance, and were on the way up when the Depression put the breadwinner out of a job. For these people, the emotional experience of losing a job may be compared with the loss of love which a child suffers when rejected by a parent, especially a child who has done nothing to deserve the loss. This feeling of rejection was especially strong among men who had worked long, arduous years for one employer, to whom, as well as to the job, they had understandably formed real attachments.

"Deprived of 'love,' their first reaction was one of fear and bewilderment, combined with optimism, born of wishful thinking, obviously over-compensatory in nature."

It was found that the shame and embarrassment of being on relief were so great that a number of families persisted in hiding the fact for years. They refused to use commodities which would at once identify them as relief recipients. This study further reports that many of the children refused to eat the hot lunches provided for them at school, since this would identify them as "reliefers." In some cases there were attempts to "cheat" on relief investigators in petty ways, affording the recipients some slight ego gratification of the kind a child gets from teasing teacher or pilfering his mother's purse for pennies.

LASTING EFFECTS OF UNEMPLOYMENT

The jobless man who eventually gets employment is not the same man he was before his unemployment experience. He has different attitudes, often colored by bitterness and disillusionment. His skills are lessened, his self-discipline is relaxed, and often habits of neatness, punctuality, and getting along with others have to be relearned. He has acquired fears that may remain with him a lifetime.

Studies show that women suffer less than men during unemployment. This may well be related to the facts that, generally speaking, women have never really been accepted in industry, that they often work on a temporary basis, and that they resign to have babies. Although unemployment may hit the woman worker just as hard economically as it does the man, psychologically women seem to be exempt from many of the problems which face men who are out of a job.

Of the many writings on the psychological effects of unemployment on the individual, practically all focus upon one basic problem: satisfaction in life comes from the *feelings of accomplishment* that the person gets from work.

MIDDLE- AND UPPER-STRATA FAMILIES

Unlike deprived families, middle-class parents make a great effort to get the child to live right, do well in school, and to think in terms of long-range goals and delayed rewards. A conscious effort is often made to subdue immediate gratifications and learn to discipline oneself. Education is designed to facilitate future achievement. In contrast to their lower-class counterparts, the children from the middle classes are taught responsibilities, independence, and self-reliance. Physical aggression is frowned upon, overt sex expression is regarded as indecent, courtship and marriage are regulated by rules of right and wrong conduct.

The middle-class person develops within a pattern of denying impulse gratifications in favor of developing initiative. He strives to learn appropriate social as well as technical skills. He struggles for improvement, but at some risk. With attainment being a dominant goal, failure becomes an ever-present threat.

What of the upper class? Here, with a strong emphasis on taste, manners, good form, and family reputation, a child is taught that he is superior. This may be an asset to the person, if he does not have to face too much of the reality of rough and tough competition. It may be a liability when exaggerated values are stressed. The secure status of an upper-class member is somewhat automatically conferred by his family. It can be retained so long as the person does not step out of line. Sometimes the individual brought up in the protection of his upper-class standing finds the going rough when finances become depleted and "family security" is gone.

WORK AND THE FAMILY GROUP

The man at work, whether an executive or a laborer, does not function alone in his industrial environment. It is almost inevitable that his problems of work are shared with his family, and the feedback from family life affects his work. Essential to the study of the whole man in his total community is the study of the family. It has been estimated that of the over forty million families in the United States about thirty-six million are connected with the labor force. About two-thirds of these families have one or more members earning a wage or salary in a nonagricultural industry.

SOCIOECONOMIC ENVIRONMENT

Industry, directly and indirectly, helps establish the socioeconomic environment within the community, even to the extent of influencing marriages. In their jobs, large numbers of men and women become acquainted. Several studies have shown that one of the primary factors related to who marries whom is proximity. Men and women who live within relatively short distances of each other tend to marry. People who live in the same neighborhood usually come from the same class and often from the same status groups. Marriages occur between people who are thrown together at work or who meet through their positions in the social structure.

The modern industrial-urban family has a high degree of equality among its members. The father is less of an authoritarian figure than

in the patriarchal family, particularly when the wife and/or children
work for pay. Although those who work may leave their problems
at the office or not talk about their work at home, much about these
problems is revealed by attitudes, particularly where feelings are
involved. Men at all levels of society concentrate daily at their
place of work, leaving their homes for a world of often different values
and traditions. In all levels of society, says our industrial sociologist,
the husband is but a part-time member of the family who must somehow
adjust his work life to the demands of the family life. Some men here
succeed but many fail. One man may see his "work self" dominate;
another may see the "family self" win out. Here one may find a key
to personal adjustment. How a man behaves with his family often reveals something about how well his needs are being satisfied at work.

WORK AND THE FAMILY

To the man in the upper levels of society with prestige and authority gained at work, there may be little carryover into his family
life. The pressure of life at the high occupational levels may mean
the man has little time to devote to his family. In either case one's
work self differs from the family self. This is particularly true if the
wife has adequate funds of her own to allow her some independence.

To the middle-class white-collar man, the situation is often different. The income of the white-collar worker is usually superior to his
wife's; hence, the family is wholly or in part dependent on the husband's
wages. But still his family has not a complete idea of what the man
has to put up with in his work. He has difficulty transferring his feelings
of accomplishment or lack of accomplishment to his family. The family
may observe the strains of his failure or try to share in his victories,
but with little real success.

The status position of the worker may be as low within his family
as it is at work. If the wife and children work as wage earners, they
may make out as well as the husband, or better. This very weakness
of the father's position may cause him to play an authoritarian role
in the family as a defensive behavior. In some culturally deprived
families women take all responsibilities and dominate the family
entirely.

FAMILY STRUCTURE AND MOTIVATION

In a manpower research program for the culturally deprived, one
basic fact was discovered by the United States Department of Labor.
There is evidence that even with good job opportunities and few eco-

nomic pressures, motivational problems might prevent large numbers of trainees from utilizing the opportunities presented to them.

The histories of job trainees show striking examples of the influence of matriarchal family structure. This structure shows itself not so much in the physical absence of the father as in the fact that the father, even when present, plays a reduced role. For example, only one out of ten trainees mentioned his father, or some other male figure, as the person who was "most important" and "influential" in his life. It is perhaps more surprising that the men trainees reported that they "take after" and "admire" their mothers more than their fathers. These attitudes are shown in Figure 9-1.

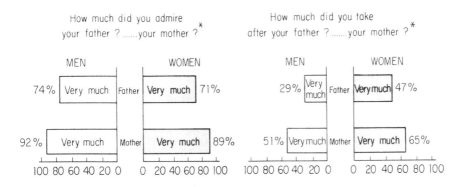

*Percentages do not total 100% because not all alternatives are included.

FIG. 9-1   A summary of the attitudes of job trainees from culturally handicapped matriarchal families. (*From United States Department of Labor. Manpower Research Program*, 1966, 1–217.)

Although most of the trainees knew that one out of three graduates of the government-sponsored training program was still working at his first job, that many had received raises, and that almost all were favorably viewed by their supervisors, still some became discouraged and left the program.

This study suggests that many trainees doubt that the "American way" applies to them. In an abstract sense, they feel that success depends on planning and hard work, but they are not certain that they are the masters of their own fate. In a survey, when asked about the need for personal planning, the majority chose the sentence, "It is not always a good idea to plan ahead, because too many things turn out to be a matter of luck."

At the core of the manpower-upgrading problem is the psychology of motivation. Studies reveal that social-psychological factors influence individual decisions in different ways for different people. Among the most culturally handicapped are those deprived of a healthy early family environment, and those who live in a depressed community. No small part of the problem is community mental health, centered around family life.

Advanced thinking and planning are bringing about a new and growing relation between psychology, the medical profession, and the community. Throughout the country, states and communities are readying themselves to try a bold new approach toward helping the mentally ill. The core of the plans now underway is to move the care and treatment of the mentally ill back into the community, rather than putting patients in distant and large hospitals.

Through research and planning the full range of mental health problems for individuals, families, and groups will be under observation, and trouble will be spotted early. Attention will be given to prevention of mental illness. Help will be provided at a time when it can do the most good. It is planned that emerging community mental health centers will be as unique as the communities to whose needs and opportunities they are responsive. In rural areas, especially, programs will be adapted to specific community needs.

COMMUNITIES

Most of our communities center around industry. Often at the core of the successful community is the college which supplies the talent for the local industries.

Social scientists have long been interested in the human problems of industry-community relations. Psychologists are interested not only in the man at work, but also in how the place where he lives affects his work, his attitudes, and his productivity. With increasing diversification within industry, with the dispersion of plants into the rural areas, and with the growth of the new suburbia, understanding the industrial community itself is becoming more and more important to the psychologist.

With the rapid growth of technology communities often grow up around research and development organizations. Cape Kennedy is an exciting example of how the space age has brought about a new type of community. For the most part, however, communities center around the city and the suburbs.

THE LARGE CITY

Within a city proper there are many and varied communities. Studies have shown that the uneven distribution of rent and occupations in the large city supports the notion that the city is made up of a lot of local and self-contained industrial neighborhoods which are relatively isolated from one another. The lack of interaction among these neighborhoods reinforces the prejudices that each group has toward the others. Some of the tensions of work may well be related to the fact that the larger the city is, the less its different segments appreciate the lives, habits, institutions, and culture of those in other areas.

LIVING ROOM AND PSYCHOLOGICAL PROBLEMS

From many sources we hear of the ill effects of crowding people into restricted quarters. We discuss the problem in terms of community delinquency and mental illness, and we ponder about what increasing urbanization will do to the psychological health of the individual. Perhaps we may get at least some feeling for the human aspects of the problem by turning to an animal laboratory study.

In one study thirty-two domesticated albino rats were placed in a 10- by 14-feet four-chambered home. These animals were observed for sixteen months without any outside interference. They went through their activities in a normal manner. But what would happen if they were forced to continue to live in the same quarters as the colony expanded through birth of new members? At first the animals behaved as do all well-housed laboratory rats. Nests were prepared and the newborn were cared for. Gradually, as the colony expanded from thirty-two to eighty, social patterns of behavior changed. Some individual rats began to show neuroses. Some males gave up mating habits. They broke into nests and on occasion ate the young who had died from earlier neglect by the mother. Other males withdrew from normal social activities of the colony. Homosexuality became common. "Happy family life," as best the experimenter could tell, was broken up. Five repetitions of the study showed the same results, with the animals becoming "withdrawn" as the conditions became overcrowded. Observed one psychiatrist, "One gets the uneasy feeling that we have heard of something not too dissimilar in our own culture." It could be a mistake to conclude that family and community problems come as a result of people having to live together under abnormally crowded conditions. The lack of enough living space may be just another of the multidimensional causes of psychological difficulty.

How a man lives may well be related to the way he works, thinks, and acts. In one large city, there are two railroads belonging to a steel empire. One railroad, which serves a number of steel mills, is located within city boundaries, and most of its workers live in crowded, run-down, tough neighborhoods. This railroad has a history of frequent labor complaints, strikes, and threats of strikes. The other railroad, owned and managed by the same people, serves as a connection between the steel mills and ore supply. It employs about the same number of people. This railroad has a history of good labor relations and few strikes. Its workers live in small settlements along the railroad, and, for the most part, own their modest homes and a couple of acres of land. Although the workers of both railroads receive the same pay rates and belong to the same national union, their behavior on the job is different. One reason for this difference seems apparent to the common management of the two railroads: the community way of living affects job satisfactions.

THE NEW SUBURBIA

What may be a threat to one community, such as the moving in of a minority group, may prove to be an asset to another. Racial or ethnic discrimination and social or economic stratification, with their related fears and resentments, help determine community patterns. The community not only contributes to the security or insecurity of the individual, but is a place where behavior can be manifested through informal organizations.

In contrast with the rigidities of the traditional community, where interlocking family relationships fix the individual's position and where he can move upward only by sanction of the next-higher group, we find that the new suburbia offers more in the way of classlessness.

Levittown, Pennsylvania, is representative of a type of the new suburbia where the goal is not to keep up with the Joneses; rather, it is to "keep down" with them. Conspicuous display is frowned upon. Even in a single neighborhood, an item which would be quite acceptable in one block might be regarded as flagrant showing off in another. True, the new suburbia is fraught with problems and conflicts, as is any other community, but here a man is more on his own in his chances for upward mobility. This melting pot of people from many industries, of men with many interests and varied backgrounds, is a growing pattern of a community life.

As the seats of economic power continue to shift from local institutions to national organizations, the middle-management group of people will move more often, some up and some out. The new suburbia provides something of a temporary home for the interim, not unlike army-post life for the family.

The new suburbia helps provide a place of declassification of people from the older standards of family background. It is a new chance for a new social order where personal tastes and even religious affiliations change. But for many there is always the fear of slipping back.

COMMUNITY TIES

One observer emphasizes the importance of knowing how people live in order to understand the relationship between community and industry. Although the tie between work and community may often be indirect, it is most important. He illustrates the point through a firsthand observation of the kinds of behavior underlying a paper mill strike. Fortunately for his study, he was accepted by both union and management. Each gave him access to records and allowed him to hold interviews both on and off the job.

The strike, it turned out, had been called by the paper-machine crew. To management it seemed strange, since this particular department was not involved in an incentive scheme which had been introduced in the cutting room. The incentive scheme was said to be the reason for calling the strike. But why would another department, seemingly unaffected, call the men out? To management, unaccustomed to thinking about the close relationship between the work situation and the community, it seemed incomprehensible that men in no way connected during working hours with the crucial department should feel themselves aggrieved.

On investigation it was found that the company's incentive scheme had its effects at a level far beyond the formal industrial relationships prescribed by the company's organization chart. The two sets of workers were bound by ties of kinship and by traditional patterns of age and occupational prestige, entirely outside the factory. The company's engineers had done far more than merely provide a better output in a single working department. They had, in fact, reversed the customary patterns of authority. The new incentive scheme had set juniors and inferiors to hurrying up their seniors and superiors. The machine-room men had struck against the disturbance of their community.

SOCIAL FORCES WITHIN THE COMMUNITY

Whether one comes from the city, the town, or the rural community, he is aware, somewhat at least, of the system of caste and class which governs American life. He is interested in getting a picture of the social influences shaping his own career. The college student has no doubt seen firsthand instances of families who have stayed at one level for generations, and of others who have risen to the top and stayed, or have fallen to the bottom. What are the factors that determine social position; what is the subtle interplay of education, money, profession, club and business associations that builds the social pyramid? What are the secrets which have made some men victims of downward mobility and carried others to high places of power and prestige? Such were the questions that led to Warner's study of a representative community in the Midwestern part of the United States. In his book, *Democracy in Jonesville,* Warner describes the social forces that make the American community run. He and his associates began their studies during World War II; they continued for most of a decade.

THE JONESVILLE STUDY

Jonesville, a code name, has a population of a little more than six thousand people. It is a town where, in terms of social hierarchy, "everybody knows everybody's place." The upper class divides into old families and new families. The first group includes those who have enjoyed wealth and position for several generations, or those who have managed to retain their social position despite loss of much of their wealth. The new families include those who have climbed into top position and have succeeded in being accepted by those already there. Not every wealthy family reaches the top position. This upper class constitutes less than 3 percent of the population in Jonesville.

Persons in the upper-middle class, active in all community activities, have less wealth than those at the top. They are the prominent, substantial people to whom common men often pay deference. But they are anxious people, fearful of doing something wrong and ruining their chances for advancement. They are constantly on the alert to enter into worthy civic enterprises, particularly those of which the elite are active sponsors.

Among the people who "belong to nice families but are nobody socially" are the small shopkeepers, the skilled workers, and the clerks. Below these are the little people, the poor but honest workers who live around the mill in the less-well-kept part of town. Finally comes a fifth lower-lower class who live across the tracks.

The young people of each class tend to marry at their own level. Their children acquire the status of the parents, learn their way of life, and help ensure the permanence of the class system. The citizens of Jonesville know and think about class behavior, and this knowledge is one of the basic guides to proper and adaptive behavior for them all.

In Jonesville, as in all American communities, the class structure is fluid. Families or individuals may not remain in one class. Mobility may be up or down. People do not quite openly admit that there are different classes, yet through their actions they place themselves and each other in a social class. While the boy from across the tracks does not often reach the mansion, he frequently ends up with a small business on Main Street. On the other hand, there is also downward mobility. Whether movement is up or down, in or out of social groups, the social class of a person's family is the zero point for indicating a change in status.

THE COLLEGE COMMUNITY

One useful exercise for the college student is to ask how the individual relates to his or her college community. Some of the answers to "Who am I?" and "Where am I going?" may be found in analyzing the groups to which one belongs.

In terms of studying the psychology of group behavior the college environment is a good laboratory—whether the problem be that of trying to relate one's individuality to a climate or to get a picture of a somewhat unique type of community.

Colleges are cultural societies with characteristics that make each one both similar to and different from every other one. In large universities, size and urbanization often encourage indifference among faculty members and students alike. Here research may be given an emphasis ahead of teaching. In community colleges teaching receives the emphasis and if classes are small enough students feel themselves as individuals, not just "walking IBM cards."

College students undergo a great deal of personal change during their tenure. Much of this change is brought about indirectly, having been learned outside the classroom. Habit patterns are formed as a result of being pushed and pulled by situations in which the student repeatedly finds himself. Attitudes are influenced by different kinds of friends, by peers versus upperclassmen, and boys versus girls. Attitude change is very rapid during the early part of the freshmen year.

College environments vary in terms of (1) how much humanistic emphasis is given in the curriculum; (2) the degree to which logical and scientific analysis is encouraged; (3) competition; and (4) the degree to which interpersonal warmth and friendliness are emphasized.

How students *perceive* their climate is important. It is quite common that students feel that they are given low grades for an unreasonably great amount of effort. They often feel that neither the faculty nor the administration is accessible enough. One study found that commuters experience more adjustment problems than those who go away to school. Their main problems stem from conflict at home and lack of counseling at the college, which offers them little to identify with. This is particularly true in large urban universities. On the other hand, community colleges that are designed for commuters may do an excellent job of counseling.

Every college has certain formal and informal groups of students, but save for very large institutions colleges differ in the kinds of students they attract. For example, community colleges and institutes of technology tend to attract the practical student who means business. Private colleges tend to attract the more rah-rah types.

STUDENT SUBCULTURES

Descriptive studies of college climates are numerous. Here we shall describe four subcultures found on practically all large campuses and sometimes in smaller colleges.

In drawing a "cultural map" of the American college one finds that the most widely held stereotype of college life pictures the *collegiate culture* as a world of football, fraternities and sororities, dates, cars, and campus fun. Students who fit into this picture, although indifferent, even resistant to the serious demands of the faculty, generate strong loyalties and attachments to the college. Part-time work, practical vocational interests, a city location, and commuter students all work against the full flowering of this collegiate subculture. Students who aspire to get into graduate or professional school can hardly afford to go collegiate.

Serious students who go to college with an emphasis on learning to make a living make up the *vocational culture*. These students usually have economic pressures on them. They show little school spirit; for them college is just an adjunct to the world of jobs.

Regardless of size, present on every college campus, although dominant on some while marginal and almost invisible on others, is the subculture of the students interested in learning. The serious students constitute the *academic culture*. Where the collegiates pursue fun and the job-oriented seek skills, these students seek knowledge. Their symbols are the library, laboratory, and seminar. These students are often oriented toward vocations. They are seriously involved in their course work beyond the minimum required for passing and graduation.

Then there are the ambivalent students which constitute the *nonconformist culture*. These students are often deeply involved with ideas and are against the *status quo*. They seek to be different, using as their status symbol some distinctive style of dress, speech, and attitude. In the aggressive nonconformists there exists a critical detachment from the college they attend and its faculty. They are often hostile to the administration and generally ready to fight the system. The precise form that this style takes varies from campus to campus, but where it exists it has a visibility and influence far beyond its usually small membership.

The student who makes a point of coming to understand the climate of his college may find that his efforts pay off when he moves into the world of making a living. Many people who find success in industry attribute it, at least in part, to discovery of climates and how they influence people in their adjustments.

Summary

We have a psychological group when two or more persons get together to influence the behavior of the others or to share something in common. A group comes into being to help achieve the wants of its members. A common goal tends to lessen behavior differences of the group which are due to the different wants of the individual members. Spatial proximity and similarity in attitudes are important in group formation.

The family is a group with strong emotional relationships that vary extensively with different class structures, ranging from the families of the chronically unemployed to the families in high socioeconomic communities. For some culturally deprived families unemployment is a way of life; for others unemployment may bring on experiences which can influence permanent changes of personality.

The jobless man who eventually gets employment is not the same person that he was before. He has different attitudes, often colored by bitterness and disillusionment. His skills are lessened, and he may acquire fears for a lifetime.

For the middle and upper classes family life centers around discipline and education, where one's work self often differs from the family self.

Most of our communities center around industries. The applied psychologist is interested in how a man lives, because this is related to how he works, thinks, and acts, and in large measure determines the problems he has. Whether one comes from the city, the town, or the rural community, he is aware of the system of caste and class which governs American life.

Studies of the social forces within the community deal with the factors that determine social position—the subtle interplay of education, money, profession, and club and business associations that build the social pyramid. Whether one is interested in movement up or down, in or out of social groups, the social class of the person's family is the zero point for indicating a change in status.

Colleges are cultural societies with characteristics that make each one both similar to and different from every other one. Each one has its student subcultures. We have the "collegiate" culture, with its stereotype of the less serious student, and the "vocational" culture, whose members see college as just an adjunct to the world of jobs. And present on every campus are the serious students who constitute the "academic" culture. And almost every college has ambivalent students who constitute the "nonconformist" culture. To which culture do *you* belong?

Suggestions for Thinking and Discussion

1   Take a look at some group on your campus. What is its history? What psychological needs does it satisfy?
2   Try to recall some group by which someone you know was rejected for membership. Can you give the real reasons why?
3   What attitude changes do you predict will be evidenced in relation to how people will view "culturally deprived families"?
4   What are the social forces operating in your home community that help determine class structure?
5   Make a subculture study of your college campus. Where do *you* fit into the picture?
6   How would you describe the influence structures in your home community?

Suggestions for Further Reading

Olmsted, M. S. *The small group.* New York: Random House, 1959. Research-oriented findings on small-group behavior.

Riesman, D., et al. *The lonely crowd.* New Haven, Conn., Yale, 1950. A classic that deals with the things that influence persons individually and in groups.

Sanders, I. T. *The community: An introduction to a social system.* New York: Ronald, 1966. A text on community life large and small; industrial and rural.

Sanford, N. *College and character.* New York: Wiley, 1964. The organizational climates of colleges.

Warren, R. L. *The community in America.* Chicago: Rand McNally, 1963. A text on community study.

PART III

ADJUSTMENTS AND CAREER DEVELOPMENT

CHAPTER 10

Personal and Social Adjustments

❖❖❖❖❖❖❖❖❖

When shaken up physically the athlete sometimes has to be carried off the field. Somewhat similarly, there are times when each of us gets hit so hard psychologically that we need help to "leave the field." One aspect of this help may be given by providing an understanding as to why *all* people have problems of adjustment. Some of us tend to repeat our own errors, and sometimes we have to pay a high price for the upkeep of our ego after it has been injured. A few people seem to live from one emotion to another. It is important to learn that some things which may be manageable intellectually are not so easily managed emotionally.

In previous chapters we have talked about how our needs and wants get blocked and how we often turn to defensive types of behavior. We have seen how the individual faces problems in childhood, adolescence, youth, middle age, and old age. How do we adjust to such developmental changes? This is the subject of this chapter. We shall begin our discussion with problems of the college-age student as he faces the very common problems of *anxiety, fear,* and *feelings of inferiority* as he finds himself in a speed-obsessed way of living. All of us, at times, have difficulty telling the difference between the rat race and the human race.

UNDERSTANDING ANXIETY AND FEAR

The concept of anxiety gives us a good example of how all college students have something in common. This statement, in itself, may be enough to provide some comfort to us. We seem to get some help just from having company in our misery.

ANXIETY AND COLLEGE SUCCESS

In one study it was found that 90 percent of college sophomores, *who had been chosen for good health and academic adjustment,* had psychological problems intense enough to warrant assistance in solving them. In most of these cases anxiety played a major role.

From many studies comes the conclusion that practically all students suffer from test anxiety. The straight-A student often has more anxiety about an exam than does the person who is below average. The A student has strong needs to achieve and to stay at his high level. One investigator found that at the lowest and highest levels of academic talent, *anxiety has little effect on academic performance.* The less academically oriented students do poorly in college regardless of their level of anxiety. Superior students are sufficiently bright to overcome any adverse effects of anxiety. One practical way to hold down anxiety is to keep busy. Hence, bright students learn to cope with their anxiety through hard work and are reinforced by the resulting academic accomplishment. For a few students, getting ahead seems to be mostly a game of mistakes. For some anxiety comes as a part of the high cost of knowing.

But what about the *average student?* Research shows that within the middle range of intellectual ability, anxiety interferes markedly with successful college performance. Since most college students occupy the middle ranges of intellectual ability, chances are that some students who could get through college successfully fail because anxiety gets the better of them. For these students college counseling and guidance programs are most helpful. We shall describe how this works out in the next chapter, but for now let us use one example.

ANXIETY AND COUNSELING

Several investigators put anxious freshmen into a group counseling situation and then compared their academic performance at the end of the first year with that of a control group of anxious freshmen who were not counseled.

The results of the study are shown in Figure 10-1. Here we see that the anxious but counseled students showed a significantly greater improvement over their own midsemester grades than the noncounseled students. (The counseling sessions began in the middle of the semester.) It is also important to note that the graph shows that those who came regularly to the counseling meetings made the greatest improvement in grades.

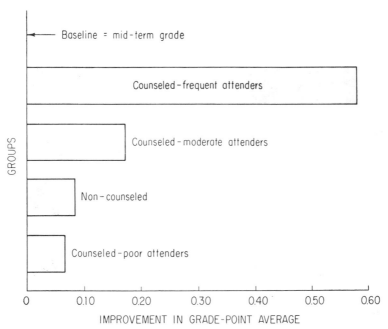

FIG. 10-1   How counseling benefits anxious college students. The counseled group had three subgroups—frequent, moderate, and poor attenders. Those who came often to counseling meetings showed the most improvement in grade-point average. [*Data from Spielberger, C. D., & Weitz, H. Improving the academic performance of anxious college freshmen: A group counseling approach to the prevention of underachievement. Psychol. Monogr.,* 1964, 78(3); *Whole No.* 590.]

Many studies show the payoff that comes from attending individual and group sessions in counseling and guidance. So important is this college service that we shall devote an entire chapter to it, Chapter 11, which follows.

NORMAL AND ABNORMAL ANXIETY

Anxiety is by no means the exclusive property of either the student or the neurotic. Anxiety is for all practical purposes a universal problem. It shows up in such *physical* symptoms as ulcers and breathing problems. *Psychological anxiety* involves such reactions as fear and feelings of depression.

An interesting aspect of anxiety is that sometimes it is "free floating," i.e., the person is apprehensive but cannot attach the feeling to any specific cause. Said one student as she came out of a counseling session, "I feel like a free-floating anxiety looking for something to tie onto." Many of us feel that we are not causing events, but rather that we are surviving them.

Normal anxiety includes, as we all know, those anxious moments before going into an exam. It entails a sense of helplessness when one is not able to find a solution to a perplexing problem. Like other emotional tensions, normal amounts of anxiety can act as a drive. A young person may react with moderate anxiety because his lack of skill in dancing prevents his or her participation in this social activity. This may motivate the person to learn to dance to overcome shyness or inconvenience. It may help in fighting that urge to flee.

Abnormal anxiety is manifested in varying degrees, but at one end of the scale it involves feelings and behavior which keep the person from functioning efficiently. At the other end it may involve panic. In this chronic anxiety the person is in a state of stress because of some internal conflict which, even by using such defensive types of behavior as are described in Chapter 2 (see page 36), he has not been able to reduce. The chronically anxious person has the usual complaints of headaches, backaches, and upset stomachs. He cannot think clearly or concentrate. *He feels tired all the time.* He has a feeling of failure and dread without knowing what it is that he is afraid of. These panic states are usually brief, though their duration is variable and they may last anywhere from a matter of minutes to days. In a later section of this chapter we shall mention some of the extremely abnormal states of pathological anxiety.

FEAR AND ANXIETY

The terms *fear* and *anxiety* are somewhat interchangeable. There is, however, one difference. Fear is usually caused by some specific thing, such as snakes. Anxiety is more diffuse and is hard to pin down to a specific cause. Fear is associated with an object that threatens us, whereas anxiety centers around the anticipation of dangers of unknown origin. Anxiety seems to thrive in a climate dominated by hostility.

Everyone, even the bravest persons, experiences fear from time to time. Fear is aroused most readily by *intense* stimuli that occur *suddenly* in circumstances where we cannot use any habit of adjustment. This can be related to our tendency to strive for a chance to indulge the cessation of time, if only for a few moments, before committing yourselves to action. As one observer put it, "If you have never been thrown from a horse, you have never ridden enough; if you rarely ever are scared, you are not adventurous enough." This is very much like saying that people who are living have problems.

FEAR THROUGH EMOTIONAL CONDITIONING

Many of our fears have origins back in childhood, e.g., fear of dogs. Social and verbal conditioning accounts for a large number of fears. A child's playmates may frighten him with stories about the dark. Parental threats, or even parental fears, may bring about emotional attitudes that persist for a long time.

Many ordinary situations of life find people being conditioned to fear some situation. Let us describe one case in which accurate observations were made of an infant.

At the age of five months, the infant was taken to a physician's office for his first inoculation. He had been in this office several times before without any notable display of emotion. The infant remained calm until after the insertion of the hypodermic needle. When it was inserted he shuddered, and then, after about three seconds, cried convulsively and could not be quieted for several minutes. On the second visit, ten days later, the infant was quiet until he saw the physician approach with the hypodermic syringe. Then, before being touched, he wailed loudly. After another ten days, a third visit produced crying immediately upon being carried into the office. The fourth call resulted in loud crying as soon as he was brought into the outer waiting room. The conditioning therefore spread gradually outward to situations more and more remotely associated with the painful stimulus. Furthermore, he now cried when placed prone upon a bath table at home, which somewhat resembled the physician's examining table. This persisted for several months. At sixteen months of age, nearly a year later, he still cried upon entering the physician's office, although no further injections or other painful treatments had been given there in the interval.

The above case was recorded in a textbook in 1940. Today this infant is a counselor. Says he, "I'm still fearful of needles. The experience of receiving many inoculations during my army service only strengthened this early fear."

ELIMINATING FEARS

Since many fears are so readily conditioned to new stimuli, it is surprising that more people are not hampered throughout life by a large number of such responses. It is fortunate that sometimes fears become lost by *reconditioning* through learning. Thus a child who had been conditioned to fear furry animals was reconditioned by the gradual introduction of a rabbit while the child was pleasantly occupied. Laboratory evidence also shows that social stimulation is useful in reconditioning emotional reactions. If a child sees that other children do not fear a situation, his fear may be overcome more easily.

On the negative side, disuse may not appreciably affect a conditioned emotional reaction. For an individual *to avoid* the emotional stimulus, therefore, merely postpones outbreaks of the fear. Fears have been known to persist through years of disuse, only to occur again when the conditioned stimulus was once more encountered. Compelling an individual to face a situation that he fears may, in fact, reinforce the emotional reaction. It is not always useful to attempt to persuade a person that his fear is groundless. To ridicule the fear may make it worse. *Ineffective methods* in getting rid of fear include (1) ignoring the fear; (2) enforced contact with the feared situation; and (3) keeping the individual away from the feared situation. *Effective methods* include (1) giving the person a chance to get acquainted with the feared situation; (2) the gradual introduction of the feared stimulus; and (3) understandable verbal explanation and reassurance.

PHOBIA

A phobia is an excessive and irrational fear of some object or situation. We may compile long lists from "claustrophobia" (fear of enclosed places) to "gynophobia" (fear of women). Many phobias are related to fears of sex and of contamination.

The sufferer from a phobia feels a strong fear of some harmless situation. He admits the fear is foolish but is unable to control it. And significantly, he cannot recall any experience that would have caused the extreme fear.

FEELINGS OF INFERIORITY

Counselors report that of all the variety of problems they hear described by college students, near the top lies one in common—*unfavorable self-evaluation*. Attitudes of inferiority are also found among adults so frequently that we regard them as a normal aspect of living.

Why are feelings of inferiority so common? One big reason is that our culture is *success-oriented*. We expect to win at games. We expect to get to the top in business. And many of us have to show somebody something.

From the time of birth the individual is compared and contrasted on everything—looks, intelligence, muscular strength, school accomplishment, and a host of other things. Each of us in our struggles to match up picks "the ideal" as our standard of comparison. We do this even though we see that it may be unfair. We compare ourselves in looks with the television star. In athletics our image of success is the professional. In academic pursuits we have parents, or an older brother or sister, to match in accomplishment. We feel inferior in the classroom because the teacher knows more than we do. There is nothing we participate in that someone is not better at than we are. By the time we have combined this ideal person, he or she doesn't exist, but we fail to realize this. Instead we try to measure ourselves by our mistakes rather than by our accomplishments.

Another reason why all of us have feelings of inferiority is that we know more about our own feelings than anyone else does. We often see only the surface feelings of others, and we observe only their many cover-ups through their role playing. In playing the role of being ourselves we come closer to our problems and see our failures. We are always aware of what other people think, and this shakes us up.

SOCIAL FRUSTRATIONS

There are two subtypes of social frustration. First, *frustration results when we fail to live up to the expectations of our social group.* Second, *social frustration ensues when some immediate drive is blocked by our habits and values.* This "blocking" or thwarting of our motives causes us to feel inferior.

The average adult male does not feel thwarted because he is not a professional football player. Neither is the average woman thwarted because she is not accomplished in all the fine arts. These accomplishments are not expected. But aside from these extremes, many other things, often beyond our capabilities, are expected of us. It is the criticisms from our equals or inferiors that hurt. Perhaps it may help our understanding somewhat to realize that often such criticism is in itself defensive. It should be recognized that we may be good judges of the other person's assets but poor judges of our own failings.

The frustration that arises when drives are blocked is usually subtle. For example, a young girl had learned to love and admire her parents. Social custom stipulates that this is the right thing to do. Now, suppose that the girl learns that her parents are unworthy, that both have been carrying on clandestine love affairs, and that they bitterly threaten each other with divorce. Her immediate reaction is to shun her parents. But this is difficult to do because of long-established habits. She is therefore frustrated and must make effective some compromise adjustment. Much of this adjustment is carried out in *thinking* as a conflict. It is carried out at the *projection* level in terms of resentment. And it is in a subtle way bundled up at the *feeling* level as inferiority.

SELF CONCEPT

Like all attitudes, feelings of inferiority are acquired by a long series of experiences. Among different persons feelings of inferiority range widely from mild to severe. Even within the individual, what we think of ourselves varies from time to time. In times of success we set our feelings of inferiority aside as being something that is really unimportant to us. On the other hand, repeated failure can build up an inferiority complex *about everything*.

A well-meaning father, by making all his son's decisions for him, by pushing him to succeed in school or in sports beyond his capabilities, may cause a defensive attitude toward himself. This may eventually become a generalized attitude toward all authority. The result for the son may show up in open rebellion. It may result in timidity. In either case, feelings of inferiority are present.

INDICATORS OF INFERIORITY ATTITUDES

There are six rather common ways to recognize feelings of inadequacy in incidents of everyday life. Up to a point we can cut down on our feelings by counterreactions to these indicators.

First, a common indicator of inferiority is marked *sensitivity to criticism*. One may overreact to direct or implied criticism. A student may devote much effort to prove that his solution to a problem is correct. On the other hand, he might more profitably search for a better method of attack. If a better method is found, reinforcement sets in to help offset the attitude of "I can't do it."

A second indicator of the inferiority attitude is *reference of all criticism to oneself*. A whispered comment or chance laughter by others, which may actually have no relationship whatever to the anxious person, may cause him to feel that he is being attacked. *Seclusiveness* is a third indicator of an inferiority attitude. In the extreme instance, the individual will cross to the other side of the street to avoid meeting people. He will not join with students gathering in the hall. He feels that he is not wanted. A note of caution, however, should be injected here. The fact that a person does not gab in the hallway is not in itself an indication of feelings of inferiority. It might be that there are more important things to do!

Fourth, the person with feelings of inferiority characteristically *overresponds to flattery*. This seems to help him improve his own feeling of adequacy. Anyone who supports it will be given a welcome reception. But, again let us point out the need to draw a line between overresponse and liking to hear good things about ourselves. The teacher's appreciation of a favorable comment about himself may be in no way related to inferiority. The chances are that such appreciation is normal in the educational climate. The professor gets mostly negative feedback from students. Those who do poorly drop the word that he is a poor teacher. Those who do well, and who quite honestly think the person is an excellent teacher, rarely if ever tell him so. Hence, it is only human nature that he may respond with good feelings to indirect flattery.

The person who feels inferior shows a fifth symptom as an indicator. He gives a *poor reaction to competition*. He is not a good loser. Every contest he enters, whether it is a game of skill or just trying to impress his girl friend, is played most seriously. He prefers, however, to compare his skill with that of someone he can defeat. He likes obscure games in which he has a high degree of competence. He avoids more conventional situations where winning is somewhat a matter of chance.

Sixth, a *tendency to depreciate others* indicates an attitude of inferiority. Pointing out the faults of others not only helps to minimize one's own defects but even involves some projection. No doubt, when we feel particular inferiority we want, perhaps unconsciously, to see that we have company in the deficiency.

INFERIORITY AS MALADJUSTMENT

Maladjustment involves the entire personality. Feelings of inferiority are a part of the whole picture.

The person who lacks confidence to a great degree makes his life miserable. His fear of himself is severe enough to repress his talents and abilities. Outwardly this person may display ability, but he actually holds back because of a fear of failure. Even mild risk taking is shunned. The individual may say in effect, "I don't have what it takes." A better statement would be, "I have what it takes but I'm afraid to take the chance of a possible failure."

Feelings of *depression* generally go along with sever inferiority. There is no prediction of moods from outward events. Friends and relatives often do not realize the extent of the depression being felt. Whereas normal feelings of inferiority relate to comparisons with the ideal, with the sick person such comparisons may turn into *envy*. He makes comparisons only about the things he is poor in, never about things he is good in. Most such people actually have a number of accomplishments, but they themselves do not realize this fact.

UNDERSTANDING FRUSTRATION AND CONFLICT

Frustration results when we are driving hard toward some goal and find our pathway blocked. Somewhat different is the state of *conflict,* which results when we must make a choice of alternatives and everything seems to be in confusion.

Since frustration and conflict often go hand in hand, we can see how we run into so many problems.

EXAMPLES OF FRUSTRATION

Let us exemplify frustration by starting with simple annoyances and proceeding to more complex examples.

A date stands one up. This produces a frustration. One is in a hurry but cannot get his car started. This is also a frustration, but the two types of frustration are different. The first of these forms of thwarting may be termed a *social frustration,* and the solution may be easy or hard. It may be easy if it turns out that the date is really ill or has some other noncompetitive excuse. But suppose the fellow sees his date with some rival? *Material frustration,* on the other hand, will not be likely to start quite so many imaginings ("What does *he* have that is better than what I can offer?"). Certainly the car failing to start upsets one, but chances are that we know how to cope with the problem. At least we do not allow our imaginations to carry us over into a world of ghost anxieties, where grumbles grow to rumbles.

Let us take a look at frustration again in an example of how sometimes we may have a material frustration under control only to find that adding social frustration to it causes an explosion.

You have a double date and are driving to a ball game when a tire goes flat. You get out the tools in preparation to putting on the spare. Your boy friend stays in the car with his date until you suggest that he help you. His help, however, turns out to be impractical advice, given freely and often, and without any effort to lend a hand. Your girl friend starts reminding you that the game is starting and implying that she could have gone with Bob—who has a better car. OK, take it from there! Here we have social frustration added to material frustration. Perhaps we should learn not to take ourselves too seriously. Humor is a good buttress against many kinds of frustration. Sitting on the ledge of a building may be a tremendous effort at communication, but is hardly the most effective way to solve most problems.

Frustrations may be *nonthreatening,* such as the cookie jar out of reach of little Ted. They may also be *threatening*. The 250-pound line backer coming in on the quarterback is an example, but here such frustration is expected and, in theory at least, a pocket of protection is formed. Preparation in training has been made for such threats. However, an unfriendly gang closing in on a stranger in an empty street is more than just an impassable barrier between the individual and safety.

Frustrations may be related to objects which are *external*—locked doors, girl friend too far away, no money for the dance. These physical barriers are specific and easily understood. Not quite so clear-cut are the *internal* barriers—personality defects, too much intellectual competition. These are the types of frustration which become related to conflicts.

CONFLICT

One counselor described conflict by saying, "You may want to, but you can't have it both ways."

The co-ed who is strongly motivated to academic attainment may find some degree of conflict in a college climate where male students rebuff the exhibition of too much cortical activity: "To get dates one must learn to ask for help with a column of figures."

Four basic types of conflict hit most of us often enough for us to be able to see the distinctions among them. First, we find the "I want it—I want it" conflict. One wants that extra helping of dessert and to lose weight. In most instances such choices are clear. We choose one alternative and forget the other. Of course, unfortunate choices may come back to increase our problem (eating the dessert). But we should also understand that losing weight is a type of reinforcement that may lead to continued decision making. Technically we speak of this as *approach-approach* conflict.

A second type of conflict has been called "I want it—I don't want it." These *approach-avoidance* conflicts have some elements which are attracting and others which are repelling. One may wish to read a sexy magazine but at the same time have some guilt feelings about doing so.

For our third type of conflict let us make things a bit more complicated by a description of the *double approach-avoidance* situation. Let us assume you have to choose between two jobs. You have studied career planning and have very intelligently asked yourself the right questions. Now you must make a choice. One job is in a part of the country where you want to live. You also will be working at the type of thing you enjoy doing. But the pay is low and requires more traveling than you would like to do. The other job is in an undesirable location and the work is less attractive. But the pay is good and you have a close friend working for the company who tells you that he likes the organizational climate of the company.

If you think this is a rough decision to make, take a look at the young woman who conceives of the ideal husband as young, attractive, full of vigor, and wealthy. She has such a suitor who has all but the wealth. But she also has another suitor, wealthy but old. Each goal has inherent within it both positive and negative characteristics.

Avoidance-avoidance is our fourth type of conflict. It involves a situation in which one can't win either way. There must be a choice between two undesirable courses of action. Thus one may have to choose between taking one of two required courses neither of which one would elect. The unmarried woman may face the choice of marrying without love or facing spinsterhood. The supervisor may face the choice between giving discipline to a friend or losing the respect of the other men.

People attempt in various ways to resolve such conflicts. Quite typically many people vacillate and are indecisive, in effect trying to solve the problem by doing nothing. But even such attempts are usually futile. Not doing anything is in itself making a decision. Other people try to make decisions by mostly talking about them. Said one observer, "He is the kind of administrator who makes decisions by clichés." Possibly most normal people choose the lesser of two evils. The "lesser" is often determined by nearness to some goal we are working toward. Just as there is a stronger tendency to "approach" a goal the closer we come to it, so we "avoid" the feared or the unpleasant with more strength the nearer we are to it.

Two generalizations about frustration and conflict can be made from observations of our daily lives. First, frustration very often leads to some form of aggression. This aggression may be good (a session at hard study following a failed quiz) or bad (telling the professor he grades unfairly). Second, conflict is often resolved by letting the pull of avoidance increase more rapidly near the time of making a decision than the pull of approach.

How a person reacts to fear, anxiety, feelings of inferiority, frustration, and conflict depends to a large extent on his personality.

THE MEANING OF PERSONALITY

No doubt we all make some errors in our understanding of people, but we also make some pretty shrewd observations about those people we know well. Most of us observe how our friends behave when they are frustrated, and we note the kinds of decisions they make when they are faced with conflict. We speak of those "with personality" and those "with personality problems." We hear people talk about those "who take life as it comes" and those who "borrow troubles." We are interested in noting that many people are compulsive in small things but calm and thoughtful in dealing with the larger, more basic problems.

The psychologist in studying personality deals with the same qualities that interest the layman. He is interested in situations which bring out the typical reactions of people. Each typical reaction he calls a *trait*. These include such characteristics as dominance, sensitiveness, and prejudice. He uses controlled observations and various kinds of tests to determine these traits. We must continue to remember, however, that personality does change, at least to a degree.

THINGS THAT DETERMINE PERSONALITY

Are we born with a set of personality traits? Does experience affect the development of our personality? Is personality determined by both nature and nurture? In answering the first question we hedge just a bit, but we do not say "No." The second question evokes the answer, "Yes, under certain conditions." And to the third question we answer outright, "Yes."

Personality has many determinants. Among the nature determinants are physiological and genetic factors that are manifested with growth. Newborn infants differ widely, and these differences soon show up. The amount of crying differs over a wide range, and the same may be said for activity. Some babies are described as happier than others. Some are quiet and others restless. A few babies even become ulcer patients.

Although research has not given us a final answer as yet, there is some evidence which makes it look as though certain children are hypersensitive to emotional stimulation.

Children certainly differ markedly in physique, right from the beginning. But what happens often is that we treat children in such a way that potential differences become greater. For example, a child may inherit an athletic body build; consequently opportunities, perhaps even pressures, are given to make him an athlete. The physique of the weaker child, who needs athletic training, may be neglected. Similarly, some children are born with more intellectual potential than others.

HEREDITY AND ENVIRONMENT

We no longer debate what percentage of our development is attributed to heredity and what percentage to environment. In earlier years the differences between children may favor heredity. Nature and nurture interact, and in complicated ways. Of course in later years environment begins to play a larger role in creating certain types of behavior. *Prenatal environmental* studies show that even the emotional state of the mother has possible effects on the unborn child. If the mother is emotionally upset the fetus becomes very active. Such activity may well last for long periods of time. Certain hormones are transmitted from the mother to the infant. The adrenal glands of the mother become very active during anger. Her gland products are transmitted to the fetus through the placenta. There is the possibility that the attitudes a mother brings to pregnancy may influence the fetus, since these attitudes involve the mother's emotional state. Research has not as yet confirmed this idea, but neither does it say that the possibility does not exist.

Infants who have been deprived of the correct amount of oxygen at birth may show intellectual deficiency, dullness, or motor retardation later on. Studies have demonstrated this. Factors associated with prenatal life and birth do have an effect on personality formation in later life.

Early childhood experiences have great influence on personality. But before talking about the environmental factors that influence human personality, let us describe some animal studies. We are, of course, able to do certain experiments with animals which no person in his right mind would ever try on human beings.

ANIMAL EXPERIMENTS

One experimenter worked with a large group of newly weaned rats on a hoarding study. Half of each litter was put in the control group and the other half in the experimental group. In this investigation the experimental animals were given only enough food for two weeks to keep them alive. The control group was given normal amounts of food. At five months of age, when the rats had become adults, hoarding behavior was studied. A significant difference was found between the groups. Hoarding of food by the deprived group was greater than by their litter mates of the control groups. Using litter mates in this study helped, of course, to even out hereditary factors.

Many studies of animals show how early experiences influence later personality. For example, puppies *raised in social isolation* are unable later to get along well with other dogs. These animals, brought up by themselves, even have difficulty getting along with human beings.

MONKEYS REARED WITH WIRE AND CLOTH MOTHERS

In Figure 10-2 we see a picture of a substitute wire mother and a cloth mother used in experiments with infant monkeys. In these re-

FIG. 10-2   An infant monkey finding comfort with a cloth substitute mother. The infant ignores the substitute wire mother. When frightened, he would run and cling to the cloth mother. (*Photograph courtesy of Dr. Harry F. Harlow.*)

search studies, infant monkeys were separated from their real mothers within twelve hours after birth. They were raised in the laboratory with two kinds of substitute mothers. One was constructed of heavy hardware cloth wire. The other "mother" was constructed of wood covered with a fuzzy cloth. Each of the mechanical mothers was provided with a nipple so that the baby monkey could nurse from it. Would the baby become attached to his substitute mother because his food and nourishment came from it? No evidence of this came out in these studies. When given a choice, the infant monkey spent more time holding onto the cloth mother. Why? It was a more comfortable place to stay. Studies also showed that this cloth mother gave the infant some feeling of security. When the baby monkey was scared he would run and cling to the cloth mother.

The infants raised with the wire mothers did not cling or even embrace this substitute. They would run away from the feared object and clutch themselves and cry. *Infants need a sense of security.* No doubt the sense of touch plays an important part in filling this need.

What will baby monkeys raised with cloth and wire mothers, completely away from their real mothers, be like when they grow up? For one thing, these animals *do not show normal affectionate behavior as adults.* Writes Professor Harlow about the adult monkeys:

> We have seen them sitting in their cages strangely mute, staring fixedly into space, relatively indifferent to people and other monkeys. Some clutch their heads in both hands and rock back and forth—the autistic behavior pattern that we had seen in babies raised on wire surrogates. Others, when approached or left alone, go into violent frenzies of rage, grasping and tearing at their legs with such fury that they sometimes require medical care.

SOME HUMAN STUDIES

One cannot, of course, deprive human beings of food, social situations, and love for experimental purposes. There are, however, many studies of deprived people that show much the same results as those found with animals. Let us indicate a few examples.

Studies have shown that among teen-age thieves who were deprived of love in infancy some grow up unable to demonstrate affection for others. Other delinquents go to great lengths in seeking affection. And still others become antisocial, refusing to establish any relationships with other people.

There have been studies of children placed in institutions and foster homes to see what influence this may have on them in later life. In one investigation two groups of teen-agers were studied. One group was well adjusted. The other group had disturbing emotional problems. The raters, in this case, were social caseworkers who did not know anything about the institutional history of these adolescents. They found later that the children who were poorly adjusted had been put in the institution around six months of age. The well-adjusted group went in at eleven months of age. The group that entered earlier remained for thirty-four months, as against twenty-five months for the other group.

Children raised in insitutions, when compared with a group raised in foster homes, showed differences in emotional responses to other persons. They were excessively demanding in attempting to get attention and in their search for affection. However, they were unable to return any love extended to them. When given problems to solve, the institution-reared children would give up quickly. The foster-home children would continue their problem-solving efforts.

What if children in institutions receive love and affection? One researcher chose for her study an institution where a deliberate effort was made by the staff from the beginning to provide the infant with love and affection. Infants were "mothered" for several weeks by soothing and holding them, playing with them, and responding to their smiles and vocalizations. Each infant was given special attention to individual needs. These infants were later compared with a control group given routine institutional care. Results showed that the children in the experimental group which had been given the special care were more responsive. At the end of a year, however, the advantages of the early stimulation had not been maintained. Perhaps one may conclude from such studies that love must be given early and continued.

In a review of hundreds of studies one writer concluded that, in general, *negative home climates are accompanied by poor adjustment in children. Home environments characterized by harmony and love are reflected in happy, confident children.* It must be concluded also that there are exceptions in both cases.

FAILURES OF ADJUSTMENT

Failures of adjustment range in degree. At the normal level we have the defensive types of behavior or substitute adjustments such as rationalization, compensation, and others described in Chapter 2.

In this chapter we shall illustrate two extremes in failures of adjustment. We shall talk about *nervousness* and *worry* and some of the things that each of us can do about them. And we shall indicate some of the serious mental disorders, the *neuroses* and *psychoses,* which need professional clinical and medical care.

NERVOUSNESS

To most of us *nervousness* suggests jumpiness, a low threshold for irritability. Nervousness occurs in degrees, and all of us are nervous in some situations. Mild nervous responses may lessen as we get used to a situation. The student who is called on in a new class will be a bit nervous. Chances are that if he responds appropriately he will gradually become less nervous. He gets positive reinforcement which aids him in handling the situation. If, on the other hand, he is sitting in the outer office awaiting his turn to receive some negative reinforcement from the dean, he may display fidgets and have distressing thoughts. When the interview is over, these symptoms will disappear, but the chances are that they will be no less pronounced later when he is again called on the carpet.

The nervous person overreacts to stimuli that many people ignore, and these kinds of behavior sometimes become *habits*—chewing finger nails, twisting one's hair, drumming on the table—you complete the list! These types of response can sometimes be overcome by recognizing them for what they are and making a conscious effort to break in on the repetitive sequence. One may overcome table drumming by putting his hands in his pocket, for example.

One type of behavior commonly described as nervousness may, in some circumstances, be beneficial; this is the *readiness to react*. Extreme sensitivity in reacting to a noise may save a soldier's life. For the most part, however, excessively quick responses to chance stimuli are more of a nuisance than a benefit.

An unresolved personal conflict may bring on "nervous stomach" or some other form of inner tension. Lacking any definite outlets, either direct or defensive, may keep the person in a nervous state.

Whereas nervous habits may be overcome, with effort, by changing responses or restraining the behavior, overcoming chronic nervousness is not so easy. Help may come through professional counseling and guidance. In extreme cases psychotherapy is required.

WORRY

Persistent nonadjustive "thinking" is the verbal counterpart of nervousness which we call *worry*. The worrier "spins his wheels" by going over his troubles again, again, and again, *without getting any closer to a solution*. When worry is concerned with a minor and *specific* problem, it is likely to disappear when the difficulty is solved or when the person directs his attention to something else.

One thing we know—persistent worry cannot be relieved merely by telling the worrier not to worry. As one well-adjusted teacher said: "I can solve problems, but I cannot solve worries. I try to convey this to my students."

SIX STEPS IN REDUCING WORRY

It is safe to say that it is impossible to get rid of *all* worry. As a matter of fact, the solutions to problems often come because of worry—at least worry may stimulate us to do something about our problems. However, it is possible to cut down on the *frequency* of worry and to some extent on the *degree* of worry. Bearing in mind that the six steps given below in relieving worry do not always work, we nevertheless suggest that you try them. (Do you have any better ideas?)

First, set a *time to consider the worry*. What is the cause? Often worry is vague and without specific cause. Taking time out to analyze it may help us find the cause. If there is no cause, this fact may help us get rid of the "ghosts." Putting off looking at worry does not reduce tension.

Second, *talk the worry out with a good listener*. Worries tend to become exaggerated when bottled up inside. An impartial observer can help us go through the stages of (1) trying to make our worry more objective by expressing it; (2) being asked questions about the cause; (3) getting some participation in the worry.

Third, *seek reliable information* about the area of the worry. Some worry is unnecessarily generated through ignorance, misinformation, or misconceptions. By talking the problem over with someone in whom we have confidence we may discover different solutions to try or we may at least find new ways of thinking about the problem. Seeking information in itself is a constructive exercise that helps to cut down on wheel spinning.

Fourth, *do something active about the source of the worry*. Low grades may be helped by guidance and efficient study. Probably the latter is enough. Solitude breeds more worry. Social worries may be lessened by some *group activity*.

Fifth, some worries have no solution. If the conditions are impossible to remedy, turn to *other types of behavior* to occupy yourself— sports, hobbies, amusements, and the like help reduce stress brought on by "no-solution" worry. And we *all* have these kinds of worry.

Sixth, *counseling centers* are good places to go to when professional guidance is necessary. But remember—most centers are overloaded with work and they hardly have time for just holding hands.

SERIOUS MENTAL DISORDERS

One often hears such statements as the following: "One in every ten persons suffers from some form of mental illness." "One-half of all hospital beds in the United States are occupied by mental patients." "One hundred thousand workers become so mentally ill each year that they enter state hospitals, lose about six months from work apiece." "Some people are not wired to handle the load."

Mentally deranged persons are not a class apart from other people. They are human beings. An unsophisticated visitor to a mental hospital is usually surprised to find how normal most of the patients seem. Very few are violent enough to be given drugs. Most of them are just pitiful individuals who are bewildered by the world and cannot adjust to it. Here we shall mention only a few neuroses and a few psychoses. One reason for including these descriptions in this text on applied psychology is that as citizens in a community we can do much to support efforts related to mental illness; the problem comes close to many of us in one form or another.

THE NEUROSES

The neuroses have as their major symptom anxiety, which was discussed earlier in this chapter. Noticeable are the physical ailments found in the *conversion hysterias*. The patient may show gross symptoms of paralysis, blindness, or deafness *which have no demonstrable physiological basis*. He may even have anesthesia, i.e., an area on the body in which pins can be stuck without producing pain. A patient may have, for example, a glove anesthesia. Hysterics seem to enjoy their illness. The term "conversion hysteria" suggests that the symptoms serve a useful purpose. The neurosis is "converted" into physical symptoms. As one psychologist says: "The neurotic is an individual who has *learned how not to learn."*

Compulsive reactions are impulses to do something over and over again. In exaggerated form they become manias. We commonly read about pyromania, the compulsion to set fires; kleptomania, the compulsion to steal; and dipsomania, the desire to go on alcoholic binges.

An uncommon dissociation reaction is *multiple personality*. These cases, in which the patient lives two or more different lives are rare, but interesting. The least rare are the *dual-personality* types, exemplified by Robert Louis Stevenson's description of Dr. Jekyll and Mr. Hyde. Although perhaps overdrawn, this story gives us a picture of the illness. If one "personality" shows one type of behavior, the other is drawn to just the opposite. A happy mood in one personality is reversed by a depressed mood in the other.

In *The Three Faces of Eve* we find a struggle between Eve White, the sweet, retiring, dignified, motherly type of person, and Eve Black, the vain, irresponsible, and mischievous individual. Eve White is unaware of Eve Black's existence. But the opposite is not true. During the months of psychotherapy there appeared a third personality, Jane. It was Jane who was able to reveal the trauma of early childhood that had produced the dissociation of personality in the first place. It was Jane who finally helped banish Eve White and Eve Black, leading to the synthesis of all three into a normal integrated personality.

THE PSYCHOSES

The psychoses are often associated with known physiological causes. For example, *paresis* caused by syphilitic infection is characterized by defects of judgment, convulsive seizures, rapid mental deterioration, and delusions.

Other serious mental disorders include the manic-depressive psychoses and the schizophrenias. *Manic-depressive disorders* are easily recognized. When manic, the patient is elated, outgoing, and aggressive and often has delusions of grandeur. Left on his own, he often indulges in alcoholic and sexual excesses, possibly involving himself in wild business ventures. On the depressed side, the patient presents a picture of depression and dejection and sometimes makes suicidal attempts. Common symptoms include blueness, a feeling of worthlessness, and hopelessness. Feelings of guilt form a part of this down phase. The manic-depressive psychosis extends beyond the normal range of being "elated" and being "blue" into three stages: (1) "hypomania—simple retardation; (2) acute mania—acute melancholia; (3) hyperacute mania—stuporous melancholia. In extreme cases the person may be harmful both to himself and to other people.

Schizophrenia, a psychosis commonly called "split personality," is characterized by four main types.

Simple schizophrenia is revealed by the person who is withdrawn and lacking in interest. It frequently begins in adolescence and progresses gradually. Persons with simple schizophrenia rarely find their way into hospitals. They may be the town eccentrics who do not disturb anyone if they have some funds. Often they live out their lives as bums, drifters, tramps, and prostitutes.

Hebephrenic schizophrenia is characterized by silly giggling, inappropriate nervous laughter, and unexplained weeping. These patients have lively hallucinations and often delusions of grandeur. They are sometimes the butt of jokes ("Give me two slices of bread. I'm a fried egg and want to go to bed.") The patient frequently deteriorates rapidly. He reaches the point of soiling and wetting himself and becomes mentally more and more withdrawn.

In *catatonic schizophrenia,* the patient may be in a stupor or he may become highly excitable. Catatonic persons in the stage of excitement are likely to be violent and dangerous. In the stupor stage they will not do what is requested of them and are very likely to do the opposite. If you offer to shake hands with a catatonic patient he may promptly put his hand behind his back. He may take a rigid posture and remain motionless for hours.

The patient with *paranoid schizophrenia* has the usual symptoms of delusions, hallucinations, and withdrawal. In addition, he has delusions of persecution. He believes that some person or group is out to get him. He "hears" voices that force him to do unusual things. Many of his feelings of persecution are farfetched and without grounds.

Paranoid people are often very intelligent, sometimes brilliant. Sometimes they have a history of having a prepsychotic personality, of resenting and distrusting others, of being excessively suspicious and hostile. They feel that they are being wronged. If they have funds and opportunity, they may seek court action against someone for little or no reason. They may demand justice where normal people perceive no injury at all.

LIVING WITH STRESS

"Stress is a normal counterpart of living," states one eminent scientist after thirty years of study. "How we react to it is important." We may even find dividends in disappointments.

Many studies of human stress show that some persons actually thrive on the same types of stressful situation that bring on health difficulties in others. Often our tensions, conflicts, and frustrations push us beyond our individual stress level. "He can't take it" may well describe the person who has exceeded his stress level. Heredity has something to do with how much stress one can take, and so do environmental factors. We know that sometimes our attempts to avoid stressful situations may even bring on more stress. We know that excessive stress over a period of time may cause such a depletion of energy that success in terms of grades, status, productivity, and money loses its meaning. There are no hard-and-fast rules to help us know when we are exceeding our *individual* stress level. For some of us the lines of stress are not quite visible. Some people struggle so hard in seeking security that they soon find themselves in the warm embrace of mediocrity.

STRESS AND RESPONSIBILITY

The parent who only half-sleeps at night waiting for the teen-age son or daughter to return home has much in common with the supervisor who has to meet a production deadline. Both are under the stress of responsibility. Likewise, the college administrator is sometimes under stress for a long period of time when he senses a growing crisis on the campus. Much of the "senior neurosis" of the student centers around the responsiblity of making career decisions. Sometimes the absence of stress in an individual may indicate lack of sophistication in anticipating problems. Perhaps it is well that the executive has an understanding of the pressures that go with a position of power. Some people, many of us in fact, may get E for excellence in pointing out the problems that cause stress, but an F for failure in coming up with our own solution.

Much has been learned about stress and responsibility from studies of men in space. Heartbeat, blood pressure, and other physiological changes have been recorded continuously over periods of days. Changes, indicating stress, have been related to stress-provoking situations. Heartbeat, for example, increases during a space walk, but it may also increase when a critical decision is being made. This "command pilot syndrome" includes a large measure of fatigue as a part of the overall adjustment system. What can each of us do about not exceeding our stress limits? Coming to understand the nature of the adjustment process can be helpful.

THE ADJUSTMENT PROCESS

The more stress a person is exposed to before he learns to cope with it, the harder it is to effect good adjustment. This is one reason why studying applied psychology early in one's college career may be beneficial. In effect much of the subject matter of psychology deals with the psychology of adjustment.

Behavior goes through four stages of adjustment: (1) motive; (2) frustration; (3) varied responses; and (4) solution. The individual has a strong *motive* which is pushing him toward a goal. Along the way he meets a baffling difficulty, i.e., a *frustration*. He tries to overcome this difficulty but cannot do so readily. Impelled by the motive, which is still unsatisfied, the individual makes various attempts to fulfill it. This process results in trial-and-error behavior, or what we call *varied responses*. Finally, comes a *solution* which, in whole or in part, satisfies the motive that started the adjustment process.

Many of us need counsel and guidance in learning to make effective adjustments in our emotional living, just as we do in choosing careers. Intellectually, or in the routine of daily living, it is not always easy to move from one problem that requires adjustment to another. Some people, however, make adjustments by moving through life sideways, though gracefully.

Summary

The college-age person faces three common problems—anxiety, fear, and feelings of inferiority. In their first and second years most students run into problems of adjustment intense enough to warrant counseling assistance in solving them.

Anxiety is for all practical purposes a universal problem. It shows up in such physical symptoms as ulcers and breathing problems, and in fear and depression. For some persons anxiety is free-floating. Anxiety ranges from those normal anxious moments before an exam to the abnormality of chronic fatigue. Fear is associated with an object that threatens us. Anxiety centers around the anticipation of dangers of unknown origin. In our success-oriented culture, unfavorable self-evaluation shows up in feelings of inferiority and a rating of our efforts in terms of unrealistic standards. These are related to social frustrations which result when we fail to live up to the expectations of our social group. They also peak in crises when some immediate drive is blocked by our habits and values. Fortunately, the indicators of inferiority attitudes hold in themselves cues for improvement in adjustment.

Frustration, which results when some path to a goal is blocked, goes hand in hand with conflict, in which we must choose between confusing alternatives. Frustrations may be threatening or nonthreatening. They may be related to objects which are external or induced internally. There are four types of conflict, to which people react in various ways.

Personality has many causes, determined by both nature and nurture, which relate to both adjustments and failures of adjustment. Mild failures of adjustment involve nervousness and worry. These are conditions that each of us can do something about. The major disorders, neuroses and psychoses, need professional medical care.

Studies of human stress show that some people actually thrive on the same types of stressful situation that bring on health difficulties in others. Often our tensions, conflicts, and frustrations push us beyond our individual stress level. Both heredity and environment have something to do with how much stress one can take.

There are no hard-and-fast rules to guide one as to when the individual stress levels are reached. However, understanding the adjustment process provides a framework for solving personal problems, as it carries the individual through the four stages of motives, frustration, various responses, and solution.

Suggestions for Thinking and Discussion

1 List the kinds of behavior you most commonly engage in when you have some anxiety. Can you find any cause-effect relationships?
2 What feelings of inferiority do you have which you are willing to discuss in a classroom setting? Assume that a class period (or some other setting) is devoted to a group therapy session; what types of feeling would you not bring up?
3 What things occur most commonly in initiating frustration in *you?* What types of choice bring on conflict?
4 Make a list of your most common worries. Select some of your fear-of-the-future worries. Keep a record for a period of time. How many of the worries worked out the way you anticipated?
5 The next time you have a worry, try to write it out in detail. What happened?
6 What are the indicators for *your* stress level?

Suggestions for Further Reading

Coleman, J. C. *Abnormal psychology and modern life*. Chicago: Scott, Foresman, 1964. The third edition of a text on abnormal psychology.

Gross, Nancy E. *Living with stress*. New York: McGraw-Hill, 1958. A popular writer puts the many technical facts from research into a readable book on adjustment to stress.

Mowrer, O. H. *Abnormal reactions or actions*. Dubuque, Iowa: Wm. C. Brown, 1966. A small volume written as part of a self-selection put-together text.

Ogg, Elizabeth. *Psychotherapy. A helping process*. New York: Public Affairs Pamphlet No. 329, 1962. A popular paperback on what can be expected from psychotherapy.

White, R. W. *Lives in progress*. New York: Holt, 1966. The development of personality of normal people. Some interesting case studies.

CHAPTER 11

Counseling and Guidance

❖―❖―❖―❖―❖―❖―❖―❖―❖

Near the center of the college campus one will usually find the office for counseling and guidance. It may be called "Personnel Counseling" or "Bureau of Measurement and Guidance," or it may have one of several other titles. It may be located in a temporary wooden structure or in the former living suite of an old mansion. Regardless of title or location, here one finds the "psychological center" of the campus. It is here that most students, at one time or another, come face to face with those all-too-familiar questions of their personal identity crisis:

Who am I?
Where am I going?
What will be the costs in getting there?
What questions should I learn to ask, and when should I ask them?

We may conclude that there is some chance that all of us will be less lonesome when we come to know ourselves.

A NATIONAL INVENTORY OF APTITUDES AND ABILITIES

In 1960 the American Institutes for Research began a study of 440,000 high school students across the nation. Students in this carefully selected sample from 1,353 secondary schools were given a comprehensive battery of tests of aptitude, ability, and achievement. They also completed detailed inventories about themselves and about their future plans. This study, called Project TALENT, has as its goal a long-term follow-up of these students. Although the careers of these male and female students will be studied for years to come, several valuable conclusions have already emerged from the study. At the forefront among the findings is the conclusion that *the great majority of young people do not make an appropriate choice of career while attending high school.* This fact often becomes recognized during the early months in college, and professional help is then sought. Says one researcher, "Bigness in education is demanding that we pay more attention than ever to the individual."

INDIVIDUAL DIFFERENCES AND LIFEWORK

The most striking fact regarding the educational achievements of the students in Project TALENT was the *wide range of individual differences.* Important, also, was the finding that it cannot be assumed that what one learns in the freshman year of high school will be retained in the senior year. For example, 20 percent of the ninth-grade students had more knowledge about spelling, capitalization, punctuation, usage, and effective expression than was demonstrated by the average twelfth grader. On a social studies test, 27 percent of the ninth-grade students achieved scores higher than those of the average twelfth-grade student.

Interest in subject matter seems to come into the picture. Whereas girls do well in reading and verbal skills, they do not show a similar pattern of growth in physical science and mathematics. A large proportion of girls forget more than they learn about physical science and mathematics in the last three years of high school. For certain language skills test scores favor the girls.

There is great variation in levels of achievement in reading reached by twelfth-grade students. For example, 15 percent of the twelfth-grade students were unable to understand what they read sufficiently well to answer correctly more than 50 percent of the multiple-choice questions based on paragraphs taken from the novels of Louisa May Alcott.

In Figure 11-1 we see a sample item from a reading comprehension test with male and female responses to four questions based on ten lines of a short paragraph.

An item in a creativity test which was answered correctly by only half the twelfth-grade boys is shown in Figure 11-2. The figure also includes an item from an arithmetic reasoning test which was also answered correctly by only half the twelfth-grade boys.

(1)   Literature is the art of selection and ruthless ex-
(2)   clusion, or, as Flaubert has said, it is "the art
(3)   of making sacrifices." Chekhov, another enemy of
(4)   the unnecessary word, says: "If in the first chapter
(5)   you say that a gun hung on the wall, in the second
(6)   or third chapter it must without fail be discharged."
(7)   He is right. The writer who seeks to emulate de
(8)   Maupassant and Poe in producing stories with pre-
(9)   cisely controlled plots cannot afford to ignore his
(10)   advice.

M	F	Who makes the sacrifices referred to in line 3?
14	20	A. Literary critics
12	8	B. Bad writers
53	53	C. Good writers
6	4	D. Bad readers
7	8	E. Good readers
9	7	Omits

M	F	What is the apparent attitude of the author of this passage towards Flaubert's view?
50	54	A. Agreement
13	14	B. Indifference
10	8	C. Mild disagreement
13	12	D. Strong disagreement
5	4	E. Perplexity
10	8	Omits

M	F	Chekhov thinks the gun "must without fail be dis- charged" (line 6) because he dislikes
7	6	A. his enemies.
13	13	B. ruthless people.
11	10	C. writers.
8	6	D. writing.
51	56	E. wordiness.
10	9	Omits

M	F	Chekhov's statement suggests that every word in a story must
5	4	A. be grammatically correct.
5	4	B. be short.
5	3	C. be familiar.
68	75	D. serve a purpose.
6	5	E. appear again.
10	9	Omits

FIG. 11-1   A sample item from a reading comprehension test used in Project TALENT. (*Courtesy of American Institutes for Research.*)

```
                 Naval landing craft sometimes become stranded on
                 sand or reefs. The situation is frequently such that
                 efforts to tow them out of the shallow water would
                 be likely to result in stranding the towing ship also.
                 The problem has been solved by towing the stranded
    M   F        craft to safety by using a
   46  41        A.  h - - - - - - - - r
   11  11        B.  j - - - - - - - - r
   12  10        C.  m - - - - - - - - n
    8  11        D.  s - - - - - - - - d
   12  14        E.  t - - - - - - - - e
   12  13           Omits


                 A salesman gets 12% commission on all items sold
                 over a quota of 5. If he sells 8 items at $30 each, his
    M   F        commission is 12% of
   25  31        A.  $240
   55  46        B.  $90
   10  13        C.  $30
    6   6        D.  $8
    2   2        E.  $5
    2   2           Omits
```

Fig. 11-2   Sample items from creativity and arithmetic reading tests used in Project TALENT. (*Courtesy of American Institutes for Research.*)

TALENTS AND CAREER PLANS

There are "families of careers" which require certain types of abilities. For example, physical scientists, engineers, technicians, and mechanics must have relatively high aptitudes in mathematics, reasoning, and mechanics. Students planning careers as artists have their highest test scores in such areas as visualization, creativity, and spatial relations. The highest scores for girls planning careers as teachers are in mathematics, literature, social studies, and vocabulary. These are only minor differences in the patterns for girls planning nursing and teaching careers. Girls planning careers as secretaries and stenographers have scores very near the average for all eleventh-grade girls on most tests, with good aptitude for learning shorthand and memory for words.

The patterns of aptitudes typical of those successfully participating in various careers should become clearer as these students are followed year after year. Project TALENT researchers conclude: "On the basis of present data it appears reasonable to expect that a large fraction of our high school graduates may be found in the top 10 percent with respect to the suitability of their pattern of aptitudes for at least one or more of the two hundred or so important career opportunities now available to young people."

It was found that students in the ninth grade had very unrealistic educational and career plans. These plans became more mature during

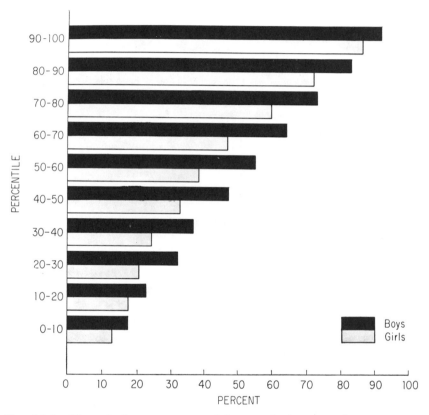

FIG. 11-3 The relative percentage of boys and girls attending college in terms of standing on a composite general academic aptitude score. Data from Project TALENT. (*Courtesy of American Institutes for Research.*)

the high school years. About half the students, however, made rather radical changes during their first year after graduation from high school. For example, 41 percent of high school seniors planning a career in law obtained aptitude scores too low to qualify for law school.

The decision to attend college seems to be more valid than plans for a career. In Figure 11-3 we see the relative percentage attending for both boys and girls in terms of standing on a *composite general academic aptitude score.*

OVERALL EVALUATION

Many factors, in addition to the individual's pattern of aptitudes and abilities, enter into the selection of a career. It is essential that the student learn early about occupations, interests, background for a career, and personal goals in choosing his or her lifework. It is here that early counseling and guidance become so important; it's hard to do the job alone.

Test scores are important, *but* they do not tell the whole story. Directors of college admissions must always face this problem. And counselors likewise face the same situation at times. They agree that there are certain minimum ability requirements to be met for success in this or that field. Beyond some given cutoff of scores, however, factors other than objective scores become important. If an individual has enough general ability and enough in the way of specific aptitudes to be a salesman, or an engineer, other factors, such as *motivation,* become important to success. The same generalization may well hold true for success in college. Let us illustrate by giving the conclusions from an experiment conducted at Harvard University.

The Harvard survey, carried out by the Admissions and Scholarship Committee, shows that a freshman who scores just so-so (500 or a little better on college boards) *but rates high on certain other qualities* is apt to rate near the top of his class in college studies. These extra qualities include such factors as energy, drive, judgment, generosity of spirit, and "old-fashioned cussedness." Such a student is likely to rank just as high as the boy who was admitted to Harvard primarily because of a top entrance exam score of around 700 to 800. The two types of student share scholastic honors about equally.

Test scores are important, but so are other factors. The college dropout world has its share of "700 goof-offs."

EDUCATIONAL AND VOCATIONAL GUIDANCE

The growing-up process of all human beings involves some form or other of guidance. Counseling, which, for all practical purposes, may be thought of as a form of guidance, really deals with the *learning process.* It presupposes that one who comes for counseling knows certain facts. He may need professional help to assimilate them in his thinking or planning. He may also need help in learning to adjust to problems. Everyone, at times, needs someone else to talk to. This is of particular importance to the person facing something new. The "something new" may be the college environment, the world of work, or a creative idea looking for a sympathetic ear.

Educational counseling is often conducted by classroom teachers, but usually in an informal sort of way. More formally, educational counseling deals with problems of study skills, reading disabilities, and other academic difficulties. Closely related is *vocational counseling* or *guidance,* in which the attempt is made to identify the particular line of work for which the person is best suited.

DECISIONS IN GUIDANCE

"Chance will take care of it." Yes, that may be true, but what really is this thing called *chance?* Chance is a way of describing all those unknown factors in a situation. Chance does, of course, influence the lives of all of us. It was "by chance" that one man who was to become a great radio announcer received his start by dropping in to a studio for an audition during his lunch hour. Said he, "Suppose I had been walking down the other side of the street?" And many must be the instances of boy meeting girl "by chance." Chance, no doubt, will continue to affect each of us because there will always be unknown factors. But, as in football or bridge, chance seems to favor the person who is prepared. There are few, if any, automatic safety factors built into the decision-making process.

Vocational decisions are a continuing process, as we shall discuss in the following chapter. But here let us say that the background for making such decisions involves getting information through measurement of a person's interests and abilities.

MEASUREMENT IN GUIDANCE

As a person considers educational and vocational guidance, three questions are basic. First, the person asks, "Do I really know what I am interested in?" Second, "Do I have the aptitudes to be able to follow up these interests?" Third, "What progress have I made so far in reaching toward my goals?" These questions involve measures of interest, tests of ability, and determination of proficiency.

VOCATIONAL INTEREST TESTS

The oldest and most widely known measure of interests is the *Strong Vocational Interest Blank.* There is one form of this test for men and another for women.

The Strong test yields scores in each of about fifty occupations in the men's form and about thirty in the women's form. Each form of the test is an eight-page leaflet listing some four hundred items that cover activities, amusements, occupations, school subjects, self-estimates of abilities and characteristics, and the peculiarities of people. Although there is no time limit involved, the blank can be filled out in a little less than an hour.

Scores on the Strong test may be translated into "standard scores," "percentile rank," or quickly read letter ranks, as shown in Figure 11-4.

An A rating means that the individual taking the test has the interests characteristic of persons successfully engaged in the occupations specified. A rating of B makes a similar implication, but with less certainty. Not much interest is indicated by a rating of C. A person so rated should give very careful consideration to other factors before planning such an occupation. Any occupation in which the rating is an A or a B+ may be worth serious consideration. The shaded areas represent the expected range of "chance scores." This means in effect that neither agreement nor disagreement is indicated.

In Figure 11-4 we see the mean scores of a group of medical students on each of the several keys. Note the high score on the "physician key" and on the "dentist key." Note also the low scores on "carpenter" and "Y.M.C.A. Secretary."

The Strong test was invented by Dr. Edward K. Strong, Jr., and his graduate students at Carnegie Institute of Technology between 1921 and 1923. Its development continued at Stanford University. Today there are many hundreds of studies showing the value of the Strong test (and other interest tests, such as the Kuder test) for counseling purposes. Interest tests are helpful in confirming stated interests. They are of value also in calling attention to occupations which the individual may have overlooked. Such tests have their limitations; in particular it is important to determine whether the person has the ability to back up his or her interests.

OTHER TESTS

The modern-day college student is rather sophisticated about other tests. Said one student, "I have been tested since my first day in school."

In counseling, *intelligence tests* are commonly employed to determine the student's general level of ability. Special reference is given to scholastic aptitude. Sometimes when the student arrives for counseling he will find his test scores already on file. Tests are often given on entering college. This gives the counselor information not only on

Report on Vocational Interest Test for Men
(See other side for explanation)

Name .... Age .... Date .... Agency or school .... Case no .....

Group	Occupation	Raw Score	Standard Score	C (0)	5	10	15	20	25	B– (30)	B (35)	B+	A (40)	45	50	55	60
I	Artist		32							X							
	Psychologist (rev.)		29							X							
	Architect		33								X						
	Physician (rev.)		46											X			
	Psychiatrist		—														
	Osteopath		—														
	Dentist		41									X					
	Veterinarian		—														
II	Physicist		—														
	Chemist		38								X						
	Mathematician		28						X								
	Engineer		35							X							
III	Production Manager		31						X								
IV	Farmer		37								X						
	Carpenter		19				X										
	Printer		33						X								
	Math. Sci. Teacher		34							X							
	Policeman		29						X								
	Forest Service		24					X									
	Army Officer		—														
	Aviator		—														
V	Y.M.C.A. Phys. Dir.		29						X								
	Personnel Manager		24					X									
	Public Administrator		—														
	Vocational Counselor		—														
	Y.M.C.A. Secretary		18				X										
	Soc. Sci. Teacher		24					X									
	City School Supt.		21				X										
	Minister		21				X										
VI	Musician		34							X							
VII	C.P.A. Partner		—														
VIII	Senior C.P.A.		26						X								
	Junior Accountant		22					X									
	Office Worker		28						X								
	Purchasing Agent		26						X								
	Banker		23					X									
	Mortician		—														
	Pharmacist		—														
IX	Sales Manager		25						X								
	Real Estate Slsmn.		33								X						
	Life Insurance Slsmn.		28						X								
X	Advertising		32								X						
	Lawyer		36								X						
	Author–Journalist		36								X						
XI	President		30						X								
	Occupational Level																
	Masculinity – Femininity																
	Specialization Level																
	Interest Maturity																

FIG. 11-4   A report form of the Strong Vocational Interest Blank for Men. Written in are the scores of a group of medical students. Ratings are given as A, B+, B, B–, and C. (*Reproduced by permission of Stanford University Press.*)

how the individual stacks up on national norms, but also on where he stands with his classmates in ability.

Achievement tests are useful in supplementing intelligence tests. Particularly valuable are scores on reading and certain quantitative skills. Special *aptitude tests* may help provide some practical answers in counseling. A person may, for example, show considerable interest in music but not sufficient aptitude to become a professional. He may, therefore, "satisfy" his interest in music through listening or playing in the band, while pursuing a career in something else. And *personality tests* are sometimes important in counseling.

The batting average in vocational prediction using tests ranges widely. Prediction is best for those vocations which are not too complex, such as clerical jobs and those using mechanical skills. There is some, but less, success in picking people who will do well in sales or in leadership. The types of behavior involved here are most complex.

COUNSELING INTERVIEWS

In the college setting, counseling may involve talking problems over with family and friends, particularly with classmates. More or less formal counseling frequently begins in the educational setting with the instructor.

THE CLASSROOM TEACHER

Some of the most effective teaching (and counseling) may occur when a student comes to his instructor. "I don't think these objective tests really measure what I know." "I study harder for this course than any other, but I can't seem to get the hang of it." Such statements often mean: "I have a problem I want to talk over and you seem to be an understanding person."

Students often want to get to know their instructor better. Some students are really lonesome. Others have strong dependency needs. But in the main, students want to talk over problems, perhaps about their parents, or about not being accepted in the group, or they are looking for tips on study habits (see Chapter 5). If professional counseling services are available on the campus, the teacher usually encourages the student to make use of these facilities. The classroom teacher is a good person to recommend services.

THE FIRST INTERVIEW

Interestingly, there are some sex differences related to counseling. Female clients express more feeling in counseling than male clients, regardless of the sex of the counselor, but male clients do not differ in expression of feeling with male and female counselors. This is true whether the counseling is educational or vocational.

Studies also show that clients who prefer counselors for their warmth and friendliness tend to focus on discussion of personal problems in the first interview. Clients preferring logic and efficiency in their interview tend to focus on the practical job aspects of educational or vocational problems.

Clients prefer a counselor who shows *empathy* in the first interview. Such a counselor seems to put himself in the position of the client. Empathy literally means "feeling into." One person "feels himself into" the action or attitude of another. Watch the stands at a football game. As the home team rushes the line, the supporters of the home team also lean forward and push with it. At a track meet, persons viewing a high jump or pole vault will often lift one foot from the ground and strain with the athlete.

The professional counselor, of course, knows when and where to show empathy or to be hard-boiled. Rapport may start with empathy and then move more in the direction of objectivity.

THE DISCIPLINARY INTERVIEW

Both in the educational setting and in industry some counseling involves the sometimes unpleasant task of discipline. Discipline may or may not strain relations between the client and the counselor. Some of the most respected people on the campus are deans, and they often gain respect by invoking discipline. The same may be said for the executive who must discipline the subordinate.

The discipline interview offers one opportunity not always present in the more voluntary situation. When discussing the discipline the counselor has opportunity to note attitudes, emotions, habits, and other behavior patterns.

One of the big problems for the supervisor, as well as for the dean, is to be able deftly to play the different roles of disciplinarian and, at the same time, of friendly confidant. In a later chapter we shall talk about industrial counseling in relation to supervision and leadership (see page 349).

ATMOSPHERE OF THE INTERVIEW

Counseling on really personal problems must be conducted within an atmosphere of confidence. Only in exceptional cases, such as the case of a seriously maladjusted person, are confidences revealed.

The establishment and maintenance of *rapport* is essential. Three elements are involved: (1) the understanding attitude of the counselor, (2) the physical and psychological climate underlying the interview, and (3) the attitude of the client.

In most instances one wishes to establish a *permissive* counseling interview. Here the client is encouraged to speak out—and without fear of reprisal. This situation is helped when the counselor listens attentively without being critical (certainly at the beginning of the interview). He knows that some things do not make logical sense, that they are only felt emotionally.

Good listening is not only an art, it is a trying experience as well. To be able to sit through talk, and often illogical reasoning, takes patience.

The interview opens with ordinary courtesy—a friendly and courteous greeting by the counselor. "How can I *help* you?" may be a better opening than, "You are the young man the dean sent down here."

Phrasing questions is important. Questions that call for a yes or no answer tend to cut down the flow of conversation. "Maybe you would like to tell me why you came in?" or "Would you like to discuss your problem?" are questions which encourage expression. Any impression of cross-examination from the counselor inhibits, or at least delays, the process of getting problems out in the open.

Many clients have difficulty in verbalizing their problems. Even people with high verbal skill hit roadblocks in expressing emotional problems. The counselor must avoid putting words into the client's mouth. The *nondirective* approach of, "I see," or, "I understand," can help the client come to point after point. Even "Yes" may serve to bridge the conversational gap or keep the client talking so that the counselor can pick up *nonverbal cues.*

Silence in the interview is to be expected. This is particularly true after the frustrations have been expressed and the client begins to think. Such silences seem to the client (and to the inexperienced listener) to be endless. Actually they are short. They may be broken by such remarks as, "Tell me more."

Experienced counselors know the importance of keeping their *vocabulary understandable.* The old pro knows the advantages of keeping the *number of ideas* per interview to a minimum. "Telling all" sometimes is just that and is very time-consuming. And the counselor is also adept at telling the difference between the sympathy seeker and the person with a specific problem. It should be remembered that he too has had an occasional ache in the back of his throat.

How to end an interview is important. Said one counselor: "I keep the clock in full view. Many clients have the tendency to just talk and talk as though time is free. Seeing how time is passing brings them more quickly to the problem." Quite often the counselor must be the one to bring the interview to a close: "Do you think we have done all we can for today?" "Is there *one* more thing we should discuss before we close?"

USEFUL GENERALIZATIONS ABOUT COUNSELING

Experienced counselors bring into summary several generalizations about counseling. Let us present them here to pull together some of the things we have implied before. We hope that in addition to providing general information, they may be helpful to the reader when next he goes for counseling.

1 *The problem volunteered by the client may be only a small part of the actual problem.* Complete frankness in the beginning of an interview is often embarrassing. The employee who asks for a transfer has to give reasons, and these may be embarrassing, even threatening. The same is true of the student who may be having difficulty with a teacher or even with "the system." Sometimes the counselor can sense the client's unvoiced questions and discuss them without becoming too specific. He knows when the client has paid his obligations to the system and he is ready to move on to his real problem.

2 *Personalities of client and counselor sometimes clash.* Most counselors ask themselves, "What does this person think of me as a counselor?" With time, conflict may be resolved. Where there is more than one counselor available, a switch may be the best way out.

3 *Much is conveyed by nonverbal behavior.* The professional soon learns to read signs. "What you fail to say tells me much." "Your facial expressions give me cues." These thoughts help to guide the counseling interview.

4 *Recurring ideas and statements are important.* One counselor added up the times that one company was mentioned in an interview about job selection. Company ABC was mentioned more than twice all others combined. Was this favorable or unfavorable? At least it had the potentials of a cue to be followed.

5 *Measuring instruments often are not called for.* Often clients come in and "want to take a test." The trained counselor knows when and when not to use measurement and diagnostic devices. After

all, testing is expensive and often unnecessary. And when tests are given they need to be interpreted.

6 *Some clients take their aggression out on the counselor.* The old pro can soon sense this and does not become disturbed.

7 *Some clients get helped without knowing it.* One counselor tells of a client who came in three times and was handled in a completely nondirective manner. He later told the dean that he didn't get any advice so he stopped going to the counseling center. "Did you get your problem solved?" asked the dean. "Yes, but I did it myself—the counselor never did anything but puff on his pipe and say occasionally, 'I understand,' or ask, 'What do you think?' "

8 *The good counselor gets the client to see his strong points.* "He comes in with his weaknesses," is the way one guidance person put it, "but in time he begins to concentrate on what he *can* do rather than what he can't do."

9 *Whatever the action planned, the client should feel it is "his" plan.* One of the difficult jobs the counselor has is getting reinforcement himself. He knows the man must feel that *he* solved the problem himself. Little wonder counselors sometimes become discouraged. If the counseling is effective, an emotional relationship may develop. The counselor must avoid giving the impression that he has gained some special advantage over the client.

10 *The professional counselor has no formulas.* Even the most sophisticated of us want a magic remedy for our problems. The counselor must make it clear that he can provide an appropriate climate for thinking but that only *the client* can solve his own problem. The guidance counselor has the particularly difficult task of helping the client to see that goals are reached step by step, not in one massive leap. A beginning is made when the client first realizes that there is no script to solve his problems, that counseling involves more than just trying to find a psychological waterhole.

SOME PRECOUNSELING THINKING

It is probably reasonable to assume that the reader will from time to time find himself *as a client* in a counseling session. Let us here give some working statements about human behavior that may help the reader think about a background for at least some of the problems he may encounter. Here we are making suggestions relative to personal problems. In the following chapter we shall be talking about the thinking one should do in preparation for vocational counseling.

1 *Know what you "bring in" to the situation.* How an individual responds to a counseling situation (or any other situation) depends

on what he *brings in* to it. This includes at least a vague knowledge of his abilities, attitudes, skills, habits, and specific problems. Of course, one of the reasons for seeking counseling in the first place is to find out about such things. But even thinking about these things provides a start.

2 *Know how someone else besides you may perceive your problems.* This may be possible only if you know your counselor well, but at least you can make some guesses about how he will look at things. In any human relationship, particularly in a problem-solving situation, one must consider the interrelationships between the parties involved. The old expression is apt here: "Consider the other fellow's angle."

3 *Find out something about the background of the counselor.* The experienced counselor is usually a person of considerable experience and wisdom: "The counselor has been there before." Just as we suggested above that you be aware of your background, it is helpful to know what the counselor "brings in" to the situation.

4 *Learn the early signs of a problem.* When an individual fails to make a suitable adjustment to a situation he becomes stirred up, disorganized, and confused. Each person has characteristic ways of showing emotional upset. The ways are often recognizable in the beginning stages. What are the typical ways in which *you* react?

5 *Be able to recognize the behavior sequences when frustration leads to aggression.* Emotional upsets vary in degree, but they all involve a build-up in tensions. The individual seeks release from these tensions by doing something. What he does may be beneficial to himself or harmful. It is helpful to know what to expect in your own behavior when you are stimulated emotionally.

6 *Accentuate the positive as well as the negative.* If everything goes well there is no need to seek counseling on emotional problems. However, since much counseling involves problems that are not disturbing, one should pay some attention to planning ahead. It is wise to review our accomplishments. Too often we think of counseling only in negative terms; we think of going for guidance only when we have a problem. Guidance often is understood best when it is free of emotional content.

7 *Be aware that stimulation without effective outlet induces tension.* When we are stimulated and have built up effective habits to deal with the stimulation, little or no tension results. On the other hand, stimulation which does not operate within the patterns of the individual's habit structures induces excessive emotion and conflict. Knowing how we let off steam or bottle up our troubles is important.

8   *Know what your dominant wants are.* Some people find it helpful to list their needs and wants and put them in a one-two-three order. Failure to understand need satisfaction can lead to defensive behavior, as discussed in Chapter 2.

9   *Recognize the relations between your "level of aspiration" and your "level of ability."* When these levels are separated too far we encounter difficulty. If the difference is in the direction of too much ambition in some area for our particular aptitude, then feelings of inferiority are generated. If, on the other hand, we have far more ability to do something than we have the desire to do it, we may be establishing lazy habits.

10   *Expect occasional failure.* What we are saying in effect is that if you have never been thrown from a horse you haven't ridden enough—at least you haven't tried enough spirited horses. The person who tries, inevitably fails in some things.

11   *Know something about your creative experiences.* The thrill of discovery is stimulating. And the reverse is true. When we no longer discover something new now and then, we are getting away from seeking things to create.

12   *Understand the nature of problem solving.* One of the main reasons in going for counseling is to practice problem solving under guidance. It takes a long time to learn how to solve problems. Trying to understand what we are doing when we work on a problem is helpful. Later we discuss an outline helpful in this respect (see page 362).

GUIDELINES RELATING PEOPLE AND JOBS

Vocational guidance demands that we not be naive about people and about jobs. From experience and from many researches, helpful generalizations are available to us for consideration in vocational guidance.

Below are ten generalizations the reader may find useful for his thinking in preparing for vocational guidance. These generalizations help form a base for considering such questions as: What kind of job do I want? What kind of job can I do? Where do I find this job? How do I get this job? How do I move ahead on this job? We are going to devote the next chapter to such questions, but before facing them, guidance may well be in order. Think through on the ten generalizations below.

1   *People differ; they differ in abilities, interests, personality, and ambition.* Where do I stand concerning each of these? Here one begins to analyze himself as an individual—a first step in answering the question, "Who am I?"

2 *Organizations differ; they differ in the opportunities they provide for taking care of individual differences.* Some people are better suited to a military organization than to business. Such a person may find the Army just right for him. Someone else may get along better working in industry. The person who likes show business may find working in a bank less stimulating although it may offer more job security.

3 *Companies, even local plants or offices, differ in their psychological climates.* A climate that may provide stimulation and satisfaction for the aggressive sort of person may arouse fear in someone else. It is important for the individual to ask of himself, "What kind of climate is most suitable for *me?*"

4 *Selection of the career job cannot readily be undone.* True, a person can usually change his job. But he is a different person by virtue of his previous job experience. When we invest time, money, and *ego* in a career it produces changes in us. These changes may, of course, be for better or for worse. That first full-time job after leaving school should be chosen most carefully.

5 *The perfect job does not exist.* Somewhere compromise has to be made between abilities, interests, values, and opportunities. The person who starts out to look for everything in a job is unrealistic.

6 *Each person has the potential for success in a large number of different occupations.* This generalization, on first thought, makes us feel that career planning is easy. True, many potentials provide for more alternatives in choice. But at the same time they produce more possibilities for conflict in making job choices.

7 *Childhood and adolescent experiences play some role in the interests we develop.* To be sure the fantasy stage of childhood and the dreamy stage of adolescence are unrealistic in many ways; nevertheless, here is where some interests begin, provided that the required abilities and opportunities are present.

8 *Possibilities for job changes will always face most of us.* The person who is "on the way up" will face changing jobs more often than the indifferent person. He should study the decision-making process—study the "whys" of failure and of success. Such experience gives guides for the future.

9 *Work is a way of life.* When we are busy, when we are tired, it is not uncommon to have thoughts of the pleasures of retirement. "I would stop work if I had enough money to live on." This thought also neglects to bring into consideration what we know about boredom. To be sure some people could be satisfied just sitting and rocking—even having an automatic rocker. But for

most people satisfaction comes through activity. Ask the man who has been out of a job for some time. Ask the energetic man who was forced into retirement. The most effective personal adjustment comes when the nature of the work itself and the way of life that goes with it—community, home, leisure-time activities, friends—are congenial to the aptitudes, interests, and values of the person in question.

10 *No job provides for complete satisfaction. No person completely fits the job.* The interaction of the individual and his environment is very complicated. Vocational guidance is helpful in providing us with opportunity to come to realize this generalization. It may cushion some of the blows.

VOCATIONAL SELECTION— A TWO-WAY STREET

Each person *selects*. We select our friends and the activities in which we engage. Each individual also *is selected*. We are selected for the band, the football team, and the dance committee. Selection lasts along the route from childhood to old age. It is a *continuing process*. At one time we are in the role of selectee and at another time we are in the role of selector.

Selection may be made with thought and preparation, or it may be made in a haphazard sort of way. As far as getting a job is concerned, most people make selections by a method somewhere between worry and luck. On the other hand, jobs may be selected with guidance or planning.

THE RECRUITMENT OF EMPLOYEES

There are several ways of getting a job. At the worker level, getting a job is largely in the hands of someone else. A union-member friend may recommend a job, or it may come from a visit to one of some four thousand employment offices in the United States. Here measurements of ability and interests may or may not be made. Supply and demand largely determine the placement of unskilled and semi-skilled workers. Above this level the job applicant is more on his own both in making decisions and in getting vocational guidance.

At the levels of technical skills in prosperous times employees are sought after by recruitment in the schools. The visit of the personnel recruiter to the campus has taken on the aspects of selling as much as of selection.

For the person who plans a career with care, getting a job is more involved. Recent researches emphasize that upward mobility depends not only on aspiration, not only on opportunity, but also on long-range planning. Many people do not get, or perceive, the chances of mobility. Most recruitment is for *the now* for the most part. There are exceptions, of course. In some managerial and professional recruiting, people are chosen with development in mind. Many people at these levels have confidence that they can get ahead through their own efforts anyway.

Workers often feel that pull and luck are necessary for advancement. Few have aspirations beyond the level of foreman. In contrast, for the person who wants to move up, getting ahead is a part of the game. It is a game in which education and guidance, formal or otherwise, are essential for the understanding of alternatives in aspiration. It is a game in which the requirements for career survival are planned. Sometimes the aggressive person fails to consider the psychological as well as the physical costs involved in moving ahead.

THE NEW EMPHASIS

Education is being upgraded. As technology has grown, specialization has become commonplace. Technical school graduates are sought after, and so are new Ph.D.'s in science and engineering. The man in sales or in management may be welcomed with open arms. But how long will this attention last? For the few, of course, it may become a way of life. For the many, however, technological and professional obsolescence comes fast. In a technological world rocking with change, vocational guidance attempts to project beyond the reef of security. And for some people there is need for help. Some are pillars of tranquillity while others collapse in jungles of neurosis. Some people are locked in by never having had an opportunity.

COMMUNITY COUNSELING AND GUIDANCE

Counseling and guidance are extending beyond the office, the school, and at work. They are extending into the community. Let us illustrate how one such program began by reproducing portions of a diary written by Pat Fulton,[1] a young man who was trying to find himself through helping others. This is a new type of counseling which bids fair to develop rapidly.

[1] This diary is reproduced here by the permission of Pat Fulton and the *Carnegie Review*.

Pat is a 21-year-old Yale dropout who recently finished a year of service in VISTA—Volunteers in Service to America, sometimes called the Domestic Peace Corps. VISTA is one of the major anti-poverty programs established by the Economic Opportunity Act of 1964. Pat was among the first group of volunteers.

VISTA is surely one of the most flexible programs ever devised by the Federal government. VISTAs (as the volunteers call themselves) simply go where they are needed and do what needs to be done. Which means that they work in cities, on farms, among migrant workers, on Indian reservations. But mostly in cities, because that's where most of America's poor people live. Pat was one of 15 VISTAs assigned to Pittsburgh's eight "poverty neighborhoods," under the Mayor's Committee on Human Resources, Inc., the administrative agency for Pittsburgh's war on poverty.

Probably no one, including Pat himself, knows precisely what he expected to achieve through VISTA. He does acknowledge having had at least two rather generalized hopes: that he would be able to reinforce his own self-respect and that of the people with whom he worked; and that he would be able to interpret the outside world to them while they interpreted theirs to him. These hopes and much more show up in the pages of a journal which he kept for a time during the summer, excerpts from which appear below.

Excerpts from a Diary

June 7. First day back from the conference and although with nothing really fresh in mind the things already there have freshened.

Morris was glad to see his pictures. Lenny and Holmes dropped by and thought the slide-viewer was hep. They talked over their recent kills in the local stores, but it seems the one they have staked out at the moment is too brightly-lit to take on. I didn't say anything.

Morris knows all about it and even appears to be in on it, in an advisory capacity. He also mentioned something about "setting them straight." I think he might be pushing pills, the boys being clientele, and they had dropped by to see what they could get. But by being there I threw a monkey wrench in whatever transaction might have taken place.

So later on I brought up William. Morris said virtually every teen-ager and man he knew has at one time or another to one degree or another, been high on narcotics. He tried to impress me with how easy it is to get stuff around here and with what a big business it is. He likes to say things like that because he wants me to know what a terrible situation he lives in, as a sort of self-justification, and also because he simply likes to be the person able to introduce me to things, my leader in other words. Then we talked of how narcotics wreck lives, specifically William's, and more generally Lenny's, Bruce's, Holmes'; and the rest in a hypothetical way. Holmes is the biggest little pusher around. Morris explained what a junk high was like.

Lenny is the clan leader, says Morris, because he is smart. That's true because he's always the one to jive me about not smoking pot with them. He has a very probing way of teasing. He experiments with people. Yet Morris said he would be depressed if I ever said yes, because though he would win a personality battle he would lose his respect for me.

Lenny asked about Neighborhood Youth Corps. I asked if this wasn't an indication that they really wanted something more than what they go after. Morris said yes, "But you'll never know what. They never talk about it." They would lose their position in the group. They find their only security there, and to admit to desires the communal attitudes preclude would be to lose importance and consequently identity, self-respect. But Morris said that basically they want to work and that they would.

Thomas dropped in. He and Morris were very impressed with Rosemary's situation, especially since she's pretty. Long talk about the South and Negroes.

Morris will go to Pitt Hospital.

I'd better soft-pedal Thomas. I hurt him the other day, I think, at the gas station, when he asked me about finding him a job. I told him he'd get a job as soon as he got himself in shape for one, and that at present he's not in shape. But that's not what Thomas needs. It's this fact he hates to face, just because everyone tells him this and he hates to have everyone tell him what is right for him. He surrenders his own individuality the day he takes their advice, and his mother allows him precious little freedom now. Thomas has aligned himself against the world and himself and he's sad to watch, because the wounds lie visibly close to the surface.

Tuesday, June 8. Among other things I went by to see Lois and Marcus. Actually I just wanted to get down to Rosedale Street again. Lois is still scared to come down to the office. She seems to be in a very flighty, undirected state of mind generally, which is symptomatic of lots. Worrying about jobs and the Employment Center acts as another confusing element, and one from which she retreats. But while she wishes the intrusion just didn't exist, her mother wishes to keep it out of the house.

I bother her. She's recovering from a nervous breakdown and only has a couple of days off per week, presumably Monday and Tuesday. She says Lois can't work and take care of her seven-month-old baby simultaneously; maybe when it gets older. . . . (She made that concession later, after she stopped being angry and tried to make me feel sorry for her. Which I did, in a cheerful way.) She said perhaps Lois could just come down for a while to register; she'll think it over. I'll go back in a week, Tuesday, to hold her to it. I think she likes me now. Lois' big concern at the time was her boy friend.

Marcus came down to the office to complete his Job Corps processing, which, as it turned out, meant starting from the beginning. He was embarrassed for forgetting to come a couple of weeks ago but we got along pretty well. How to get these guys to think the other world is relevant to them? And in a friendly way. We filled out a 511 together, me doing the spelling and he the writing. That must be a funny-looking 511, with all the hard words spelled correctly and the easy ones spelled wrong. When Marcus gets nervous he smiles a lot. Talking about his record became the funniest thing in the world. But he talks, anyway. We saw Howie Lear and a friend on the way down. Howie asked when the hell the Job Corps was going to accept him and I tried to explain D.C. to him. As usual I was a little short on answers. On our way down Marcus said most of the boys wanted out of Homewood-Brushton. He wants it very much, not to mention that he needs it just as much.

Morris said he would follow Reverend Roberts to the ends of the earth, because Reverend holds that violence must of necessity be a part of the over-all approach towards the victory of civil rights groups. Not always, but sometimes. Frustrated people identify very readily with violence. Morris wouldn't follow Martin Luther King to a church supper unless the menu was exceptional. Of course he hasn't met Martin Luther King yet, either.

We're going to go down and picket tomorrow.

Deenie's going to Homemaker's class. She seems eager. She likes Hawaii, but Morris implied it was boring. But he said he'd go to Pittsburgh Hospital so there's some enthusiasm still. I wonder if that's been weakened in favor of truck-driving. In fact, I wonder if and when he gets a job, he'll be able to fasten all his hopes on that one thing for a long time, or if his mind will turn to other dreams instead? Nothing is real to him, except dreams; will reality prove satisfying enough to absorb him?

Wednesday, June 9. Slow turgid morning at Morris' house. We were going to go downtown to picket but he got up too late and we never mobilized.

Played pool with Lenny, Howie, and someone else that afternoon. I beat Lenny two out of three and he was madder than hell. But that's good for him. Howie wanted to take me on, beat me badly three times in a row, and walked out without saying a word. Nothing could have made him happier than to beat me, and he showed it. That was bad. I'll have to practice. Then some other dude beat me twice in a row. Boy was he dumb. No reaction to each other except that he would have been nervous to talk to me, so he didn't talk. So much for pool. (Lenny spotted me as I was walking down Rosedale Street for no reason other than to be spotted. That in itself was a sort of victory, but how much I made of it is in considerable doubt.)

Homemakers' class—8 P.M. Deenie—and Joyce, which surprised me. I think she got sucked into it by circumstance, because she had been planning to get bombed. She probably wishes she had.

I decided to adopt a new personality last night. I've been getting too "nice" lately, which means everyone smiles and goes about their business when I leave. I'll play it low-key, laconic, with even an implication of menace. Marlon. Facade. OK.

Got along well with the kids last night. Felt self-conscious in front of the brass, but it was fun anyway until the relationships took on sexual overtones, at which point it became tricky.

Forge your self-respect in reality's fire.

Thursday, June 10. Nothing during the day, just incidental phone-calls. Mrs. Hines blew the whistle on the bar across the street after she heard that William had gone there, presumably for some junk. She's bothered deeply by his new attitude towards her, or rather what this new facet of it shows it has always been. I think she reacted emotionally when she made the big call.

Very interesting talk with Phyllis on the way back from the Loendi. She painted the middle-class Negroes' situation in vivid emotional hues. First of all, they resent the point of view which says that because they're Negro they should one-and-all involve themselves in the poverty/discrimination problem-complex. But, seeing as black skin feels no differently from white, they instinctively think of themselves as people first, man or woman second, job-holders third, Christians (maybe) fourth, and so on. Their skin they want to be incidental, they are neither ashamed nor proud of it, and they wish people would treat them accordingly. Second, the majority have come from the slums fighting for this right, and though they've gained some measure of financial and cultural success (by no means commensurate with the effort put out, however), they haven't yet gained universal regard as potentially dignified individuals. They haven't won as much as house and car would indicate, and they really aren't in such swell positions, emotionally. And thirdly, the wounds of the fight are so fresh, and keep on coming, in fact, that to re-involve themselves hurts a lot. That's exactly what they've suffered so much to overcome. It was a very worthwhile talk.

Saturday and Sunday: Days when my better half over-came nothing. Mrs. Palmer's, pool practice, great food, sore throat.

Monday, June 14. Too much exposure to one person or group is bad, because Morris was lots gladder to see him, which makes me more bearable and relationships easier. He asked me where the hell I had been keeping myself; also about Pitt Hospital, i.e., any news down at the Employment Center (no). I told him to call them up, which presumably he will do.

Went to William's to see what new has developed in his narcotics bout with the law. His mother said he (she) couldn't raise bond after the hearing, and that he presently resides in the City-County Building, guest of the municipality. She was very surprised to learn that Mrs. Hines had known all along, and recognized immediately why she couldn't go to court for him. She also made an interesting comment to the effect that had she known her son took junk, the affair might have had an altogether different outcome. So maybe Mrs. Hines should have told her.

I went back to Morris' later, just in time to catch some exciting events. It seems this girl had been kicked out of school a week ago, and had been so badly beaten by her father that she left home, too. She had just come to Morris' ten minutes before I showed, and as I was standing on the stoop her sister, a friend, and her sister's boy friend staged a raid. The girl wouldn't come down at first out of pure fear, for which we can't blame her because she was due for a beating on arrival, and would have gotten it right there if boy friend hadn't stepped in. Since the Missing Persons Bureau had been called, the girl's in for a long round of questions and examinations, and Morris and Deenie maybe for some trouble. For the first time I saw Morris come down with a nerve attack, and it was genuine. So was his high. He acted self-conscious about taking his pills in front of me, and was very sensitive to any comment I made about them. He was not getting high, he was getting relief. Both he and Deenie seemed pretty shaken-up.

June 15, Tuesday. Terrible day at the office, being bodyguard. Friend never showed up; presumably he couldn't split before his mother got a hold on him, but he probably never looked on Job Corps as a turning-point in his life anyway, and so feels no driving urge to hotfoot it down and confront the preliminary unpleasantries with vigor. Job Corps, to the poor—short-sighted, apathetic, basically living outside of reality as they are—must be nothing more than a pipe-dream extension of an occasionally-looming, usually-submerged-enough-not-to-count discontent with the lack of new things to do around here. But then no one around here really likes it with a deep-seated contentment, and often the deep-seated discontent surfaces enough to prompt dreams of going far, far away for a life of milk and honey. Job Corps, at least, will take them far, far away, and so the dream gathers around it. However, they want the dream, not Job Corps, and the Employment Center definitely doesn't fit into the dream. Neither does what the Job Corps really is. That's the big hang-up. Escapism presupposes no recognition of reality, but the Job Corps to them embodies the same frustrating reality they spend their lives avoiding, striking out at, escaping. Even if they see the Job Corps as the great turning point, they aren't strong enough and/or eager enough to want it. The very idea, after it sinks in, unsettles the only security, identity, they've managed to develop. Perverted romanticism.

Morris and I went to the big meeting. He was scared at first, a little anyway, but even so it seemed to generate, or uplift, what was already there, a new type of interest. He didn't want to go in to the meeting room while we were waiting. But we sat in the Y lobby talking about art, of all things, and he brought it up. He really made an effort to acclimatize himself to the "lofty" nature of the proceedings; whether to prove himself to himself, himself to me, or himself to himself through my reactions to him, I don't know. But he made the effort, instead of capitulating to the pressure, sustained it, and walked out I think a happier, more secure person, satisfied with himself. Beyond seeing a glimmer of his personal potential within the system, he even feels a desire to realize it. He wants to join the Health committee and says he'll talk to Mr. Bray tomorrow. I hope he does, and I hope Mr. Bray can give him a little extra consideration. He might never go, though. How much to burn to keep aspirations warm does he have? And then, things burn better out of the wind.

He went on to chart a new career for himself. Since medicine is beyond reach (recognized at last), chemical engineering has become it. (Only as a replacement. But in his eyes the replacement is a step down the ladder, so maybe that's an improvement.) I tried to present reality in a noncritical but convincing way. No effect. The average college board is (I said) 550, which puts him 150 points or so in arrears. That drew a reaction, although it submerged immediately. In general the meeting had a positive effect on him. He needed it all the more because Deenie has already been involved in Homemaking and he feels a bit like things have gone beyond his control, even in his own household, which is about the last bastion of his self-respect at the moment. He said the meeting was interesting, that he'd like to go again.

Wednesday. Bodyguard again.

Thursday. Took a look for a couple of guys "interested," according to Gladys, in Job Corps, neither of whom was home. Went around to Lois to see if she wanted the stroller Marcella is offering, but also to soften my image of someone who presents embarrassing problems. We did get around to discussing what Lois could do. The doctor (she spent six months in the bin) said Lois had to take care of the kid, so work seems to be out for the time being. There's no sense in having Lois come down as a statistic. It'll be hard including that family in anything. But Lois wants the stroller, anyway.

Morris and Deenie were glad to get the picture of Doodlebug. They want an enlargement. Morris' enthusiasm for the Health committee and the Homewood-Brushton Citizens' Renewal Council had waned considerably. Poverty makes hopes so transitory, a ten-minute fling with the imagination.

The quiet times around here are the deadly ones because they offer no relief or outlet for frustrations. Thursday was a very quiet afternoon until some guy took his big Doberman for a walk. They ran into three dogs at the corner of Kelly and Brushton, two small ones, loose, and a medium-sized, stocky, mustard-yellow one on a chain held by two kids. The small ones were incidental, but you could see the savage antagonism building between the Doberman and the yellow. It seemed as if after the encounter neither could accept living in the same world with the other. The four dogs raised a terrible din, barking, snapping, growling, and occasionally, when one of the little ones strayed too close to the Doberman, yelping. In the middle were the two big dogs, the two kids, and the dude. Things were at a stalemate. A crowd gathered quickly, screaming for blood. An older guy stepped in to relieve the two kids of mustard, and the crowd's pleas seemed to get to him. He stood there stupidly, not daring to hope that his dog could take the Doberman, yet not daring to back out in front of all the people. After a while he weakened and let mustard loose. The other guy continued to hold the Doberman, which was up on two legs straining against its chain. A mighty cheer went up, until the flashing tangle cleared and the Doberman emerged on top with the bleeding mustard's throat between his grinding jaws. Then it was all over and hush settled over the crowd.

Moralists would like to say that shame caused it, and to a limited extent it did. But mostly the hush came from the un-self-conscious consummation of a savage urge in the men, born and bred out of the hatred and frustration that is their whole way of life. Here was something they identified with; something very basic in their own natures that a quiet afternoon lets bubble to the surface. In a perverse way the fight washed their souls. The same thing could have happened, essentially, anywhere else, except people would be ashamed to show others their self-indulgence. (It is very important to bring out that the women reacted exactly the opposite from the men. Even in this area females seem to be more at peace with themselves and their lot.)

The night before the Education committee meeting, Monday, June 21, I had given Morris a qualified admission of difficulty in effectively spreading the Job Corps gospel. We agreed pretty much that these guys didn't want to admit to anybody that they'd lost out even before beginning, especially to me in view of my obviously different background. And yet I didn't see any other means of starting towards building any abiding motivation. Morris said to hell with that, in effect; that they'd never accept it from me anyway, and that a strong, glib, in-the-best-American-tradition sales pitch was necessary. But I can't feed anybody a very palatable line about anything, and I said as much, which gratified him greatly, which in turn burned me considerably. Never mind, never mind, he said; he'd recruit for me. I said good, and we made arrangements to start him off on his new career.

The next night, after the meeting, I brought down a folder full of OEO Job-Corps fodder, so that Morris could become as thoroughly acquainted with the setup as anyone involved in it. Which is possible inside of ten minutes; it's realizing how much you don't know about it that takes time. One thing led to another, and I reiterated my basic theory that unless you get the eligibles deeply interested in what the Job Corps really is, the program will fail in the end, if it is lucky enough to last till the end. Of course, a certain amount of motivation can take seed and grow while the kid lives at the camp, making a bit of a sales line—misrepresenting the Job Corps in a better light—permissible. But taking Headstart as an analogy, unless the boy is prepared to accept authority and consequent discipline, and to recognize them as ingredients necessary to the long-run goal of remaking him into a person with a better chance, if not a better person, he will react to them in an unconstructive way, belligerently, the way he always has. (Taking Headstart as another analogy, maybe the Job Corps should display a more enlightened attitude toward the products of prolonged and ingrained poverty. But that would make this a different essay.)

Warming to the subject, I expanded to the whole question of escapism in Homewood-Brushton, and elsewhere, from the middle class down to the depths. Morris had made a fascinating comment about a board meeting of some weeks back, saying that the members seemed more interested in protecting personal dignity and status than in taking on the area's problems. He spoke out of a feeling of economic difference, a feeling of sociological alienation, a feeling of social embarrassment and extraordinary perception. I asked if he thought that these were people on the run from their backgrounds and he said yes, and as a representative of their background he could never bring himself to accept them. I asked if he could really blame them, as who is strong enough to completely overcome himself, pointing out the other ways of running from reality that are common in his background: dope, liquor, sex (or bragging about it), music, clothes, impossible dreams. Not at all a fair question to put, and probably quite unwise, but a valid one. Yes, he said, implicitly, BUT—and that's the BUT the Renewal Council will have to answer.

We got on to the question of how to relate to the poor, and ultimately of how to interest and involve them. Morris said that more needed to be known about the Renewal Council, especially about its potential for them. This calls for a very persuasive selling job, but one that must sell honest, concrete potential. The poor must have what amounts to a religious faith in the Renewal Council, otherwise they won't even flirt with the idea of themselves as participants. There undoubtedly are individuals much easier to involve than this, however, who must be found and culled out. In any event it calls for more and deeper personal contact.

Morris said that people didn't trust me. They didn't know if I really wanted to help or if I was secretly laughing at them. He implied that I am too reserved to convince them of what I'm here for, which is probably true to a certain extent. But it's just as true that they're scared of trusting anyone, and that will take time.

Then, for the first time, we talked of how he would be received in my world. In effect, he felt that while people would be glad enough to meet him, and might try (a little hypocritically) to be friendly (which he doesn't want), they wouldn't go out of their way to introduce him to their friends. In other words, they wouldn't want to put their position in their group on the line by introducing and backing up someone who clearly doesn't fit, on the terms around which the group has coalesced—people not being that secure. He's right, in general, but there are a few socially-brave individuals. We parted with visions of Morris sipping champagne at a deb party dancing in our heads.

The bubble burst when I got robbed. But they didn't get anything. Three guys, one with a knife, in front of Mrs. Hines' house, 2 A.M. I was scared, but also exhilarated, like I'd been initiated.

Summary

The thinking college student early faces four questions of self-identity: Who am I? Where am I going? What will be the costs in getting there? "What" questions should I learn to ask "when"?

A national inventory of aptitudes and abilities of 440,000 high school students gave emphasis to the increasing need for counseling and guidance. This survey covered problems of talents and career plans, college decisions, and measurements. As a person considers educational and vocational guidance, three questions are basic: Do I really know what I am interested in? Do I have the aptitudes to be able to follow up these interests? What progress have I made so far in reaching toward my goals?

Experienced counselors bring into summary several generalizations that the student should be aware of even before going for counseling. These cover points of counselor-client relations, detailing how the client really learns to solve his own problems in a permissive atmosphere. Some dozen working statements are presented, designed to aid precounseling thinking.

For vocational guidance ten guidelines relating people and jobs are given. They are presented as a base for considering such questions as: What kind of job do I want? What kind of job can I do? Where do I find this job? How do I get this job? How do I move ahead on this job?

Vocational selection is a two-way street. Each person selects. Each person is selected. Selection is a continuing process along the route from childhood to old age. At one time we are in the role of selected and at another time we are in the role of selector.

Selection may be made with thought and preparation, or it may be made in a haphazard sort of way. As far as getting a job is concerned, most people make selections by a process somewhere between worry and luck. Others make selections with guidance or planning. Education is being upgraded. For the many, technological and professional obsolescence comes fast. In a technological world rocking with change, vocational guidance attempts to project the new.

Counseling and guidance are extending beyond the school and the conventional world of work. For the culturally deprived they are emphasizing a new world of problems.

Suggestions for Thinking and Discussion

1 This chapter began with four basic questions. (Who am I? Where am I going? What will be the costs in getting there? What questions should I learn to ask when?) Write out some short-sentence answers to each. What difficulties did you encounter in attempting these answers?

2 Assume that someone comes to you with a problem. As a good listener (and counselor) what do you do? Why?

3　Write out in outline form what you would bring in to a counseling situation that would be of value to the counselor.

4　What is meant by selection as a two-way street?

5　Describe a counseling interview which you would label as good.

6　What factors help determine the atmosphere of a good interview?

Suggestions for Further Reading

Bordin, E. S. *Psychological counseling.* New York: Appleton-Century-Crofts, 1955. Counseling techniques with minor personal problems.

Lyman, H. B. *Test scores and what they mean.* Englewood Cliffs, N.J.: Prentice-Hall, 1963. A practical book about testing.

McKinney, F. *Understanding personality: Cases in counseling.* Boston: Houghton Mifflin, 1965. Twenty college-student cases, some followed up for several years.

McLaughlin, K. F. *Interpretation of test results.* Washington: Government Printing Office, 1964. A 63-page bulletin which explains the use and limitations of tests for counseling and guidance of students.

Rogers, C. R. *On becoming a person.* Boston: Houghton Mifflin, 1961. An overall picture of normal persons faced with the identity question of "Who am I?"

CHAPTER 12

Making Career Decisions

❖❖❖❖❖❖❖❖❖❖

"Job hunting should never be hit or miss. Such a method produces nothing but weariness, discouragement, and loss of self-confidence. It is a sales campaign and it requires careful planning and intelligent development. Most people do their poorest job of selling with the most important product they will ever have to sell—themselves." These are the words of a successful personnel man. And a psychologist adds these words: "Decision making is one of the most involved processes which engages the human. It sets him in a position out in front of animals."

DECISION MAKING

It is estimated that because of rapidly advancing technology each person now twenty years of age may have as many as six careers during his lifetime. Yes, we mean careers, not just jobs. This means, for all practical purposes, that the individual who learns to make decisions appropriately early in life will have advantages over the person who moves along deciding matters by trial and error. The Federal government estimates that 50 percent of the jobs to be held in 1975 do not even exist today. More than ever, the student of today must be future-oriented. This may be helpful in keeping him from becoming emotionally unhinged in facing questions which have no built-in answers.

We all recognize that decisions cause problems as well as solve them. Getting ready to make a decision is in reality a part of the process of making a decision. It must also be recognized that the human being has limits in his ability to process information in decision making. He must also evaluate the source of his information.

INFORMATION, ATTITUDES, AND THE SLEEPER EFFECT

What is the source of the information? Can I believe it? These are questions we have to face in making many decisions. They are particularly important when the decision making involves career planning. Let us look at a study of the "sleeper effect" in getting and changing attitudes and then return to the two questions above.

Communication has most influence when the information appears to be true and complete, and when it is transmitted by a source of high credibility. Two psychologists presented college students with information about selling drugs, the future of movie theaters, and similar questions of public interest. Each communication was presented to some of the subjects as coming from a source of high credibility. For example, the information about the future of movie theaters was attributed to *Fortune* magazine, as a high-credibility source. For a low-credibility source the information was attributed to a female Hollywood gossip columnist. The actual communications attributed to the two sources were identical.

The subjects tended to judge the communication from the reliable magazine source as fairer, and 23 percent of them changed their opinions in the suggested direction. Only 6.6 percent of the subjects in the low-credibility group changed opinions. However, when attitudes were measured four weeks later there was a *decrease* in the favorability of the attitudes of subjects who had received the information from the high-credibility source. There was an *increase* in the favorability of the attitudes of subjects who had received the information from the low-credibility source. Here we find the sleeper effect operating. That is, the subjects tended with time to forget the source of the information but to remember the content. They were influenced by this remembered content. These data are shown graphically in Figure 12-1.

Now let us return to the question of evaluating sources of information about careers and jobs. In this chapter we shall talk about sources, but one point we wish to emphasize. In career decision making we should allow some time for the sleeper effect to operate. Fortunately,

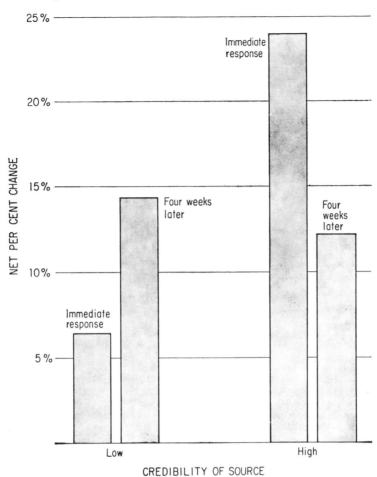

FIG. 12-1 The "sleeper effect" in changing attitudes on the basis of whether the source of information has low or high credibility. At first a source of low credibility influenced attitudes in only 6.6 percent of the subjects. Four weeks later this figure *increased* to 14 percent. In the high-credibility situation, 23 percent of the subjects were initially influenced by the information given. Later this figure dropped to 12 percent. The subjects tended with time to forget the source of the information but to remember the content. (*Data from Hovland, C. I., and Weiss, W. The influence of source credibility on communication effectiveness. Publ. Opin. Quart., 1951, 15, 635–650.*)

in most instances career planning lasts over a long period of time. Emotional components of attitudes sometimes lessen with time. This allows for thinking, and in thinking the cognitive components of attitudes become more important. Time allows us to line up and evaluate alternatives.

ALTERNATIVES IN CHOOSING

Making a decision means choosing one of several alternatives. In choosing which one of a number of cars to buy, much is involved. The alternatives actually run into many hundreds when we consider color, models, engines, and other such factors in various combinations. Chances are that we are unaware of all but a few of these alternatives, since long before the time of making the decision of what car to buy we eliminated station wagons, six-cylinder engines, dark colors, and other types and characteristics. The final choosing of alternatives may well involve a two-choice situation—perhaps we choose between a Ford and a Chevrolet and between a two-door and a four-door model.

The young married couple selecting an apartment will be likely to find the decision making more involved than in buying a car. When one is working within a limited budget, alternatives are rapidly narrowed down. The couple may consider cost, size, appearance, location, neighborhood, and a few other characteristics. Chances are that the final decision will not be so satisfying as in buying the car because more compromise is involved. The difficulty in making such decisions arises from the necessity of trading the advantages of an alternative in some characteristics against disadvantages in other characteristics. Such decisions involve rather complicated judgments and sometimes lead to hasty conclusions. Occasionally it is when we do not know where we are going that we get in a hurry. The defensive person may go through a life career with gloves on and leave no fingerprints. Sometimes each of us finds a repetition of bad decisions as we look at the cycle of our personal history, particularly when we have been through a crisis of self-confidence.

ELIMINATING ALTERNATIVES

It cannot be assumed that having more information makes a decision easier or better. Taking more and more characteristics into account in comparing alternatives brings about more opportunity for confusion. This is one reason why it is helpful to *eliminate* some alternatives as soon as one can. One way to do this is to make a list of questions, eliminate some from consideration, and combine others into a few alternatives from which a choice can be made. This, of course, is a difficult process, but all the more reason why we should start early in asking questions about career possibilities. Let us see what is involved in asking *one* such question.

WHAT KIND OF JOB DO I WANT?

This question brings in a number of alternatives. Let us list these alternatives in terms of questions.

1 *Do you want to work "with people" or "with things"?* Some students answer right off "with people" because this seems to them to be the "right" answer. Not so by any means. Some people do not have the human relations skills or potentials for working effectively with people. Do not list ability to get along with people as an asset unless you really have such ability. Some of us are just not "calibrated" to people.

2 *What studies have you enjoyed most? What studies did you have to force yourself to work on?* Such questions bring out some indicators of interest and aptitude.

3 *Which of your abilities do your friends comment on most frequently? Can you make a living at it?* Our associates usually know something about us, and we should not ignore their views. Having ability and interest in something, however, is not enough when we are considering career alternatives. We need to look at opportunities as well. No doubt there are people trying to make a living at some activity that might better have been considered a hobby.

4 *What things do people criticize you for?* Although we may not agree with the criticism, nor with the critics, they are at least "critical incidents" that should be considered in self-evaluation.

5 *There are some twenty thousand ways in which people can earn a living in the United States. If you had to choose five, what would they be? Which would you list first? Why?* In this series of questions we are going through a process of narrowing down alternatives.

6 *Do you want to work for yourself or for an employer?* This question relates to motivation and personality variables.

7 *Do you want to work for a large organization or a small one?* This question opens up an array of problems centering around organizational climates, which we shall discuss in a later chapter (see page 328).

8 *Do you prefer to work at home or away?* Here one might open up problems related to opportunities and to possible restraints.

9 *What pay level do you have in mind to attain?* Involved here is thinking about work and pay in relation to both present and future.

10 *What status level do you hope to attain?* This question is related to identification of needs and to personality.

11 *What price are you willing to pay to reach your goals?* Here we are relating ambition to the realities of what conditions are involved in goal seeking.

12 *What kind of job would your wife like to see you in?* For married men career decision making involves family considerations.

13 *What are the requirements of the kind of job you would prefer most?* This is a question of selection of a job in terms of reality rather than through fantasy.

14 *When do you wish to arrive at your goals?* Being aware of time as a decision dimension is important in setting up alternatives.

15 *Have you time, money, and desire for additional education that may be needed?* Obsolescence hits everybody in a changing organization. This question relates to the quest for knowledge, for both its own sake and for vocational reasons.

Answers to the above types of questions offer a good starting place in thinking about job opportunities in relation to what *you* have to offer an employer.

THE BEGINNING OF SELF-ANALYSIS

Where do I start? May we suggest that you sit down and carefully consider the above questions. Make a list on paper of your capabilities and shortcomings under the headings of "Assets" and "Liabilities." You may wish to check this analysis with someone on the faculty, with friends, or with your counselor. This is a test of your self-analysis, not a substitute for it.

PEOPLE AND OCCUPATIONS

Only in a rough sort of way can we take an overall look at the pattern of occupations. Effective occupational adjustment involves more than just matching individual aptitudes to job requirements. Listed below are occupational groups with a very brief statement about people who go into jobs in these groups. The examples given are listed from higher to lower levels of occupation in each group. The reader should keep in mind that the descriptions given below have their limitations and exceptions, and that some persons would place themselves under more than one grouping.

Group I: Service. This includes people who work for the "common good" or who "render service," such as educational and vocational counselors, social workers, FBI agents, hairdressers, ushers, and watchmen. Persons in this group tend to be high

in social values. High verbal skill is found at the upper level
of these jobs.

Group II: Business Contact. Salesmen, buyers, agents, interviewers,
and peddlers. These people score rather high on tests of
influence.

Group III: Organization. Industrial executives, personnel managers, postmasters, foremen, and file clerks have a high interest
in personal relationships. Economic and status values rate high
with those in the upper levels.

Group IV: Technology. Engineers, factory managers, contractors,
mechanics, and truck drivers. In the upper levels of these jobs
one finds persons with intellectual interests, of a quantitative
nature. Mechanical aptitudes and interests are high. This group
is "object-oriented."

Group V: Outdoor. Landowners, farmers, oil drillers, teamsters,
and laborers tend to come from family backgrounds of the same
sort. Intellectual and artistic interests range widely. Mechanical
interests are often high.

Group VI: Science. Mathematicians, scientists, nurses, medical
technicians, and embalmers have strong intellectual interests.

Group VII: General Cultural. College teachers, clergymen, news
commentators, librarians, and reporters. This group is verbally
oriented and usually interested in people.

Group VIII: Arts and Entertainment. Creative artists, professional
athletes, showmen, race drivers, and stagehands. Special artistic
or physical abilities play an important role. These people do
not shy away from being in the public eye.

The person who "likes people" will generally move toward occupations in which friendly, frequent contact with others is a part of the
organizational climate. Working "with things" does not necessarily mean
dislike for people. Those who like to work with things tend toward
production-oriented enterprises. The person who wants to manage finds
himself in the organizational setting which prizes practical decision making. The artistic types tend to colonize together and seek occupations
which do not demand clock punching.

SOME QUESTIONS IN CHOOSING GOALS

You probably know someone who works behind a desk all day and
likes it. And you no doubt know someone else who would be most
unhappy in the same job. He would much prefer to be on the road
selling. All of us have a certain amount of choice in the way we spend
our time *before* we settle into a job. Some people face a permanent

desk job with horror. Others want just such a position. And, of course, there are those who want it both ways. Many jobs allow both desk work and some moving around. Teaching is such an example.

Let us list here a few questions that the person may wish to think through before he finds himself in a position of choosing goals.

1 *Do you want to schedule your own time and activities?* The salesman is relatively independent in how and when he spends his time. He usually determines the appointments he keeps. His effectiveness is determined by his selling results. To a lesser extent the physician in private practice sets his own time schedule—but physicians, as well as ministers, are in some respects at the command of others.

   Some people say that they must have a fairly rigid work schedule or they won't get much done. Having independence may be good, but not for the irresponsible type of person. Textbook writers, for example, know that it takes effort to keep going during periods of discouragement, and so do college students. It requires much in the way of self-discipline and good work habits to live the independent life. The free life is not so easy as it is sometimes described to be. It is sometimes laced with one procrastination after another.

2 *Do you want to be relieved of self-prodding?* To have to work certain specified hours is some relief from making continuous choices of what to do and when.

3 *How do you want to be evaluated?* Some people like to be judged on what they accomplish each hour or each day. Others would rather be judged at the end of a month or even a year. Many of us, of course, may do better if our work is evaluated over short periods of time—this provides a cushion against laziness!

4 *What kinds of activity do you engage in that bring on feelings of accomplishment?* One person gets a kick out of promoting something. Another tries to avoid promotion at all costs. Let us rephrase this question to read, "From what do you get your kicks?"

5 *What types of enterprise do you take initiative in?* Take a look at yourself as a student. Are you an organizer? Do you read beyond the assignments? Do you know in what areas you have influence? Do you start money-making schemes and carry them beyond the requirements of necessity? Answers to questions such as these help one in planning goals by giving indicators as to what to stay away from and what possibly to follow up.

6 *Are you an idea man?* The urge to discover, to know the answer, and to come up with something new characterizes the sound idea man.

7 *Do you want to manage?* Among the several known qualities of leadership (see page 359), the desire to manage is very important.

8 *Do you enjoy a good fight?* Success in many conflicting situations entails fighting for one's ideas and principles. Do you have the psychological resources to stand both prosperity and losses?

9 *Do you want to be on your own?* This question covers a wide range. It may be related to whether a person goes into business for himself or seeks the protective umbrella of some organization. It may also be more subtle in dealing with how independent you really are.

10 *Do you like to negotiate and bargain?* These skills are basic to working effectively within organizations. Some people like such "gamesmanship," while others try to avoid it.

11 *Are you rules-oriented?* Some people like well-planned rules to follow; for example, this is characteristic of many persons who have engineering interests. Other people, writers, for example, are less structured.

12 *What factors do you feel will influence you in choosing a job?* Answers to this question are somewhat individual. Studies show, however, that most college students include eight factors near the top of the list: (1) type of job; (2) opportunity for advancement; (3) location of the job; (4) starting salary; (5) organization reputation; (6) training program; (7) educational benefits; (8) size of organization.

SOURCES OF JOB POSSIBILITIES

Each region may have a particular type of employment service, but in the main there are six different sources of information on jobs other than direct application to an organization. One place to start in is the *college placement bureau* or its equivalent. Not only will one find here company brochures, but the bureau staff sometimes can give opinions that may be useful; for example, "Our graduates in the ABC Company have received favorable promotional opportunities." *Counselors, professors,* and *college administrators* sometimes can pass along information about jobs. *Friends, relatives,* and *alumni* sometimes know about job openings. *Employment agencies,* both government and commercial, have something of the larger picture of job opportunities. It must be remembered, however, that some of the better jobs do not get listed with such agencies.

Business connections may lead to job information. Bankers, for example, usually know much about local community situations. Other ways of getting a line on jobs include *advertising* and *personal solicitation*. Letters offer one way to establish contact with an organization.

LETTERS OF APPLICATION

Once you have narrowed down the companies and kinds of job you are looking for, your next planning should include how to get to talk over job situations with the right people. The purpose of a letter of application is to *get a personal interview*. There are a number of do's and a host of don't's connected with writing such a letter. One personnel manager, after analyzing thousands of letters, concluded that most letters of application are bad. "Our company handles around 15,000 letters of application a year," said one executive. "What would you look for in such a letter?" One study shows that people have a tendency to concentrate on a few large, well-known companies, flooding them with applications. They often overlook the smaller companies where their applications not only would stand less competition but might turn up an even better job.

A GOOD LETTER

To be effective a letter of application should reveal that you are courteous, able to express yourself clearly, and qualified for the position for which you are looking. There is no one way to write such a letter. The author has reviewed many articles on the subject, a summary of which seems to be that a good letter of application should be brief and factual, should show interest, and should, where possible, be typed. The letter should be addressed to a specific individual.

One important aspect of letter writing is to get attention in the opening paragraph. Just how to get this attention may be a matter of concern. Using an unorthodox method, as in show business, may not be the best way to approach a conservative steel company. The middle paragraph of your letter of application may well include age, education, training, qualifications, and experience. The last paragraph may well be designed to elicit the desired response; namely, the interview. One way to keep the letter itself short is to accompany it with a one-page résumé or vita that gives a full, but brief, outline about you. It may be well also to ask yourself *what behavior* your letter may be likely to evoke in the reader.

In one study, made by a company which wishes to remain anonymous, all letters of the following types were classified as "bad": mimeographed letters, letters revealing defensive or egotistical behavior, and letters giving the impression that the writer is desperate for a job.

The study concluded with the warning that one should not expect all favorable replies. Even the best letter may not evoke the desired response.

INTERVIEWS

Let us begin our discussion with the *campus interview,* although only about 1 percent of employers send representatives to visit colleges, and less than one-third of most graduating classes secure employment through college recruiting.

THE RECRUITING INTERVIEWER

What are some of the general facts we can estimate about the recruiting interviewer although we know there is no typical interviewer? Chances are that he is a member of the company's personnel department, a man of some experience in interviewing, and one who is somewhat on the spot to pick the right man. A number of bad evaluations on his part and his job may even be in jeopardy. He may be talking about needing twenty men but may really be looking only for one. He has most likely been told to get men from the top quarter of the class. He may be looking for a man to fill a present need or to be groomed for a future position. The medium-sized company looking for sixty graduates may canvass forty colleges, by no more than two or three interviewers. The interviewing season is short. The interviewer must pack in as many twenty-minute interviews as possible (the usual time limit) and move on to the next college, often traveling most of the night. He frequently is physically tired, but must keep up good public relations appearances.

In the twenty-minute interview he must put the applicant at ease, get him to talk about himself, determine his interests, and try to get a line on his abilities. He must evaluate his personality, observe his dress and deportment, probe for weaknesses, and pick out the applicant's strong points. In addition, the interviewer must describe the company's training program and opportunities for advancement, explain and sell the company's pay scale, and have you leave the interview feeling that you have been treated fairly. All this he must do in twenty minutes, and repeat, and repeat, and repeat!

YOUR PART IN THE INTERVIEW

As a job applicant, you can help make the interviewer's job a little easier and possibly sell yourself at the same time. How?

First of all, have a ready answer to the request, "Tell me about yourself," or, "What can I do for you?" *Preparation for the interview* not only is getting your homework done properly, it helps put you at ease, and composure is one quality the interviewer may be looking for. A well-adjusted person knows how to stand properly, to control his movements. The suggestion is frequently made that you wear conservative, clean clothing, but be sure you feel comfortable in it. Since you have probably spent most of your school days in informal attire, it may take a while for you to get used to coat and tie. If you have two suits, wear one of them several days before the interview and get used to its feel. The other one can be worn at the proper time.

You may think it out of place to remind you of good manners, but one study indicates that many students are negligent in manners. Chewing gum during the interview, for instance, may be taken as indicating that you are not socially perceptive about the right and wrong things to do.

Take your cues from the interviewer about whether to shake hands, whether to sit down. Tell about yourself only what is relevant to the situation. Certainly the interviewer does not want to serve as a listener for your troubles unless they are relevant. By all means know something about the company being represented.

INTERVIEWS AWAY FROM HOME

Being interviewed away from your home campus is in some ways a little more leisurely process, but it is at the same time more difficult for you. Most likely you will be looked over by several persons, whether you visit the company's headquarters, plant, or educational center. Aside from the more formal aspects of being interviewed, you may well be evaluated by the secretary as you report for the interview. If you are courteous, perhaps the secretary will not mention this fact to her boss because courtesy is expected of you. On the other hand, let us say that your behavior was somewhat brash; there is a good chance that she would mention this to the interviewer, and you would have a strike against you from the beginning.

When you are trying for a job your behavior is observed in many subtle sorts of ways, just as it is on the job. The following case may illustrate the point.

ONE CASE HISTORY

The senior class of Blank University was visiting a company during the fall as a scheduled part of the class work. James M. and a friend arrived at the plant twenty minutes late and found that the tour for the students had started on time. Somewhat disappointed, James spoke to the public relations secretary in the office about his problem. She went to the trouble of making arrangements to have the two students catch up with the party. Instead of showing his appreciation for her efforts, as did the other student, he took the occasion to bawl her out for not holding the tour up for his convenience. She continued to be polite, however, asking James for his name and address so that he could be put on the mailing list.

Springtime came and James M. had decided to apply for a job at the company which he had visited in the fall. He was asked in for an interview. All seemed to be going well with the interview until a secretary handed the interviewer a note. He was soon politely dismissed and told that the company had no job for him. Later he found that the secretary to whom he had been impolite a few months earlier had recognized his name on the interview roster and had informed the interviewer of her previous observation of his behavior.

To be sure, getting a job and being promoted on a job depend on several kinds of abilities. How one *behaves* may be just as important as how much one knows, or even more important.

ANTICIPATING QUESTIONS

There are no hard-and-fast rules as to how to handle all questions in an interview. Some questions are loaded. Try to anticipate some of these questions and do some "prethinking" about them. Let us take a question that may sound innocent enough, but may well be a part of the interview technique: *What salary do you expect?* Your answer could be interpreted variously as possibly indicating modesty, conceit, wishful thinking, pride, or true value. Your employer knows within a range what he is going to pay. Most beginning positions normally have a set starting salary. A little scouting around in your preparation for the interview can give you a picture of the going rate for different kinds of jobs. In filling out an interview form in answer to the question, "What salary do you expect?" you may insert what you have learned to be about average. If you are totally in the dark, you might better write in "open." During the interview itself, some writers advise delaying until the end of the interview any questions about salary; show interest in the job first!

MOVING AHEAD ON THE JOB

During peak years of employment getting a job is not nearly so hard as getting promoted on the job. In many companies, both those with and those without a formal training program, the first year in the job is in itself a selection process. This is when the company can take a close look at abilities, personality, and ambitions. This is when they can find out if the person has patience and can handle responsibility.

GETTING ACCEPTANCE

"Being a big shot in college, belonging to the right clubs, helped me land my first job," remarked a young executive. "However, it came as quite a surprise to me to learn that these things could be a handicap in being accepted on the job," he continued. It is always difficult for a new man to get started well on a job. He must sell himself not only with the type of work he turns out, but also by the attitudes he evokes.

Much has been written on how to get promoted, ranging from the more formal researches on executive development on the one hand, to the inspirational clichés on the other.

To begin with, the new man meets with some resistance from the old-timers, if for no other reason than that he is new. With all the enthusiasm of being on the ball, new men, before they have learned about the limitations within which they must work, may push the boss too fast. It is particularly important to watch criticism when one is new on the job. Often the old-timer can get by with his frankness, even profit by it, but the new man may be set back by the same behavior. Said one executive, "A good rule on being critical is first to be sure of the security of your own position."

STUDY THE COMPANY

An advantage one gains by having studied the company before applying for a job is that what he has learned may be useful on the job. Here is where knowing the psychological climate of the organization may well give one the cue as to whether to speak up or bide one's time before letting go with feelings. Certainly the new man who bucks traditions, established practice, or customs is in for a hard time unless he has prestige or some other factor to back him in his "honesty."

Learning the lingo of the plant is a help to the new man, as is a willingness to learn. Doing a good job is important in moving up, but you may ask, "Good in relation to what?" One man may do an adequate job but operate below his level of ability, while another attempts to close the gap between ability and effort. It is the latter man who attracts favorable notice.

Some men no doubt fail to get promoted because they are potentially better than the boss. The boss may be protecting himself by holding back on promotion. One may have special abilities but if they do not fit in with company needs and the management's way of thinking, then these abilities may have no chance to be displayed. It is not very desirable to display an ability that cannot be utilized.

PROMOTION AS AN INDIVIDUAL PROBLEM

Whether one works for a promotion is, of course, an individual matter. Not everyone can get to the top, as we all know, and possibly some should not try. The setting of goals is individual. One needs to make a rational evaluation of his potentialities and set his aspiration level accordingly. For those who plan to move upward it is important to consider many factors. The large elements in decision making are usually prominent. Consideration should also be given to how one spends one's time and to the smaller elements.

MANAGING TIME EFFECTIVELY

"I have seldom found an executive who controls as much as 25 percent of his time," says one management consultant, "and the house-wife has a similar problem of managing her time." Getting ahead includes using time effectively. How do you spend your time?

The sales manager cannot tell the customer "I'm busy"; the hospital administrator cannot know what is going on unless he attends meetings with staff, doctors, nurses, and technicians. The student always has more problems than time to solve them, and often teachers find their time expenditure directed by students and deans. In terms of consuming time we are all *other-directed* in one way or another. Mostly, however, we fail to manage our time effectively because we do not realize that time has much the same value as money.

Let us list some suggestions for learning to better utilize our time:

1 Keep a daily time log for several weeks and then critically examine it.
2 Make a list of those things you do that do not have to be done.
3 Note those instances in which you stick your neck in another's business.
4 Note those things you do that waste the time of others.
5 How often do you do the work of someone else?
6 Plan warm-up time for creative work and problem solving.
7 Plan your energy expenditure. If you are most efficient in the early morning, then use this time for your more difficult tasks.

8   How much time do you waste in negative thinking?
9   Do you overplan your day?
10   Do you "oversocialize," particularly on the telephone?

SMALL FACTORS IN DECISION

Two men were being considered for one job promotion. They were about equal in background and abilities. The promotion went to the man who perceived work as an opportunity rather than to the man who somewhat exaggerated the amount of work and the importance of the job. Small attitudinal matters to be sure, but the combination of these "small" matters often determines promotional notice. It may well be that promotional consideration might be held back from the employee who has displayed that a change of his status would require considerable change in his way of living. Or again, it may be better to use an indirect approach in finding out about a job opening than to rush in and apply for it. The job may not even exist, or, for some valid reason, you might not quite fit the opening. Sometimes one can avoid the necessity of face saving by finding out indirectly what the chances are for the promotion.

DRIFTING VS. PLANNING

Since this chapter is written primarily for the student planning his vocational career, let us emphasize that promotional opportunities in a specific sense are hard to anticipate. Before taking a job in the first place one should know in a general way what the future holds. Contrast the difference between the person who drifts into a job and the person who plans his career.

A young man starts out casually enough and takes a job of average pay and with fair working conditions. It is his first job, his first real money, and the job is not too unrewarding because he hasn't given much thought to this as a problem. The years pass, he marries and takes on family responsibilities. By now he may well have discovered that his job is distasteful to him. He wants to quit but he now has responsibilities; he cannot quit for he would most likely have to start over elsewhere, and this he cannot afford. One may feel this is a situation where he is walking through vocational quicksand. At best, it is a nervous way of making a living.

Although it may not be advisable to try to select a job with promotional possibilities spelled out in detail, the man who asks the question, "What do I want to do one, five, ten years from now?" is at least meeting his future with some degree of realism. Of course, one may say that if a person doesn't like a job, he should change. This may be true, but the change should be based on planning. Frequent changes of jobs, unless each change is clearly an advancement for the individual, may be harmful to a career. Once the person gets labeled a "floater" or "job hopper," he has this stigma to buck in addition to everything else. One common complaint against college graduates is that they are impatient with slow, steady progress. On the other hand, patience may be a virtue at times, providing a link to security, but it can also entrap a person.

TIME WITH A COMPANY

There are *advantages* to sticking with the same employer over a long time. It helps the person to learn the business and become identified with the organization. Since most organizations promote from within, stability in the job may help self-development.

There are also *disadvantages*, mostly psychological, to sticking with the same company for a long time. The person may be lulled into a false sense of security and fail to broaden his experience. He may become too well satisfied and lose drive, get lost, or hit a dead-end job without realizing it until too late.

There is some evidence that there is a positive correlation between length of service and technical ability. However, studies show that promotion supposedly based on superior ability is often made for other reasons, often for personality reasons.

Promotional paths do get clogged, and the ambitious young man may find himself held back by unpromotable oldsters ahead of him. The man picking a company for job security reasons where turnover is low may find promotional opportunities lessened. These kinds of "contradictions" make it important for the person to analyze a job from every angle.

CHANGING JOBS

Changing jobs, whether or not for reasons of advancement, is of "how" importance. Chances are that each student reading this chapter will change companies several times and will change jobs many times during his career or careers. How one leaves a job may be just as important as how one performs on the job. Companies have been known to blackball men with other companies because of the manner in which they quit their job. In moving from one company to another, one should follow the protocol of submitting the resignation to his immediate superior, and in person. Sufficient notice should be given, of course, but the main thing is to leave a job with good will on both sides. Your former company may be asked about you sometime in the future. One might give planned attention to how to leave the job. One negative case may illustrate just how important this can be.

Robert S. had been a successful engineer for the ABC Company for six years. He had done a good job, had received promotions, and was on his way up. He was offered what was apparently a better job with another company. In great glee he informed his boss that he was changing jobs. He even went to the trouble to put in his letter of resignation some three pages of negative comments about the whole structure of the organization, and concluded by stating how glad he was to leave the "sinking ship." Five years later Robert decided to try to get back with his old company; he was being given serious consideration by the management for the job until his negative letter of resignation was discovered in the files!

OCCUPATIONAL CHOICE AND CONFLICT

In a nationwide survey of 4,585 college students some interesting information came out under the head of what students look for in their "ideal" jobs. The investigator found that, by and large, the student enters his occupation willingly. Actually 78 percent of the students desired to enter the occupations they expected to enter. At least they come to "want" what they realistically expect to get. Most students want a job in which they can use their special abilities, or in which they will have an opportunity to be creative and original.

How well the student can anticipate the role he must play after his college days is important in making the transition from college to occupational status. Students in this study placed a strong emphasis on the chance to work with people. Many were convinced that having a pleasant personality is an essential ingredient for occupational success. Not only do people choose a given occupation to satisfy a value, they may also choose a value because they consider it appropriate for the occupational status they expect to fill in the future. The person who "moves toward people," "who wants to be helpful," will be guided toward a general area of occupations in which friendly, frequent contact with others is inherent in the structure of the occupation. A person who needs to express control, mastery, or domination will move toward those occupations in which this need can find expression. Some people will choose occupations negatively; we find the person, for example, who wants to have as little as possible to do with people or who wishes to avoid problems. This individual will be likely to seek out an occupation that makes few demands upon him.

One conclusion from this study which may reinforce the reader's own experience is that *making a choice of an occupation involves a great deal of conflict.* This is particularly true among those planning to enter some phase of business. Another conclusion is that in terms of motivation, some people have gifts but are too lazy to unwrap them. This may be just as true for some who are born into cultural comfort as for those so deprived.

Summary

It is estimated that because of rapidly advancing technology each person now twenty years of age may have as many as six careers during his lifetime. This means, in effect, that the individual who learns to make decisions appropriately early in life will have advantages over the person who moves along deciding matters by trial and error.

Making a decision means choosing one of several alternatives. It means eliminating alternatives. It is a situation in which a so-called simple question such as, "What kind of job do I want?" may lead to a dozen other questions. Obsolescence hits everybody in a changing organization. This fact affects the quest for and use of knowledge, both for its own sake and for vocational reasons.

The questions involved in choosing goals range widely, from how one's schedule of time and activities is made to what specific factors influence the choice of a job. Self-analysis is important in dealing with questions that have to do with feelings of accomplishment, initiative, negotiation, and bargaining skill. What are the sources of job possibilities? How do I write a letter of application? What can I do to prepare for a job interview? These are searching questions, simple as they may seem.

Getting a job is often easier than the process of steadily moving ahead in it. Involved are problems of acceptance and sophistication in understanding psychological climates. The setting of goals is individual; moving ahead involves other people. By and large, students enter their occupations willingly. At least they come to "want" what they realistically expect to get. Most students want a job in which they can use their special abilities, or in which they will have an opportunity to be creative and original. Some people, such as the person who wants to have little to do with people or who wishes to avoid problems that bring on stress, choose occupations negatively.

One conclusion from research which may reinforce the reader's own experience is that making a choice of an occupation involves a great deal of conflict.

Suggestions for Thinking and Discussion

1 Try to spell out: "The kind of job I want is . . . ." Did you have difficulty doing this? Why? Why not?
2 Make a list of the sources of job possibilities in your community.
3 Describe some interview you have had in terms of ease of communication.
4 List the problems that you anticipate you will have in moving ahead on the job that you hope to obtain.
5 What conflicts do you anticipate in choosing a job?
6 What can you do *now* to prepare for career decision making later?

Suggestions for Further Reading

Greenleaf, W. J. *Occupations and careers.* New York: McGraw-Hill, 1955. An old standby, giving a background for considering careers.

New York Life Insurance Co. *Guide to career information.* New York: Harper & Row, 1957. A general description of a wide variety of careers.

Norris, Willa, et al. *Information service in guidance: Occupational, educational, social,* Chicago: Rand McNally, 1966. Sources of information about job opportunities.

Shartle, C. L. *Occupational information: Its development and application.* Englewood Cliffs, N.J.: Prentice-Hall, 1959. The third edition of a practical book about jobs.

Super, D. E. *The psychology of careers.* New York: Harper & Row, 1963. A comprehensive coverage of both research and practical problems of careers, from worker to manager and professional.

PART IV

THE
WORLD OF WORK

CHAPTER 13

The Psychology of Work

❖❖❖❖❖❖❖❖❖

What do you think about when someone mentions the word *work?* Associations range widely for most of us. We talk about work being heavy, light, strenuous, good, or poor. We think in terms of fatigue, tiredness, boredom, or monotony. We associate work with pay, with incentive, or we think of it in terms of being hazardous or safe. Work is all these things and more.

In general one may think of work as the use of the individual's physiological and mental processes in the accomplishment of some goal. The goal may be writing a theme in English or fixing a flat tire. It may be programming a computer, selling an insurance policy, or deciding to pay a stock dividend. But in each case, activity on the part of the individual is required. The utilization of the worker's skills or the supervisor's decisions means cost in terms of effort expended in reaching the goal.

WORK AND PLAY

Work may be physical or mental, or in many instances both. *Behavior involved* in trying to reach some goal is the important thing. The goal may be a managerial or an executive decision, participating in a conference, producing a steel ingot, or listening to the complaints of a frustrated student. Work for the professional may be competition in a golf tournament; for the amateur golf competition may be play.

Why can't we define work and play the same way? Does not the golf player use his physiological and mental processes in an attempt to attain the goal of winning the game? Indeed he does. But the difference between work and play centers around *motivation*. For the professional golfer making a living is the motivation. The amateur wants to do a good job for self-satisfaction, for relaxation from his real work of being a student, a teacher, or an executive. What is play to some people is work to others. Motivation makes the difference. What is play to some people may be work to others although the performance elements may be the same. We may think of the child engaging in play, but for him it may be work. For both boys and girls, toys often reflect the adult world.

COMMON CHARACTERISTICS OF WORK

A variety of changes takes place during the course of most work activities, both in physical work and in mental work. Six common characteristics of work are shown in Figure 13-1 and described below.

Changes take place in work over a period of time. In *a* of Figure 13-1 we see the *warm-up effect*. Getting started on a job is a slow process. The baseball pitcher must "warm up" to get his muscles in appropriate condition for pitching, and so it is with the worker getting everything set to run a complicated machine. Not so noticeable may be the effort involved in mental activity, but even here warm-up is necessary. The committee member must warm up to the conference situation. And the student is well aware that study involves a process of getting "into the groove."

In *b* we see a curve of *acquisition*. This type of work curve is characteristic of the person who is learning to perform a certain task. Motor skills, such as driving a car or running a crane, are usually acquired slowly. They may show improvement over a period of a day, weeks, or even, if the task requires great skill, years. Note that the "acquiring" of the skill does not result in a smooth curve. There are always some ups and downs in improving one's performance. The important thing is for the general direction of the curve to be upward. Not only motor skill is involved in reaching the peak of one's performance. Studies show that *attitudes* are important also. For example, in model changeover in the auto industry, or in the dressmaking industry, the physical skills involved may be essentially the same for the worker on a new model as they were on the old. But reaching peak performance

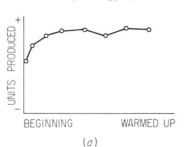

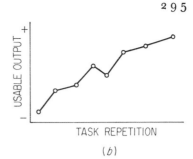

(a)

(b)

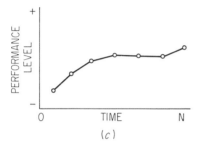

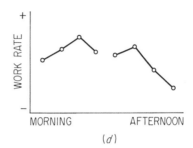

(c)

(d)

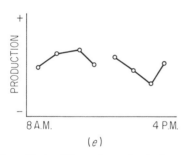

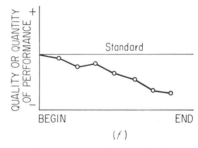

(e)

(f)

FIG. 13-1 These hypothetical curves show six common characteristics of work: (*a*) warm-up effect; (*b*) curve of acquisition, representing a person's output as he learns through repetition; (*c*) plateau of nonimprovement in performance, a common phenomenon in work; (*d*) variation in work output related to the time of day; (*e*) end spurt of increased production near the end of the workday; (*f*) work decrement, which, under certain conditions, occurs as a person continues to work.

seems to be related to an attitude that the new work is no longer new.

One of the most common phenomena in work is a leveling-off process in which performance stays the same. This period of nonimprovement is called a *plateau* and is shown in c. We described this earlier in the chapter on learning (Chapter 4). It is usually temporary.

Time of day for work output is important for productivity, mental or physical. Some people seem to be alert and to function at their best in the early morning hours. Other people function at their best later in the day. For both types of workers, however, work output seems to fall off just before noon and just before quitting time, as indicated in *d*. This *variation* in work output related to the time of day, however, is associated with another phenomenon (noticed sometimes in the closing minutes of a football game), which we call *end spurt,* shown in *e*.

Work decrement very often occurs when performance diminishes over a period of time. This work decrement is seen in *f*.

In Chapter 5 we discussed various aspects of improving study. Note how these common characteristics of work may be related to college work. It is not uncommon for class efficiency to be at a low ebb just before lunch or for fatigue to set in toward the end of the day. Scheduling study periods should include questions such as, "Am I the early-morning type or the late-evening type?" When asking these questions, however, the student should be aware that defensive behavior, such as rationalization, may come into the picture!

FATIGUE

No introduction to a chapter on work would be complete without a few words on feelings of tiredness or *fatigue.*

One of the most perplexing problems to student, worker, supervisor, and executive alike centers around the fact that different kinds of tiredness are related to different kinds of work. It behooves the individual to understand why he is tired, assuming that he wishes to understand his condition and possibly do something about it.

An emotional upset may involve a kind of tiredness different from that resulting from a hard day of physical labor free from frustration. Physical tiredness of this sort may be relieved with rest. The person may even feel a certain amount of satisfaction from "an honest job well done." But fatigue related in whole or in part to frustration and conflict prolongs recovery. Although we have no really good measures of tiredness, we know that most people learn to adjust to physical fatigue by rest pauses or changing activities. "Psychological fatigue" may be different, characterized by feelings which extend over long periods of time.

One personnel manager reports the case of a worker who frequently complained of feeling tired on the job. Following up on the suspicion that the man was not being accepted in his particular work group, he had the man transferred to a similar job with a different group of workers. Here he came to feel that he *belonged*. Complaints of fatigue lessened.

One college counselor tells of the case of a newly married male student who was having difficulty with his studies. Each night he came home determined to put in a good session of study. Although he fought the impulse, he would invariably fall asleep over his books. Unsuccessful in keeping awake he would retire with homework unprepared. Finally, he came to discuss his deteriorating scholastic performance with a counselor. Together they analyzed his past performances and changes in his living that may have been related to the worsening grades. Sometime later he and his wife moved out of his mother-in-law's home, and in two weeks the symptoms of fatigue were completely gone. Study efficiency improved. Weeks later he stopped the counselor on the capus and related the following: "I took my wife over to visit her mother last night, and minutes after we entered the house an overwhelming need for sleep came over me, the first time that has happened since we moved."

IMPROVING EFFICIENCY IN WORK

Much is being said these days about reducing the work week. Will a shorter day mean more efficiency, more production? Records show that when the work week was reduced from fifty-eight hours to fifty-one hours, hourly output increased. When the work week was reduced further, output again increased, but just how much of the improvement was due to cutting down on hours could not be determined because better equipment came in at about the same time. No one knows what the optimum work week really is. Factors enter the understanding of work that go beyond mere physical effort. Studies show, for example, that the modern bricklayer can lay 2,000 bricks per day without undue strain, but at the present time 300 is the maximum allowed by most union contracts. Complicating the problem still further are factors of boredom, wage incentives, and automation.

REST PAUSES

Numerous studies in the laboratory and in industry have shown that distributing work through the introduction of rest pauses results in increased output. In a typical laboratory study, subjects lifted weights until they were exhausted. After a five-minute rest they could lift the weights with about 80 percent of their previous ability. They returned to 95 percent of their best output after a rest of twenty minutes.

In industry the beneficial effects of rest periods on production have long been noted. A historic study conducted by the National Institute of

Industrial Psychology in Great Britain in the 1920s is significant because
it shows how a work curve may be altered by introducing rest periods.
Before the introduction of the rest pause, the work curve, averaged
from a number of workers and depicting output for each half hour
during the day, rose until 9:30 A.M., remained at the same level until
11 A.M., fell off sharply until noon, then climbed slowly until 12:30,
and from 12:30 to 1 P.M. fell off slightly. An hour's lunch break began
at 1 P.M. After a rest pause of seven minutes had been introduced
at 11 A.M., the work curve throughout the morning was generally at
a higher level, the decrement after 11 A.M. being markedly diminished
and periodic fluctuations giving way to more uniform output throughout
the morning. In the afternoon, when no rest pause was interpolated
at 4 P.M., the work curve fell sharply from 4 to 4:30, but after the
introduction of a seven-minute rest period at 4:00 P.M., the work
done during the remaining twenty-three minutes of the half hour exceeded that done in the same half hour when no rest pause was interpolated. Many recent human-factors studies have shown the same phenomena as this earlier investigation, and no doubt some readers have
experienced something similar in their own work efforts.

UNAUTHORIZED REST PERIODS

Work supervisors sometimes argue that most employees take unauthorized rests when there are no regularly scheduled rest periods.
Are there any advantages of authorized rest periods over periods of
unauthorized rest? A study of a group of comptometer operators in
a government office provides one answer to this question. The operators
were observed without their knowledge for a two-week period during
which a record was kept of the number and length of their unauthorized
rests. Later a rest schedule was formally introduced, consisting of an
eight-minute pause in the morning and a seven-minute pause in the
afternoon. Because of government regulations, the workday was length-
ened by fifteen minutes to make up for the time spent in the regularly
scheduled rest periods. Total working time thus remained unchanged.
The changed system resulted in a significant decrease in the time spent
in unauthorized rest and a 35 percent increase in work completed.

AUTHORIZED REST PERIODS

One reason for the advantage of authorized over unauthorized
rest periods is probably better placement of the rest interval during
the work period. The best way to determine how rest periods should
be scheduled is to plot production records throughout the work period
and note drops in production. Consider, for example, the production

curves shown in Figure 13-2. Since production is beginning to fall off at point *A,* this is the logical place to introduce a rest pause. The pause may be introduced at point *B* if the worker knows when it is coming, because the anticipatory effect is sufficient to keep him going during the interim. The dotted line in the figure shows the effect on production of introducing the rest period. In the afternoon, the pause is introduced at *C* or *D* and again at *E* or *F* if production falls during the late afternoon.

How can we account for the beneficial effects of rest pauses on production? A number of plausible reasons come to mind, the most

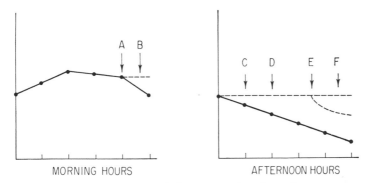

Fig. 13-2 Hypothetical curves of the proper location of rest pauses. Since production is beginning to fall off at point *A,* the pause is introduced at point *B.* If the worker knows when the pause is coming, the anticipatory effect is sufficient to keep him going during the interim. The dotted line shows the effect on production of introducing the rest period. In the afternoon, the pause is introduced at *C* or *D,* and again at *E* or *F* if production falls during the late afternoon. Shortening the hours to be worked may change these curves, but rest pauses are still beneficial. They are often written into union contracts.

obvious being that rest provides the opportunity to recover from fatigue. The physiologist has demonstrated that work causes an accumulation of waste products within the organism which reduce work capacity. Rest provides a period during which the waste products are dissipated and bodily capacity is restored. In heavy muscular work, physiological fatigue is unquestionably a major factor contributing to work decrement.

COFFEE BREAK

When work does not involve the expenditure of a great deal of physical energy, the beneficial effect of rest periods may be due to relief from a task that engenders in the worker feelings of boredom.

The worker is not physically tired—he is irritated, lacks interest, is fed up with his job. He wants a change, a break from what seems to be interminable activity. Rest pauses provide an opportunity to talk and think about nonjob activities. When the worker returns to his job, he is psychologically refreshed, so to speak, and this is reflected in increased output.

The effectiveness of introducing rest pauses may be due to still another factor—a change in attitude toward the company, including, of course, the work supervisor. A worker with a favorable attitude toward his supervisor is much less likely to loaf on the job than the worker who dislikes his boss. The introduction of rest periods may be tangible evidence that management has an interest in the welfare of the worker, and he may respond with more efficient output. On the other hand, the worker may feel differently if the coffee break, for example, is gained through union negotiations. Like other authorized rest periods, the coffee break may lead to abuse, not only in extra time taken out but in psychological time lost in getting back into the full swing of work. It is a loss somewhat related to the unproductive minutes before quitting time. One insurance company, after a study in its nationwide offices, defined the time from 4 to 5 P.M. as "the most expensive hour in America."

BOREDOM

The introduction of rest periods is not the only way to alter the shape of the work curve in the direction of increased output. The nature of the job itself has to do with how long a person can maintain a high rate of production. We "stay with" interesting jobs longer than with uninteresting ones, and repetitive jobs appear to be least interesting. We reflect this lack of interest when we say that the job is boring. Actually the job itself is not boring. *Boredom is the worker's reaction to the job.* More specifically, boredom arises from a conflict between the necessity for doing a dull job and wanting to turn to more interesting activities.

Attention requirements have much to do with the degree of boredom engendered by repetitive tasks. A highly repetitive job to which the worker becomes habituated elicits relatively little boredom in some workers if they do not have to pay close attention to what they are doing. If the worker can do the job without thinking, he is free to talk to his fellow workers about yesterday's football game or next month's vacation. Or, if conversation is impossible, he can daydream. Boredom will be pronounced on a repetitive job like an assembly-line operation where the continuous work flow and the task requirements occur over and over again but permit few lapses or shifts in attention. Boredom is not a problem in a complex and varied task which because of its intrinsic nature tends to hold attention.

ELIMINATING BOREDOM

The problem of eliminating the effects of boredom is acute in present-day industry, where many repetitive tasks result from the fractioning of work into smaller and simpler units. An obvious but naive answer to the question of how to eliminate boredom is to do away with tasks of a repetitive nature. This is not only impractical but to a considerably extent unnecessary.

A promising lead on how to reduce boredom comes from the finding that repetitive tasks do not give rise to the same degree of boredom in all persons. For example, in an investigation of women sewing-machine operators, those reporting the strongest feelings of boredom disliked routine activity, more often preferred active leisure activities, and indicated lack of satisfaction with their home and personal life. Operators who were least susceptible to boredom were placid and generally contented with the existing state of affairs.

Another study of women performing repetitive work in a chemical factory showed that those experiencing the most boredom tended to be more extroverted than introverted, desired opportunities to use their own ideas, and attached great importance to promotions. There is also evidence that persons of low normal intelligence are less bored by repetitive work than persons of higher intelligence. Additional study of the personality characteristics associated with feelings of boredom is necessary. The available evidence indicates that production decrement resulting from boredom can be reduced by selecting persons who will not be bored with the jobs to which they are assigned.

NEED FOR CHANGE

Although rest periods tend to reduce the deleterious effects on production resulting from boredom, the effect is due not so much to a need for rest as to a need for change. The bored worker is satiated with doing the same old thing. Rest periods provide an opportunity for change, of course, but boredom can frequently be relieved by giving the worker another kind of job. *Variety* is the spice which makes work interesting, and the interested worker is never bored. One observer reports a practical application of the principle of variation concerned with two types of maintenance jobs, dusters and solderers. The workers complained of overwork and were apparently bored with the tediousness of their routine tasks. They were eventually given the opportunity to exchange jobs, and all of them accepted. Half the workers dusted and half soldered, but every two hours they exchanged jobs. Feelings of boredom were reduced, and, significantly, the dusters now dusted as much on a half-time basis as they had previously on full time.

Exchanging jobs is not a general cure-all for boredom. The effectiveness of the practice depends at least in part on the amount of similarity between the jobs and the frequency with which the exchanges are made. If two jobs are perceived as highly similar, changing from one to the other will do little good. On the other hand, if they are so highly dissimilar that great versatility in skill is required, boredom may be reduced but at a great loss in efficiency. Where there is a moderate degree of similarity which allows the use of the same skills but the experience of doing something different, the beneficial effects will be maximized. Even in this situation confusion in operations may ensue if the jobs are alternated too often.

BATCHING

The bored worker frequently says that he has the feeling of not making any progress. He perceives his work as endless and unmeaningful. Routine inspection of the same kind of machine parts as they come off a conveyor will not be likely to engender feelings of progress in the inspector. One part is like another, and there are thousands of them. These feelings can sometimes be reduced by the foreman or supervisor who takes time to point out to the worker the relation of his routine or part work to the total job picture. He might explain why, for example, certain tolerances must not be exceeded. Or he might ask for suggestions on the improvement of methods of inspection, or discuss waste costs resulting from the rejection of parts. Giving the worker responsibilities and opportunities for judgment makes his work more meaningful and hence reduces the feelings of boredom which occur when he is looked upon as a robot who is told to do a job and ask no questions. In some situations a technique used to help correct boredom is "batching." No new work is given to the employee until he completes the batch he is working on.

STIMULATION AND BOREDOM

What will *more* leisure do to people? Boredom, even fatigue, may increase with shorter work hours. Many workers are even now taking on second jobs, and for reasons in addition to bringing in more income. Such moonlighting is one way to deal with the problem of additional leisure time; for some persons it is perhaps a better way than developing new and more expensive tastes. Boredom is affected not only by individual personality but by job perception and even by mood. On the job, in addition to job rotation and job enlargement, introducing subgoals that allow for task completion may sometimes help to lessen boredom.

In one individual low threshold for boredom may be offset by a low threshold for stimulation. In another person low threshold for boredom may be accompanied by a high threshold for stimulation. In the second instance, boredom may become a serious psychological problem for the individual.

TIME-AND-MOTION STUDY

One obvious way to maintain production, or increase it, is to see that the worker is using the best possible method for doing a given job. A worker may get a job done, and the end product of his efforts may be satisfactory. But what about the nature of the various operations performed in getting the job done? Did he waste time and energy performing unnecessary movements or standing around waiting for a machine to finish an operation? Are the activities of several men working on a job distributed properly? Men left to their own devices on a job seldom consider these questions, with the result that their true job efficiency is never maximized. For example, an analysis of an inspection job revealed that when left to their own devices, most inspectors put their attention on the wrong aspect of the operation. The inspectors' job was to examine a pile of tin plates for defects and to remove any imperfect plates from the pile. They examined each plate as they turned it. Thus as the first plate was being turned, the side coming up was examined, and after the plate was turned, the side going down was examined; then the second plate was picked up, and both of its sides were examined, the one side while it was coming up and the other side while it was going down. Inaccuracies occurred because the inspector was always looking at moving surfaces. A new method was developed in which the inspector ignored the moving plate and examined the one at rest. The new method cut down inspection errors considerably. This illustration shows the importance of investigating the best way to do a job. The general name given to the process of finding better methods for doing a given job is *time-and-motion-analysis,* or *study*.

USE OF MOVIES

In time-and-motion study occupational movements are broken down in order to determine the fewest and simplest movements necessary to do the job and the time required for each movement. The motion picture is now standard equipment in time-and-motion analysis. Through an examination of the films showing precisely what is done by each of the operator's hands and the time spent on each operation, the analyst rearranges some movements, eliminates others, and comes up with the fastest and least wasteful work pattern.

TIME-AND-MOTION PRINCIPLES

Time-and-motion analysts are guided by a body of rules and principles which are treated in detail in standard works on the subject. Some examples of the major time-and-motion principles are:

1 Minimize the number of motions by eliminating unnecessary movements.
2 Minimize the length of motions by reducing reaching distances to tools, supplies, and machine operations.
3 Provide for continuous curved motions instead of zigzag or straight-line motions involving sharp changes in directions.
4 Arrange work to permit an easy and natural rhythm wherever possible.
5 Distribute action among the used members of the body in accordance with the inherent capacities of the members.

SOME CRITICISM

At first glance time-and-motion analysis appears to be a good technique for maximizing efficiency. Certainly there is considerable merit to the general argument that production is at least to some extent a function of the way the job is done. Even in such a simple physical task as lifting a heavy steel bar, there is a right way and a wrong way. The worker with lifting know-how can lift all day. The worker who does not know how to lift tires quickly and may even injure himself. In more complex manual tasks and also in mental tasks there are poor, better, and best ways of performing jobs. Yet despite the apparently sound case that one can establish for time-and-motion analysis, it has been subject to numerous adverse criticisms as a technique for maximizing production.

One weakness of the technique as generally practiced is the worker's misunderstanding and suspicion of it. The time-and-motion analyst is usually perceived as an outsider who is trying to put something over on the worker. "The trouble with this place is that there are too many efficiency experts," is a common complaint of many workers. Employees fear that the efficiency expert is mainly interested in speeding up production and that if this happens, there will be a drop in rate of pay and probably a dismissal of some workers. With this attitude prevalent among the workers, time-and-motion analysis is not likely to result in improved production.

Another criticism of time-and-motion study, with its objective of discovering the best way to do a job, is the questionable standard or criteria used to determine the best way. Traditionally, time-and-motion analysts have assumed that there is one best way for performing each job. But astute observers of worker performance have learned that what may be the best way for John Doe is not the best way for Bill Smith. Physical and psychological differences among workers must be recognized. For example, there is evidence to show that older workers with declining perceptual and motor skills modify their work methods to compensate for their deficiencies, so that the best way for them is different in many respects from the best way for a younger worker.

WAGE INCENTIVES

Some form of incentive wage is offered to about 60 percent of all industrial workers in the United States. Let us take a look at the broad outlines of a fairly typical incentive system that has been in operation at the Procter & Gamble Company since 1928. Consider the case of Frank Handy on his job of sealing boxes of soap in the packing room. Frank's job requires him to put glue on the flaps of the boxes and push them into the sealing belt as they pass down the line. The job has been studied to find both the correct method of doing the work and the average time normally taken to do it. The standard time for this job has been set at thirty-six seconds, or 0.01 hour per box. The rate of 100 boxes an hour means 800 boxes per eight-hour day. However, since Frank can and does seal 125 boxes an hour, or a total of 1,000 boxes, he gets credit for two extra hours, for which he receives a bonus of two hours' pay. So much for the overall picture. The kind of job study on which the system is based is worthy of more detailed treatment in view of what we shall say later about some of the shortcomings of incentive systems.

JOB STUDY

In an actual job study, an examination is made of the various ways or methods of performing the task; this is followed by the selection of the best method. This method is written out in terms of specific job elements, and the employees are trained in this correct method. Next, there is a determination of the average time it takes the employees to do the job. Thus as Frank Handy seals boxes, the job-study engineer records by stopwatch the time for each element of the job. The worker's performance is considered in terms of how *smooth* his operations are, how *quickly* he seals the boxes, how *accurate* he is in applying the glue, and how *careful* he is in lining up the flaps. How well he *plans ahead* in filling the gluepot is also considered. Is Frank physically fit to do the lifting required? Is he the right height to reach the machine? All these factors are critical in the job study.

After studying Frank's job performance, the engineer finds that Frank's skill and effort are above normal. On the basis of company skill and effort values, it is judged that 16 percent more time should be added to make Frank's actual time equal to a fair normal time. This addition amounts to 7.2 minutes per 100 boxes.

In addition to the time required to do the work, an allowance is made in the standard for personal needs and tiring. A fatigue allowance is added to compensate the worker for the effects of getting tired when he maintains a consistent work pace throughout the day. By comparing Frank's job with typical fatigue allowances based on company experiences, the job-study engineer determines that this allowance should be 15 percent of the normal time. This addition amounts to 7.8 minutes per 100 boxes.

When we add together the time for each step in the study of Frank's job, we get the final standard time that is allowed for doing the work:

	Minutes per 100 Boxes	Hours per Box
1. Frank's actual average time	45.0	0.0075
2. Allowances for skills and efforts	7.2	0.0012
3. Personal needs and fatigue	7.8	0.0013
Final standard time	60.0	0.0100

The analysis described above shows the extent to which a job can be objectified. It sets up a standard and provides the worker an opportunity to earn extra money. The company benefits by employing what seem to be the most efficient work methods. At first glance, some kind of incentive system would seem to be an ideal way to step up production and make more money for both employee and employer. Yet despite the apparent objectivity of an incentive system based on a job analysis, important judgment and value questions enter the picture, which give rise to a variety of problems. What is normal job production? What is a fair rate of pay for achieving it? What about employees displaced by production increases?

WHY INCENTIVE SYSTEMS SOMETIMES FAIL

When an incentive system fails, the reasons are sometimes psychological. The announcement of an incentive plan based on a job study such as that exemplified in the case of Frank Handy may be reacted to with distrust. As was pointed out in our earlier discussion of time-and-motion study, the job analyst is often seen as a management man who sets arbitrary rates in order to compel the worker to produce more for the same amount of money. Many workers feel that the analyst will establish a standard production rate that is too tight. Hence even though a bonus is provided for exceeding the standard, the extra pay is not worth the effort. Or if the production rate is not too tight and many workers exceed it and thus make more money, the company will cut the rate. This suspiciousness may cause workers to hold back on production. In a nationwide poll of workers, nearly 75 percent said that a worker should hold back on production because his piece rate would be cut if he worked to full capacity. From a psychological standpoint, it is interesting to note that workers also hold down output in order to protect the less skillful members of their work group. Apparently their loyalties to fellow workers outweigh the desire for financial gain.

An overall appraisal of incentive systems in general would be that sometimes they work well and probably just as frequently they do not. The details of the various incentive systems now in operation are probably of minor importance in determining their success. The important thing is how the worker *perceives* the system in relation to all his needs, psychological and material. The value of incentive pay cannot be viewed in isolation. Work behavior cannot be manipulated solely by the manipulation of money. Financial rewards are part of a total picture. They are effective when other basic needs are also satisfied.

MERIT RATING

On so-called production jobs, proficiency is usually evaluated in quantitative terms. Quantity is often considered to be the only variable. If Frank produces 100 units per hour, he is viewed as being more proficient than John, who turns out 80 units per hour. But of course, in actual practice, most items vary in quality. Thus in measuring worker proficiency, it is necessary to set up a standard which requires that the product be of specifiable quality in order to be acceptable. If units produced are rejected because of qualitative deficiencies, they must be considered waste and subtracted from the output measure. Plotting a work curve is meaningful only to the extent that the counting of units produced is based on a consideration of both qualitative and quantitative aspects.

When we come to the problem of measuring proficiency on non-production jobs, difficulties arise. Nonproduction jobs are those in which quality plays a predominant role. On nonproduction jobs proficiency is usually measured through the use of judgment techniques, which, although subject to some degree of error, have proved useful. Evaluation of a worker's proficiency by a qualified second party familiar with the job is termed *merit rating*. A wide variety of merit-rating systems is used in industry, each with special features. Let us examine three of the most error-free systems.

THREE RATING METHODS

One of the most widely used methods of employee rating is the *employee-comparison* system. In this plan, each employee working under a given supervisor is compared with every other employee. The workers are arranged in pairs. Periodically the supervisor checks the man in each pair who is better in overall performance. The system, however, has limitations. It cannot be used for promotional purposes, counseling, employee improvement, transfer, or layoff, because it cannot show the reasons why a man was rated low. However, in layoffs it may be enough to identify the lowest in the group.

Another system of rating, the *forced-choice* method, requires considerable preliminary work in developing the scale. Pairs of statements about job performance must be found, both of which express equally favorable or unfavorable things about a man; but only one of the statements in each pair actually differentiates between the men known to differ in job performance. The statements are then printed on the rating form in groups of four. Two of the four statements are favorable (and equally favorable), and the remaining two are unfavorable (and equally unfavorable). The rater is asked to check two of the four statements— the one which most accurately describes the man being rated and the one which least accurately describes him. The plan has not had widespread use in industry because of the preliminary work involved and the difficulty encountered in keeping scoring secret. It deserves greater consideration because it produces objective evaluations, yields a more nearly normal distribution than most rating methods, can be scored by machine, and yields ratings that are related to valid indices of good and poor performance.

An increasingly popular and useful method for evaluating proficiency is the *critical-incident* technique, in which there is a determination, through interviews of superiors, of those types of behavior which workers exhibit or fail to exhibit that are critical to success or failure in a given job. Once such a list is compiled, supervisors are asked to watch for these kinds of behavior during work performance. If a considerable number of good critical incidents is noted about a worker over a given period of time and few negative critical incidents have been observed, the man's rating will be high. Conversely, if most of the incidents observed are negative, his rating will be low. In this rating we are getting reports on actual behavior, not just opinions about behavior.

MERIT IS MORE THAN OUTPUT

Although some system of merit rating must be resorted to in evaluating proficiency on nonproduction jobs, performance on production jobs should also be evaluated in terms of merit. Merit is a far more general aspect of proficiency than production in terms of items turned out per time unit. Merit includes a variety of characteristics which make a man a valuable employee, such as his attitude toward other employees and the supervisor, observance of safety regulations, assumption of responsibility, and the like. Systematic merit rating brings to the supervisor's attention many aspects of the employee's performance that can be improved and often suggests the appropriate course of action.

WORK AND ACCIDENTS

Of the many and varied problems related to men working, one of the most costly is industrial accidents. A report of the National Safety Council indicates that industrial accidents cost well over 3 billion dollars a year, with an average cost to industry of about $50 a worker. The monetary cost is enormous, but in terms of life and limb the situation is tragic. Accidents and safety are obviously critically important areas of inquiry for the industrial psychologists.

Even in the relatively safe environment of a college campus accidents occur. In one year one university reported that twenty students fell off curbs, eighteen tripped on shoelaces, and thirty-eight walked through windows. Thirteen students hurt themselves by dropping cafeteria trays on their feet, one fell off a laboratory stool, and ten fell out of bed. Yes, and forty-four students sustained injury by running into other people.

Some people behave as if they were spring-loaded for an accident. In many instances, the problems related to accidents seem to grow by increments, where one risk-taking bit of behavior leads to another.

THE NUMBER ONE CAUSE

It is not uncommon to read in the news of someone who has been hurt by walking through a glass door. Markings on the door at adult eye level may not help the small child. Safety glass, of course, can help reduce the severity of the accident. This example illustrates that safety involves both people and things.

At work and at home, falls lead in accident causes. This chief cause is followed by handling objects, being struck by falling objects, and contacting harmful substances. Electricity, heat, explosives, and machinery account for most other accidents. Practically all studies in the field of accidents have indicated that *human factors rank number one in causing accidents.*

DEFINITION OF AN ACCIDENT

If a workman falls off a ladder and is not injured to the slightest degree and does not cause any damage to equipment, is this an accident? Frequently the answer is "no." Suppose he sprains his ankle in falling off the ladder. Is this an accident? What about the worker who falls off the ladder and rubs the skin from his elbows; shall we call this occurrence an accident? Indeed, in each of these instances we have an act or instance of behavior which we must call an accident. There are of course differences. In one case the results are inconsequential, in another there is a skin abrasion, and in still another there is an incapacitating sprained ankle. However, common to each of these instances is the act of falling off the ladder. The differences lie in the *results* of falling off the ladder.

There are instances of behavior involving acts with common features and different results. There are other instances in which the acts are different but the results are similar. A complete understanding of the nature of accidents and their prevention requires that a careful distinction be made between acts and the results of these acts. The appropriate distinction is made in the descriptive statement that defines an accident as *an unexpected, incorrect, but not necessarily injurious or damaging event that interrupts the completion of an activity.*

ACCIDENT RESULTS

Some of the major classes of accident results can be enumerated without difficulty. First, there are results which do not involve injuries of any consequence. These are no-injury accidents. A workman bumps against a piece of moving machinery. Result: just grease on his overalls and a button ripped off his suspenders. Second, there are minor-injury accidents. A workman bumps against the same piece of machinery and suffers a slight laceration of the skin on his forearm. Third, there are accidents involving major injuries. Contact with moving machinery results in a mangled hand which has to be amputated. And of course there are accidents in which there is damage to equipment. A workman bumps into the moving machinery, and his recoil causes a nearby wrench to fall into revolving gears. There is a damaged machine although no bodily injury. Widely different results are apparent in each of these cases, but each result stems from the same or nearly the same happening.

THE CAUSES OF ACCIDENTS

Every enlightened student of behavior knows that behavior is caused; accident behavior is no exception. A close examination of accident causes reveals two general categories—unsafe conditions and unsafe acts. *Unsafe conditions* involve some aspect of the physical environment which sets up or makes probable the occurrence of an accident. Cluttered arrangement of machinery, poor lighting, unguarded moving parts, and oily floors are examples of unsafe conditions. *Unsafe acts* are those kinds of behavior which lead to an accident or those failures in performance which result in an accident. In the cases previously cited in which three workers bumped into a piece of machinery, the unsafe act was the act of making contact with the machine. The results were different in each case, but if the act of bumping had not occurred, there wouldn't have been any result to worry about. Failure to engage a safety device is an example of neglectful behavior which frequently leads to an accident.

INTERACTION OF ACTS AND CONDITIONS

Unsafe acts and unsafe conditions may interact in such a way that an accident may be caused by both. Too, an accident may be caused by a number of unsafe conditions or by a number of unsafe acts. The careful investigator always seeks to determine all the factors which lead to an accident.

Let us now push our analysis of causes a little further and ask what causes the unsafe condition or the unsafe act. Since we are getting further and further removed from the actual accident, we may call these matters indirect causes of accidents. The unsafe-act and unsafe-condition categories we may conveniently call the direct causes of accidents.

What causes a man to perform an unsafe act? A number of possibilities are immediately apparent, such as faulty vision, illness, worry, intoxication, poor coordination, lack of job know-how, and the like.

All these states or conditions reside within the individual; they make up the so-called "human element," and we may justifiably call them human factors.

Analyzing the nature of causes to the point where we are dealing with human factors is helpful in understanding accident causation because we are now dealing with something which can tell us why the unsafe act was performed. If we can isolate a human element responsible for the unsafe act, we are in a position to do something constructive. Thus if one of the human elements responsible for the unsafe act is lack of job know-how, we may be able to eliminate this causative factor by training. If the cause is faulty vision, corrective glasses may remedy the situation. If the human factor is incorrectable, the offender can be removed from the job and placed in a less hazardous type of work. Usually, however, we are just a bit more cautious of safety when doing hazardous work. Statistics show, for example, that the accident record of professional window washers is low, much lower, in fact, than the percentage of accidents found among housewives cleaning around the home.

Unsafe conditions usually stem from human factors. A worker overloads a conveyor belt and leaves the scene; later the belt breaks, and the result is an accident to someone in the immediate vicinity. The direct cause of the accident, the broken belt, is an unsafe condition caused by an unsafe act. But why did the worker commit the unsafe act of overloading the belt and walking away? Was he distracted by worry over unpaid bills or the illness of a member of his family? If we trace the accident back to its source, we find that the worker's state of mind was the indirect cause out of which the direct causes originated.

As a matter of fact it is not hard to present a strong case for the contention that all unsafe conditions have their origin in human factors. Worn-out machinery can create an unsafe condition which might cause an accident. But if the machine had been properly maintained and the wearing parts replaced soon enough, the wearing out would have been avoided, and the unsafe condition would never have occurred. Why did a worker fail to maintain the machine in proper working order? What human factor in him caused the neglect? A steampipe may burst and be the cause of an accident. This looks like an unsafe condition in which no human factor is involved. But steampipes are supposed to be tested periodically for stress potential, and failure to do this is an unsafe act by a human operator. Once again we may ask: Why was the operator negligent? Cases like these are frequently classified as unsafe conditions caused by nonhuman factors, but it is obvious that the classification is arbitrary. It is used where the causative human agent is not readily identifiable.

The year 1966 was one that related highway accidents to a chain of events. This was the year the Congress established the National Traffic Safety Agency to protect passengers in automobiles. Can it be that an automobile accident has its origin in Michigan? In Berlin? In faulty brakes? In power systems? It is a fact that cars made on a Monday are more prone to defects: plant absences are high on this day, and second-string men have to be put on the assembly line. Can this type of behavior be regulated by legislation? How far can one go in controlling driver behavior? Perhaps we may get some cues to these questions by taking a look at programs of safety in industry.

If all accidents are caused, then careful analysis and observation should lead to the discovery of the causes. The next obvious step is to remove the causes. Accident prevention has been retarded by the failure to identify in some systematic fashion the conditions which cause accidents.

THE ACCIDENT REPORT

Where shall we turn to obtain reliable data or information useful for an accident-prevention program? The basic source of such information is the accident report. A good accident report should include data on such items as the following:

1 *Date, hour of the day, shift, and location.* Working conditions often change, sometimes in a systematic manner from day to day, from hour to hour, and from shift to shift. For example, the day-shift worker usually comes to work after a full night's sleep and breakfast. The preceding activity of the night-shift worker is usually more varied. Fatigue effects are more pronounced during the latter part of the working day. These and other factors under this category may influence accident behavior.

2 *Job classification, job operation, and job unit.* These data give specific information about the type of work in which the accident occurs. The hazard potential of different jobs and operations within jobs can thus be determined. Suppose that a painter fell from a ladder while descending with his back to the rungs of the ladder. His job classification would be painter; his job operation, using a ladder; his job-operation unit, descending the ladder.

3 *Accident type.* Information in this category should include an exact description of the nature of the accident, including a description

of the contact agent. These descriptive data are not necessarily extensive and detailed. For the painter who fell from the ladder, a statement such as "fell to the floor" would be sufficient.

4   *Immediate cause of the accident.* This information covers the cause of the accident in terms of specific unsafe acts or conditions or both. Among other findings, we get from this information an answer to the question: What violation of a commonly accepted safety procedure resulted in a particular accident? We need to know what actually was done or was not done that contributed to the accident.

5   *Results of the accident.* Data under this heading cover bodily location of the injury, description of the injury, and extent of property damage. Frequently the person who fills out the accident report cannot immediately describe the injury or property damage precisely. Medical assistance and help from someone responsible for assessing property damage are needed.

6   *Experience.* How important experience on the job is in relation to type of accident can be determined only by a careful analysis of reliable data, the source of which must be the accident report. Data such as these can be of great help in planning a safety training program.

7   *Psychological data.* If available, scores on aptitude tests, personality inventories, and achievement tests should be included in the accident report. The analysis of such data may provide information for identifying some of the personal factors contributing to accident behavior.

ACCIDENT REDUCTION

Accident reduction is achieved through training only if the worker learns to behave safely on the job. If a new worker who does not know the company safety regulations is given this knowledge and demonstrates that he knows it, has he been trained in accident prevention? Not necessarily. Knowing will not always ensure doing. The problem of training clearly involves two phases: first, the worker must learn how to behave the safe way; second, he must be stimulated to do it. Thus the safety slogan of the United States Steel Corporation— "Knowing's not enough."

Basic accident-prevention strategy calls for:

1   *A cause analysis of accidents.* Speculation that an accident was the result of worry, lack of attention, or carelessness has no place in accident-prevention strategy. Strategy requires observation of men at work and, from these observations, an identification of unsafe acts and unsafe conditions.

2   *A distinction between accidents per se and their results.* To define an accident as "an act in which someone gets hurt" makes cause

analysis difficult if not impossible. It is poor policy to wait for an injury before making a cause analysis. The same principle applies to cause analysis resulting in loss of time.

3 *Elimination of unsafe acts.* When the cause analysis points to an unsafe act, appropriate action must be taken to correct this factor. This may require training, and the nature of the training depends on the need. It may be that the trainee does not know what to do, or he may know and not put into practice what he knows. If the unsafe act cannot be eliminated by training, placement of the employee in a less hazardous job is necessary.

4 *Elimination of unsafe conditions.* If some factor in the physical environment is leading to accidents, steps to nullify it should be taken. Wearing safety equipment may be the nullifying step. Proper maintenance of machinery is another possibility. A guard or other safety device on a piece of machinery is still another. Research on the design of equipment will lead to the discovery of additional unsafe aspects of the physical environment.

Accidents now outrank diseases as a leading cause of death from age one to age thirty-four. Industry is now increasing its attention to the off-the-job accident as a major step in preserving the working effectiveness of its employees. Major strategies include the control of exposure to risk, the reduction of accidents during risks, the prevention of injury when accidents occur, and minimizing the residuals of injury.

PERSONAL FACTORS RELATED TO ACCIDENTS

Most of us as adults are aware that it is necessary for children to be protected until they are mature enough to govern certain aspects of their own behavior. We keep poisons out of their reach, and we prevent them from running into the street. Yet, as adults we climb on stacked boxes, take other risks, and behave in ways that we do not allow in the child. We require the three-year-old to rest when he is tired, yet many of us insist on driving the car well beyond a safe fatigue level. We try to calm the child when he is overexcited but rarely govern our adult behavior in similar manner. We do not expect the five-year-old to be able to use potentially dangerous tools, yet we have no hesitancy in using a power saw when we are angry. What does research say about the personal factors related to accidents?

RISK TAKING

A promising new area of research has to do with the concept of risk as a basic human factor in accident causation. A new term is now being used to describe the behavioral trait of engaging in an activity in which failure is quite likely. We call this personal trait *risk acceptance*. Immediately we think of gamblers who range widely in how much risk they will take. At one end of the scale we find the calculated-risk taker (who may often succeed), and at the other end of the scale, the wild-chance taker who reacts as though he can beat all odds (he often fails).

In one study a simulated laboratory situation was used in which the subjects were classified into a "low-risk" group and a "high-risk" group on the basis of personality tests. Following this classification the subjects were put on jobs with the same possible accident hazards. After a period of time it was found that the subjects in the high-risk group had incurred more accidents, were less skillful, and possessed greater variability in task performance than the low-risk group.

FATIGUE

The critical point at which fatigue becomes an accident cause in an individual has not been determined. We do know, however, that extreme fatigue leads to increased accident frequency. For example, in a shell factory in England during World War II the accident rate among women workers was reduced by more than 60 percent when the factory changed from a twelve-hour to a ten-hour day.

Caution must be exercised in attributing accidents to fatigue if there is an accompanying change in production rate. What may seem to be a fatigue factor may really be a tendency to overlook accident dangers because one is working faster. The way to separate these two factors may be illustrated by an analysis of accidents made by the United States Public Health Service in which the effect of production rate was held constant. The technique was to divide the accident index by the production index for a given work period; in other words, to report in terms of accidents per unit of output. Results showed that in the *earlier hours* of the day the index rises and falls with the output rate. Increases in production bring a corresponding increase in the number of accidents. However, this relation breaks down in the *closing hours* of the working day. Here the accident rate remains high relative to the production rate. Such an analysis makes it possible to show the importance of the fatigue factors. Formal studies have shown essentially the same thing as the experience many people report. On the highway, at work, and in the home fatigue interferes with our psychomotor coordination and lessens our alertness. One observer put it this way, "When I get very tired and keep going I'm just an accident looking for some place to happen."

COORDINATION

It would seem reasonable to suppose that slowness of response and clumsiness would contribute to accident frequency. Yet speed of reaction in and of itself has been found to have no significant relation to accident frequency in industry. However, more complex reaction tendencies are important.

One investigator used a battery of tests consisting of a dotting test, a device for measuring speed of reaction to a signal. Another test required the subject to change his muscular performance in accordance with changing signals. When 500 employees were divided into two groups on the basis of high and low test scores, the poorer performers had 51 percent more accidents than the better three-quarters. Other investigations support the conclusion that poor muscular coordination has a bearing on accident susceptibility.

VISION

How well a person can see would appear to be a factor contributing to accident susceptibility. Research supports this contention. For example, one investigator found that only 37 percent of a group of machine operators who passed visual tests had accidents during a given year. On the other hand, 67 percent of those who did not pass the vision test had accidents.

PERSONALITY CHARACTERISTICS

There is mounting evidence that the personality and temperament of the individual have a great deal to do with the susceptibility to accidents.

A relationship between emotional cycles and frequency of accidents has been reported from a study which showed that the average worker is emotionally low about 20 percent of the time and that more than half of the 400 minor accidents studied occurred during these low periods. In another study it was shown that the high accident rates were found among the men most disliked by their fellow workers. Men well liked by their associates tended to be accident-free. Other studies show that when one is excessively elated he is subject to being in accidents more than when he is in a neutral emotional state. On jobs with high attention requirements introverts are less likely to have accidents than extroverts.

What about intelligence scores and accidents? The literature on this subject is not clear. Dull people do not seem to have any more accidents than bright people in some situations, but they do have more in other situations. Intelligence seems to be related to accidents involving errors of judgment, but not to accidents involving only manual skills. Very likely a minimum amount of mental ability is necessary for accident-free behavior in all occupations.

FUTURE RESEARCH

As stated above, accidents now outrank diseases as a leading cause of death from age one to age thirty-four. These statistics include both on-the-job and off-the-job data. Only recently has the public become ego-involved in safety research, automobiles and highway accidents making the overall problem more dramatic. The growth of accident clinics, where emphasis is placed on human causes of accidents, is adding to the engineering of safer equipment. Major strategies include the control of exposure to risk, the reduction of accidents during risks, the prevention of injury when accidents occur, and minimizing the residuals of injury. But at the core is the human element. We are becoming more aware that safe performance, in the home, at the job, or on the highway deteriorates if there is either too little stimulation or too much. Both extremes subject the individual to an increase in the potentials of an accident.

Summary

One may think of work as the use of the individual's physiological and mental processes in the accomplishing of some goal. The difference between work and play centers around motivation. What is play for the amateur golfer may be work for the professional.

There are numerous practical ways of making work more efficient, less fatiguing, and sometimes more pleasant. Efficiency is related not only to rest pauses and coffee breaks but to how these programs are established and managed. Boredom, the worker's reaction to the job, arises from the conflict between the necessity for doing a dull job and wanting to turn to more interesting activities. The student may find that the several ways found effective in eliminating boredom in work situations may well apply in the educational environment. In the main, the individual should look at his own behavior in terms of what stimulates him or fails to provide incentive. In one individual low threshold for boredom may be offset by a low threshold for stimulation. In another person it may be accompanied by a high threshold for stimulation. In the second instance, boredom may become a serious psychological problem for the individual.

Many analyses have been made of time-and-motion study, of wage incentives, and of merit rating. Here again the reader may well find that the problems involved in pacing work, paying for work, and being evaluated are not too different from those found in an educational setting. In particular one may conclude that industry has never really solved the problem of merit rating. The same is true in attempts to evaluate student performance on examinations.

Of the many and varied problems related to men working, one of the most costly is accidents. Practically all studies in the field of accidents have indicated that human factors rank number one in causing accidents. Unsafe acts and unsafe conditions interact in such a way that an accident may be caused by both. Some practical information is known about what causes a man to perform an unsafe act. There are also many ways in which accidents can be reduced.

Suggestions for Thinking and Discussion

1 Make a list of activities that you would regard as work. Make another list that you would regard as play. What are the differences between the two lists?
2 With reference to the incident of the student who would fall asleep over his books (page 297), describe from your experience some situations of fatigue brought on by a psychological situation.
3 What kinds of situation bring on boredom in *you?* What do you do when you become bored?
4 Compare grade determination in a particular course with merit rating in industry. Why is evaluation in both situations so difficult?
5 Describe some "near accident" that you have observed. What situations brought on the near accident? What prevented it from becoming an actual accident?
6 Evolve a theory relating accidents to risk taking.

Suggestions for Further Reading

Barnes, R. M. *Motion and time study*. New York: Wiley, 1958. The fourth edition of a book on techniques of time-and-motion study.
Barrett, R. S. *Performance rating*. Chicago: Science Research Associates, 1966. A summary of research and techniques on work evaluation.
Gellerman, S. W. (Ed.) *Motivation and productivity*. New York: American Management Association, 1963. A book of readings integrated with text. Covers some of the practical problems of work.
National Safety Council. *Accident facts*. Chicago. Various editions keep up to date on research and accident prevention.
Whyte, W. F. *Men at work*. Homewood, Ill.: Irwin, 1961. Case materials about work.

CHAPTER 14

The

Working Environments

❖◆❖◆❖◆❖◆❖◆❖◆❖

No discussion of work would be complete without descriptions of the *places* where people work—home, school, college, office, shop, plant, laboratory, or down on the farm. In one sense of the word, working environments are all around us.

Home environments have their physical descriptions in terms of houses or apartments, spiit-level homes or those without basements. They also have their psychological environments, described in such terms as friendly or formal; permissive or tense; or as being a nice place to come to or a place to avoid as long as possible. Colleges have their environments in terms of different climates, as we mentioned in Chapter 9.

For the salesman, who must do much of his work on the road, hotel climates become important, and different people may have quite different reactions to the same hotel. One person may like a hotel because it is sophisticated; another may dislike it for the same reason. Tour agencies have long been aware of the importance of matching individuals with appropriate accommodations suitable to their status, demands, and pocketbooks. One person may like the small friendly hotel where he is called by name and known individually. Another person may prefer the large hotel where he can get lost.

In much the same way that we can describe the atmosphere of the place we live in, we can describe work environments on the job. We are interested in the psychological atmosphere or "climate" of these places because it is related to problems of satisfaction and dissatisfaction, to problems related to success and failure.

Individual personalities and school or job requirements *interact* to produce a climate that affects both the individual and the organization. The psychological environment is in effect what we react to—the frustration as well as the pleasures derived from the "collegiate culture," or the whole context of stimulation and confusion where we work.

Let us take a look at physical environments first. This will be followed by descriptions of psychological environments.

INDUSTRIAL PHYSICAL ENVIRONMENTS

Many studies have been carried out on the effects of noise, illumination, temperature, ventilation, music, and related conditions on work output. Both in the office and in the plant these physical aspects of the environment are related to psychological climates. Let us take a look at some conclusions as to how noise and other conditions affect work.

NOISE

Noise is usually regarded as distracting and therefore as interfering with work efficiency. "I can't do my job properly around this place because it's too noisy," is a common worker's complaint. Actually, clear-cut evidence that noise reduces work output is very scant. We do know, of course, that many people find different kinds of auditory stimulation irritating. Thus high tones and very low tones are judged almost universally to be more annoying or irritating than tones in the middle ranges. Unexpected noises, intermittent noises, and reverberating noises are also irritating to most people. Such knowledge as this has made it possible to sound-treat work areas in order to reduce the irritating effects of noise.

An interesting study of the effects of noise in a work situation has been conducted in England in a film-processing plant. Different measures of efficiency were made in untreated workplaces and in the same places after the noise level was measurably reduced by acoustical treatment. The results of this study showed that rate of work was not improved by noise reduction but that *error was significantly less frequent when the noise level was lower.*

Another study had to do with the output of weavers over a period of twenty-six weeks during which the workers wore ear defenders on alternate weeks. The protective devices reduced the noise from 96 to 87 decibels. There was an increase of 12 percent in speed of production while the workers were wearing the ear defenders.

In view of the universal dislike of noise it seems probable that deleterious effects exist, but much additional research must be conducted before definite conclusions can be drawn regarding the effects of noise on work output in different kinds of jobs.

M U S I C

Within recent years, the practice of introducing music into the workplace has become common. Music is alleged to have salutary effects on attitudes, to improve morale, and to increase production. In two investigations, significant increases in production were associated with the use of music. In both these studies the workers performed relatively simple tasks. Before it can be assumed that all productive effort will be enhanced by music, the effects of music on different kinds of tasks must be determined.

In one study of the effects of music on a complex industrial task, attitudes were revealed as important. This investigation was conducted in a rug-manufacturing factory and dealt with a task known as "setting." Setting is a relatively complex job involving the preparation of material for rug looms. The work requires a high level of mental and manipulative skill and considerable physical endurance. Music was found to have no favorable or unfavorable effects upon the production of workers in the setting operations. Despite these findings, questionnaire results showed that the workers were favorably disposed toward music and, perhaps more significantly, that they believed that it increased their actual production.

It is not entirely clear why simple task performance is sometimes improved by music and complex task behavior is not. One possibility is that the workers in the setting operation, being highly skilled and experienced, had developed stable habits of production and adequate adjustments to the work environment and that music effects were not sufficiently strong to break these well-established habit patterns.

I L L U M I N A T I O N

Despite a voluminous literature on the effects of illumination on work efficiency, solidly established relationships are practically nonexistent. Studies have been conducted in actual work situations. In some cases changes in illumination appear to be related to output, but so many variables have been left uncontrolled that it is impossible to assess the effect of the illumination variable per se. There have been well-controlled laboratory studies, but in these cases the tasks were often not of the kind performed in the industrial workshop. Where there does appear to be similarity between the laboratory tasks and workshop tasks, it is possible to make educated guesses as to the probable effects of various illumination levels on industrial output. Tentatively, it has been concluded that the majority of industrial operations could be carried out with maximum efficiency in the neighborhood of 10 footcandles. In exacting visual tasks such as drafting and typesetting, as much as 40 footcandles is required, and spectral qualities are often important.

COLOR

The color dynamics of the workplace is often claimed to be an important determinant of work efficiency, but supporting evidence is conspicuously nonexistent. One of the few experiments related to the color problem is that dealing with the effects of colored illumination on perceived temperature. This study was prompted by the almost universal tendency to speak of green and blue as "cool" colors and red and orange as "warm." The experimental question was: Can a person's judgment of the temperature of the air around him be biased by the hue of his surroundings? Subjects performed a number of tasks illuminated by different spectral lights and were asked to indicate by a switch when the temperature rose to a point at which they began to feel uncomfortably warm. The findings showed no change in the levels of heat they would tolerate as a function of the colors of illumination, but nevertheless, when asked to rank the colors they had experienced, the subjects persisted in the conventional belief that blue and green are cool colors. It appears, therefore, that despite beliefs about color efficiency, any attempt to change the comfort of persons in a work environment through variations in colored illumination may be unsuccessful.

ATMOSPHERIC EFFECTS

Every worker at one time or another has complained about the heat or the cold in terms which imply that his efficiency is being affected adversely by the temperature of the working environment. A determination of temperature effects on work efficiency would seemingly be an easy matter. The problem actually is complicated because almost always when atmospheric temperature varies, other conditions such as humidity do not remain constant. There are a few studies which enable us to pinpoint temperature effects uncontaminated by uncontrolled variables. These studies have been summarized by one investigator, and he concludes that the desirable temperatures for sedentary work in winter are from 68 to 73°F and for the same kind of work in summer, 75 to 80°; for moderately hard work in all seasons, the desirable temperature is 65°, for strenuous work, 60°. Humidity effects are considered negligible because in the range of temperatures investigated relative humidity is an unimportant variable.

HUMIDITY

The role of humidity has been demonstrated in a number of studies, so that there is a factual basis for the common expression that "it's not the heat, but the humidity" which causes discomfort. In one of these studies workers were exposed for one hour to different combinations of humidity and temperature. Temperatures as high as 140°F were judged to be tolerable when the humidity was only 10 percent. On the other hand, when the humidity reached 80 percent, a temperature of 110°F was judged to be intolerable.

AIR CIRCULATION

Besides temperature and humidity, air circulation is another atmospheric condition that is critical in a good work environment. An example is a study in which electric fans were operated on alternate days for a period of six summer weeks and the effects on a weaving operation were observed. For every hour of the working day, production with the fans stopped was less than when the fans were running. The beneficial effects of the fans were greater in the afternoon than in the morning, for the most part, although the third hour of the morning and the second hour of the afternoon showed the greatest production increases.

Altering atmospheric conditions in order to create a favorable working environment is nowadays frequently accomplished through the installation of air-conditioning systems. Indeed, these systems are now under such precise control that humidity, temperature, and air-circulation problems would appear to be amenable to ready solution. However, the problems are not so simple as they appear. The complicating factor is the worker's reaction to or his perception of the change brought about through the manipulation of physical variables. A case in point is the reaction of workers in a blackout factory built in Texas during World War II. The building contained no windows or skylights but was conditioned to control temperature, humidity, and air circulation.

Since the ceiling was 50 feet from the floor, most of the air vents were located near the top of the walls.

From the beginning employees complained about the bad air. It was too hot, too humid, and too close. A thorough check of the system was made, and it was found to be in excellent working order. Complaints persisted until it was recognized that the workers were rural people unaccustomed to industrial work and air conditioning. They felt cooped up in a windowless plant where they could not feel a breeze. Since the vents were too high for the workers to feel the moving air, they needed some visual indication of stirring air. When tissue streamers were fastened to the ventilators high on the walls, the workers could see that the air was moving. The frequency of employee complaints soon became negligible.

THE ANATOMY OF THE MODERN COMPANY

The administrative anatomy of a company is designed for the purpose of making decisions most effectively. This is an essential part of the working environment. Only in the smallest of firms are decisions made by a single individual. Ordinarily, even though the final responsibility for taking an action may rest on one particular person, usually a number of people make the formal and informal preparations that lead to the decision situation.

The decision-making process of converting policy into practice necessitates an administrative setup in which each division of a company is headed by someone who has both authority and responsibility for its supervision and control. Similarly each division may be broken down into a framework of departments with an operating head for each.

No two companies are identical. Company organizations vary not only in size but also in the character of the people making up the company. However, there are five principal types of administrative organizations into which most firms can be placed.

LINE ORGANIZATION

This is a very simple structure. Responsibility and control stem directly from general manager to superintendent to foremen to workers.

LINE AND STAFF ORGANIZATION

As companies get larger, they become more complex, and top executives can no longer be personally responsible for such different functions as research, engineering, testing, planning, distribution, public relations, and other activities requiring special training and experience.

In this type of organization executives and supervisors retain authority and control over activities in their particular departments. But this *line* function is aided by *staff* assistance from engineers, budget officers, and other specialists.

FUNCTIONAL ORGANIZATION

This structure is an extension of the line and staff organization; here more attention is given to specialized skills, mainly at the supervisory or foreman level. One foreman may serve as the production boss to meet quotas, another as inspector, and a third may be responsible for maintenance. In this system the clear-cut lines of responsibility and authority of the line organization have been lost, but gains have been made in terms of getting more specialized work supervision.

LINE AND FUNCTIONAL STAFF ORGANIZATION

This type of organization gives the functional staff more responsibility and authority in consultation with the line organization in such specialized functions as inspection, purchasing, and shipping.

LINE, FUNCTIONAL STAFF, AND COMMITTEE ORGANIZATION

In order to facilitate communication involving decision making, some large companies construct a network of committees to work with the line and staff organization. In certain companies these committees are permanent and meet regularly. In others they are organized to serve a temporary function only.

LINES OF RESPONSIBILITY

In theory at least, organizational structure demands that the lines of responsibility do not require too many men to report directly to one man. In large organizations, industrial psychologists employed by the company often operate in the department of industrial relations. Their duties may range from those of human-factors specialist to those of consumer researcher. Consulting psychologists may work at any level within the organization. Consulting organizations function in an advisory capacity to the president and to other officers.

In the company of moderate size, employing some two thousand or fewer personnel, the organizational structure is less spread out. For example, a works manager rather than a vice-president may be in control of such staff functions as industrial relations, product development, and purchasing.

SIZE OF COMPANY

As one comes to understand business organizations of different magnitudes, it soon is apparent that each size has characteristic strengths and weaknesses. Since no one man in the large company can have the personal knowledge of what is going on and the personal contact with his workers that an owner-manager has, the large company is forced more in the direction of coordination and group action. Personal ego interests, though always present in the so-called "company man," may be placed more in the background in the larger organization.

The organizational structure of most companies of medium or large size has an inherent problem. There is not enough flexibility to meet emergencies when perfect coordination fails. Supervision at the foreman level finds itself in a myriad of what appear to be impossible demands coming down from the top. There is insufficient flexibility to overcome the gremlins of distribution, material shortage, and machine breakdowns. However, modern management is attacking such problems with systems analysis, mathematical programming, automation, communication control, or what has recently been called "information technology." Yet the biggest problem of the entire industrial scene involves the human element. Asks one observer, "What will happen to the individual? Most organizations in the world are getting larger while the world itself is getting smaller. . . . We will grow bigger and alas for all of us, not just for the young, facelessness will follow bigness, as the night, the day."

SIZE AND PROBLEMS

When we think in terms of size of an organization, it is important at times to distinguish between the overall size of the corporation and the company's subunits, such as divisions or departments. In terms of overall size, large companies have many technical and financial-resource advantages, they have more community and international prestige than smaller companies, and they offer self-fulfillment opportunities for a small number of persons in the middle and upper levels of management. Bigness also has disadvantages—delay in decisions, ego-satisfaction problems for a large majority of people, and problems of bureaucratic power for the subordinate. There is evidence that productivity and profitability are lower in the large divisions of a company than in the small divisions and that workers in small work groups or departments are better satisfied than workers in large groups or departments. More absences and turnover are found among larger work groups, but the general belief that communication is better in the smaller organization is not necessarily true. Size is a variable in identifying and handling people problems, but it is important to specify whether we are talking about company size or the size of subunits. Failure to do so may lead to some beliefs contrary to facts.

The anatomy of the modern company also includes psychological climates. Let us take a look at these.

PSYCHOLOGICAL CLIMATES

One way to think of the psychological climate of an industrial organization is to speak of the *company personality*. One may be described as "democratic" in contrast to another which is "authoritarian." One may be very "aggressive" and another "passive." One may be described as "friendly" and another as "impersonal."

AN IMPORTANT QUESTION

"What kind of climate is best for *me* to work in?" If the individual is an outgoing person who is full of ideas and likes to participate, he may be better satisfied working in a democratic or permissive climate. On the other hand, if he prefers to be told what to do and does not relish taking part in decision-making conferences, he may be better off in an autocratic climate.

Some organizations seem to be permeated with fear, and some function in an atmosphere of permissiveness. Psychologists who have worked with different industries believe that companies fall into psychological patterns. One young computer programmer says, "In my company I am well paid, but I have the feeling that I never know where I stand." A secretary says, "I dislike being made to feel just like another piece of furniture." There are those who, in seeking a good climate, find the balance between chaos and order is easy to tilt, and some of us find it difficult to regain our position in a climate that has left us behind.

The personality of a company, in many respects, is a composite of the varied ways of behaving of the people within it. Let us take a look at this picture.

PERSONALITY TYPES

Some people may be described as "tender-minded" and others as "tough-minded." Some people are very practical, others are idealistic. The practical individual accepts rules and customs *as they are*. The idealist is concerned with how things *ought to be*. We can see these different types of people on any campus or in any large work situation. Such disparities of personality often make for stimulating classroom discussions. At work they sometimes are related to conflict.

Studies show that there are three general types of personality in any organization of an appreciable size. Found at or near the top of the organization pyramid are the "upward mobiles," who react positively to the large bureaucratic situation and succeed in it. The uncommitted majority in the organization are the "indifferents," who see their jobs as mere instruments toward obtaining off-work satisfactions. Then there is a small, perpetually disturbed minority composed of persons who can neither renounce their claims for status and power nor play the disciplined role to get them. These type descriptions are oversimplified and idealized, but useful in better understanding organizations and people.

Though one may not wish to place people rigidly in pigeonholes, their types of behavior do *point in directions* leading to the assumption that the large organization provides a more sympathetic workplace for the upward-mobile person (who is less critical of some of those values that lead to success) than for the person who wishes to escape through indifference or the one who wishes to contest the *status quo*. We shall give some generalized descriptions of these three personality types, which will possibly not give an adequate picture of any one individual. It might be well, also, to keep in mind that there are perhaps individuals who combine some of the characteristics of all three types. One person may play an upward-mobile role to reach a position of relative security where he can afford to be indifferent to the job and yet induce change by indirect means.

Many researchers say that both upward mobility and indifference are functions of class and education as well as of personality. It is also true that attitudes toward "pyramid climbing" are complex and contradictory. Within this frame of reference we give the following brief descriptions.

UPWARD MOBILES

These people have tendencies toward high job satisfaction and identify strongly with the organization. Typically they get a disproportionate share of the organization's rewards in power, income, and ego reinforcement. A lack of success is more likely to be interpreted by them as personal failure than as system failure. The upward mobile is an organization man. He is a conformist who can act without much self-analysis. He plays at human relations as a career utility, is sensitive

APPLIED PSYCHOLOGY

to feedback, and behaves accordingly. This driving type thinks in strategic terms and will use ritualistic behavior to conceal resentments. He realizes that power is potential influence.

The upward mobile is rule- and procedure-oriented and often views individuals in detached terms. He places personal advancement before group acceptance, feels little sense of conflict, and goes in heavily for the paraphernalia of organizations. His interests and aspirations are tied to the organization so much that he finds little difficulty in rationalizing organizational claims. He seeks out the sights and sounds of power. Often he lacks broad or national perspective on problems. Upward-mobile people generally are not hampered by any desire for obscurity. Sometimes when they fall they go down hard.

INDIFFERENTS

The great mass of wage and salary employees come within the category of the indifferents. These are the people who withdraw from system participation when possible. In one sense they sometimes regard organizations, especially large ones, as "planned systems of frustration." Compared with the upward mobiles, they do not compete strongly for rewards. Since this is a typical pattern of the majority in an organization, the upward mobiles get more chance to operate. In effect, then, the indifferent shares in neither the ownership and profits nor the ego involvements of the organization. He must therefore seek off-the-job satisfaction. He rejects the values of success and power, paying lip service to the system only when he has to. Nevertheless, the indifferent person still wants to be treated as an individual. He does not want to be analyzed, he does not want to be computerized, he wants to be recognized.

Many indifferents, both blue-collar and white-collar, pay lip service to getting ahead but transfer their expectations to their children. They "expect less" and, therefore, may be "less disappointed." Status anxiety, success striving, and self-discipline, which are characteristic of the upward mobile, are rejected by the indifferent. After he puts in his required hours of work, he jealously guards the remaining time as his, because he separates his work from his personal life. On the job, anything that is not routine worries the indifferent person.

It is noticeable in the mass-production type of industry that the indifferent person may depreciate the things he makes. ("If people only knew how shabby those things are they wouldn't buy them.") He has become conditioned not to expect much from the organization and not to identify strongly with it. This may be related to the fact that he gradually becomes immune to discipline and seeks to identify himself with his immediate work companions. Labor economists say this attitude allows the small group to play a protective role and thus, through the union, shields this man from real or imaginary threats from management.

Sometimes, as his organization changes, the formally upward-mobile person shifts to a role of indifference. This is related in some respects to the "middle-age revolt" which was described in Chapter 8. The man may reject advancement because of the added responsibility it entails. The indifferent person frequently has generally satisfactory interpersonal relations, since he is not perceived as a threat by his colleagues. Even in his large union, the indifferent worker only helps provide numerical support for decisions made by others. For the indifferent person, blue-collar or white collar, people, jobs, and organizations are not much different; *he tends to adjust to each.*

AMBIVALENTS

These people are described as both creative and anxious. They usually find themselves in a marginal position, with somewhat limited career chances. They can neither reject the organization's promise of success and power nor play the varied roles required to compete for them. While upward-mobile anxiety is usually adaptive, the ambivalent attitude tends toward the neurotic. While the upward mobile likes the *status quo* and the indifferent person accepts it, the ambivalent person wants to change it.

Intellectual interests of the ambivalent person tend to run high. He is frequently found with limited interpersonal facility, not knowing how to get along with people. He is often subjective, withdrawn, or introverted, but may attack "the system" when sufficiently shaken up. The ambivalent person honors theory and knowledge, and he has a high verbal skill. He is in no way system-oriented, even resisting bureaucratic rules and procedures. His career expectations are idealistic, often unrealistic, and he often finds himself unable to bargain effectively. Repeated frustration on the job tends to increase the *psychological distance* between the ambivalent individual and the organization.

The ambivalent person rejects authority and cannot bring himself to believe that those who reach authoritative positions merit them in terms of talent, wisdom, and morality. This attitude may be related to the finding that in a number of companies studied, there was no relationship between intelligence and aptitude, on the one hand, and rank and salary, on the other.

Instead of playing a role, the ambivalent person plays himself and consequently may be out of step with the system. He cannot conform to folkways, often rejects work-group values, and cannot condone the compromise that people make in status seeking. Whereas the upward mobile is sustained by status rewards and expectations and the indifferent person adjusts by limiting his aspirations, the ambivalent individual becomes disturbed. He may develop a compulsive interest in his work, not primarily for its intrinsic value but as a means of obtaining sufficient recognition to set him off from the rank and file. The ambivalent is not good in practical decision making and in a sense is unsuited for the large organization in all but one respect—his critical function as an agent of change.

DETERMINERS OF CLIMATE

Five dimensions are important in determining the psychological climate of an organization: (1) goal directions; (2) size and shape; (3) leadership patterns; (4) communication networks; and (5) decision-making procedures.

GOAL DIRECTIONS

One of the main differences between a college, a military organization, and a company are the differences in their reasons for being—respectively, education, fighting and keeping the peace, and making a profit.

Among companies, climate descriptions are related to the answers to a variety of questions: What does the company make? What underlies a company's approach to human relations? What are the ways in which the organization seeks change? Does the company actually help the individual to grow? Who sets the goals in the organization?

These are some of the questions important to determining climate. Questions and answers vary with other dimensions, but particularly with size. The small company may be able to specify its goals more clearly and, in effecting change, may be able to relate cause and effect more closely.

SIZE AND SHAPE

One may easily appreciate the difference in size between the 160-acre farm and the vast million-acre spread of the King cattle ranch in Texas. But it may be more difficult to get the full impact of the fact that the Federal government employs more people in engineering than in typing jobs and that more and more persons are going to work for the larger industries. In the past two decades the number of self-employed declined; during the same period the number of private wage and salary workers almost doubled, and the number of government workers increased more than twofold. The chief merit of the large organization, whether an industrial, governmental, or research bureaucracy, is its technical efficiency, with a premium on precision, speed, and control. Today, big corporations and the Federal government account for 70 percent of all patents issued.

As a business grows, the old face-to-face techniques are no longer adequate; new and different ones are required. Such factors as the kinds of skill and the location of pools of skill within the organization, the decentralization of authority, and the development of new kinds of communication networks may change radically as the company grows. Often there is a tendency to perpetuate solutions that were successful in the past, trying to solve tomorrow's problems with the techniques that worked yesterday. Size, of itself, is not necessarily harmful; however, size has a seductive quality in that it may lead to the belief that the organization is strong and powerful just because it is big. Whereas the smaller organization may be able to maintain an agility and flexibility in adapting to changed conditions, the larger one may be handicapped in this respect, thus hindering some individuals within the organization.

The shape of the organization in some companies is changing from *pyramidal,* with workers in the majority at the base, to *hexagonal,* with the blue-collar workers at the base about equaling the number of men in the management teams at the top, and the majority portion including large numbers of professional staff persons. Certainly the vertical communication system of the old up-and-down pyramid is in for changes, and no small part of the problem involves effective supervision and coordination of these highly individualistic staff professionals. When bureaucracy is the end product of increased size and complexity, and when the personality pattern of the bureaucrat is often centered on impersonality, one can easily see the likelihood of conflict within the organization as well as with customers and the public.

Figure 14-1 represents the pyramid type of organization, typical of most companies, on the left. On the right is the six-sided figure representative of the newer type of research and development organization.

Psychologically, the size of the organization may be thought of as one dimension of organizational climate, and one may picture the individual being treated more and more impersonally the larger the organization becomes. Yet, as we shall note in a later chapter, size alone, important as it may be, does not determine job satisfactions. The level

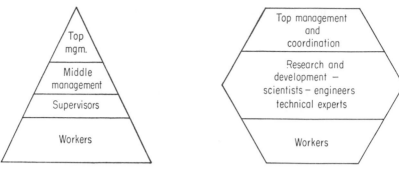

FIG. 14-1 The pyramid-structure type of organization on the left, with the majority of people being the workers at the bottom. On the right is the six-sided structure hypothetically representative of the growing research and development organization, where the number of workers at the bottom about equals the number of persons in the top management-coordination team shown at the top. The majority of people are in the middle. They are the scientists, engineers, technical experts, and a host of specially trained people who support them.

at which a person finds himself in the organizational structure, whether the organization is large or small, is a most important variable, as is the size of the subunit in which the individual finds himself.

LEADERSHIP PATTERNS

After years of research, psychologists have concluded that there is no simple relationship between morale and productivity, in the office, the plant, or the laboratory. High job satisfaction does not necessarily mean high productivity. Much depends on other variables—types of incentives, supervision, hierarchy status, personal-need achievement, occupational levels, and a host of other factors. We know well that good supervisory practices must be the concern of all levels of the organization. A local foreman will have some difficulty trying to exert a democratic type of leadership pattern when his bosses and the structure above him are autocratic. One plant superintendent, speaking before an assembly of lower supervisors gathered to take a course in human relations, passed out a set of specific rules telling the men how they were to become more permissive in their leadership roles. He concluded, with emphasis, "We will have good human relations in this plant even if I have to demote each of you." Certainly in such a situation a democratically oriented instructor may experience difficulty, to say the least.

In a study of four managerial levels it was concluded that the leadership hierarchy, like any other social structure, has role differentiation. Each role player, whether a foreman or a top manager, contributes only a segment of the necessary conditions that will lead to organizational effectiveness. We seem to be heading toward a condition in which leaders will be judged more on how well each performs his personal obligations, and less on how well the organization as a whole performs. This may be one reason why industries are now laying so much emphasis on individual performance appraisal. It must be recognized that not every promising recruit is a potential member of top management. Some persons will become outstanding leaders as foremen, as plant superintendents, or as professional specialists, but not necessarily in top management. We should seek to enable people at all levels to develop to the fullest their potentialities in the role they can fill best. It must also be recognized that in an era of computers, expert teams, and government by consensus, leadership patterns are changing in ways that put demands on the individual.

There is some evidence to support a situational approach to leadership. In one study, for example, employees in small work groups, which were characterized by a great deal of interaction among workers and between workers and their supervisor and by a high degree of interdependence, had more positive attitudes toward equalitarian leaders. On the other hand, employees in large work groups, in which opportunities for interaction among workers and between workers and their supervisor were greatly restricted and in which individual employees were highly independent, were found to have more positive attitudes toward authoritarian leadership.

At one extreme, the leadership pattern may be very rule-centered and bureaucratic. At the other extreme, it may be very group-centered and democratic. In between are found authority-centered or autocratic patterns of leadership and individual-centered or idiocratic leadership patterns. There is growing evidence that organizations, in considerable measure, may be reliably described in terms of typical leadership practices.

COMMUNICATION NETWORKS

The consultant frequently asks the department head, "What do *you* think is the main problem here in the plant?" Quite often he gets the reply, "Communications." One writer points up the problem by concluding that what we call communication problems are often only symptoms of other difficulties which exist among persons and groups in an organization; communication, other than the most formal kinds, flows along friendship channels. When trust exists, content is more freely communicated and more accurately perceived by the recipient. When individuals have different goals and value systems, it is important to create understanding about needs and motives. Often the free flow of ideas and information is restricted by the feeling that one may not receive credit for the contribution or by fear that his idea will be stolen. Basic to free (and accurate) communication in an organization are questions of task assignments, authority and responsibility, status relationships, and the question, "Where do *I* stand?" One observer reports the instance in a university of a professor with high status who, though for years he had been a good source of information, a good sounding board, and a champion of unpopular causes, literally stopped communicating. Later he explained that he wanted to see where he fitted into a yet ill-defined climate. He had a new department head, a new dean, and the president had just announced his own retirement.

Basically the firm, as a communication system, may be defined in terms of four elements. First, there are the characteristics of the information taken into the firm from the outside in a wide variety of ways, ranging from sales orders and reports of salesmen about competitors to a family problem told to a foreman. Second, there are the firm's rules for doing something about the information. What happens to the sales order? What will be done about the word concerning the competitors? What will be done, if anything, about the worker's family problem? Third, there are rules about handling information generated inside the organization. What parts of the organization make decisions, issue orders? How does the information move through the firm? Fourth, there are the characteristics of information leaving the firm, through orders to suppliers, deliveries to customers, and public relations releases. It makes a difference who gathers the information, who filters it and for what purpose, and how various people perceive and interpret the information.

Getting accurate information upward through the organization is particularly difficult. The foreman may sense the feelings of a group of workers, filter out that which makes him look at fault, and pass the information to his boss, who in turn follows a similar screening procedure. The use of the problem-solving approach not only stimulates less-filtered upward communication but also helps to create a climate more favorable to decision making and helps remove sources of resistance to change. When people near the bottom of the pyramid feel that their views are getting to the top unaltered, they are more receptive to the orders coming down through channels.

An important question to ask about the best way of communication is, "Communication for what?" One experimenter set up a laboratory situation in which A talked to B without return talk, which he termed one-way communication. Two-way communication was set up similarly; this time there was conversation, that is, communication from A to B and from B back to A. Later the same format was followed involving more people. Several practical findings emerged from the studies. One-way communication was much *faster,* but two-way communication was *more accurate,* and the receivers felt more sure of themselves in the two-way system. The sender found himself more vulnerable in the two-way condition because the receiver picked up his mistakes and oversights and told him about them. The two-way system, in some college classrooms, for example, is more noisy and disorderly; there are interruptions, expression of feelings, asking for clarifications, and so on. The one-way method, on the other hand, appears neat and efficient to the outside observer, but communication is less accurate. The same patterns have been found in nonacademic situations. If speed alone is of primary importance, for example, in a military situation, then one-way communication has the edge. If appearance is important, when one wishes to look orderly and businesslike, the one-way system is preferable. The same is true if the sender wishes to keep his mistakes from being recognized or wants to protect his own power by blaming the receiver for not getting the message. In a two-way system the sender may be criticized but he will also get his message across. Said one observer, "It's easier to give a speech than to induce appropriate behavior in others." No doubt feedback types of communication are sometimes avoided because of the psychological risks that may become involved. Communication is in part what the speaker says, but it is more what the listener hears. There are those people who hear only what they want to hear.

DECISION-MAKING PROCEDURES

Centralization of decision-making power, long established on the management side of single organizations, seems to be increasingly characteristic of industrial unions. And more recently companies have united, to some extent, in industry-wide bargaining. University scholars are giving more attention to the basic problems of the nature of decision making, and some industrial organizations are studying their own structures to determine the hierarchy of influence in both policy and operating decisions. For example, a study in one large corporation led to the conclusion that decision influence is multidimensional; no single individual actually makes a company-wide decision.

Psychologists have long been interested in problems about the impersonal quality of a decision, on the one hand, and its degree of acceptance, on the other hand. Many studies have been conducted on leader behavior and the amount of influence which various persons have in decision making and on both systems and personality variables involved. Hundreds of studies have dealt with such problems as group participation in problem solving, authoritarianism of supervisors, concepts of autocratic, democratic, and laissez-faire leaders, locus of organization control, decision rules, individual adjustment patterns, and a host of other problems about decisions and what they do to people. Top management recognizes the need for large hierarchic structures, and sometimes it recognizes the problems that such structures impose on individuals. Recently there has been some concern about the place of the computer in decision making. "It is of great value *below my level*," is not an uncommon reaction. Some people use the computer as an excuse for not making decisions themselves.

EFFECTS OF CLIMATE ON PEOPLE

Familiar to the student is the accuracy with which a sophisticated upperclassman can describe the diverse environments between the authoritarian class situation and the permissive one where the instructor encourages class argument. The worker's reaction to a new supervisor and the speculation that goes on in middle management when a vice-president has a heart attack are both illustrations of the fact that people react to climates and climate changes. It is not uncommon at any level to hear words to this effect: "I did not object so much to *what* was done, but I did object to *how* it was done." Organizations sometimes change because individuals change. A modification of climate also offers one good way to observe the effects that climate has on the people in the organization.

HOW PSYCHOLOGICAL CLIMATES CAN CHANGE

The psychological climates of organizations change sometimes for good and sometimes for bad. A change may happen even where there is no turnover in company personnel. Let us illustrate how the character of one organization became different as the president modified his behavior over a period of some five years. The president initially worked cooperatively with his executives, often taking their advice and sharing in the give-and-take of conference behavior. The business expanded, profits increased markedly, and so did problems. Then gradually the climate of the organization began to change from permissive to auto-cratic. Fewer and fewer conferences were held, and the president made more and more decisions without consultation. One observer described the process as "decision by desperation." Both staff and line officers, who had previously been free and open with constructive criticisms, now found that criticisms not only were not wanted, they were in effect forbidden.

What had happened? When the president began his term of office, he never considered suggestions and criticism to be a reflection on his ability. A few years later, however, he was taking all such comments personally. He read into them an implication that he personally had failed for not having foreseen and forestalled the situation which was being criticized. Whether he also suffered from the ego inflation that goes with prolonged occupancy of a top administrative post is not so clear. It may be that he just grew tired of facing new disruptive problems.

The effect on the organization all the way down the line was one of clamming up. People began to censor what they would say and consider to whom they would talk. A few of the top people resigned, but on the whole the organization became adapted to the new climate.

Some recent studies aimed at determining the main variables which differentiate the activities of organization have shown that individual labor-union locals show differences in character. Sometimes a clash in personalities between the company and the union may be a precipitat-ing cause for strikes. Sometimes such clashes may change the climates of both organizations. There is evidence that certain industries are con-sistently strike-proof, while others are consistently strike-happy. Keen observers of the labor-management scene report that some regions of the United States are known to be strike-happy, while others are rela-tively strike-free. Often these strike-happy communities are the cities or towns where industry has not been very progressive in research on human relations.

THE INFLUENCE OF CLIMATE

Conflict between individuals and organizations is inevitable. People with strong needs to be independent find that most organizations do not provide a proper setting. Learning theorists and training directors have long known that in general rewards are better motivators than punishments, yet most industrial organizations provide for much punish-ment. One training program may succeed because it is operating in a climate of rigid and formal rules with people who are rules-oriented. In the same climate the program may fail if the trainees involved are unstructured and ambivalent. With some people conflict increases with the number and concreteness of regulations; with others it may even decrease. The training director who receives the assignment to help develop a future executive might well ask, "For what kind of climate?"

Two kinds of influence of climate on individuals may be distinguished. First, there is a *direct influence* that affects all or almost all members of the company or of a subunit. The second kind of effect, termed *interactive influence,* exists when a climate has a certain effect on some people, a different effect on others, and possibly no effect at all on still others.

Some types of behavior never occur because the stimuli that would elicit them are never presented. Organizations themselves place constraints on people through rules and regulations, routine practices, and taboos. It is not uncommon for the ambitious person to find himself in a climate that puts restraints upon freedom, thus narrowing his alternatives of action. One psychologist has emphasized that in any organization of human beings there accumulates through time a common fund of experience. Out of it develop ways of behaving, ways of working, ways of loafing, ways of cooperating, and ways of resisting. A newcomer to an established subculture may rebuke the old-timers as being cynical about the system, apparently unaware that there is at times a thin line between cynicism and wisdom. He may find to his embarrassment that hasty evaluation of people and established practices can backfire.

How the individual *perceives* his climate is governed by personality factors. This perception is related to the satisfaction of one's needs and to the satisfactions or dissatisfactions one gets from his job. For the supervisor and the executive it is most important to understand how individual personalities and job requirements interact to produce a climate.

Summary

Working environments are of two kinds. We are well aware of physical environments because it is easy to observe noise, lighting, temperature, and ventilation. We are also aware of the formal structures of the environment in terms of who reports to whom, who is his boss, and so on. There is also a second kind of environment that we call the "psychological climate." In an industrial organization we may think of it in terms of the company personality.

Many conclusions come from studies of physical environments. The rate of work, for example, may not be improved by noise reduction, but error is less frequent when noise level is low. When workers are performing simple tasks music may increase production. However, this does not hold when tasks are complex. Illumination and color are related to work output and to attitudes, and so is air circulation.

Companies normally fall into one of five types or organization, determined largely by size. Large companies have technical and financial-resource advantages, more prestige, and more opportunities for a small number of people in the middle and upper levels of management. Bigness also has disadvantages—delay in decision, ego-satisfaction problems for a large majority of people, and problems of bureaucratic power for the subordinate.

There is a close relationship between personality of the individual and the type of psychological climate for which he may be best suited. Each individual should face the question, "What kind of climate is best for me to work in?"

Five dimensions are important in determining the psychological climate of an organization—goal directions, size and shape, leadership patterns, communication networks, and decision-making procedures.

Conflict between individuals and organizations is inevitable. People with strong needs to be independent find that most organizations do not provide a proper setting. There is a direct influence of climate on individuals that affects most people. There is also an interactive influence, which exists when a climate has a certain effect on some people, a different effect on others, and no effect on still others. How a person perceives his climate is governed by personality factors.

Suggestions for Thinking and Discussion

1 Why is there so much controversy about the benefits of listening to music while working?
2 List those factors which favor working for a large company and another list favoring the small company. If everything else was equal, which would *you* prefer and why?
3 Jot down some typical facts about yourself—likes and dislikes, your feelings about people, your ambitions, and the like. Add to this an evaluation of your assets and liabilities. We realize that personality evaluation is much more involved than this, but nevertheless, which description fits *you* the closest: upward-mobile, indifferent, or ambivalent?
4 Describe some organization you know in terms of the five determiners of climate: goal directions, size and shape, leadership patterns, communication networks, and decision-making procedures.
5 Describe a class you have had in terms of a communication network.
6 Describe some situation you know in which the psychological climate has changed.

Suggestions for Further Reading

Borow, H. (Ed.) *Man in a world at work*. Boston: Houghton Mifflin, 1964. Papers related to individuals in their working environments.

Karn, H. W., & Gilmer, B. von H. (Eds.) *Readings in industrial and business psychology*. New York: McGraw-Hill, 1952 and 1962. Each edition contains four articles on the psychology of work and work environments.

Leavitt, H. J., & Pondy, L. R. (Eds.) *Readings in managerial psychology*. Chicago: University of Chicago Press, 1964. Some of the readings relate to managerial climates.

Turner, Majorie B. *Women and work*. Los Angeles: University of California, Institute of Industrial Relations, 1963. An eighty-page booklet which describes women in industry in a review of where they fit in and where there are prejudices against them.

Vroom, V. H. *Work and motivation*. New York: Wiley, 1964. Theories and facts about work attitudes and climates.

CHAPTER 15

Supervision and Executive Leadership

❖ ❖ ❖ ❖ ❖ ❖ ❖ ❖ ❖

The first direct contact between management and the workers is made by the foreman, or first-line supervisor, as he is also called. His position has been described in a number of ways: he is the key man in production; he is a man who always feels that he has more responsibility than authority; he is the pivotal factor in human relations; he is accepted neither by management nor by the worker. But his lot is improving somewhat. He has been elevated from "bull of the woods" to a person who holds the key to industrial morale. However, he is still in a position of "walking the tightrope of multiple loyalty." In this chapter, we shall analyze the principles of human relations in industry as revealed through the problems of the foreman and the executive. Let us begin with the foreman. The male student who plans to enter industry may well keep in mind that in a short period of time he will become a supervisor, and possibly, eventually an executive. Some readers may even now be supervisors or executives.

A HISTORICAL PERSPECTIVE

Around the turn of the century, the foreman held a position in industry quite different from that which he holds today. Almost alone he had

343

the responsibility and authority for running the shop. He hired and fired at will, acted as timekeeper, controlled production, and was, in effect, his own wage-and-hour administrator.

All this changed rapidly with the growth of unions, with the expansion of companies in size and complexity, and with increasing automation. Engineers and other trained specialists became essential as technology advanced. Hiring was taken over by the personnel department, and union stewards became buffers between the foreman and his men. As the supervisor's authority and responsibility split in varying directions, management, for the most part, did little to help the situation. The foreman was bypassed in the chain of command, the worker found himself taking orders from a dozen bosses instead of from one.

A CHANGE OF STATUS

Then, once again, as industry continued to grow in complexity, the supervisor's position became a key position. But this time it was different—*the foreman was now an interpreter of policy,* not a maker of policy. Training courses were established for him as he took on more and more responsibility for job instruction, accident prevention, and worker morale. This was the end of the bull of the woods who had become a supervisor only because he had been on the job a long time. Technology has only confounded the problems of supervision. We have computers with instant chemical memories, pneumatic systems giving rapid response, but the same old human relations problems are still with us.

Now, whether the supervisor comes from the ranks (a yardmaster on the railroad, let us say, who slowly works his way up from trainman) or whether he is given his supervisory post shortly after joining the company (for instance, a young graduate, expertly trained in technology or science, who rises swiftly in the chemical industry), a new dimension is added to his job—human relations.

THE NATURE OF GOOD SUPERVISION

Information on the nature of good supervisory practices has come in recent years from a number of sources. Programmed experimental research from such organizations as the Survey Research Center of the University of Michigan has given us answers to questions involving the relationships between supervision and productivity. Reports of the Foreman's Institute include analyses of numerous case studies of industrial relations problems. Personnel associations and training societies have concentrated much of their efforts on supervisory selection and training. The National Industrial Conference Board, the various associations of business colleges, and government agencies have been focusing more attention than before on human relations in supervision. In this section we shall review experimental and observational studies of the human aspects of supervision.

MEASURING SUPERVISORY RESULTS

Often two groups of workers, doing the same work under similar circumstances, produce results that differ significantly both in quantity and quality. If other factors are about equal, researchers have tried to answer the question: How does the way these groups are supervised affect their productivity?

One writer has summarized the results of supervision on high-producing and low-producing groups in two diverse kinds of work: clerical work in an insurance office and section-gang work on the railroad. He found that the more secure the first-line supervisor felt with his superiors, the greater the group productivity; but the greater the amount of pressure exerted on the supervisor from above, the less the section productivity. There was more productivity from groups of workers *when the supervisor assumed a leadership role* than there was from groups whose supervisor acted as just another employee. Of particular interest was the finding that where supervision was employee-oriented, production was higher than where supervision was production-oriented. One has to interpret these findings with caution, however. There must always be some emphasis on production, or little will get done. But exclusive emphasis on production without consideration of the employees may be self-defeating. Other investigators report virtually the same results from studies made in a large utility company. Employees who felt free to discuss personal problems with supervisors were more highly motivated to turn out work than were employees who did not have such freedom. Being sensitive to employees' feelings, voluntarily letting the employees know where they stand in an informal way, and giving recognition were described as the behavioral evidences of the employee orientation.

INFLUENCE OF SUPERVISOR

In a series of studies it was found that greater production resulted when the supervisor had influence with his superiors and used this power to help the employees achieve their goals. When power is used to block the achievement of the employees, the achievement of the

group suffers. These studies support the contention that close supervision of the section heads is not so effective for productivity as more
general supervision, a factor related to the feelings of security of the
supervisor.

An attempt to summarize the many findings of the Survey Research Center led to the observation that the effectiveness of the supervisor was not a problem to be solved only at the first-line supervisory
level. If a superior emphasizes production with the supervisors beneath
him, those supervisors are, in turn, more likely to emphasize production
with their workers. This emphasis frequently results in a production
record lower than that achieved when supervisors and superiors emphasize personal relationships with employees. Good supervisory practices
must be a concern at all levels of the organization. We must realize,
however, that employee orientation is no magic solution to productivity;
naive interpretation of these findings can be disastrous.

Other writers, in summarizing studies on office employees, forest
personnel, and skilled tradesmen, concluded that supervisors in the
more effective work groups were more democratic and more likely
to share information with subordinates, who were thus kept in the
know. Such supervisors were effective in planning, in organizing, and
in demanding adherence to regulations. They made decisions consistently and decisively.

One industrial relations professor, reporting on several studies,
concluded that supervisors who achieved good teamwork in their groups
were also loyal to the company. Those supervisors who perceived and
prepared for future needs were found to be good counselors and good
organizers. In general, the more effective supervisor felt that his authority was commensurate with his responsibility. In decision making, the
better supervisors were reported to have good judgment and to be
consistent; poorer supervisors were often considered overcautious.

SUPERVISORY COMPLEXITIES

When over one thousand insurance agents from five different companies were asked for suggestions on how their managers could improve
their jobs, the most frequent recommendations centered around closer
and more understanding agent-manager relationships. Several studies
have shown that the employee-oriented practices of the supervisor, combined with other skills, resulted in greater agent effectiveness. It was
found that attitudes toward the company and how it was managed
were favorable when attitudes toward the immediate supervisor were
favorable. In college settings, situations occur when the department
head or dean leaves a professor out of the decision-making process.

Under these conditions, it is usually the organization that suffers if the professor has tenure. He becomes less organization-oriented and follows his own personal interests to a greater extent.

Permissiveness, democracy, and flexibility in supervision do not automatically lead to good supervision. A study of the engineering department of a company illustrates how a work environment may become too flexible. Supervisory practices may be ineffective when policy practices of top management do not concur with those of immediate supervision.

This study reported bad morale in an engineering department of a company with the reputation of being an engineers' paradise. The structure of the department was such that each man had almost complete freedom; the major source of supervision was a committee which passed on research plans and checked on progress. In effect, there was no supervision save the vague pattern of control from top management, which gave the engineers no chance for advancement in responsibility. In fact, the environment was so flexible that the men felt insecure in their positions.

HUMAN RELATIONS

Much has been written on the techniques of good supervision, and it is of interest to note that many of the do's and don't's accumulated through practical experience serve as behavior samples of good human relations principles. Almost every book written on industrial supervision includes such good suggestions as: avoid getting into arguments with your men; learn to say "no" without harming the man's ego; praise people in advance so that they will try to work toward your expectations; be honest in admitting your errors; tell the employees in advance of impending changes that will affect them; and be efficient without becoming abrasive.

Whether one regards human relations as an art, a science, or a combination of both, there is evidence to show that good human relations in supervision come only with hard work. Maintaining good human relations is a continuing problem.

How well one can go from effectiveness on the verbal level to effectiveness on the behavior level depends in part upon one's depth of understanding and one's ability to sense the local psychological climate. Good supervision is found at the *behavior level on the job*. Some men talk better supervision than they practice. As one observer put it in describing a certain supervisor: "He is big talk, little do." No doubt much money and effort are wasted on training programs that get no further than the verbal level.

A SUPERVISOR'S CHECKLIST

One way to appreciate the many and varied demands placed on the supervisor in modern industry is to make a checklist of his day-to-day activities. A review by the author of several such checklists taken from large industries and small industries, from office situations and plant situations, from closely confined workplaces and from the transportation industries shows that the human relations problems are the same, though activities from job to job may vary extensively. This checklist puts questions to the supervisor in a straightforward way. Each question is phrased for a positive answer:

1 Do you know each of your men well enough to tell where he lives, where he came from, and what his interests are?
2 Do you know the general aims of the company?
3 Can you list in order your men who are ready for promotion?
4 Do your men work together well?
5 Do you know how to give an order?
6 Have you obtained better working conditions for your men?
7 Have you corrected the sources of grievances before they came up?
8 Do you listen to complaints?
9 Do you reprimand without building up ill feelings?
10 Do you avoid talking behind a man's back?
11 Do you reprimand in private rather than in public?
12 Do you have a check sheet for introducing a new man to his job?
13 Do you guide the new employee over rough spots?
14 Do you keep a progress chart on the new man?
15 Do you have good criteria for judging performance?
16 Are you a good listener?
17 Are your records useful?
18 Do you know how to get a man to talk in an interview?
19 Do you keep up to date on company policies?
20 Do you keep up to date on union activities?
21 Do you plan work schedules in advance?
22 Do you have adequate inspection procedures?
23 Are you familiar with the technical side of the men's jobs?
24 Does work go on efficiently in your absence?
25 Do you keep your superiors informed of your department's activities?
26 Do you avoid taking up bothersome details with your boss?
27 Do you answer correspondence on time?
28 Do you see where your job fits into the overall organization?
29 Do you have a man who could take your job?

30 Do you know what the accident hazards are in your department?
31 Do you train for safety?
32 Do you give recognition to the man who does good work?
33 Do you ask workers for suggestions before attacking a new job?
34 Do you spread overtime work fairly?
35 Do you allow conversation at work on routine jobs?
36 Do you ever ask a worker to criticize his own work?
37 Do you admit your mistakes?
38 Do you believe that ability to handle workers is learned?
39 Do you know what goes on in departments other than your own?
40 Do you use conferences in getting ideas over to workers?
41 Do you keep cash and production records for your department?
42 Do you ever explain company policies to your men?
43 Do you keep your people informed on business conditions of the company?
44 Do you spend part of your time listening to worker complaints?
45 Do you believe the worker wants more from his job than just pay?
46 Do you believe that most workers will cooperate in helping solve problems?
47 Do you believe that a worker who does not get promoted should be told why?
48 Do you believe in giving workers rest periods?
49 Do you believe people want to know where they stand on a job?
50 Do you believe in trying to sense how the worker feels?

Knowing what to do at the verbal level and actually carrying through at the behavior level is one of the big problems of supervision. Studies show that practically no supervisor does all the things which he knows should be done. For our purposes here the list is useful in emphasizing in another way the many demands put on this man of many roles.

FORMAL AND INFORMAL COUNSELING

Almost every individual relationship between the supervisor and the worker involves some form of counseling. By taking a look at the now classic Western Electric studies which were begun in 1927, we can get a picture of how counseling in industry took on at least a degree of formality.

WESTERN ELECTRIC STUDIES

These studies set out to discover the effect of the working environment, including such factors as illumination, working conditions, rest pauses, and the length of the working day, on production. Through a series of circumstances one investigator of the studies found himself in the role of a supervisor in a department. Trying to obtain information from the workers, he noticed, as their comments were solicited, that they began to lessen their unfavorable attitudes toward management. As time went on it became apparent that factors other than working environment and working conditions were having an effect on the productivity of the employees. What was happening here?

At first, the investigators thought that asking workers about their job was the key. A series of systematized, structured interviews was set up, but with little success. Next came a more informal type of interviewing where the workers were allowed to discuss any topic of interest to them. The theory underlying this approach was that the worker would tend to talk about what was bothering him most. But no ready-made system of effective counseling resulted from this approach; it did little more than give the workers a chance to get things off their chests. Finally, it was discovered that the key to the formalized employee counseling lay in giving the worker a chance to effect some *personal problem solving*. Thus in 1936 Western Electric instituted employee adjustment counseling by hiring full-time professional counselors.

In this program each counselor was assigned a given department or area within the plant. He had no supervisory or administrative responsibilities; his sole function was to acquaint himself with the employees with whom he was working and to counsel on personal problems in any informal situation: at the bench, at the desk, in hallways, washrooms, as well as in private counseling rooms. Experience showed that the interviews averaged a little over an hour; the employees were not docked in pay for the time they spent in the counseling sessions. Counseling could be initiated by the worker, his supervisor, or the counselor.

EVALUATION OF FORMAL PROGRAMS

How effective have these formal counseling programs been? Are they worth the money they cost? Answers to these questions, within and without Western Electric, are many. At one end of the continuum we find those in management highly endorsing such programs. At the other end, some managers have thrown the program out. Some other companies have established similar programs of counseling, some have tried them and later dropped the idea. Union reaction has, by and large, been negative to formalized counseling services. Spokesmen for unions regard them as a sop on the part of management to get more out of the worker.

Perhaps one may conclude that the lack of adequate objective evaluation procedures has led to the many pros and cons about formalized industrial counseling. There really is no clear answer to the question as to the effectiveness of the formal programs. The author, in conversation with a plant manager where a program had been well received for several years, heard the explanation of the sudden discontinuance of the program in these words: "We got a new vice-president, and he has interests other than the counseling program instituted by his predecessor."

WHEN DO WE HAVE COUNSELING?

Regardless of the pros and cons for specific programs of counseling, much has been learned about the psychology of industrial counseling. The principles involved are much the same as in college counseling. Whether formal or informal, counseling is an important aspect of management-worker communication. Let us take a look at this communication of feelings, bearing in mind that in most companies the counseling that does take place is done informally by the worker's immediate supervisor. Often the foreman does not even think of it as counseling. The author had this brought to his attention when he spent a day with an industrial supervisor as part of a job-description study that was being made.

During the day, along with giving orders, making inspections, and planning for the next day's work, this particular supervisor helped six of his employees to work out solutions to individual practical problems. The six problems involved such diverse activities as listening to grievances about working conditions and handling a telephone call from the wife of a worker who wanted advice on a domestic problem (which wasn't given, by the way!). I mentioned to the supervisor that he was carrying out a good load of counseling during the day. His reply was to the effect that he didn't do counseling because this really wasn't part of his job. He did not regard the six individual problems he gave his time to as counseling. The writer would, however, for in each instance the foreman let the employee unburden himself by talking through his problem. In three of the cases, I received the impression that the employee *himself* worked out a solution to his problem as he talked and responded to the supervisor's questions. Since another interpreter might hesitate to call these informal instances counseling, let us describe a little more fully what goes on in the counseling situation, beginning our description with the use of professional counselors operating within a formal framework.

NONDIRECTIVE COUNSELING

The formal counseling interview is, by its very structure, worker-oriented. The counselor listens, does not argue, records what he hears, and uses the information he gets to try to help dispel anxieties. He does not discipline the worker, as the supervisor has to do at times. The counselor presents information to management which he believes is in the interest of the worker, not for use against the worker. Adherents of these formal programs have described them as "adjusting rather than paternalistic," "counselee-centered rather than authoritarian," "clinical rather than disciplinary." The method is essentially the nondirective approach in which the subject himself does the most talking. Pauses of long duration sometimes occur, but the properly trained person will recognize these pauses to be good omens. Many times during these pauses the counselee is working out solutions to his problems. Often following long pauses the counselee says things which reveal that he is beginning to grope toward understanding.

In essence the nondirective approach in counseling is designed to provide opportunity for the counselee to work through his problems to his own satisfaction, without being given advice or guidance. Here the counselor establishes rapport, listens, and talks very little himself. He reflects his acceptance of the client's feelings and attitudes and lets the counselee himself break up the silent intervals, lets him bring out his own problems. Some counselors find the nondirective approach difficult because it does not allow for advice, argument, lecture, or cross-examination. It does not allow the counselor to ride his position of prestige or to take responsibility for final action.

Nondirective counseling demands that the counselor be secure and well adjusted himself, and that he be a good and interested listener who can use a language level appropriate to the occasion without losing the dignity of the counseling relationship. If the counselor can get the counselee to state his problem, give its history, and develop the problem—without having to ask leading questions—he has developed quite an art.

DIRECTIVE COUNSELING

There are times and places where directive counseling gets best results. Here the counselor takes an active part in bringing about an understanding or solution to a problem. He does not give the man the solution, but directs him toward a solution. And it must be remembered that there are times when people need to be told what to do.

How best to do this relates to personality differences between workers who are "grievers" and those who are "nongrievers." Grievers are more thin-skinned, as shown in Figure 15-1. They are also more aggressive and critical of supervision than are nongrievers.

RANKS WITHIN THE COMPANY

Determining who outranks whom is important in understanding any work situation and the problems of supervision and leadership. One way to picture status differences in industry is to describe the work situation of men in different ranks. We shall begin with the worker and come up the line through a description of the jobs of the foreman, the department head, the superintendent, the vice-president, and the president of a mythical manufacturing company.

WORKER STATUS

It is through his identification with the union that the worker has status. It is through the union that he feels strength and has a means to fight power with power. Whereas the man in management possesses symbols of status represented by titles, executive dining rooms, and company airplanes, the union man identifies himself with the heroic figures of union movements and the folklore of struggle. He can express himself through such traditional songs as "I'm a Union Man." The union leader, regardless of his power and prestige, is never allowed to forget that he has risen to his position through his ability to get and maintain the support of his fellow union members. This is quite a contrast to the management executive who attains position through the approval of his superiors.

THE FOREMAN

The foreman is the first-line supervisor of the workers. In some companies he is definitely accepted as a part of management; in some he feels he is a part of labor. In other companies the foreman is in the awkward position of not being quite accepted by either management or labor. He spends a considerable part of the day on the floor, carrying out orders from above and seeing that work gets done. Though technically considered in the first level of management, the foreman often feels that he really isn't in the know. At the same time, the foreman is not accepted as a worker. Rarely does he belong to the workers' union, and he must maintain a status position above those whom he supervises. His ability to maintain a distance from the workers and

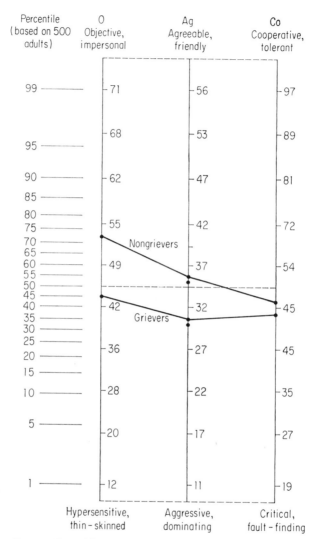

FIG. 15-1   Personality differences in "grievers" and "nongrievers." On the Guilford-Martin Personnel Inventory, grievers and nongrievers differed significantly on trait O ("objectivity"). The grievers tended more toward thin-skinned sensitivity; e.g., their feelings were hurt more easily. There was a slight tendency for the grievers to be more aggressive and critical than the nongrievers. (*From Stagner, R. The psychology of industrial conflict. New York: Wiley*, 1956.)

an identification with them at the same time is an indication of his degree of success as a foreman.

The foreman usually starts the day at his desk looking over the work orders. After he has done his turn around the shop, getting work started, he sometimes talks with neighboring foremen and with his department head about plans for the day and about yesterday's difficulties. Much of the foreman's time is taken up listening to problems and making decisions as he circulates among the workers. To the workers, the foreman is the boss. He judges their work, maintains discipline, enforces the rules, gives orders, listens to their troubles, and tries to maintain smooth relations with the shop steward (the workers' union spokesman).

The foreman often finds himself in a position so close to the work and the workers that he fails to get an overall view and becomes impatient with those in the hierarchies above him. He feels that many of the orders which come down from above are unreasonable, while at the same time he feels that the workers do not understand the company's problems. The foreman is usually as impatient with paper work as is the enlisted man in the army.

Of course, foremen differ widely in their personalities and attitudes. Some of them try to cover up for their men and their mistakes and resist putting in changes that upset established routine. Other foremen play the company-man role and are critical of the workers.

Management often claims that the foreman needs more training, particularly in the area of human relations. (The foreman's superiors often fail to tell him that what they mean by "human relations" is that he is to follow orders, get the work done, and keep the problems at a minimum.)

As the workers see him, the foreman is to represent their views to management and to protect them from excessive pressures from above. He is viewed as the vital first link in labor-management relations and is expected to know all the answers.

And what does the foreman think about his status? There seems to be one universal attitude: he feels that he never has enough authority to carry out his responsibilities.

THE DEPARTMENT HEAD

The department head, or chief, as he is sometimes called, is unquestionably a part of management. His relationship to the workers is quite different from that of the foreman. Whereas the foreman deals directly with the workers in getting the job done, the department head uses the foreman as the buffer for his demands. In problems of discipline of the workers, failure to meet production quotas, or worker complaints, the department head centers his attention on the foreman. He thus avoids becoming involved in many energy-sapping frictions with the men, while at the same time he can play the role of the big boss.

The department head spends much of his time at his desk away from the work location. He reads reports, screens the type of information that should be passed up the line, and filters out the communications coming down which he feels should be passed along to the foreman. The head is in a position to know what is going on, since he spends a great deal of time in conferences with other department heads, with design and test engineers, with inspectors, and with other staff people. He has his ego boosted by showing VIPs through the department and by having his advice sought as a line officer.

The department head is actually too busy to find out firsthand what is going on in the shop. Hence he is quite dependent upon the foremen to keep him informed. This dependency is a club which the foremen may hold over the chief in order to get his cooperation when it is most needed. It is through the department head that foremen indirectly have a voice in the lower-level decision making.

The workers see just enough of the department head to know that he exists; hence they often let the foreman know that he, too, has a boss. The head can overrule the foreman, or he can make a decision without having to cope with its consequences. If the chief is friendly, the workers feel he is a last resort to hear serious complaints. If he is unfriendly, then the workmen feel that no one will listen to them directly, and they turn their complaints into formal channels through their union steward.

Psychologically, the department head is in an awkward position. He frequently does not possess as much formal education as the engineers with whom he works, but he is above the level of the foremen, the group from which he was most likely chosen for his present job. He is the last visible authority for the workers. He is consulted in some decisions and left out of others. Though primarily management-minded and officially a part of management, the department head is nevertheless in the quandary of not quite knowing just where he stands. "The brass" decide at any given time whether or not he is to be included in making policy or procedural changes.

THE SUPERINTENDENT

The superintendent, or works manager, is in the top-management bracket. Psychologically, at least, he is quite far away from the actual work of the plant. He keeps in touch with its activities through conferences, reports from department heads, memos, and data sheets. In the larger companies the superintendent often functions under the vice-president in charge of manufacturing and so is the eyes and the ears for his boss, helping to make policy recommendations above the level of everyday details. He is in a status position which allows him to disagree with the ideas of vice-presidents (up to a point!) as he upholds the importance of getting the work turned out. The manufacturing superintendent is often a case-hardened old-timer who has risen through the ranks from foreman. He may or may not have much formal education, but he knows the plant and as a consequence has good cause for feeling secure in his job. At the same time the superintendent sometimes shows defensive behavior in resisting changes suggested by the top brass. In some respects the superintendent holds a status position, at least in the plant, above that of vice-presidents, even though they outrank him.

THE VICE-PRESIDENT

Vice-presidents are frequently in an awkward status position. They have often come into the company from outside or have come through staff positions in sales, engineering, accounting, or some other specialty, and hence do not have a detailed knowledge of the operations of the company as a whole. Vice-presidents sometimes hold the rank for public relations reasons (this is particularly true at the assistant-vice-president level) and are the attenders of meetings and luncheons. They are often active in community affairs. Vice-presidents, save those who merely hold the title for prestige reasons, are in policy-making positions and hence have much power. By the time a man has reached the level of vice-president, he "is high enough to be shot at," as one observer put it. He has status, but he has to continue the competition game to hold his power—a situation clearly portrayed in the novel *Executive Suite*. It is at the vice-president level, as well as at certain lower executive levels, that we find the man's industrial status carrying over into the community. He is named to important civic committees and to boards of directors, and he usually expends much energy in playing the role of the important man around town.

THE PRESIDENT

"The most lonesome man in the organization" is one way in which this man has been described. He has status, and he possesses so many symbols of his status that he can afford not to flourish his rank for prestige purposes. Most presidents are professional managers and have attained their position because they have real ability and a strong constitution. The president is a lonesome man for several reasons. In the first place, he faces certain problems that only he can deal with. Not only does he have to steer his organization so that it will meet the ever-present problems of competition; also, he must keep abreast of the social, economic, and political changes that affect business. Second, the president has virtually no one of his own status who can listen to his complaints or share his frustrations. He cannot become too confidential with other people in the organization for fear of revealing some of his own weaknesses. He must be very cautious of his statements, because his every word may be interpreted as a commitment or policy indication. The new president soon finds that his old vice-presidential acquaintances gradually begin seeing less and less of him as he expands outward, as he attends more and more dinners and business meetings. These outside contacts, which make it possible for him to get to know other top executives in other companies, mean that he has less time for his old friends. Let us also add that top ranking even in science can relate to being lonesome. One internationally honored scientist put his feelings this way: "My own experience is that fame imposed a social distance where people would not talk to me regardless of availability."

Although the president's attention is focused outward, he still must keep informed about how things are going within the company. Although he receives information prepared especially for him and is given advice by his staff, much of the problem solving is still his. With all that he has to do to keep up with his many jobs and the demands placed on him by his status, as well as by the company, the president soon finds his time and energy taxed to the limit.

FUNCTIONS OF EXECUTIVES

Defining the term "executive" is difficult, as anyone will recognize who has ever tried to write a formal description for the job. One popular conception is given by the wife of a newly promoted man: "More money, more status, new clothes." Another, just about as useless, is that of the employee who identifies executives as "the ones who are allowed to use the private company parking lot." Likewise, though having a key to the private washroom may provide an indication of a man's status in the organization, it is hardly a workable description of the executive's job. What do people think executives do? What do they actually do?

WHAT EXECUTIVES DO

There are those who picture the executive as a person who sits at a great walnut desk surrounded by telephones, masterminding the fate of his company and its employees. This mythical executive spends his day making split-second decisions and issuing directives, like a master puppeteer who decides what each act shall be and who shall do the performing.

Then there is the conception of the executive, probably equally hypothetical, as the master expediter who is always on the go, never in the office. He has few, if any, scheduled routine responsibilities. If he were suddenly to leave for a six months' tour of Europe, his absence would scarcely be noticed, save by those members of the organization who were perceptive enough to observe that things were not running quite so smoothly as usual and that morale was suffering a little. In general, we might say that in the absence of this executive, communication was more difficult, objectives were not quite so clearly defined. In other words, the primary function of this second mythical person is to maintain a favorable environment for effective work by other people in the organization. This role requires that the executive be an expert to an almost impossible degree in the motivation of human behavior.

What executives actually do is a little less romantic than the picture given above. Much time is spent in planning and in the preparation of procedures and methods for getting things done. Time is spent in the supervision of technical operations, in personnel activities, and in public relations.

The executive must provide inspiration and create an organizational climate in which the followers willingly accept the leader as their agent in cooperative endeavor. The executive must spend time in keeping up with, or ahead of, his competition. He stands not only as a leader but also as a symbol—almost everything the executive does and says counts in some way.

Perhaps the best way to describe what an executive does is to talk about the characteristics of successful executives.

CHARACTERISTICS OF SUCCESSFUL EXECUTIVES

The attributes of successful executives have been studied by hundreds of researchers. Here we shall list ten characteristics found important.

1 High drive to get ahead.
2 Willingness to move if it means promotion.
3 Respect for superiors.
4 Ability to organize.
5 Ability and willingness to make decisions.
6 A lot of self-confidence, but willingness to listen to other people.
7 Some fear of failing. This attribute makes the executive plan in ways that will prevent failures.

8   A strong reality orientation.
9   Loyalty to the overall goals of the organization.
10 Ability to handle people. Good executives are high in human rela-
    tions skills, in working with both groups and individuals.

It is to be remembered that one price of executive leadership is
that the leader bears a heavy part of the burden. In one person, leadership may be manifested by aggressive actions, while in another leader,
influence may come through a quality of stillness. Effective leadership
means generating participation as well as obedience.

GROUP-DECISION PROCEDURES

The development of human relations programs in industry has been
approached from two directions. The impetus on improving the job
satisfaction and morale of workers has come largely through attempts
to improve first-line supervision by emphasizing the friendly personal
touches. From the direction of the higher and intermediate levels of
management has come an emphasis on the techniques of *problem-solving conferences.* Fortunately, the two approaches have a common base,
since they deal with attempts to satisfy such psychological needs as
status, recognition, and feelings of personal worth. Group-decision procedures, which have been proved so successful at the higher-participa-
tive management levels, are being used more and more at the first-line
supervisory levels in dealing with a wide range of problems, from the
coffee break, desk arrangements, and vacation schedules in the office
to overtime work, safety practices, and job modifications in the plant.

PROBLEM-SOLVING CONFERENCES

Some of the very best work in the application of the principles
of behavior to group decisions has been conducted by study conferences.
Group problem-solving conferences are useful in several ways: (1)
developing awareness of basic problems, (2) getting different points
of view on problems, (3) providing for permissive participation of
the people involved in any given problem, and (4) developing approaches to solving problems.

It is important, of course, that any given supervisor work out
techniques best suited to his personal mannerisms and the psychological
climates in which he finds himself. Conducting an effective problem-
solving conference is a skill that has to be learned through experience.

One researcher has described four stages of effective group decision-making procedures:

I. *Studying the Problem.* In this stage the leader checks his own responsibility to see if this is a problem he should deal with. He analyzes the situation to see if it is a problem to be brought before the group. It is important that the leader check his own attitude to see if he feels that the group is capable of solving the problem, if he is willing to encourage the group to solve the problem. Following this comes a plan for presentation of the problem to the group, telling *why* there is a problem.

II. *Sharing the Problem.* First comes a statement of the question, presented in positive terms, never in terms of objecting to something. It is presented to the group as "our" problem rather than "my" problem, in a way that will stimulate interest rather than give rise to defense reactions. Facts are presented in this stage.

III. *Discussion of the Problem.* This is the stage that requires the leader's skill in human relations. Here he must establish an atmosphere of permissiveness, in which everyone will feel free to talk without criticism. Here is where the supervisor pays as much attention to how people feel as to what they say. Every effort is made to get people to talk without putting anyone on the defensive. Even such behavior as eyebrow raising or a shrewd glance on the part of the leader of the session may destroy the atmosphere of permissiveness.

IV. *Solving the Problem.* The supervisor or executive must recognize that group solutions come slowly because each person has to "catch up" with the thinking of others. He must sense group agreement on a solution without calling for a formal vote. Many solutions do not find everyone agreeing, and they should not be put on the spot by vote. An informal check or agreement can be obtained by such questions as: "We have had some good suggestions here. Do you feel they provide the answer to our problem?" Finally, it is important that each solution should specify some action. Discussion is often concerned with *what* should be done, but unless the *how* is included misunderstandings may occur.

CONFERENCE LEADERSHIP

Those who have used the group problem-solving procedures point out several do's and don't's that group leaders should follow. Let us list twenty merely to show how important it is to understand how people feel in conference situations, and to get an appreciation of why resistance sometimes gets out of hand.

The manager who is leading a group-decision conference should:

1 Know the general types of subjects he intends to include in the discussion.

 2 Have something prepared to start the meeting off.
 3 Have brief warm-up sessions at the beginning.
 4 Present the general problem area, and let the participants express their ideas on the way they see the problems involved.
 5 Expect some resistance at the beginning of any session.
 6 Let the men get aggressions off their chests.
 7 Recognize all suggestions, but influence *direction of thinking* by asking further questions.
 8 Protect individuals from criticism by other group members by interpreting all remarks in a favorable light.
 9 Recognize his own position and prestige, and try never to be defensive.
10 Freely admit that he is wrong, if he is.
11 Keep the discussion *problem-centered.*
12 Respect minority opinions.
13 Have a recorder keep a list of suggestions.
14 Keep the discussion going by asking such questions as: "How do you see the problem?"
15 Not try to come to a solution too soon.
16 Not give personal suggestions as to a solution too soon.
17 Make his objective one of resolving differences.
18 Keep an optimistic attitude that the problem can eventually be solved.
19 Try to round out each meeting with the feeling that something has been accomplished.
20 *Listen*—let the others do most of the talking.

A PROBLEM-SOLVING OUTLINE

Whether one is a student, a supervisor, or an executive, problem solving is much the same when one is dealing with human behavior. *How can we handle the human relations problem when it comes up?* There is nothing new or unique about the outline below on problem solving. It phrases questions to "you" as a matter of convenience. An examination of this outline offers one systematic method of working out solutions in human-relations problems and often in personal problems also:

  I Defining the problem
     A First indication that problem exists
       1 What is bothering you?
       2 Is it a real problem?
       3 Is it a problem of your concern?
       Objective: To recognize a problem

B Selecting the problem
    1 Does the problem need to be solved?
    2 Is the problem made of a number of problems?
    3 Is the problem within your capacity and knowledge?
    Objective: To differentiate main problem from subproblems
C Stating the problem: Can you write the problem out clearly and accurately?
    Objective: To state the problem
D Setting up tentative solutions
    1 What ways can be thought of by which the problem may be solved?
    2 Why did you include these tentative solutions?
    3 What outcomes might be anticipated?
    Objective: To see several ways of solving problem with possible consequences of each

II Working on the problem
A Recalling what you know: What do you already know that is vital to the problem?
    Objective: To see what is at hand in the way of information
B Getting more information
    1 What additional information is needed?
    2 Where do you get it?
    3 How can you get it?
    Objective: To get all the facts
C Organizing the information
    1 In what kind of order could you write down the information?
    2 Is any of the information irrelevant?
    Objective: To have only pertinent information for use
D Interpreting the information
    1 How does the information relate to principles that may be involved?
    2 Does an examination of the information lead to other problems?
    3 If so, what problem should be solved first?
    Objective: To see relationships

III Coming to a conclusion
A Stating possible conclusions
    1 What are the possible conclusions?
    2 How do these conclusions stack up with your tentative solutions in I,D?
    Objective: To clarify the alternatives

  B   Determining the best conclusions
      1   What conclusions can you eliminate?
      2   What conclusions do you want to draw?
      3   What conclusions seem most logical?
      4   What conclusions can you draw?
      5   What do you think will happen if you put the first-choice
          conclusion into effect?
      Objective: To draw a logical and reasonable conclusion
IV Carrying out the conclusion
  A   Doing something about the conclusion
      1   What *action,* if any, does the conclusion call for?
      2   If action is indicated, how and when can it be put into
          effect?
      3   If no action is indicated—what then?
      Objective: To act on the conclusion
V   Learning from above activity
  A   Reviewing your behavior
      1   Did the problem solving work?
      2   If so, what do you think made it work?
      3   If not, what made it not work?
      4   What would you do, or not do, the next time you have a
          problem similar to this one?
      Objective: To learn from experience

Summary

Human relations in industry and the nature of leadership are revealed
through the problems of the foreman and the executive. Both jobs
have changed extensively in the last few years. Good human relations
come only with hard work and represent a continuing problem. Knowing what to do at the verbal level and actually carrying through at
the behavior level constitute a big problem.

Almost every individual relationship between the supervisor and
the worker involves counseling, both nondirective and directive. In essence, nondirective counseling provides opportunity for the counseled
person to work through his problems himself. It demands skill of the
counselor, who is often the supervisor himself. In directive counseling
the supervisor may well take an active part in helping the employee
arrive at a solution to his problems.

The hierarchy of ranks within an organization is important in
supervision and leadership. For the worker, status comes largely through
union membership. The foreman often feels that he is between two
power structures. The union regards him as management, and management often rejects him as such. He feels that he never has enough

authority to carry out his responsibilities. Management includes the department head, the superintendent, the vice-president, and the most lonesome of all—the president. He has rank, status, power, and all the amenities that go with his high office. He must make decisions within the lonely confines of his own thoughts and feelings.

The attributes of successful executives have been studied extensively. They are people who have high drive to get ahead, a willingness to move for promotion, and respect for their superiors. They have ability to organize, to make decisions within a framework of self-confidence. The executive plans, in part, because of his fear of failure. He has a strong reality orientation and is company-oriented. Good executives are high in human relations skills, in working both with groups and with individuals.

The executive type of person has skills in conference leadership. Both he and the supervisor understand the fine art of problem solving through its five stages of problem definition, working on the problem, coming to a conclusion, carrying out the conclusion, and learning from each attempt at problem solving.

Suggestions for Thinking and Discussion

1 Evaluate *yourself* in terms of potential for success as a supervisor. What three points would be near the top as assets? What three points would be near the bottom as liabilities?
2 What are the common elements between counseling in college and counseling in industry? In what ways do they differ?
3 Psychologically, why is the president of an organization in a position of loneliness?
4 After studying the characteristics of successful executives, how would you evaluate *yourself* in terms of being groomed for such a spot?
5 On your next opportunity for observing some group problem solving, check out the behavior of the leader in terms of the twenty items on page 361.
6 Note section V in the outline above (page 364). Review some problem *you* have solved in terms of the four questions. At the same time, review some problem you have not solved in terms of the same questions.

Suggestions for Further Reading

Gardner, B. B., & Moore, D. G. *Human relations in industry*. Homewood, Ill.: Irwin, 1964. The fourth edition of an old standby for practical suggestions on supervision.

Haire, M. *Psychology of management.* New York: McGraw-Hill, 1964. Covers human needs, leadership, communication, training, pay, and organizations.

Jennings, E. E. *The anatomy of leadership: Princes, heroes, and super-men.* New York: Harper & Row, 1960. Leaders driven to dominate, men dedicated to causes, and iron-willed individuals.

Kay, B. R., & Palmer, S. *The challenge of supervision.* New York: McGraw-Hill, 1961. The development of human relations skills in supervision.

Maier, N. R. F. *Problem-solving discussions and conferences.* New York: McGraw-Hill, 1963. The many aspects of participating in or leading conference groups.

CHAPTER 16

Getting Satisfaction from Work

❖ ❖ ❖ ❖ ❖ ❖ ❖ ❖ ❖

What does the worker want from his job? What does the manager want from his job? How do personal attitudes affect what we do on the job? These questions are related to job attitudes, job satisfactions, and morale. They are important to each person—housewife, technical expert, supervisor, or executive. And, what is even more important to the individual, we know some practical answers to the question, *How can I prepare myself for liking my job?*

There have been some two thousand research studies about what people think about their jobs in terms of the *feelings* they have. From these studies came the conclusion that there is urgent need for a better understanding of the attitudes of people toward their jobs *and of how education is related to good job satisfaction.*

THE EXTENT AND NATURE OF JOB DISSATISFACTION

The average percentage of persons dissatisfied with their jobs in various industries is around 13 percent. Age as a factor has been shown from twenty-three studies. In general, job satisfaction is high among young workers but tends to go down during the first few years of employment. The low point is reached when workers are in their middle and late twenties, or early thirties. Then it increases steadily until a temporary middle-age revolt sets in. Initial enthusiasm for work is apparent among the younger group, but any failure to get ahead lowers job satisfaction for a period. Gradually, really dissatisfied workers are weeded out, and the rest struggle to survive and move ahead. In late middle age, positive attitudes toward the job are found in the man with seniority. For most of us, there is the realization that life does not tie up into neat bundles. For some, dissatisfaction results from the frustration of being ignored.

THE DISSATISFIED WORKER

There is considerable evidence that job dissatisfaction is often associated with generalized maladjustment of some kind. People who are dissatisfied with their jobs are less outgoing and friendly, are more emotionally unbalanced, and show more boredom, daydreaming, and general discontent than do their satisfied coworkers.

The dissatisfied worker finds it difficult to adjust to arbitrary standards of work or to rigid requirements of the employer. For example, in one study of nearly 1,400 workers, in seven different occupations, it was found that people dissatisfied with their jobs had levels of aspiration far exceeding their levels of ability and opportunity.

OCCUPATION LEVEL

One review of almost two thousand articles reports the unequivocal fact that the higher the level of occupation, the higher the level of job satisfaction. One study, conducted on a large national sample, showed that 25 percent of unskilled workers were dissatisfied with their jobs compared with 0 percent of businessmen. Sustained job-interest studies have shown that professional people lead the list in degree of job satisfaction, that salaried workers are next, and that factory workers are least interested in their jobs.

Follow-up studies of college graduates show that dissatisfaction is directly related to income. Often it is a matter of comparative incomes, rather than the absolute rate of pay, that affects feelings. It has been discovered that among executives in the middle-pay bracket, the best morale is found in small companies. This apparently is because middle-management executives in the small company are not isolated either from the workers or from decision-making top management.

It is not at all uncommon to find low job satisfaction among workers in the lower social strata where family ties are weak, housing is substandard, and the opportunities for achieving stable work habits are limited. Such habits as shiftlessness, irresponsibility, and lack of ambition are normal responses which the worker has learned from his physical and social environment. The well-educated girl from a professional family may scorn a job as a waitress, whereas someone from a lower social class may be happy with it. There is considerable evidence that the attitude people have toward their jobs is more than just an individual matter; it is related to the value system of the class.

EFFECTS OF ATTITUDES ON PRODUCTIVITY

Within the past thirty years, the writings in the area of worker productivity have shown a shift from an emphasis on wage incentives and environmental working conditions to an emphasis on human relations.

This shift is due, in part, to the fact that working conditions and wages have been improved in recent years. Mainly, however, industry leaders are finding that there is another important side to the economic man. A poll of the executives of several hundred companies emphasized that business leaders are beginning to realize how important worker attitudes are.

WORK AND ATTITUDES

Do attitudes affect the amount and quality of work production? This is an involved question. What are the facts? In one report twenty-six studies were cited in which some quantitative relationship between productivity and job attitudes in a variety of jobs had been measured. Fourteen of these studies found that workers with positive job attitudes showed higher productivity than those with negative attitudes; for nine studies, there was no relationship; and in three studies, workers with positive job attitudes actually showed poorer production records than those with negative attitudes. The contradictions in these studies may be due in part to differences in the research methods involved, or in the workers surveyed, or in their work situations. One basic consideration is that high productivity accompanies high morale only when the attitudes of the work group favor maximum output. This is particularly true when the work group is very cohesive, when the atmosphere is friendly, and when belonging to that specific work group is highly desirable to its members. A group of this kind can either restrict or raise output independently of the degree to which its members are satisfied with their jobs.

JOB TURNOVER AND ATTITUDES

The findings of studies relating attitudes to job turnover and absenteeism are in general in agreement. Twenty-one of twenty-four studies cited in the literature report that workers with positive job attitudes have less turnover and absenteeism than workers with negative attitudes.

Two studies report no effects, and one study showed workers with positive job attitudes as having more turnover. One investigator has shed some light on the problem in his investigation of telephone company employees. He found that those who quit their jobs felt that they were less personally involved in their jobs than those who stayed; they left, in part, because they had had no chance to help make decisions, and they felt they had not contributed to the success of the company. Another investigator found virtually the same situation with bricklayers and carpenters who were less likely to leave their jobs when they were given some say in the composition of their work groups.

It has been found that the critical employee is not always a poorer producer than the uncritical one, but the preponderance of evidence adds up to the conclusion that workers with positive job attitudes outproduce workers with negative job attitudes when the psychological climates favor high production, where there is good supervision, and where the employee really wants to produce and get ahead.

ASPIRATION AND PRODUCTIVITY

One researcher has made the point that employee satisfaction is a function not only of how much a person receives from the job situation but also of where he stands with respect to his level of aspiration. When the environment provides little possibility for need satisfaction, those people with the strongest desires, or highest aspirations, will be the least happy. Or, as this researcher has put it, "The greater the amount the individual gets, the greater his satisfaction, and, at the same time, the more the individual still desires, the less his satisfaction." From her interview studies of white-collar clerical workers and supervisors, she makes the point that if an employee is in a situation where he is not making any decisions, *and does not want to make any,* he will tend to be highly or moderately satisfied with his work, but if he is not making any decisions, *and would like to make some,* he will tend to derive little satisfaction from his job.

With satisfaction seen then as a function of both the strength of needs in a particular area and the amount of "environmental return," we can see how *education increases the strength of needs for pay and for job status.* This factor is of vital consideration to the college student in planning his career. As the person grows older, the need for pay and job status increases. This can lead to job dissatisfaction when the discrepancy between levels of aspiration and possibilities of attainment becomes too great.

THE PSYCHOLOGICAL CLIMATE FOR WORK

The social aspects of the job-work groups, leadership, and organization of the company all add up to a psychological climate for the person to work in (see page 328). It is known, for example, that work groups which are cohesive, whose members have a sort of pride in the group, have higher morale than those which are not cohesive. However, it appears to be substantiated that high morale is not always associated with high productivity. Why? In part, we will get an answer to this question as we take a look at the complexities of how people work together or fail to work together.

INFORMAL GROUP STRUCTURES

Logically, we may think that all people are ambitious, but they are not. We may think that people are motivated to keep accidents from happening; statistics show otherwise. We may think that work which is planned for convenience and efficiency will be accepted by the work groups, but experience sometimes proves otherwise.

Both the formal and the informal structures of an organization may be described by the *roles that the people play,* by the ways in which they communicate, and by the final decisions that are made. Formal structures are, of course, the official way in which a company is organized. Informal organizations, on the other hand, result from friendships, car pools, nearness of workplaces, community interests, union associations, and the like.

KINDS OF INFORMAL ORGANIZATIONS

One scientist, writing on the social psychology of industry, describes three kinds of informal organizations. First, we find the formation of groups based on some *issue.* For example, a revolt in the ranks of the United Steel Workers lined up people for and against existing policy-making groups. Second, we have the *clique,* which, for example, may be based on a common workplace or on the sharing of some common task. The group consisting of *intimate friends* constitutes a third kind of informal organization. How these groups interact determines the morale of an organization to a large extent and often serves as the key element in productivity. Many informal groups have leaders who may actually set production norms. The real power of these informal groups was first adequately observed in the Hawthorne studies. These studies pointed out that such devices as trading jobs, helping one another, talking, engaging in horseplay, and teasing were all prohibited by management rules; but the foremen did little more than wink at them. As a matter of fact, some studies have shown a high degree of labor turnover in jobs where there was little opportunity for conversation among workers.

On mass-production jobs in the automobile industry, one investigator has explained low job satisfaction among the workers on the basis of the lack of social contact due to the impersonal pressure of the assembly line. A number of findings have revealed that work situations in which the formation of informal work groups is inhibited are not conducive to optimal employee morale.

THE SOCIOGRAM

The sociogram was developed in the early thirties to describe relations among people. This unique instrument offers a graphic way to look at communication. One can see how these "who works with whom" structures can have a bearing on morale, either at the worker level or at the management level. Let us illustrate some patterns which these relationships may take.

Figure 16-1 shows kinds of sociograms found among workers. A diagram of a cohesive group without a strong leader is shown in

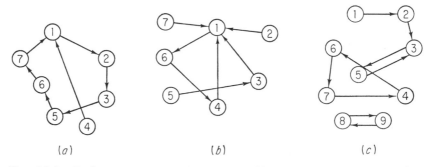

(a) (b) (c)

Fig. 16-1 Sociograms representing one graphic way to portray communication among people: (a) a cohesive group without a strong leader, contrasted with (b), one with a strong leader, and (c), an unstructured group with cliques, isolates, and mutual-admiration societies. (*From Blum, M. L. Industrial psychology and its social foundation. New York: Harper, 1956.*)

a. The sociogram of a group with a strong leader is represented in *b.* An unstructured group with cliques, isolates, and mutual-admiration societies is shown in *c.*

ORGANIZATIONS AND MORALE

The manipulation of the variables affecting morale in a "live" business organization has certain limitations as to experimental control. Hence, why not build a miniature organization in the laboratory? True, such laboratory experimentation has limitations when it comes to relating results to real organizations. But the laboratory situation holds the advantage that one variable at a time may be manipulated and it is possible to get at some of the relatively isolated factors operating in job satisafction.

LABORATORY STUDIES

In a series of laboratory experiments, answers were sought to such questions as:

> What difference does it make in an organization if communication is limited to certain channels?
> How will the morale and performance of an individual member be affected by the centrality of the position he occupies?
> What is it about a central position in an organization that is so satisfying?
> Does the position of "autonomy" affect job satisfaction in the individual?

Communication networks were established in which subjects in any one group were seated around a circular table separated from one another by radial partitions which extended so that the subjects could not see one another. They communicated by means of written notes passed through slots in the partitions. The communication network of any group was controlled by having some slots open and others closed. Problems were provided by the experimenter. The groups developed their own system of pooling information and working out answers.

The drawings in Figure 16-2 represent the "organizations," or different groups. In the "star" group all information is sent to a central person, who then transmits the answer back to each individual member. In the "chain" network, the information is sent by the end men, the men on the periphery (P), to the middle men (M), and then in turn to the man in the center (C). The "Y" network is a combination of the star and the chain. The "circle" network lacks centralized organization; thus problem solving is made more difficult. In such a network, pieces of information could bounce around for some time before someone accumulated all of them and took the leadership in sending out answers.

Results of the experimentation showed, first, that for efficiency in problem solving the star and Y nets did better than the chain and circle. Second, the members differed both within and across nets in the amount of satisfaction derived from their jobs in the group, and in the amount of status accorded them by other group members, as measured later by questionnaire. Even in these experimental situations, devoid of much reality, the persons occupying central positions

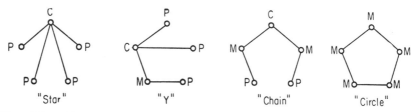

Fig. 16-2 Four communication networks showing how the group is hung together. In the "star" the men on the periphery send information to the central person, who then transmits answers back. In the "chain," middlemen are interposed between the center and the periphery. The "Y" network combines the star and the chain. Problem solving is more difficult in the noncentralized "circle" network. (*After Leavitt, H. J. Some effects of certain communication patterns on group performance. J. abnorm. soc. Psychol., 1951, 46, 38–50.*)

expressed greater job satisfaction and were seen as having higher status than the occupants of middle positions. The latter, in turn, expressed more satisfaction than the occupants of the peripheral positions.

SATISFACTION OF INDIVIDUAL NEEDS

The descriptions above represent only a few of the experiments on this problem. As far as job satisfaction is concerned, they add up to the following conclusions:

1 A central position in a communication net usually has associated with it a larger amount of autonomy. Its occupant can decide for himself what to do next. The person on the periphery has to be *told* what to do. In our culture, at least, being able to decide for oneself what to do is more satisfying than having to be told.

2 Being autonomous has more effect on satisfaction than does merely being central.

3   In positions in which the person is in a position of being both central and autonomous, satisfaction is highest.

4   Members of the groups whose personalities (measured before the experiment) showed strong psychological needs to be independent were more dissatisfied with positions of low autonomy than were members who had weaker independence needs.

Why do people get together in certain groupings, derive satisfaction from belonging to a particular group, and leave it only with reluctance? It is here that the *individual* finds a climate suitable to his needs and one where other members of the group help him satisfy his desires for recognition and status, his feelings of being wanted, and most of all, his feelings of security. When these needs *in the individual* members of the group are satisfied, group cohesiveness produces high morale, and, in turn, high productivity, especially where leadership and company loyalty are also a positive part of the psychological climate. When there is good reason for suspicion, the group can sometimes limit production *and* get by with doing so. A good example of this may be found in the Hawthorne series of studies.

GROUP BEHAVIOR

In the Bank Wiring Observation Room study, an observer was placed in the room to record as much as possible of the group's behavior as the people worked at wiring, soldering, and inspecting switchboard banks. In due course of time it became apparent that the men had become distrustful of the observer. The informal structure of the group began to operate. They set a low standard of output, which was rigorously enforced by group pressures. The men worked hard in the morning and early afternoon until they had reached their "informal quota." From then on, the day was filled in with trivial work, helping the slower fellow worker. Social pressure was exerted on the chiselers to maintain their quota by stepping up their work; it was exerted on the rate busters to slow it down.

A number of studies of rate busters have been reported in which it has been shown that the work group can close ranks against these deviates. Another investigator, in a study of the individual rate buster, describes him as a person who is relatively maladjusted socially and unable to gain acceptance in the work group on a personal basis. Another writer has found that highly cohesive groups tend to enforce the group standard of productivity more rigorously than do less cohesive groups, but high productivity results only where the attitude toward the company is favorable.

RESISTANCE TO CHANGE

There is some tendency, both within and without industry, for people to resist change, even though the change may be best for the individual or for the group. As simple a situation as introducing safety devices on machines to prevent accidents has even caused strikes among workers when the devices necessitated changes in work habits.

One investigator describes how a wage-incentive system was introduced into an automobile factory without any explanation of the reasons for it, or of the results it was supposed to produce. The plan was a failure. Others tell of the failure to increase production in coal mines by changing from technical obsolescence to the use of modern machinery which had been shown to be effective in other mines. The workers not only resisted verbally, but they failed to produce with any appreciable change in output. The modern machinery caused the men to lose identification with their jobs. They had not been consulted about the change, and therefore, they were not conditioned to accept it.

In a somewhat similar situation in a textile plant, a proposed change in production operations was put to the workers *as a problem*. The workers themselves, thus being involved in a solution affecting them, accepted the change. The workers also increased their productivity during the course of the problem solving.

WORK ENVIRONMENT AND MORALE

What of the feelings of people who are exposed to working conditions deleterious to man's well-being? This is a problem of increasing concern in this day of rapidly advancing technology. Can people be found who will be willing to work in high-noise-level areas around jet aircraft and guided missiles? What about absenteeism and turnover among workers whose jobs might possibly cause illness or even death? Are other factors in the work environment more displeasing to the man than physical discomfort? Are there positive factors in a job situation which counterbalance the negative factors?

MORALE AND WORKING CONDITIONS—
AN EXPERIMENT

A series of studies has been made of the morale of workers exposed to high levels of occupational noise and other undesirable work conditions. These studies indicate two important facts. First, in this day of technological change more attention than ever needs to be given to the scientific selection of people for hazardous jobs; consideration must be given to both their technical skills and their ability to work with others. Second, in the evaluation of worker morale it is very important to know the psychological conditions of work before predicting that bad physical work conditions per se will cause low morale.

The investigation was made at Tinker Air Force Base in Oklahoma, a jet plane base, where the noise exposure was at times as high as 140 decibels (db). (For comparison, a pneumatic drill has a loudness level of 80 db, a boiler factor, around 100 db, and loud thunder, around 120 db. A level of 140 db can induce severe pain.) In control rooms the noise levels were around 88 db; in the ready room the level reached 109 db; inside the test cell one jet engine at idle speed reached 119 db. The maintenance of jet aircraft just prior to flight reached 140 db. In this study, however, no subjects were exposed to these painful levels at 140 db. The subjects were aware, however, that even medium-range intensities could be a hazard to health.

The problem was simply to determine whether a high degree of morale can be maintained in the presence of intense noise, and if so, why? Some previous studies in the navy, made aboard an aircraft carrier, showed that maintenance and other personnel engaged in servicing and operating jet planes are efficient in their work and willing to continue in their jobs, even without using earplugs.

The Air Force study was planned so that 100 jet-engine testers could be studied and compared with 100 welders and grinders. The two groups worked under different environmental conditions. The engine testers worked as a team under bad physical conditions. The welders and grinders worked in isolation under less severe physical conditions. The groups were matched for age, race, sex, pay status, and length of service. The experimental design of the study included personal interviews, environmental noise measurements, psychological tests, sociometric investigations, and reviews of absence due to illness, injury, and frequency of visits to the industrial medical dispensaries on the base.

The noise to which the experimental engine-tester group was exposed reached a maximum of 119 db. The control group (the welders and grinders) worked in a much less-intense noise area of 76 db, about the average of factory noise. The skill requirements of the workers were classified as repetitive, average, and diversified, and the "social geography" of the jobs was identified. About three-fourths of the workers had received only a high school education, most of them were born in the state, and they were in the middle-age range.

In the personal interviews the workers were encouraged to talk about their social contacts and their attitudes toward each other, as well as about their jobs. Sociograms were developed which described a knowledge of the group structure, the leaders and dominant figures, the integration and cleavages, the clique formations, the amount of social interaction, and the hierarchical status of each member.

The experimental group (engine testers), because of the very nature of their jobs, was highly integrated; cohesiveness among them was intense. There was just no place for isolates on the test teams. The job requirements were diversified. On the other hand, the welders and grinders operated alone. They worked in booths, behind protective eye wear, and completed a work assignment on a single engine part. To them, their work seemed unrelated to the engine as a whole. Their jobs, although requiring some skill, were quite repetitive.

The results of the study showed *very high morale* among the engine testers, although these workers were exposed to levels of noise not far below the threshold of pain. The welders and grinders were found to have *low morale,* although their noise-environment level was no more than that of the average factory. Why the difference in morale?

Among the engine testers there was common motivation: the group goals were to turn out good engines which could be sold to the inspector. "Selling an engine" meant protecting a pilot's life, building a stronger air force, and making a better country. Leaving the men to work out the details of procedure, supervisors gave the assignments to the workers in groups, but stood by to offer help when needed. Since these workers felt an overall satisfaction at accomplishing something worthwhile, they complained very little about the unpleasant features of the work situation. There was little or no complaint about the exposure to noise and outside temperatures or about the job's being greasy and the area slippery. Little was said about the ever-present vibrations, the threat of engine explosions, and the potential danger of hearing loss. Complaints stemmed not from the work per se or from the physical environment. They came from such things as favoritism, inequities in giving raises, ratings, overtime, loan-outs, and demotions.

In short, these engine testers had to work together. Cooperation was basic to getting the job done. The purpose of their job was clear to them, the work itself was tangible, concrete, and easily grasped.

The welders and grinders were physically separated; the work was individual and repetitive and required no cooperative effort in any way. Many of the workers were found to be isolates or near-isolates. Their morale was low. Complaints from these men were numerous and centered around their isolation, their being dealt with arbitrarily, or their being discriminated against. They described their work as strenuous, unhealthful, nerve-racking, and fatiguing. They expressed deep feelings of job insecurity. For the most part the sociogram of these people demonstrated a sparseness of friendship choices, tenuous connections. The grinders, in particular, expressed no satisfaction in their jobs. There was no ego involvement or identification with the work. Although the physical hazards involved were less than in the engine testing, the dangers were mentioned more frequently. There were many complaints about dust, flying steel particles, impaired illumination, eyestrain, and standing; and believe it or not, these workers complained far more about noise than did the more cohesive group of engine testers.

Although most of the welders and grinders were highly dissatisfied with their jobs, a small minority were found to have a high morale. These were a group of nine welders who were found to belong to an informal clique. Although their jobs were separated, they got together at lunch and at other times. There was no common goal for these men such as that which existed among the well-integrated engine-testers group. Their clique had a clear status hierarchy dominated by a few individuals, but nevertheless this group complained far less than did their nonclique counterparts.

THE PERCEPTION OF WORKING CONDITIONS

Several important conclusions may be drawn from these studies for our understanding of industrial morale. First of all, the results substantiated some earlier work that such factors as noise, exposure to bad weather, slippery operational areas, and other undesirable physical working conditions *do not* determine morale per se. Morale results from the worker's *perception* of his working conditions and his job. How the job is perceived is a function of his ego involvement with it. Associated with ego involvement is a feeling of belonging, a sense of responsibility, and an opportunity to contribute knowingly to a worthwhile effort.

Through worker selection and placement, adequate programs of training, and work situations favoring cohesiveness, workers' needs have a better chance of being fulfilled. When one feels that he is needed as a part of the organization, then his morale may be high in spite of the undesirable aspects of the physical environment.

But why, we may ask, do men work in the first place? One man may feel that something important needs to be done and that he is the man to do it. He needs no other motive to get the task completed. In the upper levels of the industrial hierarchy we may find economic forces pressuring an executive to work hard purely for financial reward. At another time he may work to avoid a penalty for shirking. But generally he works, as do most people gainfully employed at any level, not for some special reward or for fear of penalty, but for a *combination of reasons*. We work for different reasons at different times, but in the main we are all after very much the same things in our work.

TEN FACTORS RELATED TO LIKING THE JOB

"What do you want most from your job?" "What things give you satisfaction in your work?" "What causes the most dissatisfaction for you?" Studies show that when thousands of persons were asked many questions such as these, some ten factors emerged. The data were summarized by using computers.

INDIVIDUAL DIFFERENCES

The studies showed that most people like and dislike much the same things about their work and their jobs. However, when a person is asked what factor is the most important *to him,* the next most important, and so on, some individual differences are found. For example, for a newly married man wages may be of primary importance. At some other time, or under other conditions, it is quite possible for wages to be placed low in any comparisons. Opportunity for advancement or some other factor may well take first place.

Where, for example, does money fit into the picture? Do we each value it differently? Probably each of us could say something like the following:

Money is a way of rewarding behavior.
Money is an anxiety reducer in making one feel more secure.
Money is an instrument for gaining certain things.
Money is important but not what I most want.
Money isn't everything.

All these things may be true, yet we often behave as though money is number one with us. Says one psychologist: "We talk about money more than anything else and behave as though it comes first—executives sacrifice health for it, entertainers work toward more and more lucrative arrangements; bankers embezzle; robbers rob; employees strike; and professors publish to earn increased salary and enjoy royalty checks. Yet we must not conclude that bankers embezzle *only* for money and professors publish *only* for financial return."

We know that money can be lowered in value by what we have to do to get it. We know also that people tend to exaggerate what someone else may make. Studies show, for example, that secret pay policies contribute to job dissatisfaction because we usually overestimate the pay of others and we don't like it.

Money acts as a symbol in different ways for different individuals. A person's desire for money, or choice not to struggle for it, tells something about his personality, past history, and how well certain nonmoney needs are being satisfied. Let us look at satisfaction and dissatisfaction of pay in relation to the nine other job factors when we consider the list below.

THE AVERAGE RANKS

Although individual differences are important in how people react to work and express how they feel about their job, we can still give some "average ranks." We shall present such ranks below. It is possible, of course, that you, or any other single individual, would not rank these factors in the order in which they are presented. It is also possible that a person would shift these rankings from time to time. Nevertheless, average ranks are useful in seeing how one compares with other people.

1 *Security*. This factor deals with the steadiness of employment, with the feeling of the manager or worker that he has a reasonable chance of working under conditions of company stability. The man with security feels that he is valued by the firm and that he has the abilities and the opportunity to keep his job. Security is a strong reason for liking a job and is generally mentioned first by men and women as contributing to job satisfaction. The lower one gets in the occupational scale, the greater the importance attached to the security factor. The greater skill and responsibility demanded in higher-level jobs give the employee more "salability" and hence create a demand for his services, both within his own company and in others.

   Security is a job-attitudes factor which increases slightly in importance with an increase in age. There is evidence that security is less important to employees with more education. It seems to be equally important to employees regardless of their dependents, with the possible exception of the single man who is entirely on his own.

2 *Opportunity for Advancement*. What are the chances of getting ahead? This factor ranks high in importance, particularly to the person striving for upward mobility. Opportunity for advancement is quite a different problem for persons at opposite ends of the socioeconomic scale. The professional man and the corporation executive have this factor primarily within their own individual control. To the man in middle management, however, the problem

of opportunity is of greater concern, for his future is tied in largely with what happens to and within his company. To the worker, advancement is related to merit, to be sure, but seniority plays a big role where union contracts are in effect. The young, ambitious, good worker may find advancement held back because of seniority agreements.

Once a man has reached his "opportunity level," and becomes adjusted to his situation, other factors become more important to him—length of service in a stable company, for example. Intelligence and education are substantially related to the opportunities factor.

3 *Company and Management.* What constitutes a good company and management? To one employee it may mean how well the company gets along with the union. Another man may rate the company on its sponsorship of athletic teams. Whether we are dealing with the size of the organization, reputation, earnings, or public relations, the employee believes that a good company is one which helps him feel some stability in his job. Like security, this job factor is seldom a strong reason for dissatisfaction, but it contributes substantially to the employee's satisfaction.

In terms of occupational level there is some evidence that the higher the skill level, the greater the satisfaction with the company. Older workers show a slightly greater concern for the rating and reputation of the company than young workers do. Perhaps their years of service to the company have made them a little more ego-involved with it.

4 *Wages.* When this factor is ranked with the nine other job factors, employees give it fourth place. It is interesting that employers generally rank this factor near the top when they are asked what the employee wants. Although there is some indication that wages and opportunity for advancement are related through the element of money, employees consistently have rated wages as much less important than either opportunity for advancement or security.

Studies show that the factor of wages contributes more to the dissatisfaction than to the satisfaction of the worker. Rarely ever does a man express satisfaction with the amount of money he is making.

Wages are more important to men than to women workers, and are generally more important to factory workers than to office workers.

5 *Intrinsic Aspects of the Job.* There are many reasons why people like their job simply for the sake of the job. One man may like what he is doing because he has just the right ability and training

for it. Another may like his job per se because it brings him recognition; a third person may like his job because it is easy, gives him an opportunity to travel, or is free of tension and pressure. Whatever the reason, what the man does at his particular job contributes to both satisfaction and dissatisfaction.

There is an important relationship between a person's skill and education and the requirements of a job. It has been found, for example, that a reduction in the skill requirements of a job increases the dissatisfaction of the more skilled worker, whereas it would not affect the less skilled worker. The higher the occupational and skill level of the person and the higher his education, the more important the challenge of his job becomes. Most people in executive or supervisory positions say that they like their job because intrinsically it challenges and stimulates them. One difficult thing for successful leaders to realize is that employees in lower-status jobs often do not like jobs with challenge. For them, other factors must be involved if the job is to lead to satisfaction.

6 *Supervision.* To the worker, his supervisor is both a father figure and an irritating boss who is an equally strong contributor to both satisfaction and dissatisfaction. Women seem more sensitive to supervision than do men, but for both, bad supervision may be a primary reason for absenteeism and labor turnover.

Supervision seems less important at the high levels, even though people in high positions have a greater tendency to verbalize what is wrong with their particular supervisory structure.

7 *Social Aspects of the Job.* This is one of the most difficult of the job-attitudes factors to describe. It involves such needs as belonging and social approval. This factor contributes to both satisfaction and dissatisfaction of the employee. A man who feels himself a member of a productive, cohesive group is happier with his job than is someone who finds himself a misfit. The social factor appears only slightly more important to women than to men; it is relatively independent of age and occupational level.

8 *Communication.* An old military expression, "There is always someone who does not get the word," is expressive but hardly a complete definition of the factor of communication. The lack of good communication may be a reason for disliking a job, but it is never a specific reason for liking a job. What, then, is really meant by communication? To be sure, it means the formalities of conveying information, giving orders, turning out annual reports. But to the employee it also means being listened to, receiving recognition, and "knowing why." Good communication, as far as feelings go, means the opposite of being ignored. The factor

of communication seems to be more important at the higher educational levels.

First-line supervisors list the lack of good communication as one of their chief annoyances. Perhaps this is because they feel that they are "told" by higher management, rather than "conferred with." In one company an attitude survey was made among 120 foremen. When asked to describe their biggest problem, most of these supervisors listed communication. In a few months these men were brought together to discuss company policies and problems. After a one-day session they returned to their jobs. One year later when they were asked to identify problems, communication was far down the list. A follow-up study showed that merely being brought together and asked for views on company problems had made the men feel that communication was now good. Recognition that he is a part of management may well be what the supervisor wants when he asks for improved communication.

9 *Working Conditions.* Temperature, lighting, ventilation, parking facilities, cafeteria, toilets, and the like always afford a chance for criticism when the employee wishes to let off steam. Actually working conditions have been found to make an equally low contribution to both satisfaction and dissatisfaction. They are substantially more important to women than to men. Hours are more important to men than any other specific aspect of working conditions; but among women, especially married women, this aspect has even more significance. To the more educated and higher-level employee, hours are almost negligible in importance. Few, if any, executives work the limited hours of the union man! To workers in hazardous jobs, safety conditions are most important; but when they are ranked with the nine other job factors, working conditions come in next to last.

10 *Benefits.* Retirement provisions, hospitalization, leaves, vacations, and holidays are now somewhat standard features of most jobs; there is greater uniformity throughout industry in these factors than in any of the other major factors. Benefits have not been mentioned as a real contributor either to satisfaction or to dissatisfaction in the many studies of job attitudes. It is interesting to note, however, how much attention is paid by union representatives to fringe benefits at the time of contract negotiations.

HOW TO PREPARE FOR JOB SATISFACTION

The student giving serious consideration to his or her career may find the ten factors described above useful in helping him to establish an individual "need hierarchy." He will no doubt find that he wants all these factors in the job that he chooses, but he will want them in different degrees. As time goes on, he will find his attitudes shifting, but it is important that he have a base of understanding from which to operate in making decisions about his life's work. Planning ahead may help break the cold wind of failure.

A LOOK AT ONE'S SELF

A good time for the person to try to answer three basic questions is while still in school, as we described in Chapter 11. The questions were: (1) Who am I? (2) Where am I going? (3) What will it cost me to get there? Few people can come up with complete answers to these questions, and sometimes we change our answers. Do you think differently about these questions now? What about the fourth question we asked, back on page 240?

Who Am I? Here one should take a look at his *personality* characteristics. Along some scale of "bossy to submissive," where do I stand? Am I more interested in "things" or in "people," or am I equally interested in both?

Next, take a look at your *habits.* Which ones do you believe are assets? Which ones are liabilities? Which ones could be changed easily? Which ones seem too deep-seated?

Ambitions play a big role in getting or not getting satisfaction from work. If a person's level of aspiration is in line with his *abilities,* level of *education,* and *opportunity,* then job satisfaction may be more in the cards.

Where Am I Going? Taking a look at one's ambitions leads to the next consideration: What influence does "climate" have in determining where I am going?

It may be good for one person to try to *match* his individual personality with company personality. For example, if you are a hard-driving person with a permissive personality, you may get more satisfaction from the democratic type of organization. If you have a permissive personality but lack drive, it may be better to *mismatch* yourself with the climate. An authoritarian climate may better stimulate you to action. We must remind ourselves at times that people usually don't change unless they become uncomfortable. Ask then: What is the best climate *for me?*

What Will It Cost? This is a question usually without a complete answer. In effect, we should ask: To get where I want to go, what will it cost in money, in time, in energy, and in terms of sacrifices?

Our degree of work satisfaction depends in large measure on how well we can *integrate* the answers to these three basic questions.

Summary

Do you like what you are doing? How can you prepare yourself for liking your job? Such questions get at the feelings people have about satisfactions and dissatisfactions in work. Age is a factor in job satisfaction; education and occupational level are other factors. Employee satisfaction is a function not only of how much a person receives from the job situation, but also of where he stands with respect to his level of aspiration. "Environmental return" for effort expended means much for satisfaction. Work groups which are cohesive have higher morale than those which are not cohesive. And morale is related to the roles that people play.

In general, job satisfaction is related to autonomy. Being able to decide for oneself what to do is more satisfying than having to be told. Members of groups who have strong psychological needs to be independent are more dissatisfied with positions of low autonomy than members with weaker independence needs.

There is some tendency, both within and without industry, for people to resist change. But when most people are allowed to participate in change, resistance is lessened and more satisfaction is expressed than when change is forced from the outside. Through selection and placement, adequate programs of training, and work situations favoring cohesiveness, people's needs have a better chance of being fulfilled. When one feels he is needed as a part of the organization, morale has a chance of being high, even in spite of any undesirable aspects of the physical environment. Morale results from the individual's perception of his working conditions, and his ego involvement with them.

Ten factors are related to liking the job. They include security, opportunity for advancement, company and management, wages, the intrinsic aspects of the job, supervision, social aspects of the job, communication, working conditions, and benefits. A person will put these factors in one rank order at one time and in another under different conditions.

Getting satisfaction from work depends not only on the conditions of work but on personality characteristics, habits, ambitions, abilities, levels of education, and opportunity.

Suggestions for Thinking and Discussion

1   Write out statements of what you like *most* about what you are now doing in college. Make other statements about what you like

least about college. What can this tell you about your satisfaction as a student?

2 Set up on paper an experiment somewhat like the laboratory studies described on page 373. What position would *you* like best for solving a problem in which you wanted everyone to help?

3 With reference to the ten factors for liking a job (page 380), how would you rank them now? Ask some older person to rank them. Find any differences?

4 What factors would you like to know more about in trying to match *your* personality with some company personality?

5 What are the *outside* (people, situations) influences on your likes and dislikes?

6 What are the *inner* (feelings, thoughts) influences on your likes and dislikes?

Suggestions for Further Reading

Herzberg, F. *Work and the nature of man.* Cleveland: World Publishing, 1966. Attitudes of workers toward their jobs and their company.

Krech, D., et al. *Individual in society.* New York: McGraw-Hill, 1962. A text which includes material on attitudes.

Levinson, H., et al. *Men, management, and mental health.* Cambridge, Mass.: Harvard, 1962. Interviews with 874 employees at all levels by a Menninger Foundation team.

Maier, N. R. F. *Creative management.* New York: Wiley, 1962. Conflict between man and the organization.

Zweig, F. *The worker in an affluent society.* New York: Free Press, 1962. Aspirations of the British working classes.

PART V

OTHER
PROFESSIONS
AND PSYCHOLOGY

CHAPTER 17

Applications of Psychology in Other Areas

❖━❖━❖━❖━❖━❖━❖━❖━❖

All people relate to psychology through the problems of childhood, adolescence, youth, and old age. In addition, most people find useful applications of psychology through programs of counseling and decision making and in work. These relationships we have covered rather completely in preceding chapters. Although few of us are involved directly with the use of psychology in specialized business areas, such as advertising and selling, and in professional areas, such as law, no description of applied psychology would be complete without a few pages on psychology as it relates to the consumer, to engineering, to unions, and to the professions of education, medicine, and law. Let us give some sample descriptions of how psychology is used in each of these areas.

PSYCHOLOGY IN THE MARKETING MIX

All of us as consumers are influenced both directly and indirectly through advertising and selling. We react in varying ways to the radio jingle and the television cartoon. But we also are concerned with problems in buying and customer service, and with those other factors that make up psychology in the *marketing mix.*

INGREDIENTS OF THE MIX

At the heart of the marketing mix is *advertising.* It is defined as any paid form of nonpersonal presentation and promotion of ideas, goods, or services by some identified sponsor. The media of advertising include magazine and newspaper space, trade papers, billboards, throwaways, programs and menus, car cards, catalogs, and local and national radio and television.

Advertising is designed to *influence* people and the decisions they make in a world of competition. Because Americans use some 20 tons of aspirins daily, many firms pursue this market. There are 1,500 ads per day assaulting the eyes and ears of the American consumer. He shuts out more than 1,400 of these daily pitches, reacting to only thirteen. The psychologist is interested in which ones and why.

The power of *habit* dominates all of us, and advertising attempts to control the ways in which we change our behavior through learning. The bases of changing behavior through learning are described in Chapter 4.

The American consumer is being peeped at, shadowed, and grilled, and even analyzed in terms of his personal habits during the hourly and half-hourly station breaks on TV. Researchers are using mathematics and high-speed computers to help manufacturers understand why people buy, or do not buy, a particular brand or product. And the housewife is surveyed over and over about her peeves. Sometimes she is more concerned with *little* frustrations than with bigger problems. Of one survey of 1,100 women, some one-third complained about difficulty in opening packages, another 10 percent found fault with reclosing, and 10 percent complained of deterioration of packages. Less than 1 percent complained about false label information.

In one study, canned soups were arranged in alphabetic order by the type of soup—asparagus, bean, chicken, etc.—with the original amount of display space retained for each brand and type. Previously, canned soups had been grouped together by brand rather than by type. Although several signs were placed at the soup section telling the customers that the cans had been rearranged alphabetically, 60 percent of the customers were foiled by the new arrangement *and by their own habits.*

The power of habit was noted in another way. Under the original shelf arrangement there was no indication that consumers switched brands when the leading brand of tomato soup went out of stock. When the soup display was rearranged and the leading brand was out of stock, sales indicated that the next leading brand picked up from 50 to 80 percent of the sales which normally went to the leader.

Advertisers not only want to reinforce habits, they at times want to change them. (Note this type of battle among cigarette brands.) The success of a new product depends on whether customers can be induced to shift away from their former brands ("new low cost" or "new standard of performance"). The continued success of an established leading brand depends on the ability to strengthen existing habits ("the taste to stay with").

Selling involves both sales promotion and personal selling. In most companies, it involves the largest part of the marketing mix. As in advertising, the psychological factors in selling involve the sequence of perceiving, understanding, and feeling. The sales interview involves interaction between the salesman and the customer. Each provides a continuing stimulus for the other. What the salesman says and does must be perceived by the customer and responded to favorably if a sale is to take place. Thus, the focus of the salesman's attention is the customer. He must catch the small cues in the customer's behavior which indicate what to stress and what to gloss over. And good selling is *planned in advance*. One experienced Detroit car salesman put it this way: "I have found that most men who bring their car in for service are mad at the car. They are also mad at the manufacturer. This is particularly true if they have broken down on the expressway. They start taking out their anger on the service manager. He calls me in to take the beating. After the potential customer simmers down I let the mechanic tell him the car can be fixed. This turns his thinking from complaints to listening. I give him a cold coke and take him over to a new car. He starts the new car conversation and then I make my sales pitch."

The thinking processes induced by the salesman must be considered. Concreteness of language and aptness of illustration, for example, often spell the difference between success or failure in selling. The mind works somewhat like a motion picture camera. It doesn't take in abstractions easily. When the stimulus word or phrase is abstract, the individual hearing it translates it according to his own ways of perceiving, of feeling, and of thinking. For example, if a salesman says of his product that it is of high quality, the associations aroused in any given customer may vary. One may conclude, "It is too expensive for me"; another may think, "It is overengineered for my simple use"; or another may think, "It's trouble free, just what I have been looking for."

The salesman may also base part of his strategy on rationalization. Here the customer is eased into believing what he wants to believe. It is just human nature to justify our behavior in our own eyes. The advertiser or salesman can help this along: "Order some now before the supply is exhausted." "The coats would cost twice as much in the regular season." "The amount you save will pay your youngster's tuition for a whole year."

Customer service is a growing part of the marketing mix. "I don't mind buying it if I can just get it fixed," is not an uncommon remark. The selling of services in one form or another has grown until money now paid out for services exceeds that paid out for things. Service activities include maintenance and repair of products, technical and professional assistance in problem solving, help in training the customer's personnel in operating equipment, and marketing research on the customer's products.

In theory sales and service are supposed to complement each other. In practice the two are often in conflict. "Sales" makes commitments that "service" has difficulty in supplying. The car salesman promises one thing, and the service man says it cannot be done. The warranty on a new car, for example, may be honored without question by one dealer and virtually ignored by another. The sophisticated buyer studies service before determining where to buy.

One homeowner who maintained a contract with an exterminating company expressed the importance of service (feelings for the lack of it) this way: "When I originally signed the $700 contract to rid my house of beetles the company adhered to my every wish. The house was gassed, but to be on the safe side I took out their insurance policy against failure. Two years later bugs reappeared. It took me three visits, two long distance calls, and threat of a law suit to get the company to even come and look at the house."

Another part of the mix includes *public relations*. All employees informally contribute (for good or bad) to the public relations of a business. The larger organizations employ a specialized staff or outside agency to coordinate this aspect of the marketing mix.

Credit is involved in buying and selling as a part of the mix. It becomes important as the value of the purchase increases. And for most of us *pricing* is important in the mix. It has not only an economic base but involves psychological values as well, when status becomes important: "It costs a little more when you serve the best." And no small part of the mix involves *delivery*.

Purchase behavior by the consumer is related to psychological and sociological factors as well as to economic ones. Age of the buyer is important. From the "six-year-old purchasing agent" to "middle-age impulse buying," the psychologist is taking a look at the behavior of people. Scientists are concerning themselves with the "why" of purchasing behavior; researchers are investigating motivation and personality differences.

Beliefs are important in purchasing. In one study on consumer preferences for beef, two different displays were put on the counter. One was an economical product from cattle fed on grass. The other display was from cattle that had been more expensively grain-fed. The fat from the grass-fed cattle was slightly off-white in color, in contrast to the fat on the grain-fed beef. When the more expensive grain-fed beef was identified as such, it outsold the cheaper brand, but when neither was identified, and both were marked at the same price, each sold equally well.

In a follow-up study, customers said there was no difference in taste in the beef bought from the unidentified racks. But when identified, the customers said there was a difference—favoring grain-fed beef. Maybe it pays to *tell people what they like!*

PSYCHOLOGY IN ENGINEERING AND SYSTEMS

The space age has united the professions of engineering and experimental psychology in dealing with the problems of man-machine systems. Human-factors engineering is concerned with how people *receive* information through the eyes, ears, and other senses. It is concerned with how people *store* this information and *use it* in making decisions. It is also concerned with how people *react*. The computer, in particular, has introduced both complexity and "all-at-onceness" to which the human must adjust. For progress, modern machines are not enough. There must be modern attitudes as well.

For the housewife the engineering psychologist has made studies on the speed of reaction and the errors that people make in turning knobs. They have, for example, come up with a virtually error-free design for a four-burner cook stove on which each control knob is placed with its burner. This is shown in Figure 17-1.

Engineering psychologists helped design the L-shaped desk for the secretary, to bring an enlarged work space within easy reach. Study has gone into the design of automobile seats, which must accommodate persons of various shapes and forms. Researchers have studied aircraft accidents and come up with cabin designs for both comfort and safety.

Psychology in *engineering* is interested in the principles involved in how men and machines can be made to work together efficiently. This covers a wide range of problems, from the design of a household appliance to the design of a manned space vehicle. Psychology in *general systems* covers a broader area. Here problems center around how to bring large groups of men and machines together for some human purpose. Designing the cooking stove was an example of psychology in engineering. Coordinating thousands of people, ships, radar stations,

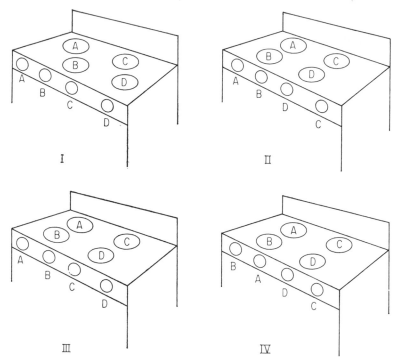

FIG. 17-1   The control-burner arrangements of a simulated stove used in the study of human reactions. There were zero errors for design I in the upper left-hand corner. This design also had the shortest reaction time of the four models; it has better compatibility with the subject. The other three arrangements induced errors and long reaction times even after much practice. (*From Chapanis, A., and Lindenbaum, L. A reaction time study of four control-display linkages. Hum. Factors, 1959, 1, 1–7.*)

and equipment of all sorts for a space mission represents a "systems" problem, part of which involves psychology.

EQUIPMENT DESIGN

Almost everyone who has had experience in reading meters knows that some can be read rapidly while others are seen with difficulty. Engineering psychology is concerned with designing equipment which is *easy for the human operator to run.* This is just the reverse of designing a machine so complicated that it takes great ability and long training for the operator to learn to operate it.

With advancing automation it is essential that visual displays (speedometers, pressure gauges, thermometers) be designed so that the human operator can read them efficiently. Let us see how experiments help with this problem.

The most common types of display involve dials. They range from simple scale markings on a yardstick to the more complex instrument panels of a modern spacecraft. Dials vary in size and shape, in length of scale units, and in the number of space markings. They also vary in the spacing of markers and in the size and style of letters and num-

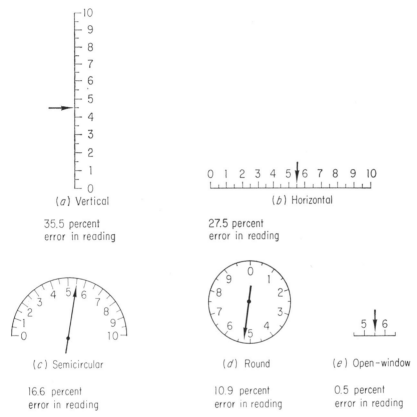

(*a*) Vertical

35.5 percent
error in reading

(*b*) Horizontal

27.5 percent
error in reading

(*c*) Semicircular

16.6 percent
error in reading

(*d*) Round

10.9 percent
error in reading

(*e*) Open-window

0.5 percent
error in reading

FIG. 17-2 The percentages of errors in reading five types of dial. (*Data from Sleight, R. B. The effect of instrument dial shape on legibility. J. appl. Psychol., 1948, 32, 170–188.*)

bers. Some dials are designed for rapid reading; others are designed differently for very careful reading.

For *rapid* reading, greater accuracy is achieved with a dial having *few scale markers*. On the other hand, a dial with *individual markers* corresponding to each scale unit yields better results when there is plenty of *time for reading*.

In Figure 17-2 we see the percentage of errors in reading five types of dial.

Several conclusions have come from such studies:

The open-window type provides the most compact design.

The semicircular and horizontal scales require the eye to cover increasingly more ground.

On semicircular and horizontal scales, errors are more common at extreme positions.

Horizontal eye movements are easier and faster than vertical eye movements.

Reading habits tend to favor the horizontal type of scale.

In qualitative or check reading (to see whether equipment is functioning in a safe range) the dial and moving-pointer display is superior to the open-window type.

Time required to identify different dials increases with the number of dials in the panel. However, the increase in time is greater when the normal pointer positions are not aligned.

EXAMPLE OF A MAN-MACHINE SYSTEM

In Figure 17-3 we see the control system between the pilot and the airplane. The *input* to the pilot comes from the air-speed indicator as he reads the dial. He *decides* to advance the throttle. This constitutes the *output* as the pilot moves the throttle. This example in Figure 17-3 represents a *closed-loop* system, since the output modifies the input.

In contrast to the above example we have the *open-loop system*. An automatic system for turning lights on and off is an example. Thus, when daylight gets below a given level of brightness it activates a photoelectric cell which turns on the lights. When the out-of-doors illumination (the input) increases again at dawn, the quantity of light entering the photocell exceeds the level set for turning off the lights, and the control switch is deactivated. Once the switch is so deactivated, further changes in the input do not influence it.

PSYCHOLOGY IN UNION-MANAGEMENT RELATIONS

Psychologists are becoming increasingly interested in *group conflicts*. On the American scene, union-management relations offer an excellent example of such conflict. As put by one United States Secretary of Labor: "You have to understand not only that the other fellow has a point of view, but that he probably has pretty good reasons for having it."

It is difficult for many employers to accept the fact that they are not completely free to run their own plants and that their employees are unwilling to rely on competition among themselves to uncover and reward the most productive member. It is difficult for many workers to accept the fact that the employer has responsibilities to keep the plant profitable and moving ahead.

Although it has many other functions, a union is basically a *fighting organization*. Anything that limits the union's ability to stand up to

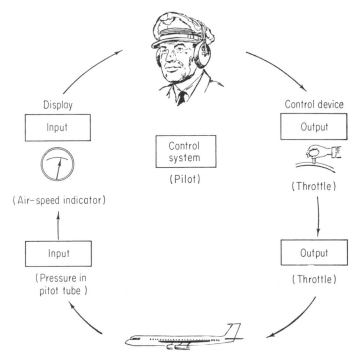

FIG. 17-3 Controlling air speed of an aircraft. The pilot is a control system, receiving inputs from the display (air-speed indicator) and providing outputs to the control device (throttle).

management in a crisis will weaken its ability to bargain with management in a crisis. It is difficult for the public to realize that beyond the fringes of friction there is much understanding and cooperation between unions and management. It is important to understand that collective bargaining is more than just arithmetic.

WHY WORKERS JOIN UNIONS

The positive reasons for joining a union are four: (1) the desire for job security, (2) the desire to be a member of an organization which is powerful, (3) the social pressures demanding that one join the union, (4) the feeling of belongingness that comes with being a union member.

Labor unions believe that they must stick together and get things for their members if they are to survive. Research shows that irrespective of the reason for joining, most workers accept unions with some degree of conviction.

Labor unions also feel that employers remain a strong potential threat to their survival. The future of the labor movement will depend upon its ability to attract members in the expanding sectors of the economy. They are working hard to organize white-collar employees and to expand their membership into the professions. Teachers' unions have been growing rapidly in those cities where experience shows that success depends on functioning within the climate of a power structure. The old feeling that unions are for blue-collar workers only seems to be passing.

One example of an insecure type of business is commercial television. An analysis of personnel changes in one TV station, owned by a network, showed a very high rate of involuntary turnover among nonunion management people. Among union members (cameramen, stage hands, engineers, newscasters) turnover was low. Of the entire union membership 70 percent had been with the station eighteen years. This was in contrast to the finding that only one manager had been with the station more than three years. Some managers, of course, move out and up. Some, however, move only out.

THE UNION ORGANIZATION

Most people know that in a management structure, power "comes from the top." It is just the opposite in a labor union, where power comes from the membership. Even when the officers are advancing the organizational goals of the union, they must protect their own positions. Dependence on the membership forces labor leaders to keep one eye on their political fences. Unlike their management counterparts, they have no single measure, such as profits, with which to evaluate their performance.

Union leadership is made more difficult, particularly at the local level, because of wide differences in the members' interests and attitudes. Union locals are made up of several groups with different backgrounds of age, levels of skill, and years of service with the company. Each group has its own demands. More for one group may mean less for another. Better opportunities for promotion in one group will make it more difficult for others to move ahead. More job protection for older workers may mean fewer jobs, or promotions, for younger workers.

CONFLICT AT THE CONFERENCE TABLE

Bargaining is basically a *power relationship*. Much of the table pounding and strong language that the negotiators use may be more to impress stockholders or union membership than to gain points in argument.

If one of the parties can succeed in convincing the other that it is unable to retreat from a certain solution, the act of commitment may force the opponent to give ground. Both management and labor negotiators go to great lengths to convince each other that they are firmly committed to particular positions. The nature of bargaining helps explain why facts and logic are often bypassed in all the confusion.

GRIEVANCES

Most grievances are settled at a local level between the union committeeman or steward, the foreman, and the man with the grievance. At this level, the process is very informal. Here much group conflict is avoided, for two basic reasons. First, the steward may be able to get something for the man; at least he defends him in the eyes of his fellow workers. Second, the foreman gains greater flexibility, which helps prevent worse grievances. It guards him against the actions of his superiors, who like to have the supervisor solve his own problems. This informality helps to stabilize industrial relations.

ARBITRATION

What happens if conflict cannot be resolved at the local level? Outsiders are brought into the picture. In addition to providing a method for getting together on the solution of differences, arbitration helps to make the grievance steps more meaningful. Arbitration provides, for the most part, a fair method of determining whether or not rights have been violated and makes the contract something more than a temporary halt in the power struggle. Arbitration, of course, is not always accepted.

As job security gains prominence as a union demand, it runs headlong into management's need to increase efficiency. For the psychologist, union-management relations provide an excellent situation for studying group conflicts.

PSYCHOLOGY IN EDUCATION

The applications of psychology in education cover a wide range of problems, from helping with the overly shy child to counseling parents on appropriate programming of activities for the exceptionally bright child. For the most part we can classify applications in the field of education as coming within the framework of school psychology and teacher education.

THE SCHOOL PSYCHOLOGIST

The functions of the school psychologist are much like those described in Chapter 11 on counseling and guidance. One specific is that the school psychologists perform their duties almost exclusively in the *school setting*.

The school psychologist works closely with teachers. He gives and interprets psychological tests and discusses problems with parents. He studies records and makes observations of student behavior in the classroom, on the playground, and in other parts of the school environment. Under certain conditions he functions in ways to help improve the child's home climate.

School psychologists are in measure *coordinators*. They organize and administer testing programs and often are associated with in-service teacher training. They also may be thought of as "community psychologists," participating in PTA meetings, performing on boards of directors of guidance centers and mental health societies, and, as one psychologist put it, "Giving a speech when the program chairman cannot find anyone else." Said one long-experienced professional, "My chief skill is availability."

Many kinds of problems are referred to the school psychologist, among which are difficulties of emotional adjustment, psychological aspects of physical handicaps, and problems in remedial reading, speech, and arithmetic. This person of many roles is also concerned with enriching the educational climate for the gifted child.

One applied psychologist put the job of the school psychologist in a nutshell: "He works not only *in* a school but *through* it."

TEACHER EDUCATION

At the heart of teacher training lies the psychology of learning. Important for learning is the *climate* in which it takes place. At the core of this classroom atmosphere is the teacher. And in some respects we may say that psychology is the science underlying education, much as the physical sciences provide the foundation for engineering. Regardless of the teaching medium—audiovisual aids, educational television, or teaching machines—the psychology of learning is fundamental. In Chapter 4 we discussed some of the basic elements of changing behavior through learning. Here let us talk a little more specifically about applying learning principles to teaching.

PROGRAMMED LEARNING

The use of teaching machines excites some educators and upsets others. Some see programmed learning, in which students happily push buttons to answer questions and are rewarded by the machine, as a great boost to individual learning. Critics see programmed textbooks or sliding-door machines as gadgets that do little more than old-fashioned workbooks. There are also those who are critical of elaborate systems which show objects or problems on a television screen, ask the student a question, and have him reply by pushing a keyboard wired to an electronic computer. The computer evaluates the answer and decides what next should appear on the screen.

Whether programmed learning makes use of specially prepared textbooks or computers, in either case it requires *an active response by the student*. And by a continual trial-and-correction process, an answer is *immediately scored*. More important, the material is presented in sequence, so that every question will elicit a response readily available to the student. This feedback provides for immediate reinforcement in the learning process.

Utilizing the *step-by-step* principle each question moves only a small distance beyond the questions the pupil has already answered. After exposing the learner with hints leading to the right answer, the programmer can remove some of these hints, or cues, and ask him to respond again. In theory, at least, it is possible for one to learn without making an error. Figure 17-4 illustrates the learning of a spelling word.

"If programmed learning has done nothing more than stimulate research and interest in the teaching process it has been worth every cent," remarked one educator.

REINFORCEMENT

Busy schedules of teachers often prevent "immediate feedback" on examinations. Likewise many learning situations have payoff coming late, or not at all, and we know how these experiences often lessen motivation for work. We all know that learning is facilitated when the learner is stimulated by the successful consequences of his behavior. The *reward,* which either depends upon or follows from the performance of a task, is referred to as *reinforcement* (see page 67).

Reinforcement may take many forms in work as well as in education. It may be a money reward or some psychological reward, such as a pat on the back or the feeling of accomplishment that sometimes goes with doing a good job. There are both positive and negative reinforcers.

Positive reinforcers work because they are presented as a consequence of having done something, e.g., a good test score or a smoothly

---

1. **Manufacture** means to make or build. *Chair factories manufacture chairs.* Copy the word here :

    □ □ □ □ □ □ □ □ □ □ □

2. **Part** of the word is like part of word **factory.** Both parts come from an old word meaning *make* or *build.*

    manu □ □ □ □ure

3. **Part** of the word is like part of the word **manual.** Both parts come from an old word for *hand.* Many things used to be made by **hand.**

    □ □ □ □ facture

4. **The same** letter goes in both spaces:

    m□nuf □cture

5. **The same** letter goes in both spaces:

    man□ fact□re

6. **Chair** factories □ □ □ □ □ □ □ □ □ □ chairs.

Fig. 17-4 The small-step principle in programming the learning of a spelling word. (*From Skinner, B. F. Teaching machines. Science,* 1958, 128, 969–977.)

running engine that one has just overhauled. *Negative reinforcers* are effective because *they are withdrawn* as a consequence of doing something. Examples include removing a trainee from a job he dislikes as a result of the successful completion of a training course.

LEARNING TO LEARN

Teacher education involves understanding how people learn. In Chapter 4 we talked about transfer in learning and we talked about set to learn. We have all had experiences in which practice on one muscular skill led to faster learning of a second, quite different skill. How does this happen? Let us turn to researches on monkeys. Studying the monkey has an advantage in that we can *control his environment from birth,* so that we know what cues he has had a chance to use.

The monkey is placed in a special cage for a training session. A shutter is raised and he sees before him two objects, a yellow cube and a blue cube. Just underneath each object is a cup. One cup holds a raisin. The monkey explores the situation and knocks one cube aside.

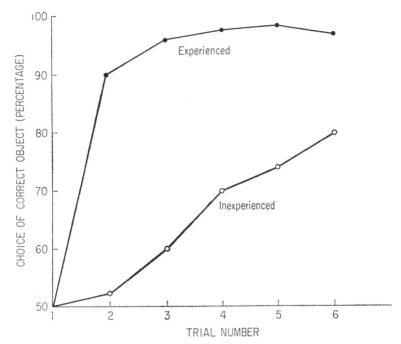

Fig. 17-5 The results of monkeys' learning which of two objects conceals a food reward. The lower curve is an average for the performance of inexperienced monkeys on their first eight problems. The upper curve represents the average of performance after experience with 200 previous problems. (*From Harlow, H. F. The formation of learning sets. Psychol. Rev., 1949, 56, 51–65.*)

If he exposes a raisin he is permitted to keep it as a reward. The shutter is then lowered to end the trial. How long does it take the monkey to discover that the raisin is always under the yellow cube? This depends on the past history of the monkey.

The monkey learns slowly in his first problem. Note the bottom curve in Figure 17-5. If the monkey has fifty trials with the yellow and blue cubes, then fifty trials on a second problem of a different sort (e.g., a pyramid block versus an oblong block), and so on, he eventually becomes expert at solving *choice* problems.

If trial 1 is a *new problem,* the monkey has only a 50 percent chance of success. If, however, he uses the information gained from this trial, he can succeed on trial 2. A monkey who has done 200 problems succeeds 90 percent of the time in getting the raisin on trial 2. He has learned to take advantage of his first-trial experience. He has learned that *success* depends on his effort to detect a cue, not on accident. Some way or other the monkey learns to make comparisons of objects in a way that indicates where the raisin is.

Psychology contributes to education by suggesting factors to be taken into account in influencing people to learn. It checks out beliefs and hypotheses in experiments and tries out many ideas that the teacher in the classroom does not have time to explore. Psychology in education explores problems of evaluation and measurement, and problems of how the individual grows in his or her intellectual, emotional, and social life. And the problems are becoming more extended and complex. From the standpoint of the amount of money spent, education in all its aspects is today the biggest business in the United States. Psychology in education is central in the stretch for excellence.

PSYCHOLOGY IN MEDICINE

For the most part psychology in medicine means *clinical psychology* and basic research in physiological and comparative psychology. Here the psychologist may work in private practice, in medical schools, in hospitals, for the Veterans Administration, or in various programs of rehabilitation.

Clinical psychologists work in many settings with physicians on the problems of the individual. The problem may involve helping a mentally handicapped child or evaluating the personality of a neurotic patient. Research work may range widely from trying to develop workable ways for testing the effects of a new drug on the behavior of animals to devising scales for measuring behavior changes in an emotionally disturbed person.

Clinical psychologists are also interested in the behavior of normal people. They know that people do not like to be pushed around, and they are interested in learning how each person reacts. For example, some anxiety reactions do not manifest themselves immediately. Feelings of fatigue, irritability, and even hostility may come on us slowly and without apparent cause. The clinician looks for the accumulated causes. Often when the normal person understands that we all experience these symptoms, the symptoms slowly disappear. Even creative effort sometimes brings on sleepless nights and overaggressiveness. These behaviors may well vanish when the creative product is achieved.

PUBLIC HEALTH

Psychologists working in public health systems may apply some of the methods and research findings used in advertising and selling. For example, the psychologist may try to help answer questions as to why many people will not take free polio shots, or why they even actually resist city programs for fluoridation of water to prevent tooth decay.

The psychologist, working along with others, has found that straight factual presentation on certain health programs among high school students is more effective than the more emotional fear-arousing presentations. He may become involved in persuading mass response to appeals. For example, the Veterans Administration had expected that 70 percent of some 1½ million veterans who were sent literature on higher benefits would respond, but only 19 percent did. Certainly there is no fear involved in filling out and mailing in a self-addressed form. What does happen when fear may be a part of the picture?

Why will some people who have been told they have cancer not report for treatment? One investigation studied several hundred patients who had received a diagnosis of cancer but did nothing about treatment. After their death (from cancer) the families were contacted. In one-third of the cases the reasons given for not seeking treatment or not returning for it were fear and unwillingness to admit the diagnosis. Other studies show that fear of knowing is quite common among people, particularly among the less well-educated. Some people are "psychologically closed" when it comes to facing problems of personal health.

COMPREHENSIVE MEDICINE

In some places emphasis is put on studying and giving treatment *to the whole person.* This approach in medicine is the opposite of the narrow specialization of medical practice. Such comprehensive medicine views the problems of the individual, particularly those involving mental health, in an environmental setting. The psychologist joins the team of physicians, nurses, social workers, and others in dealing with the problems of patients. Family-care programs and programs in child guidance and rehabilitation center so much on teamwork that psychologists have been added to the faculties of some medical schools.

COMMUNITY PSYCHOLOGISTS

Psychologists, in increasing numbers, are working as mental health consultants, mental health educators, human relations counselors, and as community-oriented clinicians. They work on a wide variety of problems, from helping to organize child guidance centers to setting up "halfway houses" for gradually getting the ex-mental patient back into work and into the community. Community psychology is becoming more and more involved with programs for the rehabilitation of alcoholics and drug addicts.

SOME TESTS USED BY PSYCHOLOGISTS

For the most part, clinical psychologists are concerned with people with intellectual handicaps and with people who have emotional difficulties. They give and interpret *intelligence tests* and help determine the nature of personality disorders through *interviewing, case histories,* and the use of *projective techniques.* The clinical psychologist is interested in a detailed personality description of the patient who combines a variety of problems of adjustment, as described in Chapter 10.

Practically all students are familiar with the nature of intelligence tests and of interviewing, and in one way or another they may have become a subject in some organization's case file, and hence are familiar with case histories. Somewhere along the line the student may have taken an "MMPI" given by a psychologist.

The *Minnesota Multiphasic Personality Inventory* (MMPI) is a self-report inventory. The individual responds to a series of written questions about his typical feelings. He reports on his attitudes and his actions. The MMPI consists of 550 statements which the subject is to classify as "True," "False," or "Cannot Say." It is primarily designed to indicate those traits that are commonly characteristic of psychological abnormality.

In the individual form of the test, each statement is printed on a card, and the subject places the card in a box under a category that he thinks is appropriate. The items range widely, covering such areas as health, psychosomatic symptoms, sexual attitudes, and motor disturbances. The inventory deals with items related to delusions, phobias, and a host of other abnormalities.

Sample items of the MMPI include:

I do not tire quickly.
I am worried about sex matters.
When I get bored I like to stir up some excitement.
I believe I am being plotted against.

Scores come out in ten scales, such as: "Masculinity-femininity" (commonly understood!); "Hypochondriasis" (anxiety about some part of body); or "Depression" (unhappiness and feelings of worthlessness).

Items for the Masculinity-femininity (Mf) scale, for example, were selected in terms of frequency of responses by men and women. Interpretation of MMPI "profiles" is complex and involves careful professional use.

Projective techniques, although used in some places in personnel selection, and even in advertising research, are used principally in the clinical setting. One of the best-known instruments is the Rorschach Inkblot Test. The subject is shown each of ten cards made up of a bilaterally symmetrical blot *standardized* on many cases. (You can make an inkblot by putting a glob of ink near the center of a sheet of paper and then folding over once, pressing down lightly.)

Some of the Rorschach cards are in black, white, and gray, and others are in color. Subjects tell what they "see in the inkblots." Such associations are scored and interpreted for meaning.

Another common projective technique uses pictures as stimuli. Most familiar is the *Thematic Apperception Test* (TAT), which employs black and white pictures as stimuli. The subject is told to make up a story to fit each picture, to tell what is happening in the picture, and what the characters are feeling and thinking.

Projective tests are useful to the clinician in providing leads for further probing about problems. They are also useful in getting data on long-range research problems. Below we shall describe a summary of several such projects involving the normal stress of work and living.

STRESS AND PERSONALITY PATTERNS

Longitudinal studies, using the MMPI and other clinical evaluations, found that those who developed coronary heart trouble fourteen years later had originally held higher scores than most people on such scales as "hypochondriasis," "masculinity," and "activity."

It was found in a nationwide sample of persons at various occupational levels that *psychological tension increases with rank and with income.* This does not mean, however, that one will escape tension by becoming a failure. The gradual increase in tension as one moves upward is well known to anyone who has experienced increasing responsibility. Coordinating the work of others is a factor in management stress, not unlike the confusion surrounding the administration of a program in education. There is a relationship between a person's rank in an organization and the amount of pressure on him. The college department head may feel more pressure than the instructor, but less than that of the dean. Who survives best?

A TWELVE-YEAR STUDY

The Public Health Service's report on a twelve-year study of business executives shows that their average life span *is above normal*. How can this be?

It could well be that the worker who worries about a layoff feels more stress than the vice-president whose job is in jeopardy. For one man a performance review may be a big threat, something which he dreads. For another person, who differs in personality and ambition, it may be a promise and a challenge. Patterns of reaction to stress relate to general health and to personality. The executive who understands his job and realizes that problems and pressures are "a part of the game" may thrive on stress. This executive without conflict expresses much the same dislikes for his job as does the manager with conflict. Whereas the leader without conflict accepts pressure and isolation as something to be expected as a part of the job, the leader with conflict tries to fight the windmill.

One reason why top organizational people can withstand stress lies in *natural selection*. That is, many of those whose stress levels do not favor survival as executives do not reach this position. The clinical psychologist is interested just as much in people who succeed as in those who fail. Making comparisons between the characteristics of the two leads to understanding.

PSYCHOLOGY IN LAW

The class had been in session for about twenty minutes when suddenly the door opened and in rushed two men. The small man pointed a banana at the large man. The firing of a shot was heard as the large man fell to the floor. Two students (who had been briefed on the demonstration) carried the fallen man out a side door. The other man made an exit at the rear of the room. The instructor, who had fired a blank shot from behind his desk, immediately passed out notebooks and asked each of some thirty students to write out what they had just witnessed. The entire episode lasted less than one-half minute.

Reports of the incident varied greatly. Many students "actually saw" the banana as a gun. Others saw things that happened and things that did not happen.

AUSSAGE TESTS

The Aussage test is known by its original German name, meaning "testimony" or "report." The description of the classroom event above illustrates how formal studies have been made about descriptions given at automobile accidents and at murder scenes. Of the many studies on eye-witness testimony, research has found that *reports without error are rare indeed*. People usually "fill in" the gaps of their observations. They "recall" the scene with plausible detail, in accord with some of the principles of perception discussed in Chapter 3.

Versions of Aussage tests have been found useful in the training of law students; the students play various roles—witness, judge, prosecuting attorney, defense council, and court reporter.

ON THE STAND

Studies have shown that when witness reports are given under conditions of free description there is more accuracy in the report than there is under conditions of direct questioning. Most people give more details when asked to answer specific questions than when they are allowed free recital, *but more of their report is wrong*. Accuracy drops very low under hostile and confusing types of questions in cross-examination.

Studies show that questions can be asked in ways that encourage a particular answer of false recall. If asked whether the defendant held the pistol in his right hand or his left hand, many witnesses may honestly come to believe they saw a gun that was not actually there. One study found that the mere grammatical form of a question may direct the response. "Wasn't there a car parked in front of the bank?" is more *suggestive* than the question, "Was there a car parked in front of the bank?" "Did *you* see a car?" tends to increase caution and accuracy in answer.

When subjects are asked which facts they would be willing to report under oath, error is reduced somewhat but not eliminated.

LABORATORY STUDIES

From experimental laboratories come conclusions useful to legal psychology. The inaccuracy of visual illusions and localizations of sound offer common examples. It is known that people will overestimate vertical distances more than they do horizontal distances. Likewise one will overestimate a filled space more than an unfilled one. Accuracy in estimating the speed of moving vehicles is subject to much error. Strong emotion at the time of observation tends to decrease the accuracy of a report.

Can false confessions be induced in the calm environment of the college laboratory? Yes, under three conditions. First, an individual's attitudes *and beliefs* can be manipulated by getting him to play some particular role. Second, beliefs of the individual can be changed by getting the person to deliver some persuasive argument. Third, attitudes and beliefs can be manipulated by getting subjects to behave in ways that imply endorsement of a particular set of beliefs.

College students were asked to participate in experiments disguised as research on lie detection. They were asked to cross out certain words in a list. Each subject was trained to give true statements in the presence of a "truth light." The same subjects were trained to give false statements in the presence of a "lie light." Each subject was then required to state aloud that he had previously crossed out certain words and had not crossed out others. Half these "confessions" were false. Each was made in the presence of either the truth light or the lie light.

When the subjects were asked later to recall what they had done, a significant thing happened. False confessions in the truth light caused more errors of recall and less confidence in remembering. There were fewer errors and more confidence of recall when "confessions" were given in the lie light. What does this mean? One practical interpretation says that a false confession can distort a person's recall of his past behavior *if* the confession is given in the presence of cues previously associated with *telling the truth*. Cues previously associated with *lying* can create self-disbelief in *true* confessions.

From these, and similar types of studies, one may question the accuracy of "confessions," whether they be in laboratory situations, in the stress situations of prison confines, or even in courtroom climates.

THE POWER OF SUGGESTION

An individual may be told to place his hand in an elaborate-looking apparatus, with dials, controls, and lights that change in intensity; he is then instructed to tell when he feels warmth. Several switches are thrown. Most people will report a sensation of slight warmth although no physical warmth is present. Through suggestion warmth is perceived in the absence of the real stimulus.

Leading questions often elicit responses by suggestion. In one experiment, a subject who has looked at a certain picture is asked: "Is the man holding the dog by a leash or by the scruff of the neck?" Most subjects answer one or the other, but in the picture the man is not holding the dog at all!

There is no mystery attached to suggestion. It is a simple stimulus-response activity. A suggested response is a direct reaction to an external stimulus. The response occurs without the presence of the internal or self-directive intermediate stimulus that is present in voluntary activity. In *voluntary action,* a command, an invitation, or some other social stimulus arouses an intermediate response of "inner speech," or thought, which in turn arouses the act. In *suggestion,* the external stimulus elicits the act directly, as it were, "without thinking." *Hypnosis* represents a form of suggestion.

Members of a jury may be influenced by suggestion as it is related to prejudices, or even to appearances and mannerisms. *Suggestion does not have to be given verbally to be effective.* Studies show that the personality of the foreman influences some jury decisions. Even the order of the presentation has an effect on persuasiveness of evidence. For example, one investigation showed that the judgment of guilt *rose* with successive presentation of prosecution evidence and *dropped* with successive presentation of defense evidence. Studies show that two things are important under ordinary courtroom conditions, *primacy* and *recency*. They tend to be equally strong. Getting there "first with the most, and last with the suggestion has won me many a case," said one lawyer.

CONFORMITY AND INFLUENCE

A jury situation offers opportunity for the study of how some people yield to suggestion and persuasion. In *conformity,* a person changes his behavior in a way to comply with situational pressure. Any response in which the individual yields to the pressure of the group is a conforming response. *Influence* involves a personal change of attitude or opinion. Whereas conformity is an outward change, influence is private or a change inside the person. Both are important aspects of legal psychology.

In the laboratories of social psychology much has been learned about factors that affect both conformity and influence:
1   In face-to-face groups conformity is greater than when the individual votes anonymously.
2   Conformity can be reduced somewhat by having a person express his feelings in writing before joining a group.
3   A subject tends to conform more when he feels himself a part of the group.
4   Influence is related to status.
5   Conformity and influence tend to work together.

On the one hand, there is a tendency for a person to *conform* to the judgments of others. Following this the individual tends to try to influence deviate members of a group to come along in agreement.

LIE DETECTORS

No description of psychology in law would be complete without a word about the practical application of so-called lie detectors. Several conclusions may be made from the results of hundreds of studies. *First,* lie detectors are useful in preliminary examinations and in initial screening of police suspects. *Second,* lie detectors are not free of error. Most errors are, however, failures to detect guilt. Reports show that rarely has an innocent person been shown to be guilty by the lie detector. *Third,* it is very rare that lie detection data are admitted as evidence in court trials. *Fourth,* in any setting, legal or elsewhere, a lie detector should be employed only with the examinee's consent. *Fifth,* it is possible that a thorough understanding of lie detector principles and of the physiology involved may help a person "beat the test." *Sixth,* only technically competent people should administer and interpret test data.

HOW THE LIE DETECTOR WORKS

Why has there been so much controversy about lie detectors? In part, the lie detector is misnamed. It is not a detector of lies, but rather it involves the use of instruments for measuring physiological changes in breathing, blood pressure, and the galvanic skin response. It does not measure lies, *it measures emotional upset.* Telling an untruth usually causes some increase in blood pressure and pulse rate and an irregular rhythm in breathing. The galvanic skin reaction is related to sweating of the hands. A small electric and imperceptible current is sent through the palms. When the palms perspire, electrical conductivity is increased. Or in other words, electrical resistance is lowered, and this resistance can be measured. All the physiological measures are recorded on an instrument called the "polygraph."

The lie detector compares the subject's responses to both neutral stimuli and critical stimuli. Suppose that rare books are missing from the library. Several persons are suspected of taking two valuable volumes of Shakespeare, each in a yellow jacket. Neutral stimuli could be chosen which closely matched the critical words of "number," "Shakespeare," "yellow," etc. The critical words given in a free-association test would be scattered at random among the neutral words. To the innocent subject, the critical and neutral words are indistinguishable.

Guilt may be indicated if the subject's responses to the critical words are significantly different from his responses to the neutral words. Measures are made in several ways; in terms of reaction time, repetition of stimulus word, or failure to respond. Sometimes instead of using free-association words the experimenter may ask questions requiring answers of "yes" or "no," or he may even use multiple-choice questions.

For the student of human behavior the applications of psychology can be found in all professions. They are most noticeable, however, when they can be observed in day-by-day situations.

Summary

Psychology is applied in specialized and professional areas—marketing, engineering and systems, union-management relations, education, medicine, and law. These applications extend beyond the problems we have covered with childhood, adolescence, middle-age, youth, and retirement. They go beyond problems in adjustment, counseling, and work. However, they relate only indirectly to the individual.

Psychology in marketing covers a mix of advertising, selling, customer service, and purchase behavior—in short, the problems of influence.

Psychology in engineering deals with problems of how machines can be designed to relate better to man's senses and muscles, making it easier for the human operator. Systems problems concern inputs and outputs.

Group conflicts have many psychological aspects, such as power struggles, grievances, and arbitration, which come out in union-management relations.

Psychology in education covers a wide range of problems in the areas of school psychology, teacher education, and programmed learning. It probably relates to more people in more ways than it does in any of the other professional areas. Attention is given to the gifted as well as to the handicapped child, and to the many aspects of applying learning theory to the daily problems of the classroom.

Clinical psychology is closely related to the profession of medicine and to research in the physiological areas, e.g., testing the effects of drugs on behavior. Psychologists work in programs of public health, in community relations, and on teams studying and giving treatment to the whole person. Much of their work centers around testing, the use of projective techniques, and varied studies of stress and personality.

Psychology in law is concerned with the accuracy of testimony, with the power of suggestion, and with how it is possible to sway juries. It is also concerned with conformity and influence. It is interested in the many aspects of the uses and misuses of so-called lie detectors.

For the student of human behavior the applications of psychology can be found in all professions. They are most noticeable when they can be observed in day-by-day situations.

Suggestions for Thinking and Discussion

1 Spend one day reading and listening to ads; count them. Which ones did you "shut out"? Which ones had an influence on *you?* Do you know why?

2 Examine some home appliance or other piece of equipment for ease of operation. Do you see some ways in which the appliance can be improved by human engineering?

3 Study some strike situation. Can you tell the difference between the economic and the psychological factors involved?

4 Make a list of those things *you* have found to be important in "learning to learn."

5 Make an "inkblot." Have a number of observers tell you what they see in it. How would you plan a study to find out if a series of such inkblots could be made into a test?

6 List the arguments for and against the use of lie detectors.

Suggestions for Further Reading

Bruner, J. S. *Toward a theory of instruction.* Cambridge, Mass.: Harvard University Press, 1966. How teachers can keep alive the child's "inner urge to know."

Gagne, R. M. (Ed.) *Psychological principles in systems development.* New York: Holt, Rinehart and Winston, 1962. Twenty psychologists talk about systems, computers, tasks, selection, training, performance appraisal, and experimental design. For the most part presented in technical language.

Goldstein, M. J., & Palmer, J. O. *The experience of anxiety: A casebook.* Oxford University Press, 1963. A paperback of twenty-four unanalyzed cases of raw clinical data.

Guilford, J. P. (Ed.) *Field of psychology.* Princeton, N.J.: D. Van Nostrand, 1966. This third edition includes chapters on five professional areas where psychology is applied.

Hughes, J. L. *Programmed instruction for schools and industry.* Chicago: Science Research Associates, 1962. The principles and construction of programmed materials.

Inban, F. E. *Lie detection and criminal investigation.* Baltimore: Williams & Wilkins, 1942. An old standby on the practical uses of lie-detection methods.

Katona, G. *The mass consumption society.* New York: McGraw-Hill, 1964. An overall view of marketing at the consumer level.

McCormick, E. J. *Human factors engineering.* New York: McGraw-Hill, 1964. A text on engineering psychology.

Marshall, J. *Law and psychology in conflict*. Indianapolis: Bobbs-Merrill, 1966. Psychological studies show that perception and recollection of situations are imperfect. Shows the human failings of the individual witness.

Mayer, M. *Madison Avenue USA*. New York: Pocket Books, 1959. A popularized image of American advertising.

Purcell, T. V. *Blue collar man*. Cambridge, Mass.: Harvard, 1960. Shows that workers can be loyal to both the company and the union in some climates.

Sachs, B. M. *The student, the interview, and the curriculum*. Boston: Houghton Mifflin, 1966. Counseling in the elementary and secondary school setting.

Stagner, R., & Rosen, H. *Psychology of union-management relations*. Belmont, Calif.: Wadsworth, 1965. A paperback on the rapidly growing field of the psychology of conflict.

CHAPTER 18

Psychology
in the Military

❖—❖—❖—❖—❖—❖—❖—❖—❖—❖

The one place where the many aspects of applied psychology come together is in military settings. Scientific psychology has unfolded during the same time that international conflict has become worldwide. This has created a climate favorable to the study of human behavior in very large systems. For example, psychologists have found that soldiers who are informed about a dangerous mission before it takes place will commit themselves to higher risks. If they learn about the impending action several days before H-hour, fear will be present but emotional shock will be absent. Risks can be calculated and the psychological preparation that follows will lessen the fear.

The military applications of psychology in the United States began during World War I, with the development of two types of intelligence test: the Army *Alpha* for those who could read and write and the Army *Beta* for illiterates. The tests were widely used, and they contributed in measure to the effective selection, classification, and assignment of Army recruits.

With United States entry into World War II psychologists entered all branches of military service. They worked on a wide variety of psychological problems. From the field of experimental psychology came answers to practical questions about the efficient use of the human senses and motor skills in combat. Much was done to improve the use of human resources through programs of selection and training, to which contributions were made by industrial and educational psychologists. Counseling and clinical psychologists became involved in the many problems of adjustments to military life. Social psychologists gave of their talents to problems of group behavior and leadership.

The application of military psychology, in peacetime as well as during war, has provided a vast laboratory and clinic for researchers. Much of the content of applied psychology described throughout this text has come from military settings or later from hundreds of psychologists who gained valuable experience as members of the armed forces. It is important to remember that military organizations function in peacetime as well as in wartime.

PERCEIVING AND PERFORMING

From experimental psychology has come much information about the human senses important to the armed forces. In terms of practical rules, let us talk about efficient use of the senses.

THE EYE

Visual fatigue is caused when the eyes are used too long or when they are strained to perceive near or beyond their limits of acuity. Change of focus back and forth for long periods causes the eyes to tire because the various muscles used become fatigued.

Work in very uneven illumination causes eyestrain. Looking from a bright instrument panel to outside darkness is fatiguing. Readers experience a similar strain when they look back and forth from a well-illuminated book to a darkened room. Looking at unclear objects, such as fine print, causes undue fatigue, as does glare.

Some practical rules for *day* vision are:
1 When possible, avoid looking at small objects.
2 Use good illumination without glare.
3 Do not look back and forth between far and near objects too often.
4 Blink when the eyes seem to need lubrication.
5 Avoid general fatigue. The small muscles of the eye are affected quickly by waste products.
6 Remember that an excessive amount of alcohol affects the visual nerve centers.
7 Avoid emotional upset (if possible!). The person in a "blind rage" can be just that.

Some practical rules for *night* vision are:

1 Have night vision tested. Some people are night-blind in varying degrees.
2 Stay in the dark for thirty minutes before night observation. Dark adaptation takes time. (Remember sitting on someone's lap in the theater?)
3 Try to avoid looking directly at a light.
4 Look to the side of what you want to observe. Seeing out of the corner of the eyes utilizes the rods (night receptors in the eye). Avoid the straight-ahead look because this stimulates the cones (daylight and color receptors).
5 When possible, choose a contrasting background for observing an object.
6 Practice recognition of targets. Familiarity helps with the "fill in" of what you observe.

Some practical rules for *not being seen:*

1 Avoid movement; this attracts attention.
2 Avoid lights. Blackout is the best camouflage.
3 Keep small. A man standing on the ground is much more obvious than a head above the foxhole.
4 Avoid uniqueness. Being different compels attention.
5 Avoid patterns. Certain forms (lines, circles) are conspicuous. For example, a circular pond among a number of irregular ponds would be noticed first.
6 Avoid brightness contrast. Light on dark, for example, produces contours.
7 Avoid texture differences.
8 Avoid shadows.
9 Match the background as much as possible.

THE EAR

Whereas the eye is primarily a "spacial" sense, the ear is a "temporal" sense. Space location by ear may be very inaccurate.

Some practical rules for good hearing are:

1 Colds cause dull hearing by producing unequal pressures in the ear.
2 When flying keep swallowing to help equalize the pressure on the two sides of the eardrum.
3 Loud sounds mask out faint noises. Repeated loud sounds, such as one's own rifle fire, cause temporary deafness.
4 In the midst of loud noise sticking one's fingers in one's ears improves the hearing of shouted speech.

5   Become familiar with certain sounds. You will hear them better.
6   When a loud sound is expected, be on the ground if possible. Explosion vibrations generally go up from the ground.
7   Open the mouth when an explosion is coming. This helps equalize eardrum pressure.

SENSE OF SMELL

Smell is a ground sense. Walking erect cuts down on the efficiency of smelling; crawling is better. Smell adapts very rapidly, particularly when we sniff hard. Most people are either uninterested in odors or reject foul ones. Hence special attention has to be given to learning the characteristic odors of certain war gases.

Rules about detecting war gases by smell:
1   Note individual differences in sensitivity to smell; some people have very little.
2   Adaptation to smell is rapid. Colds may abolish it entirely.
3   Some fumes, particularly those from gasoline, dull the olfactory sense temporarily.
4   Tobacco smoke and some explosives dull olfactory sensitivity.
5   Do not try to test for gas on high ground. Gases tend to settle in low places.
6   Learn the odors of different gases from weak dilutions of the gases themselves.
7   One odor may mask out another. Learn which types dominate.
8   Odors are often mixed. Learn to detect such combinations.

MOTION

Motion sickness is quite common. Nausea is caused not only by disturbances of the vestibular organs associated with the ear, but by visual disturbances as well. Odors may be nauseating; even imagination adds to the picture. *Suggestion* plays a big role in causing motion sickness. It is easier to be sick when other people are sick, when you think about it, or when you expect to get sick. It is possible *to learn* not to be sick.

Here are some rules for avoiding motion sickness:
1   Get used to motion. Sailors and flyers do.
2   Think about things that do not stimulate sickness.
3   Try to avoid associating sickness with specific situations.
4   Breathe fresh air.
5   Avoid overeating, hangovers, and fatigue.
6   Use only pills which have been prescribed.

SOME SPACE TRAVEL PROBLEMS

Research into space travel has added something new to the old problems of equilibrium. Under conditions of *weightlessness* motion sickness and extreme fatigue accompany long space flights. Even return to normal conditions of gravity may be accompanied by marked debility and impaired psychomotor performance. Fortunately, through training and the use of instruments, astronaut *disorientation* can be overcome. This is a situation where sensory cues are misperceived and the equilibrium sense gives distorted information. The "gravity receptors" of the inner ear upset spatial orientation in ways we rarely experience on the ground.

Even the effects of confinement in a spacecraft cause feelings of *detachment,* a situation characterized by feelings of separation and loneliness. This is called the "breakoff effect." Here the pilot feels not only alone but actually separated physically from the earth. Reactions differ. Some observers report exhilaration and a sense of power; others anxiety and insecurity.

One generalization has emerged from studies of both real and simulated space travel. *People who adjust well in everyday life situations can learn to adjust to the stresses of space through programs of habituation and training.*

SENSE OF TOUCH

Military organizations, along with organizations devoted to the study of communication for the deaf-blind, have recently been conducting research on "talking through the skin." Although such cutaneous communication has not as yet provided rules for improving perception through the sense of touch, we wish to describe briefly some of the research that has been going on in the military, in universities, and in other experimental laboratories.

We believe it important to point out that military organizations sponsor much research in both basic and applied psychology. We use the description below as one of many examples.

COMMUNICATION THROUGH THE SKIN

The practical needs for a tactile communication system have whetted the imagination of many persons. Research is now underway to find ways of communicating with frogmen by using mechanical vibratory codes sent to them from a distance. With vibrators attached to the body, secret transmissions are quite feasible. Studies are being made on efficient ways of communicating with tank drivers via coded electrical "pulses" tuned for reception through the skin. These can be felt when noise masks out speech. Work is being conducted to improve aircraft landings on carriers by supplementing the eyes and ears with information supplied through the skin.

Research is being conducted with astronauts for communication in space under conditions where sight and sound may be distorted. It has been found that *seven* classes of information can be conveyed through the skin using such signals as mechanical vibrations (similar to the feelings one gets from touching a tuning fork) and electrical pulses (very mild "taps" on the skin). Some research is going on in the use of small air jets as stimuli.

It has been found out that *amounts* can be presented through the skin, providing quantitative information or giving quantitative instructions, such as, "add three more pounds of pressure." *Coordinates* can give relational information; e.g., "The target is located where coordinate A crosses coordinate B." In landing an aircraft both *directions* and *rates* can be transmitted through the skin.

Research is being carried out utilizing the attention-demanding qualities of vibration or an "electrical nudge." Such stimuli can always break through noise or inattention, giving *warning* to the pilot that he is to be ejected from the spacecraft. The Navy has been using cutaneous vibrations in studying the *vigilance* of sailors on watch.

The primary demand for a cutaneous communication system has been for its use in transmitting *language*.

The skin as a sensory channel for communication has one unique advantage; it is rarely ever "busy." Even though there is a wide range of individual differences in skin sensitivity, for all practical purposes there is no such thing as complete "skin deafness." The skin, of course, has a long history of serving as a communication channel for the blind, Braille having been invented in 1826. Braille, however, even when thoroughly mastered, is still slow and cumbersome. Recent researches indicate that much more efficient systems for communicating through the skin are not far off. This indicates once again that many research projects undertaken to find answers to practical military problems also give answers to peacetime problems.

SKILL AND EFFICIENCY

In some ways we may think of human efficiency as the ratio of output to input. Input may be the number of man-hours spent, and output may be the number of airplanes serviced or potatoes peeled. But such inputs and outputs are difficult to measure.

A great deal of work has been devoted to *psychomotor* skills. The word "psychomotor" suggests that some thinking preceeds the muscular, or motor, response. Measures of movements have been made, and it has been found useful to speak of several kinds of movement when we are talking about efficiency of muscular work.

First come the basic movements, called *simple positioning.* An illustration would be the hand moving from one location to another; e.g., twisting a knob from one setting to another.

A second class involves *tense* movements. In tense movements the arm, for example, is caused to shift in position but finds opposing muscles operating. In driving a truck over smooth roads steering involves only "simple positioning" movements. However, driving over rough country of rocks and ruts causes forces to be applied that either add to or subtract from the force produced by the driver. This leads to a "tense" kind of movement pattern.

Third come *ballistic* movements, as in throwing a football or swinging a golf club. Here no opposing muscles are functioning. And here we find one disadvantage—the unpracticed amateur can "throw his arm out." Flipping a switch is an example of a "ballistic" movement.

Static movements are a fourth class. They are similar to positioning movements but differ in being very small; e.g., pushing a brake pedal.

Fifth come *sequential* movements in which actions are repetitive. Wheel turning or tapping tasks are of this sort. While we are learning to make such responses we must think about what we are doing. Once these habits have been established, they go on automatically without our having to think about them. This is one reason why we should learn such skill movements correctly from the beginning.

There are many motor-ability tests to find people with abilities in wrist-finger speed, aiming ability, manual dexterity, and some forty other skills involved in psychomotor coordination. A person may be very good in doing one kind of movement and poor in some other kind. Fortunately, different jobs demand different skills. What the instrument maker has to do and what the ballplayer has to be skilled in are different. There are some general suggestions, however, for increasing motor skill and efficiency.

Some of the rules for determining the best method of work are similar to points discussed about work in Chapter 13. They include:

1 Keep the number of movements to a minimum.
2 Arrange movements so that each ends in a position favorable for beginning the next.
3 Make sequence of movements in rhythm.
4 Minimize the number of parts of the body involved.
5 Arrange for the use of both hands as much as possible.

6 When possible provide for intermittent use of different muscles.

7 Provide for symmetrical motions of both arms.

8 Arrange the work space efficiently.

SELECTION AND TRAINING

Selection and training of military personnel differ basically very little from the processes involved in civilian occupations. In the military, selection involves the measurement of aptitudes and skills to pick the best people for training in some two thousand occupational specialties. One problem which is acute in both civilian and military jobs is skill obsolescence.

PERSONNEL SELECTION

Selection may be careful or careless, systematic or haphazard. And in the military one will find many instances repeated of selection "snafus." They range widely. One example is that of the stock broker who was sent to cook-and-bakers' school because some corporal read his civilian occupation on the personal history sheet as "baker" instead of "banker." He later became a high-ranking officer, quite knowledgeable in army food problems.

Research data from World War II support the conclusion that personnel selection in all branches of the Armed Forces is the best mass programming ever done in matching peoples' potentials to jobs. The development of psychological tests, together with other selection procedures, owes much to the work accomplished in military settings.

INDIVIDUAL DIFFERENCES

People differ in many ways. They differ in height and weight, in size of the feet, and in reaction time. They differ in educational background and in interests.

Men differ widely in *general intelligence,* and these differences begin in childhood, as shown in Figure 18-1.

Men also differ in *special aptitudes,* such as music and mechanical ability. They differ in their *reactions* for flying airplanes and driving jeeps. And they differ in *perception,* ranging from color blindness to the speed of receiving code. Men differ in *trade knowledge* and in *educational achievement.* They also differ in *personality,* in *interests,* and in many other ways. But for the most part, all these differences can be measured. This allows the military to "classify" people appropriately.

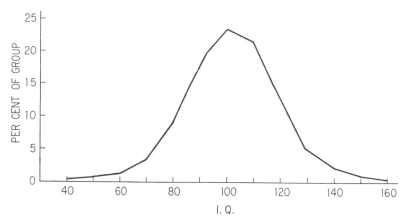

FIG. 18-1   The distribution of intelligence quotients of some three thousand children tested on the Stanford-Binet. They range from the gifted (140 I.Q. and above) down to the mentally defective (below 60 I.Q.). The majority fall in the average range of 90 to 110 I.Q. For the most part these children will show the same range of general intelligence when they reach military age.

EXAMPLE OF SELECTION RESEARCH

In Figure 18-2 we see the results of one investigation using a battery of some twenty tests to select airplane pilots. The tests measured such factors as ability to read maps, to make mathematical calculations, to make coordinated movements, and to perceive relationships. The figure illustrates the percentage eliminated from primary flight training for each of nine aptitude levels called the pilot *stanine*. These results, based on a sample of over 153,000 cases tested in World War II, employed many applied psychologists. It may be seen from examining the graph in Figure 18-2 that by selecting only those candidates whose pilot stanine was 6 or above, 70 percent of the potential failures would have been eliminated.

TRAINING AND EDUCATION

There is much evidence to support the conclusion that some of the best teaching that is done is found in military settings. Yes, no doubt there are exceptions, perhaps similar to those we find in college. In most civilian occupations it is important to distinguish between "training" and "education." In the military, with the exception of higher-level positions, training predominates.

"Training" is defined as *the teaching of specific skills*. "Education" usually refers to a broader type of teaching in which the objectives relate to *proficiency in future situations* by providing a basis for learning through experience or future training. The teaching of typing illustrates training, as does instruction given to the mechanic in running a new machine. Instruction given to officers in the Army War College is education. This textbook in applied psychology is designed for education, hopefully providing a broad base for dealing with future applications of psychology to specific problems.

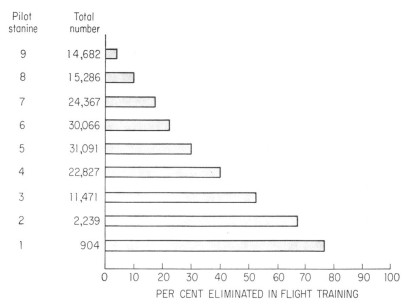

FIG. 18-2   A sample of 153,000 subjects given a battery of twenty tests for the prediction of success or failure in pilot training. All the cadets, regardless of scores, were sent to primary training. It may be seen that of those who scored the lowest stanine (aptitude index) of 1, over 70 percent failed in training. With a stanine of 5, about 30 percent failed. With the highest index of 9, only 5 percent failed. The number of subjects in each stanine bracket is listed in the second column of figures. (*From Staff, AAF Training Command. Psychological activities in the training command. Psychol. Bull.,* 1945, 42, 46.)

PREPAREDNESS IS BOTH TRAINING
AND EDUCATION

Within the control center of the Air Defense Command, beneath the Colorado Mountains, one will find a mass of equipment and many levels of men—each dependent on the other, and on "the system." Behind the orange consoles sit officers giving commands, officers with years of experience and education. Nearby, is the "display specialist," with months of specialized training, who knows his special job perfectly—"what" buttons to push "when." Computers calculate data fed to them from thousands of miles away by men trained in their given specialties. Missile crews are ready, as are other men specifically trained. In this man-machine system there are those who are highly trained in specific jobs that no one else can do. There are those who are educated in knowing the overall picture, trained also in some specifics, and in the delicate processes of decision making. In one sense, then, we may think of the differences between training and education as somewhat academic. Efficient "systems" demand both. In the military, one cannot afford the luxury of irresponsibility.

TRAINING AIDS, DEVICES, AND SIMULATORS

The military services have policies which require the development of training devices to accompany the construction of new equipment. A major portion of time spent in some training programs is spent in using training devices—flight simulators, oxygen deprivation equipment, and teaching machines. Hundreds of hours are spent by astronauts in all aspects of space travel without leaving the ground.

Some training devices are built to provide measures of how proficient a person is in doing his job. Some devices are designed to facilitate effective transfer of training to the job situation. Some devices provide "work samples" for learning an actual job situation.

From the standpoint of the psychologist, training aids, devices, and simulators offer a means of automatically controlling many of the variables which facilitate learning and transfer.

CLASSIFICATION OF TRAINING

Training occurs at various levels in the military. When a man enters the service he undergoes *orientation and indoctrination* training, during which one is supposed to learn rules and regulations, become familiar with the formal structures of the organization, and start on the development of appropriate attitudes. Needless to say, much of the understanding of the organizational climate does not come through such formal settings.

Newly inducted recruits are often separated into categories based on selection and classification procedures. Some are sent in the direction of *vocational and job-skill training*. Semiskilled individuals may well fall in this category. By contrast, professional and technically trained people find themselves in *advanced* schools. All organizations, the military included, require a variety of persons with *specialized* training, such as computer programmers or laboratory technicians. The military also offers training and education in *supervisory, managerial,* and *executive* activities comparable to those described in Chapter 15. Many statistics show the value of military training for career development in later life.

ADJUSTMENTS IN MILITARY LIVING

Psychologically, adjustments to miltary life are much the same as in civilian life. As one chaplain put it, "Problems are the same, only more so."

The general foundations of adjustment problems were described in Chapter 10. Let us here describe how they are related to the military environment.

In our democratic society many men have not had to make the adjustments which must be made to military life. Some men find the "authoritarian climate" to their dislike, others enjoy the new experience. Military living involves a controlled life of cooperation under discipline, a life of taking orders, a life without privacy, and a life with projected fears. In civilian life one can often resist change and get by with such resistance. This is more difficult within the military climate.

Two sets of problems of adjustment face the man who is new to a military organization. Some men get shaken up by one or the other or both of these. First, there is the problem of the new recruit. The second set of problems comes with facing the dangers of combat.

THE NEW RECRUIT

Arrival in training camp begins with a confusion of rules and discipline. Ego needs suffer a blow as the individual loses his identity among the masses. He is told, and told, and told (yes, the author is a former service man—World War II). Participative experiences *of his own choosing* are hard to find. Many things the recruit is asked to do make little sense to him. He is told the "what," the "how," and the "when," but rarely is he told the "why." When he tries to find out he often gets taken for a ride in some form or other.

Homesickness is normal for the recruit. Some psychiatrists call this *cryptic nostalgia.* While preoccupied with thoughts of home he seems inefficient, unreliable, slow to learn, awkward in drill, and not yet with appropriate ways of beefing about military life. The big send-off from home only adds to feelings of frustration and the anxieties of failure.

As time goes on in training the recruit finds he has company in misery, and he finds relief in griping and in humor. Gradually the normal person begins to enjoy some aspects of military life (this is true particularly of those who like to try to beat the system) when he gets some reinforcement. Knowing and understanding "what to expect" help adjustment.

ADJUSTMENTS TO COMBAT

Even the bravest of men get scared. Below we shall summarize, from many descriptions, some ways of adjusting to combat:

1　There is always the fear of death. It can be met in part by accepting the possibility of death as a part of the military job.
2　The old pro understands statistics. Of the many in combat, a small number are wounded and a still smaller number killed.
3　Faith is a strong supporter of morale in combat.
4　Most men become accustomed to the sight and smell of death.
5　Comradeship aids morale.
6　Understanding the reasons for fighting aids morale.
7　Action has a tendency to dispel fear.
8　Habit makes fear less effective.
9　Knowledge of the situation lessens fear.
10　Calm behavior lessens fear.
11　Humor fights fear.
12　Companionship decreases fear.
13　Good physical condition works against fear.
14　Knowing about fear reduces fear.

One marine summarized an attitude of adjustment in a short answer. When asked what he wanted, he replied: "Give me tomorrow."

THE CHAPLAIN AS COUNSELOR

All chaplains, through their training and experience, have done some sort of counseling. Every chaplain has studied psychology in addition to religion.

In Chapter 11 we described the concepts and methods of counseling. Here we shall list samples of problems brought before the military chaplain:

1　Moral problems in which the serviceman wants to do the right thing but finds it difficult.
2　Moral conflicts and confusion in which different forces contend from within.

3   Marriage problems, whether premarital indecision or adjustment after marriage.
4   Emotional problems, such as doubt, feeling of futility, or sexual difficulties.
5   Job frustrations.
6   Antagonisms toward others.
7   Feelings of guilt.
8   Resentment against alleged injustices.
9   Physical and mental handicaps.
10 Adjustment to discipline.

RUMOR

In Chapter 2 we mentioned that the starting of rumors, and sometimes spreading rumors, may be thought of as common defensive behavior in all walks of life. In the Armed Forces rumor thrives—the climate is just right for it. Such an environment also provides a favorable opportunity for studying rumor.

In times of stress rumor emerges to add to the confusion. Military operations require secrecy; this gives cause for rumor, and rumor in war can lead to panic. Rumors are repeated even by those who do not believe them. They *provide a chance for emotional expression which otherwise would be suppressed.* Somehow the hostile person seems to feel better if he spreads a rumor.

A study made during World War II showed that "hate rumors" spread against sources of frustration and prejudices—officers, defense workers, profiteers, rationing boards, to name a few.

Rumors can readily become something to attach one's free-floating anxieties to when everything else is lacking. In 1944 there sprung up rumors about "very large numbers" of men being sent home from overseas because they were "insane." A few had been returned to the States who had been unable to stand the strain of combat. But this rumor was spread out of all proportion by the anxiety of loved ones back home. Such *bogey* rumors are common during wartime.

Pipe-dream rumors are spread because they apparently make people feel happier:

"The Japanese do not have enough oil to last six months."

"There will soon be a revolution in Germany."

RUMORS AND MORALE

Both pessimistic rumors (a big defeat) and optimistic rumors (record production) indicate low morale. Communication of rumors through certain "group channels" indicates the needs of different groups.

Prevalence of rumors may also mean that the group does not trust the formal communication channel.

Studies show that a commanding officer may learn something of the morale of his men by getting answers to three questions:

1 *Among whom are the rumors current?* This gets at the troubled groups of men.

2 *What are the rumors about?* Here is a cue to thinking, to fear, and to hope.

3 *What emotions do the rumors express?* Here one can find out whether feeling is positive or negative.

Rumors spread most easily *horizontally* in a homogeneous group. *Lack of information* favors rumor, as does *idleness.* Rumor is fostered by *expectation.* A rumor tends to get more *concrete* with spreading, and it becomes assimilated into cultural traditions with time.

REACTIONS TO DISASTER

Disaster has been studied both in wartime and in times of peace. Investigations have been made of what happened to people in civilian and military populations during the bombings of the Battle of Britain, the atomic attacks on Hiroshima and Nagasaki, and the sieges of Malta and Stalingrad. Analyses have been made of people's reactions to such disasters as fires, earthquakes, tornadoes, and even the "realistic" radio report by Orson Welles of the "invasion from Mars" in 1938. From these studies and others come several conclusions of value to the Armed Forces. Let us remember that the Armed Forces are called out for peacetime disasters.

People behave much the same in one situation of disaster as in another. When a major catastrophe strikes, a *sequence* of kinds of behavior occurs:

1 There is a condition of *behavioral bankruptcy* in which the individual has no reactions "on tap" to deal with the situation. He is stunned into silence and immobility.

2 After extricating himself, and his neighbor, the individual goes into a *state of shock,* in which he is passive in the extreme.

3 Later comes *extreme curiosity,* when people go "sightseeing" to watch the rescue work.

4 An increased perception as to the *cues to danger* next arises.

5 People join with others with increased *interpersonal communication* and "togetherness."

6 *Compulsive rituals and superstitious practices* begin to emerge. Many Japanese rubbed onions on their heads to prevent bombs from seeking them out.

7 *Planning* finally gets into the sequence, and people begin to organize aid, restore communications, and ward off further disaster.

PANIC AND MOB BEHAVIOR

Panic is not foreign to disaster or to war. The psychology of panic is closely allied to *mob* behavior. Fortunately, the members of the Armed Forces rarely become parts of mobs. As a matter of fact they are brought in to quell mob behavior.

A mob is more than just a crowd. A crowd turns into a mob when the *common emotion* is intense, especially when it is intense anger. A mob acts when there is some *goal* which gives direction. But in some ways, mob behavior resembles a riot. Psychologically, to a certain extent, a riot is the language of the unheard, of rebels who want a crisis and a chance to hold the center of the stage rather than the resolution of a conflict.

Often the goal must be put in focus by someone who assumes leadership: "Burn the store," "Tear down the flag." Impelled by emotion the mob has a narrow field of attention. People behave in mobs in ways they would not behave as individuals.

Some rules for preventing mob action ahead of time include:

1 Stop grievances and frustrations before they pile up.
2 Prevent the allegiance of large numbers of persons to troublesome (or potentially troublesome) leaders.
3 During social tension prevent crowds from forming.
4 Disperse the crowd before the leader takes control.
5 Redirect the mob instead of trying to stop it by reason.
6 Be decisive by suggesting positive action rather than what not to do.
7 When in a mob seek personal self-control.

BRAINWASHING

Stress techniques in war have no doubt been in existence since the beginning of time. Various methods have been employed over the centuries to coerce prisoners of war. These have involved inducing emotional disturbance and intellectual disorganization by intense physical and psychological stresses, ranging from semistarvation to isolation. *Individuals differ in their responses to these kinds of treatment.* Some people give in, others resist. Personality factors and home background seem to be of importance. Of importance also is the *esprit de corps* that may exist within a group of prisoners.

MILD STRESS

Some students when called before a discipline committee report feeling under stress. Examinations put some individuals under stress but seemingly have little emotional effect on others. *Stress situations* have been set up as a part of certain selection programs. These contain unsolvable problems to be done under time pressures. They may also include "unfriendly" stress interviews.

SELECTION FOR ESPIONAGE

One realistic system for weeding people out of spy service was set up during World War II in the Offices of Strategic Services. Here the purpose was to select candidates for the OSS who could stand the stress of espionage and other dangerous military assignments. The procedures involved putting the candidate in a realistic and complex lifelike situation. The intent was to select persons who were likely to think effectively and provide leadership under conditions of pressure and privation. For example, in a *stress interview* the candidate had to imagine he had been caught stealing secret files. He was given twelve minutes to construct an alibi and to explain his presence in the government office with the files. This defense was carried out under rapid and hostile questioning. At the end of each interview the candidate was told that he had failed. His reaction to this disappointing news was carefully observed. He was also told not to reveal his experiences to anyone.

Later on, in a *post-stress* interview, conducted by a friendly interviewer in an informal manner, the candidate was made to feel better. Would this unexpected release from tension cause the candidate to violate security?

INTENSE STRESS

The first extensive study of brainwashing was made of American prisoners captured by the Chinese during the Korean War. Agencies studied prisoners' reactions to extreme privation, inhuman treatment, and to interspersed-reward types of situations. Studies were made of what happens when leaders were separated from their men. Seminars for confession were established so that each man became his own informer.

During the war some seven thousand American service men were captured by the North Korean–Chinese Communists. A little less than half of them died in prisoner-of-war camps. All but a few who remained were eventually returned to the United States, where they told how they had been treated.

The prisoners had been starved, tortured, beaten, and put on public display. They were humiliated before the civilian population as a part of the "thought control," or brainwashing. This extreme stress caused some prisoners to sign "confessions" admitting to various atrocities. Even larger numbers reported that they engaged in at least one act of cooperation with the enemy, such as making a tape recording for their captors or signing a petition. It is also to be noted that among some groups of prisoners, who maintained their own military organization within the prison compounds, there was no known collaboration. Each man took an interest in his fellow group members. They gave assistance to their comrades who were in trouble.

The methods and types of stress used by the Chinese involved application of well-known principles of *learning and motivation*. Stress was characterized by three things. First, the prisoners were made physically weak through semistarvation and physical punishment. This resulted in a "debility" produced by extreme fatigue. Second, the prolonged periods without sleep and food caused a condition of "dependency" on the captors. This dependency was made worse by placing the prisoners in social isolation, bringing out in them the strong need for companionship—or even the need just to be close to other people. Thus through both physical and psychological deprivation the Chinese captors saw to it that they alone became the objects of dependency. Finally, a chronic fear, or "dread," became a part of both day and night living. The fears induced in the prisoners were real, and they were many.

THE DDD SYNDROME

Through it all many of the prisoners kept a sense of humor. They named the "debility-dependency-dread" components the *DDD syndrome*.

The fact that there was some relief from punishment at times kept the men's hopes alive. This, too, was a part of the brainwashing. The Chinese provided the prisoners with relief from hunger, pain, fatigue, and fear if they depreciated themselves and denounced their fellow prison mates. For spying on fellow prisoners they were given rewards of alcohol, candy, food, parties, and the privilege of sleeping late. Thus, through such *reinforcement,* patterns of conformity to the enemy's demands were gradually built up.

Even the mere talking to one's interrogator (on the surface a quite innocent thing to do) after a period of social isolation served as a reinforcement for further communication with the enemy. As time went on, some prisoners lost their power to resist. They began believing the enemy propaganda as it was presented, dose by dose.

PSYCHOLOGICAL WARFARE

By the nature of its instruments, and its mission, psychological warfare begins long before the declaration of war and may last long after. In psychological warfare one must fight an enemy who does not answer back directly. One is fighting an enemy that he does not see, fighting along the edge of nightmare, as it were. Psychological warfare and propaganda are as old as mankind. Their roots lie deep in history.

In 1245 B.C. Gideon used lamps and pitchers in the great battle against the Midianites to cause *confusion*. He had his 300 men lined up around the enemy camp, breaking pitchers, concealing all the lamps at one time, accompanied by trumpet blasts. The startled enemy went into panic and fought one another.

The antecedents of propaganda leaflets can be traced to the days of the early Greeks:

> Themistocles, having selected the best sailing ships of the Athenians, went to the place where there was water fit for drinking, and engraved upon the stones inscriptions—"Men of Ionia, you do wrong in fighting against your fathers and helping to enslave Greece—."

The above text is very much like leaflets dropped during World War II, over Korea, and over Vietnam. The history of psychological warfare fills volumes. Cortez used horses to spread terror among the Aztecs. The American forces at the Battle of Bunker Hill used handbills to emphasize the class distinctions then existing between British officers and enlisted men. Fear was exploited as an aid to persuasion.

PROPAGANDA

Psychological warfare uses propaganda as organized persuasion by nonviolent means. Psychology gets into the picture in four ways. First, the propagandist presents to the fighting man those mental elements which are usually kept out of sight. He can show how to change lust into resentment, individual resourcefulness into mass cowardice, friction into distrust, and prejudice into frustration. Second, psychological warfare means setting up techniques for finding out how the enemy really feels. Third, it is important that the propagandist keep his private emotions out of the picture, play the cold role of complete objectivity.

Psychology helps with this by selection and training. Fourth, using all mass media down to whispering campaigns, psychological warfare dwells on influence.

Of all the arts and sciences that contribute to psychological warfare, psychology deals most with *human needs.* Psychological warfare cannot outlast war. Its mission is the improvement of the function of war.

CONQUEST OF THE MIND

It is natural to think of war in terms of military action and the many aspects of effectively utilizing human resources. These aspects of war are reinforced to us everyday through news media. Except for being told that "leaflets were dropped behind enemy lines," we hear little about how psychology relates to propaganda and morale.

Few men will continue fighting, at least none but the fanatics, when victory is clearly impossible. In the concluding chapter of the book, *Psychology for the Armed Services,* prepared by a committee of the National Research Council, the following paragraph appears which sums up propaganda and psychological warfare:

Defeat in war is ultimately a conquest of the mind. The infliction of death and suffering on the enemy and the destruction of property have only one purpose—surrender. And surrender is a state of mind, a psychological attitude which makes a man want to abandon aggression.

Men and nations fight for some goal. When the goal is found to be unattainable, they may accept a lesser goal. Even when victory is at last seen to be impossible, fighting may continue. Hope remains for obtaining less harsh terms of surrender. In general, they will stop fighting, they will surrender or allow themselves to be captured, when the material disadvantage of defeat is no longer greater than the disadvantage of continued resistance. Psychological warfare attempts to influence thinking. The means for this activity is called propaganda.

Propaganda, to be effective, must be aimed at a particular target. *Military men* are an important target. Soldiers, for example, are united by a common psychological climate in that they share common fears, anxieties, gripes, frustrations, and doubts. *Women* in an enemy's country form another target. They are anxious about their men, believing that there may be no tomorrow.

Through espionage the propagandist tries to get at the *needs* of the enemy and what he is *thinking about.* Propaganda is often based upon some recent event, for two reasons. First, *attention* for the propaganda already exists. *Second,* propaganda is likely to be believed when attached to an event that is known to be true.

Propaganda cannot create a situation or an event. These must be seized upon quickly. Otherwise propaganda may be so late that it becomes only counterpropaganda. Counterpropaganda is at a disadvantage because it may be vague and defensive.

TACTICS OF PROPAGANDA

Propaganda works best under the following rules, says a committee of experts:

1 *Remember the audience.* Address propaganda to some specific group. Use words and other means of communication which the audience will easily understand. Use familiar names, places, and events that have prestige for the audience.
2 *Deceive.* Treat the enemy for the moment as if he were a friend. Respect his heroes and admired public figures. Be objective about enemy defeats. Describe them without hostility.
3 *Start rumors.* Put material in a form that will get itself repeated. Familiar terms and simple ideas through anecdotes can be easily communicated. Tell news suppressed by the enemy. Give facts and figures. Spread rumor by acknowledging it as rumor. It will soon be spread as fact, not rumor.
4 *Attack weak points.* Arouse guilt feelings by playing up enemy mistakes. Magnify disagreement and discontentment.
5 *Be timely.* Seize every opportunity to exploit an event immediately.
6 *Use suggestion.* Short, catchy statements are best. Describe without recommending—the listener may adopt the suggestion and think it is his own idea. Statements should be positive rather than negative. Providing the building material for rationalization should be subtle. Capitalize on anxiety, and suggest positive action only after anxiety, doubt, and guilt have become strong.

Summary

The one place where the many aspects of applied psychology come together is in military settings. The armed forces have always provided a climate favorable to the study of human behavior in large systems.

From experimental psychology has come information about the human senses and psychomotor skills providing many practical suggestions for efficiency in perceiving and performing.

Selection, training, and education have had a long history of research and practice in military settings. Much of applied psychology in civilian occupations has its basis in the military. It is here that the problems have been demanding, and during wartime professional talent was available to work on the problems.

From clinical and counseling psychology have come applications enabling personnel, from the new recruit to the combat soldier, to adjust to military living. Brainwashing has been given study. Knowing and understanding what to expect helps adjustment.

From social psychology comes knowledge about rumor, reactions to disaster, and psychological warfare.

In times of stress rumors provide a chance for emotional expression which otherwise would be suppressed. They have both their positive and negative aspects. Rumors may be used to attach one's free-floating anxieties to when everything else is lacking. They are also indicators of morale.

Disaster has been studied both in wartime and in times of peace. From these studies we find that behavior goes through a predictable sequence, from stunned immobility to planning.

Much of what we know about panic and mob behavior has come from studies in military settings. And from stress techniques used on prisoners we know much about brainwashing. From studies of thought control, psychology has learned much about the effects of extremes of human maltreatment.

By the nature of its instruments, and its mission, psychological warfare begins long before the declaration of war and may last long after. Much of what we know of influence behavior has come from studies of propaganda in the conquest of the mind. Propaganda provides the subtle building material for rationalization, and it capitalizes on anxiety, doubt, and guilt.

Suggestions for Thinking and Discussion

1 Some practical suggestions are given for perceiving and performing (page 419). How many of these suggestions do you see followed in your day-to-day activities? Which ones may be appropriate?
2 If you were planning to go into business for yourself, how would you select the people to work for you? Assume you would be employing five people; and again, fifty people. How would your problems compare, and contrast, with problems of military selection?
3 Start some rumor (harmless, we hope!) on the campus and study how it is spread.
4 How do you believe *you* would react to brainwashing?
5 How do you believe a person can prepare (to some degree) to best meet threats of death or disaster?

6 Why is the chaplain such an important person in a military organization?

Suggestions for Further Reading

Boring, E. G. (Ed.) *Psychology for the armed services.* Washington: Combat Forces Press, 1945. A practical book on military psychology extending some of the content of this chapter.

Brown, J. A. C. *Techniques of persuasion: From propaganda to brainwashing.* Baltimore: Penguin Books, 1963. A paperback covering many aspects of the psychology of influence.

Grinker, R. R., & Spiegel, J. P. *Men under stress.* New York: McGraw-Hill, 1945. Psychological and medical aspects of men pushed beyond normal levels of stress in World War II.

Linebarger, P. M. A. *Psychological warfare,* Washington: Combat Forces Press, 1948. The history and techniques of psychological warfare before, during, and after war.

Porter, E. H. *Manpower development.* New York: Harper & Row, 1964. Manpower development for large-scale military operations.

Bibliography

CHAPTER 1

Anastasi, Anne. *Fields of applied psychology.* New York: McGraw-Hill, 1964.

Boynton, P. W. *So you want a better job?* New York: Socony-Vacuum Oil Company, 1947.

Foulkes, D. *The psychology of sleep.* New York: Scribner, 1966.

Gilmer, B. v. H. *Industrial psychology.* New York: McGraw-Hill, 1966.

Havemann, E. *The age of psychology.* New York: Simon & Schuster, 1957.

Hinton, W. M. Serendipity in psychology. *Va. J. Sci.,* 1966, 17, 57–64.

Kleitman, N., & Kleitman, H. The sleep-wakefulness pattern in the Arctic. *Scientific Monthly,* 1963, 76, 349–356.

Leuba, C., & Bateman, D. Learning during sleep. *Amer. J. Psychol.,* 1952, 65, 301–302.

Olin, C. H. *Phrenology.* Philadelphia: Penn, 1910.

Ross, S., & Lockman, R. F. *A career in psychology.* Washington: American Psychological Association, 1965.

Routtenberg, A. Neural mechanisms of sleep: Changing view of reticular formation function. *Psychol. Rev.,* 1966, 73, 481–499.

Segal, J., & Luce, Gay G. *Sleep.* New York: Coward-McCann, 1966.

Simon, C. W., & Emmons, W. H. Responses to material presented during various levels of sleep. *J. exp. Psychol.,* 1956, 51, 89–97.

Stevens, S. S. (Ed.) *Handbook of experimental psychology.* New York: Wiley, 1951.

Stewart, M. Resistance to technological change in industry. *Hum. Organ.,* 1957, 16, 36–40.

Webb, W. B. (Ed.) *The profession of psychology.* New York: Holt, 1962.

Whitehead, A. N. *The aims of education.* New York: Macmillan, 1929.

Wolfle, D. The spirit of science. *Science,* 1966, 152, 1699.

CHAPTER 2

Ginsburg, S. W. What unemployment does to people. *Amer. J. Psychiat.,* 1942, 99, 439–446.

Goode, W. J. A theory of role strain. *Amer. Soc. Rev.,* 1960, 25, 483–496.

Haire, M., et al. Psychological research on pay: An overview. *Industr. Relat.*, 1963, 3, 3–8.

Hall, J. F. *Psychology of motivation.* Philadelphia: Lippincott, 1961.

Hoyt, Mary F. *American women of the space age.* New York: Atheneum, 1966.

Lawler, E. E., III, & Porter, L. W. Perceptions regarding management compensation. *Industr. Relat.*, 1963, 3, 41–49.

McClelland, D. C. *The achieving society.* Princeton, N.J.: Van Nostrand, 1961.

Miller, D. R., & Swanson, G. E. *Inner conflict and defense.* New York: Holt, 1960.

Patchen, M. *The choice of wage comparisons.* Englewood Cliffs, N.J.: Prentice-Hall, 1961.

Patton, A. *Men, money, and motivation.* New York: McGraw-Hill, 1961.

Rothe, H. F. How much incentive in incentive pay? *Supervisory Mgmt.*, 1960, 5, 11–15.

Stewart, G. R. *Ordeal by hunger.* Boston: Houghton Mifflin, 1960.

Stricker, G. Scapegoating: An empirical investigation. *J. abnorm. soc. Psychol.*, 1963, 67, 127–131.

chapter 3

Adam, June. The relationship between visual illusions and figural aftereffects. *Australian J. Psychol.*, 1966, 18, 130–136.

Boring, E. G. The moon illusion. *Amer. J. Physics,* 1943, 11, 55–60.

Dember, W. N. *Psychology of perception.* New York: Holt, 1960.

Fargus, R. H. *Perception: The basic process in cognitive development.* New York: McGraw-Hill, 1966.

Gibson, J. J. *The perception of the visual world.* Boston: Houghton Mifflin, 1950.

Gibson, J. J. The perception of visual surfaces. *Amer. J. Psychol.,* 1950, 63, 367–384.

Henneman, R. H. Vision and audition as sensory channels for communication. *Quart. J. Speech,* 1952, 38, 161–166.

Immergluck, L. The role of set in perceptual judgment. *J. Psychol.,* 1952, 34, 181–189.

Ittelson, W. H. Size as a cue to distance: Radial motion. *Amer. J. Psychol.,* 1951, 64, 188–202.

Jones, E. H., & Sumner, F. C. Relation of the brightness differences of colors to their apparent distances. *J. Psychol.,* 1948, 26, 25–29.

Koffka, K. *Principles of gestalt psychology.* New York: Harcourt, Brace & World, 1935.

Köhler, I. Experiments with goggles. *Sci. Amer.,* 1962, 206, 62–72.

Smith, G. H. Size-distance judgments of human faces (projected images). *J. gen. Psychol.,* 1953, 49, 45–64.

Smith, K. U., & Smith, M. W. *Perception and motion.* Philadelphia: Saunders, 1962.

Solley, C. M., & Murphy, G. *Development of the perceptual world.* New York: Basic Books, 1960.

Witkin, H. A., et al. *Personality through perception.* New York: Harper & Row, 1954.

Wohlwill, J. F. Developmental studies of perception. *Psychol. Bull.,* 1960, 57, 249–288.

Young, P. T. Auditory localization with acoustical transposition of the ears. *J. exper. Psychol.,* 1928, 11, 399–429.

CHAPTER 4

Battig, W. F. Transfer from verbal pretraining to motor performance as a function of motor task complexity. *J. exp. Psychol.,* 1956, 51, 371–378.

Cook, T. W. Massed and distributed practice in puzzle solving. *Psychol. Rev.,* 1934, 41, 330–335.

Duncan, C. P. Transfer in motor learning as a function of degree of first-task learning and inter-task similarity. *J. exp. Psychol.,* 1953, 45, 1–11.

Ferster, C. B., & Skinner, B. F. *Schedules of reinforcement.* New York: Appleton-Century-Crofts, 1957.

Harlow, H. F. The formation of learning sets. *Psychol. Rev.,* 1949, 56, 51–65.

Harris, I. D. *Emotional blocks to learning.* New York: Free Press, 1961.

Hilgard, E. R. *Theories of learning.* New York: Appleton-Century-Crofts, 1956.

Krueger, W. C. F. The effect of overlearning on retention. *J. exp. Psychol.,* 1929, 12, 71–78.

McGehee, W., & Thayer, P. W. *Training in business and industry.* New York: Wiley, 1961.

Miller, G. A., & Selfridge, J. A. Verbal context and the recall of meaningful material. *Amer. J. Psychol.,* 1950, 63, 176–185.

Mowrer, O. H. *Learning and behavior.* New York: Wiley, 1960.

Spence, K. W. *Behavior theory and conditioning.* New Haven: Yale, 1956.

CHAPTER 5

Bartlett, F. C. *Remembering.* Cambridge: Cambridge, 1932.

Bennett, M. E. *College and life.* New York: McGraw-Hill, 1952.

Bruner, J. S. Learning and thinking. *Harv. educ. Rev.,* 1959, 29, 184–192.

———, et al. *A study of thinking.* New York: Wiley, 1956.

Carter, H. D. The mechanics of study procedure. *Calif. J. educ. Research,* 1958, 9, 8–13.

Crawford, A. B. *Incentives to study.* New Haven: Yale, 1929.

Dewey, J. *How we think.* Boston: Heath, 1933.

Flesch, R. *A new way to better English.* New York: Harper & Row, 1958.

Gerken, C. *Study your way through school.* Chicago: Science Research, 1953.

McGeoch, J. A., & McDonald, W. T. Meaningful relation and retroactive inhibition. *Amer. J. Psychol.,* 1931, 43, 579–588.

McKeachie, W. J. *Teaching tips.* Ann Arbor, Mich.: Wahr, 1956.

Newman, E. B. Forgetting of meaningful material during sleep and waking. *Amer. J. Psychol.,* 1939, 52, 65–71.

Pennington, L. A. Shifts in aspiration level after success and failure in the college classroom. *J. gen. Psychol.,* 1940, 23, 305–313.

Ryans, D. G. *Chàracteristics of teachers.* Washington: American Council on Education, 1960.

Taylor, P. H. A study of the effects of instructions in a multiple-choice mathematics test. *British J. Educ. Psychol.,* 1966, 36, 1–6.

Thouless, R. H. *How to think straight.* New York: Simon and Schuster, 1939.

Vernon, J. A., & Badger, D. H. Subliminal stimulation in human learning. *Amer. J. Psychol.,* 1959, 72, 265–266.

Volks, V. *On becoming an educated person: An orientation to college.* Philadelphia: Saunders, 1957.

CHAPTER 6

Ames, L. B. The development of the sense of time in the young child. *J. genet. Psychol.,* 1946, 68, 97–125.

Bakin, H. Thumb and finger sucking in children. *J. Pediatrics,* 1948, 32, 99–101.

Billig, A. L. Why children bite their nails. *Hygeia,* Dec., 1942.

Bravelas, A., & Lewin, K. Training in democratic leadership. *J. abnorm. soc. Psychol.,* 1942, 37, 115–119.

Gilmer, B. v. H. An analysis of the spontaneous responses of the newborn infant. *J. genet. Psychol.,* 1933, 42, 392–405.

Halverson, H. M. Studies of the grasping responses of early infancy. *J. genet. Psychol.,* 1937, 51, 371–449.

Hayes, J. R. The maintenance of play in young children. *J. comp. physiol. Psychol.,* 1958, 51, 788–794.

Hoffman, Lois W., et al. Parental coerciveness, child autonomy, and child's role at school. *Sociometry,* 1960, 23, 15–22.

Hooker, H. F. The study of the only child at school. *J. genet. Psychol.,* 1931, 39, 122–126.

Moyer, K. E., & Gilmer, B. v. H. Attention spans of children for experimentally designed toys. *J. genet. Psychol.,* 1955, 87, 187–201.

Piaget, J. How children form mathematical concepts. *Scientific Amer.,* 1953, 188, Nov., 74–79.

Pintner, R., & Lev, J. Worries of school children. *J. genet. Psychol.,* 1940, 56, 67–76.

Pratt, K. C., Nelson, A. K., and Sun, Kuo Hua. *The behavior of the newborn infant.* Columbus: The Ohio State University Press, 1930.

Sears, R. R., et al. *Patterns of child rearing.* New York: Harper & Row, 1957.

Sewell, W. H. Infant training and the personality of the child. *Amer. J. Sociol.,* 1952, 58, 150–159.

Shirley, M. M. *The first two years.* Vol. 2. Minneapolis: University of Minnesota Press, 1931.

CHAPTER 7

Agnes, Sister Mary. Influence of reading on the racial attitudes of adolescent girls. *Catholic educ. Rev.,* 1947, 45, 415–420.

Bandura, A., & Walters, R. H. *Adolescent aggression.* New York: Ronald, 1959.

Bossard, J. H. S. Residential propinquity as a factor in marriage selection. *Amer. J. Sociol.,* 1932, 38, 219–224.

Burgess, E. W., & Wallin, P. *Engagement and marriage.* Philadelphia: Lippincott, 1953.

Coleman, J. S. *The adolescent subculture.* New York: Free Press, 1961.

Coombs, R. H., & Keukel, W. F. Sex differences in dating aspirations and satisfaction with computer selected partners. *J. Marriage & Fam.,* 1966, 28, 62–66.

Crane, A. R. Pre-adolescent gangs: A socio-psychological interpretation. *J. genet. Psychol.,* 1955, 86, 275–279.

Fleege, U. H. *Self-revelation of the adolescent boy.* Milwaukee: Bruce, 1945.

Hurlock, Elizabeth, B. *Adolescent development.* New York: McGraw-Hill, 1955.

Jersild, A. T. *In search of self.* New York: Teachers College, Columbia University, 1952.

Lewin, K., et al. Patterns of aggressive behavior in experimentally created social climates. *J. soc. Psychol.,* 1939, 10, 271–299.

Linder, R. *Rebel without a cause.* New York: Grune & Stratton, 1948.

Miller, D. R., & Swanson, G. E. *The changing American parent.* New York: Wiley, 1958.

Reevy, W. R. Premarital petting behavior and marital happiness prediction. *Marriage & Fam. Living,* 1959, 21, 349–355.

Remmers, H. H., & Radler, D. H. *The American teenager.* Indianapolis: Bobbs-Merrill, 1957.

Strang, R. *The adolescent views himself.* New York: McGraw-Hill, 1957.

Tarr, J. *Operation match.* Cambridge, Mass: Compatibility Research, 1966.

Winch, R. P. *Mate selection: A study of complementary needs.* New York: Harper & Row, 1958.

CHAPTER 8

Bergler, E. *The revolt of the middle-aged man.* New York: Wyn, 1954.

Birren, J. E. *The psychology of aging.* Englewood Cliffs, N.J.: Prentice-Hall, 1964.

Bowman, C. C. Loneliness and social change. *Amer. J. Psychiat.,* 1955, 112, 194–198.

Chown, Sheila M., & Heron, A. Psychological aspects of aging in man. *Annu. Rev. Psychol.,* 1965, 16, 417–450.

Dennis, W. The age decrement in outstanding scientific contributions: Fact or artifact? *Amer. Psychologist,* 1958, 13, 457–460.

Dorian, F. *Commitment to culture: Art patronage in Europe. Its significance for America.* Pittsburgh, Pa.: University of Pittsburgh Press, 1964.

Gardner, J. W. *Self-renewal: The individual and the innovative society.* New York: Harper & Row, 1964.

Goffman, E. *The presentation of self in everyday life.* Garden City, N.Y.: Anchor Books, Doubleday, 1959.

Harvey, O. J., & Consalvi, C. Status and conformity to pressures in informal groups. *J. abnorm. soc. Psychol.,* 1960, 60, 182–187.

Jacobson, A. H. Conflict of attitudes toward the roles of the husband and wife in marriage. *Amer. soc. Rev.,* 1952, 17, 146–150.

Kastenbaum, R. (Ed.) *New thoughts on old age.* Berlin: Springer, 1964.

Kleemeier, R. W. (Ed.) *Aging and leisure.* Fair Lawn, N.J.: Oxford University Press, 1961.

Meltzer, H. Age differences in happiness and life adjustments of workers. *J. Geront.,* 1963, 18, 66–70.

Michael, D. N. *The next generation: The prospect ahead for the youth of today and tomorrow.* New York: Random House, 1965.

Morris, W. *When you've lost a job after forty.* Englewood, N.J.: Knabe-North, 1963.

Pressey, S. L., & Kuhlen, R. G. *Psychological development through the life span.* New York: Harper & Row, 1957.

Reichard, Suzanne, et al. *Aging and personality: A study of eighty-seven older men.* New York: Wiley, 1962.

Selye, H. *The stress of life.* New York: McGraw-Hill, 1956.

Williams, R. H., & Wirths, C. G. *Lives through the years.* New York: Atherton, 1965.

CHAPTER 9

Arlitt, A. H. *Family relationships.* New York: McGraw-Hill, 1942.

Baker, R. E. *Marriage and the family.* New York: McGraw-Hill, 1953.

Bendix, R., & Lipset, S. M. (Eds.) *Class, status, and power.* New York: Free Press, 1961.

De Neui, D. The growing Canadian community college movement. *Educ. Rec.,* 1966, Spring, 199–202.

Faris, R. E. L. The middle class from a sociological viewpoint. *Soc. Forces,* 1960, Oct., 1–5.

Form, W. H., & Stone, G. P. Urbanism, anonymity, and status symbolism. *Amer. J. Sociol.,* 1957, 62, 504–514.

Goldberg, S. C. Influence and leadership as a function of group structure. *J. abnorm. soc. Psychol.,* 1955, 51, 119–122.

Handel, G. Psychological study of whole families. *Psychol. Bull.,* 1965, 63, 19–41.

Havighurst, R. J., et al. *Growing up in River City.* New York: Wiley, 1962.

Kent, H., & Davis, D. R. Discipline in the home and intellectual development. *Brit. J. Med. Psychol.,* 1957, 30, 27–33.

Kohn, M. L. Social class and the exercise of parental authority. *Amer. sociol. Rev.,* 1959, 24, 352–366.

Lifton, W. M. *Working with groups.* New York: Wiley, 1961.

McCord, J., et al. Effects of maternal employment on lower class boys. *J. abnorm. soc. Psychol.,* 1963, 67, 177–182.

Marrow, A. J. *Changing patterns of prejudice.* Philadelphia: Chilton, 1962.

Mowitz, R. J., & Wright, D. S. *Profile of a metropolis.* Detroit: Wayne State University Press, 1962.

Mumford, L. *The city in history.* New York: Harcourt, Brace & World, 1961.

Okun, A. M. (Ed.) *The battle against unemployment.* New York: Norton, 1965.

Olmsted, M. S. *The small group.* New York: Random House, 1959.

Pace, C. R. Five college environments. *Coll. Bd. Rev.,* 1960, 41, 24–28.

Rosecrance, F. C. *The American college and its teachers.* New York: Macmillan, 1963.

Rossi, P. H. The organizational structure of an American community. In A. Etzioni, A. (Ed.) *Complex organizations.* New York: Holt, 1961.

Schein, E. H. Interpersonal communication, group solidarity, and social influence. *Sociometry,* 1960, 23, 148–161.

Seeley, J. R., et al. *Crestwood Heights.* New York: Basic Books, 1956.

Smith, M. B., & Hobbs, N. The community and the community mental health center. *Amer. Psychologist,* 1966, 21, 499–509.

Stern, G. G. Student ecology and the college environment. *J. med. Educ.,* 1965, 40, 132–154.

Sutherland, R. L., et al. (Eds.) *Personality factors on the college campus: Review of a symposium.* Austin, Tex.: University of Texas, Hogg Foundation for Mental Health, 1962.

Walters, J. A review of family research 1959, 1960, and 1961. *Marriage & Fam. Living,* 1962, 24, 158–178.

Warner, W. L. *Democracy in Jonesville: A study in quality and inequality.* New York: Harper & Row, 1949.

Whyte, W. H., Jr. *The organization man.* New York: Simon and Schuster, 1956.

CHAPTER 10

Blatt, S. F. An attempt to define mental health. *J. consult. Psychol.,* 1964, 28, 146–153.

Bosselman, B. C. *Neurosis and psychosis.* Springfield, Ill.: Charles C Thomas, 1953.

Friedman, A. S., et al. *Psychotherapy for the whole family.* Berlin: Springer, 1965.

Gibson, J. E. Science looks at your job: A ten-year study at General Motors. *Today's Hlth,* 1960, 38, 14–15.

Goldfarb, W. Infant rearing as a factor in foster home placement. *Amer. J. Orthopsychiat.,* 1944, 14, 162–167.

———. Variations in adolescent adjustment of institutionally reared children. *Amer. J. Orthopsychiat.,* 1947, 17, 449–457.

Gordon, G. *How to "live" with your job.* Montreal: National Office Management Association Conference. May, 1960.

Harlow, H. F. The heterosexual affectional system in monkeys. *Amer. Psychologist,* 1962, 16, 1–9.

———, & Harlow, Margaret K. Social deprivation in monkeys. *Scientific Amer.,* 1962, Nov., 3–10.

———, and Zimmerman, R. R. Affectional responses in the infant monkey. *Science,* 1959, 130, 421–432.

Hilliard, Marion. *Women and fatigue.* Garden City, N.Y.: Doubleday, 1960.

Jackson, D. D. (Ed.) *The etiology of schizophrenia.* New York; Basic Books, 1960.

Kahn, R. L., & Katz, D. *Social psychology of organizations.* New York: Wiley, 1964.

Lancaster, E., and Poling, J. *The final face of Eve.* New York: McGraw-Hill, 1958.

Lindzey, Gardner. *Projective techniques and cross cultural research.* New York: Appleton-Century-Crofts, 1961.

Maier, N. R. F. *Frustration: A study of behavior without a goal.* New York: McGraw-Hill, 1949.

Mowrer, O. H. *Abnormal reactions or actions (an autobiographical answer).* Dubuque, Iowa: Wm. C. Brown, 1966.

Plimpton, G. *Paper lion.* New York: Harper & Row, 1966.

Ray, W. S. Mild stress and problem-solving. *Amer. J. Psychol.,* 1965, 78, 227–234.

Riesman, D., et al. *The lonely crowd.* New Haven, Conn.: Yale, 1950.

Selye, H. *The stress of life.* New York: McGraw-Hill, 1956.

Shaffer, L. F. Fear and courage in aerial combat. *J. consult. Psychol.,* 1947, 11, 137–143.

———, Gilmer, B. v. H., & Schoen, M. *Psychology.* New York: Harper & Row, 1940.

Thigpen, C. H., and Cleckley, H. M. *The three faces of Eve.* New York: McGraw-Hill, 1957.

Thorne, F. C. Directive counseling in psychotherapy. *Amer. Psychologist,* 1948, 3, 160–165.

Wolfe, D. M., & Snoek, J. D. A study of tensions and adjustment under role conflict. *J. soc. Issues,* 1962, 18, 102–121.

CHAPTER 11

Barrett, R. S. Guide to using psychological tests. *Harv. Bus. Rev.,* 1963, 41, 138–146.

Biesheuvel, S. Personnel selection. *Annu. Rev. Psychol.,* 1965, 16, 295–324.

Brozek, J. Symposium on adjustment to aging. *Bull. int. Ass. appl. Psychol.,* 1966, 15, 22–29.

Daniels, H., & Otis, J. A method of analyzing employment interviews. *Personnel Psychol.,* 1950, 3, 425–444.

Demman, Rosamond R. Counciling in the classroom: The teacher's role. *Amer. Voc. J.,* 1966, Oct., 33.

Flanagan, J. C., et al. *The American high school student.* Pittsburgh, Pa.: University of Pittsburgh, Project TALENT Office, Technical Report, U.S. Office of Education, Project 635, 1964.

Gribbons, W. D., & Lohnes, P. R. Shifts in adolescents vocational value. *Personnel & Guidance J.,* 1965, 44, 249–252.

Hobson, J. R. Sex differences in primary mental abilities. *J. educ. Res.,* 1947, 41, 126–132.

Lofquist, L. H., & England, G. N. *Problems in vocational counseling.* Dubuque, Iowa: Wm. C. Brown, 1961.

Magoon, T. Innovations in counseling. *J. counsel. Psychol.,* 1964, 11, 342–347.

Moser, L. E., & Moser, Ruth S. *Counseling and guidance: An exploration.* Englewood Cliffs, N.J.: Prentice-Hall, 1963.

Myers, W. High school graduates choose vocations unrealistically. *Occupations,* 1947, 25, 332–333.

Nash, A. N. Vocational interests of effective managers: A review of the literature. *Personnel Psychol.,* 1965, 18, 21–37.

Prien, E. P. Personality correlates and changes in proworldmindedness and antiworldmindedness following an intercultural experience. *J. Soc. Psychol.,* 1966, 68, 243–247.

Ramsay, G. V. The initial counseling interview. *Pastoral Psychol.,* 1966, 17, 27–34.

Rogers, C. R. *Client-centered therapy.* Boston: Houghton Mifflin, 1951.

Rust, R. M., and David, J. S. The personal problems of college students. *Ment. Hyg., N.Y.,* 1961, 45, 247–257.

Seashore, H. Academic abilities of junior college students. *Junior College J.,* 1958, 29, 74–80.

Shriver, S. Two years of the Peace Corps. *Foreign Affairs,* July, 1963.

Spiegel, Rose. Women's quest for identity. *AAUW J.,* 1962, May, 244–247.

Steinberg, E. R. A new life-pattern for the college-educated woman. *The Eleusis of Chi Omega,* 1965, Sept., 535–540.

Stewart, L. H. Characteristics of junior college students in occupationally oriented curricula. *J. counsel. Psychol.,* 1966, 13, 46–52.

Strong, E. K., Jr. Satisfactions and interests. *Amer. Psychologist,* 1958, 13, 449–456.

CHAPTER 12

Bernard, Jessie. *Academic women.* University Park, Pa.: Pennsylvania State University Press, 1964.

Bingham, W. V., et al. *How to interview* (4th ed.). New York: Harper & Row, 1959.

Boyd, J. B. Interests of engineers related to turnover, selection, and management. *J. appl. Psychol.,* 1961, 45, 143–149.

Boynton, P. W. *So you want a better job?* New York: Socony-Vacuum Oil Company, 1947.

Cassara, Beverly B. (Ed.) *American women: The changing image.* Boston: Beacon Press, 1962.

Dill, W. R., et al. How aspiring managers promote their own careers. *California Mġmt Rev.,* 1960, 2, 9–15.

Geister, Janet. Our new young are different. *Amer. J. Nursing,* 1964, 64, 102–104.

Ghiselli, E. E. *Theory of psychological measurement.* New York: McGraw-Hill, 1964.

Gilmer, B. v. H. Psychological aspects of women in industry. *Personnel Psychol.,* 1957, 10, 439–452.

Hunter, Thelma. Industrial courts and women's wages in Australia. *Economic Record,* 1962, 38, 438–447.

Jephcott, Pearl, et al. *Married women working.* London: G. Allen, 1962.

Kennedy, J. E. A general device versus more specific devices for selecting car salesmen. *J. appl. Psychol.,* 1958, 42, 206–209.

Maier, N. R. F. *The appraisal interview: Objectives, methods and skills.* New York: Wiley, 1958.

Manle, Frances. *Executive careers for women.* New York: Harper & Row, 1961.

Mead, Margaret, & Kaplan, Frances B. (Eds.) *American women: Report of President's Commission.* New York: Scribner's, 1965.

National Manpower Council. *Womanpower.* New York: Columbia, 1957.

Peterson, E. Are women taking men's jobs? *Personnel J.,* 1962, 41, 83–84.

Schein, E. H. How to break in the college graduate. *Harv. Bus. Rev.,* 1964, 42, 68–76.

Smith, L. J. *Career planning.* New York: Harper & Row, 1959.

Smuts, R. W. *Women and work in America.* New York: Columbia, 1959.

Steinberg, E. R. What about womanpower in the space age? *Space Dig.,* 1962, Aug. 56–58.

Winter, E. *A woman's guide to earning a good living.* New York: Simon and Schuster, 1961.

Zander, A., & Curtis, T. Effects of social power on aspiration level and striving. *J. abnorm. soc. Psychol.,* 1962, 64, 63–74.

CHAPTER 13

Ashby, W. R. *An introduction to cybernetics.* New York: Wiley, 1956.

Atkinson, J. W. Motivational determinants of risk-taking behavior. *Psychol. Rev.,* 1957, 64, 359–372.

Barnes, R. M. *Motion and time study.* New York: Wiley, 1958.

Blaire, R. N. A fresh look at the principles of motion economy. *J. Industr. Engng,* 1958, 9, 3–5.

Brower, E. J. Fatal accidents in the home. *Canad. J. Publ. Hlth,* 1956, 49, 6.

Dankert, C. E., et al. (Eds.) *Hours of work*. Englewood Cliffs, N.J.: Prentice-Hall, 1965.

Davids, A., & Mahoney, J. T. Personality dynamics and accident-proneness in an industrial setting. *J. appl. Psychol.,* 1957, 41, 303–306.

DeReamer, R. *Modern safety practices*. New York: Wiley, 1961.

Flanagan, J. C. The critical incident technique. *Psychol. Bull.,* 1954, 51, 327–358.

Floyd, W. F., & Welford, A. T. *Symposium on fatigue*. London: H. K. Lewis, 1953.

Ghiselli, E. E., & Brown, C. W. Learning and accident reduction. *J. appl. Psychol.,* 1947, 31, 580–582.

Griew, S. A study of accidents in relation to occupation and age. *Ergonomics,* 1958, 2, 17–23.

Haddon, W., et al. *Accident research: Approaches and methods*. New York: Harper & Row, 1964.

Heron, W. The pathology of boredom. *Scientific Amer.,* 1957, 196, 52.

Hersey, R. B. Emotional factors in accidents. *Personnel J.,* 1936, 15, 59–65.

Kephart, N. C., & Tiffin, J. Vision and accident experience. *Natl Safety News,* 1950, 62, 90–91.

McFarland, R. A., & Moore, R. C. Accidents and accident prevention. *Annu. Rev. Medicine,* 1962, 13, 371–388.

McGehee, W., & Owen, E. B. Authorized and unauthorized rest pauses in clerical work. *J. appl. Psychol.,* 1940, 24, 605–614.

National Safety Council. *Accident facts* (1965 ed.). Chicago: National Safety Council.

O'Connor, R. B. The impact of emotions on production and safety. *Menninger Quart.,* 1958, 12, 1–6.

Opsahl, R. L., & Dunnette, M. D. The role of financial compensation in industrial motivation. *Psychol. Bull.,* 1966, 66, 94–118.

Procter & Gamble Company. *Time bonus*. Cincinnati: Author, 1946.

Speroff, B., & Kerr, W. A. Steel mill "hot strip" accidents. *J. clin. Psychol.,* 1952, 9, 89–91.

Spragg, S. D. S., & Rock, M. L. Dial reading performance as a function of brightness. *J. appl. Psychol.,* 1952, 36, 128–137.

Vernon, H. M. Prevention of accidents. *Brit. J. industr. Med.,* 1945, 2, 3.

Whisler, T., & Harper, Shirley F. (Eds). *Performance appraisal: Research and practice*. New York: Holt, 1962.

Whitelaw, J. L. *Highway traffic safety*. East Lansing, Mich.: Reprinted from *U.S. Publ. Hlth Serv. Bull*. May, 1964, 1–103.

Wyatt, S., et al. *Incentives in repetitive work*. London: Industrial Health Research Board, No. 69, 1934.

CHAPTER 14

Bavelas, A. Some problems of organizational change. *J. soc. Issues,* 1948, 4, 48–52.

Berry, P. C. Effect of colored illumination upon perceived temperature. *J. appl. Psychol.*, 1961, 45, 248–250.

Broadbent, D. E., & Little, E. A. J. Effect of noise reduction in work situation. *Occup. Psychol.*, 1960, 34, 133–140.

Burnham, R. W. *Color: A guide to basic facts and concepts.* New York: Wiley, 1963.

Forehand, G. A., & Gilmer, B. v. H., Environmental variation in studies of organizational behavior. *Psychol. Bull.*, 1964, 62, 361–382.

Gellerman, S. W. *People, problems and profits.* New York: McGraw-Hill, 1960.

Gilmer, B. v. H., & Forehand, G. A. Recent research on organizational climate. *Training Directors J.*, 1964, 18, 2–8.

Glorig, A., et al. Hearing loss in industry. *Laryngoscope*, 1958, 68, 447–465.

Haire, M. Size, shape, and function in industrial organizations. *Hum. Organization*, 1955, 14, 17–22.

Judd, D. B., & Wyszecki, G. *Color in business, science, and industry.* New York: Wiley, 1963.

Kahn, R. L., & Katz, D. *Social psychology of organizations.* New York: Wiley, 1964.

Kerr, M. D. Effects of music on factory production. *Appl. Psychol. Monogr.*, 1945, No. 5.

Levinson, H. *Emotional health in the world of work.* New York: Harper & Row, 1964.

McGehee, W., & Gardner, J. E. Music in a complex industrial job. *Personnel Psychol.*, 1949, 2, 405–417.

McMurry, R. N. Recruitment, dependency, and morale in the banking industry. *Admin. Sci. Quart.*, 1958, 3, 87–117.

Mann, F., & Williams, L. Some effects of the changing work environment in the office. *J. soc. Issues*, 1962, 18, 90–101.

Marcus, S. New weapons against bigness. *Harv. Bus. Rev.*, 1965, 43, 100–108.

Meltzer, H. Mental health realities in work situations. *Amer. J. Orthopsychiat.*, 1963, 33, 562–565.

Porter, L. W. Where is the organization man? *Harv. Bus. Rev.*, 1963, 41, 53–61.

Presthus, R. *The organizational society.* New York: Knopf, 1962.

Sells, S. B. (Ed.) *Stimulus determinants of behavior.* New York: Ronald, 1963.

CHAPTER 15

Argyris, C. *Executive leadership: An appraisal of a manager in action.* New York: Harper & Row, 1953.

Davis, K. *Human relations in business.* New York: McGraw-Hill, 1957.

————. *Human relations at work* (2d ed.). New York: McGraw-Hill, 1962.

Dill, W. R., et al. *The new managers.* Englewood Cliffs, N.J.: Prentice-Hall, 1962.

Dyer, F. C. Myths about women bosses. *Supervision,* 1959, 21, 18–20.

File, Q. W., & Remmers, H. H. *How supervise?* New York: Psychological Corporation, 1948.

Flanagan, J. C. A new approach to evaluating personnel. *Personnel,* 1957, 34, 45–50.

Gardner, B. B. Executives: Their personality and its appraisal. *Advanc. Mgmt,* 1953, Jan., 13–15.

Ghiselli, E. E. Managerial talent. *Amer. Psychologist,* 1963, 18, 631–642.

Goetz, B. E. Avoiding managerial obsolescence. *California Mgmt. Rev.,* 1965, 7, 91–96.

Guest, R. H. *Organizational change: The effect of successful leadership.* Homewood, Ill.: Irwin, 1962.

Hawley, C. *Executive suite.* Boston: Houghton Mifflin, 1952.

Hersey, R. *Better foremanship.* Philadelphia: Chilton, 1955.

Hulin, C. L. The measurement of executive success. *J. appl. Psychol.,* 1962, 46, 303–306.

Jerdee, T. H. Supervisor perception of work group morale. *J. appl. Psychol.,* 1964, 48, 259–262.

Kay, B. R., & Palmer, S. *The challenge of supervision.* New York: McGraw-Hill, 1961.

Likert, R. *New patterns of management.* New York: McGraw-Hill, 1961.

Maier, N R. F. *Principles of human relations.* New York: Wiley, 1952.

Miles, M. B. Human relations training: Processes and outcomes. *J. counsel. Psychol.,* 1960, 7, 301–306.

Pfiffner, J. M. The effective supervisor: An organization research study. *Personnel,* 1955, 31, 530–540.

Schlender, W. E., et al. (Eds.) *Management in perspective.* Boston: Houghton Mifflin, 1965.

Scott, W. G. *Human relations in management.* Homewood, Ill.: Irwin, 1964.

Stryker, P. On the meaning of executive qualities. *Fortune,* 1958, 57, 116–119.

————. *The character of the executive: Eleven studies in managerial qualities.* New York: Harper & Row, 1961.

Tilles, S. The manager's job: A systems approach. *Harv. Bus. Rev.,* 1963, 41, 73–81.

Vroom, V. H. *Work and motivation.* New York: Wiley, 1964.

Whyte, W. F. *Human relations in the restaurant industry.* New York: McGraw-Hill, 1948.

Wilson, A. T. M. The manager and his world. *Industr. Mgmt Rev.,* 1961, 3, 1–26.

CHAPTER 16

Arensberg, C. M., & McGregor, D. Determination of morale in an industrial company. *Appl. Anthrop.,* 1942, 1, 12–34.

Bavelas, A. Communication patterns in task-oriented groups. *J. Acoust. Soc. Amer.,* 1950, 22, 725–750.

Berelson, B., & Steiner, G. A. *Human behavior: An inventory of scientific findings.* New York: Harcourt, Brace & World, 1964.

Blauner, R. *Alienation and freedom.* Chicago: University of Chicago Press, 1964.

Brayfield, A. H., & Crockett, W. H. Employee attitudes and employee performance. *Psychol. Bull.,* 1955, 52, 396–424.

Coch, L., & French, J. R. P., Jr. Overcoming resistance to change. *Hum. Relat.,* 1949, 1, 512–532.

Dalton, M. Worker response and social background. *J. political Econ.,* 1947, 55, 323–332.

Festinger, L. *A theory of cognitive dissonance.* New York: Harper & Row, 1957.

Friedlander, F. Job characteristics as satisfiers and dissatisfiers. *J. appl. Psychol.,* 1964, 48, 388–392.

Friedmann, G. *The anatomy of work.* New York: Free Press, 1961.

Guion, R. M. Industrial morale: The problem of terminology. *Personnel Psychol.,* 1958, 11, 59–61.

Habbe, S. Job attitudes of life insurance agents. *J. appl. Psychol.,* 1947, 31, 111–128.

Herzberg, F., et al. *Job attitudes: Review of research and opinion.* Pittsburgh, Pa.: Psychological Services of Pittsburgh, 1957.

Kornhauser, W. *Scientists in industry.* Berkeley, Calif.: University of California Press, 1962.

Leavitt, H. J. The effects of certain communication patterns on group performance. *J. abnorm. soc. Psychol.,* 1951, 46, 38–50.

Likert, R. *New patterns of management.* New York: McGraw-Hill, 1961.

Mann, F. C., and Hoffman, L. R. *Automation and the worker.* New York: Holt, 1960.

Mausner, B. Ethical problems in the development of a technology for changing attitudes. *Bull. int. Ass. appl. Psychol.,* 1966, 15, 76–84.

Morse, Nancy C. *Satisfactions in the white collar job.* Ann Arbor, Mich.: University of Michigan, Institute for Social Research, 1953.

Myers, M. S. Who are the motivated workers? *Harv. Bus. Rev.,* 1964, 42, 73–88.

Remitz, U. *Professional satisfaction among Swedish bank employees.* Copenhagen: Munksquard, 1960.

Turner, A. N., & Lawrence, P. R. *Industrial jobs and the worker.* Cambridge, Mass.: Harvard, 1965.

Uhrbrock, R. S. Music on the job: Its influence on worker morale and production. *J. appl. Psychol.,* 1961, 14, 9–38.

CHAPTER 17

Ash, P. (Chairman) Psychology in labor relations: A symposium. *Personnel Psychol.,* 1964, 17, 361–383.

Barbash, J. (Ed.) *Unions and union leadership.* New York: Harper & Row, 1960.

Becknell, J. C., Jr., & McIsaac, R. W. Test marketing cookware coated with "Teflon." *J. Adv. Res.,* 1963, 3, 1–8.

Bem, D. J. Inducing belief in false confessions. *J. Personality & soc. Psychol.,* 1966, 3, 707–710.

Bennett, E., et al. *Human factors in technology.* New York: McGraw-Hill, 1963.

Bliss, P. (Ed.) *Marketing and the behavioral sciences.* Boston: Allyn and Bacon, 1963.

Borko, H. (Ed.) *Computer applications in the behavioral sciences.* Englewood Cliffs, N.J.: Prentice-Hall, 1962.

Britt, S. H. The rules of evidence: An empirical study in psychology and law. *Cornell Law Quart.,* 1940, 25, 556–580.

Bruner, J. S. *On Knowing: Essays for the left hand.* Cambridge, Mass.: Harvard, 1962.

Chalupsky, A. B., & Nelsen, D. D. Programmed learning: Better than regular text books? *Personnel J.,* 1964, 43, 542–547.

Chapanis, A. Men, machines, and models. *Amer. Psychologist,* 1961, 16, 113–131.

Cherry, C. *On human communication:* New York: Wiley, 1957.

Cole, D. L. *The quest for industrial peace.* New York: McGraw-Hill, 1963.

Cozan, L. W. Type of mailing and effectiveness of direct-mail advertising. *J. appl. Psychol.,* 1960, 44, 175–176.

Cummings, T. F., et al. *The development and use of three self-teaching books.* Poughkeepsie, N.Y.: International Business Machines Corporation, 1962.

DeCecco, J. P. (Ed.) *Educational technology: Readings in programmed instruction.* New York: Holt, 1964.

Edelman, M. Concepts of power. *Labor Law J.,* 1958, Sept., 623–628.

Flagle, C. D., et al. *Operations research and systems engineering.* Baltimore: Johns Hopkins, 1960.

Flaherty, B. E. (Ed.) *Psychophysiological aspects of space flight.* New York: Columbia, 1961.

Fogel, L. J. *Biotechnology: Concepts and applications.* Englewood Cliffs, N.J.: Prentice-Hall, 1963.

Folley, J. D., Jr. (Ed.) *Human factors methods for systems design.* Pittsburgh, Pa.: American Institutes for Research, 1960.

Gilmer, B. v. H. The third crisis in industrial training. *Training Directors J.,* 1962, 16, 4–11.

Glaser, R. (Ed.) *Teaching machines and programmed learning.* Washington, D.C.: National Education Association, 1963.

Haire, M. Projective techniques in marketing research. *J. Marketing,* 1950, 14, 649–656.

Hathaway, S. R., & Meehl, P. E. *An atlas for the clinical use of the MMPI.* Minneapolis: University of Minnesota Press, 1951.

Hoffer, E. *The ordeal of change.* New York: Harper & Row, 1963.

Hughes, J. L. *Programmed learning: A critical evaluation.* Chicago: Educational Methods, Inc., 1964.

Husband, R. W. *The psychology of successful selling.* New York: Harper & Row, 1953.

Ivey, P. W. *Successful salesmanship.* Englewood Cliffs, N.J.: Prentice-Hall, 1947.

Jacobs, P. *The state of unions.* New York: Atheneum Publishers, 1963.

Judge, G. G., & Chuang, Y. H. The flow of feed grain changes. *Livestock Breeder J.,* 1962, Feb., 102–107.

Katona, G. *The powerful consumer.* New York: McGraw-Hill, 1960.

Keller, M., & Efron, C. The prevalence of alcoholism. *Quart. J. Stud. Alcohol.,* 1955, 16, 619–644.

Kornhauser, A. W., et al. *Industrial conflict.* New York: McGraw-Hill, 1954.

Lester, R. A. The changing nature of the union. *Mon. Labor Rev.,* 1960, Aug., 843–845.

Lippert, S. Designing for comfort in airport seats. *Aeronaut. Engng. Rev.,* 1950, 9, 39–41.

Lomov, B. F. Engineering psychology in the Soviet Union. (In English.) *Bull. Ass. int. psychol. appl.,* 1965, 14, 81–89.

Lumsdaine, A. A., & May, M. A. Mass communication and educational media. *Annu. Rev. Psychol.,* 1965, 16, 475–534.

McDermott, T. J. Use of fact-finding boards in labor disputes. *Labor Law J.,* 1960, Apr., 285–304.

McFarland, R. A. Human factors engineering. *ASSE J.,* 1964, 9–20.

Milton, A. W., & Briggs, G. E. Engineering psychology. *Annu. Rev. Psychol.,* 1960, 11, 71–98.

Miner, J. B. Personality and ability factors in sales performance. *J. appl. Psychol.,* 1962, 46, 6–13.

Peterson, Florence. *American labor unions: What they are and how they work.* New York: Harper & Row, 1964.

Porter, E. H. *The system thinkers: Parable and paradigm.* Santa Monica, Calif.: System Development Corporation, SP-285, 1961.

Reynolds, W. H. The role of the consumer in image building. *Calif. Mgmt Rev.,* 1965, 7, 69–76.

Rice, A. K. *The enterprise and its environment.* London: Tavistock Institute, 1963.

Rich, S. U. *Shopping behavior of department store customers.* Boston: Harvard Graduate School of Business Administration, 1963.

Science News Letter. Eye witnesses can get facts twisted. 1954, 66, 68.

Seidman, J., et al. *The worker views his union.* Chicago: University of Chicago Press, 1958.

Sells, S. B., & Berry, C. A. (Eds.) *Human factors in jet and space travel: A medical psychological analysis.* New York: Ronald, 1961.

Skinner, B. F. Teaching machines: *Science,* 1958, 128, 969–977.

Stagner, R. *The psychology of industrial conflict.* New York: Wiley, 1956.

Steiner, G. A. *The people look at T.V.* New York: Knopf, 1963.

Twedt, D. W. Consumer psychology. *Annu. Rev. Psychol.,* 1965, 16, 265–294.

Weiss, E. B. *The vanishing salesman.* New York: McGraw-Hill, 1962.

CHAPTER 18

Allport, G. W., & Postman, L. *The psychology of rumor.* New York: Holt, 1947.

Armstrong, H. G. (Ed.) *Aerospace medicine.* Baltimore: Williams & Wilkins, 1960.

Bray, C. W. *Psychology and military proficiency.* Princeton, N.J.: Princeton, 1948.

Carlson, E. R., & Abelson, H. I. *Factors affecting credibility in psychological warfare communications.* Washington: Human Resources Research Office, 1956.

Farber, I. E., Harlow, H. F., & West, L. J. Brainwashing, conditioning and DDD (debility, dependency and dread). *Sociometry,* 1957, 20, 271–285.

Janis, I. L. *Air war and emotional stress.* New York: McGraw-Hill, 1951.

Lazarsfeld, P. F. The American soldier—an expository review. *Public opin. Quari,* 1949, 13, 377–404.

Lifton, R. J. "Thought reform" of western civilians in Chinese communist prisons. *Psychiatry,* 1956, 19, 173–195.

McFarland, R. A., & Moore, R. C. The prevention of accidents in the armed services. *Military Med.,* 1963, 128, 1190–1195.

McGuire, W. J. Persistence of the resistance to persuasion induced by various types of prior belief defenses. *J. abnorm. soc. Psychol.,* 1962, 64, 241–248.

Melton, A. W. Military psychology in the United States of America. *Amer. Psychologist,* 1957, 12, 740–746.

OSS Assessment Staff. *The assessment of men.* New York: Rinehart, 1948.

Segal, J. Correlates of collaboration and resistance behavior among U.S. Army POW's in Korea. *J. soc. Issues,* 1957, 13, 31–40.

Smoke, K. L. An objective study of concept formation. *Psychol. Monogr.,* 1932, 42 No. 191.

Stouffer, S. A., et al. *The American soldier: Adjustment during army life.* Princeton, N.J.: Princeton, 1949.

Stressman, H. D., Thaler, Margaret B., & Schein, E. H. A prisoner of war syndrome: Apathy as a reaction to severe stress. *Amer. J. Psychiat.,* 1956, 112, 998–1003.

Tuddenham, R. D. Soldier intelligence in World Wars I and II. *Amer. Psychologist,* 1948, 3, 54–56.

Watson, G. (Ed.) *Civilian morale.* New York: Reynal & Hitchcock, 1942.

Glossary-Index

❖❖❖❖❖

Ability—*The power to perform a task successfully, such as giving a speech. It differs from "aptitude" or "capacity" in that it refers to what an individual does do rather than what he might do if given the correct training:*
general, 131
and occupational choice, 175
special, 132
Absenteeism, men and women, 22
Accident(s), causes of, 311–313
and coordination, 317
definition of, 310
and fatigue, 316
future research into, 318
human factors in, 312–314
personal factors and, 315–318
and personality, 317
reduction of, 314–315
report of, 313
results of, 310
and risk taking, 315
and vision, 317
and work, 309–311
Acquisition in work, 294
Adjustment—*Attempting to satisfy needs by overcoming both inner and outer obstacles. Fitting oneself to circumstances, such as student getting along with the group in which he finds himself. The process of trying to bring about a balance between needs, stimuli, and opportunities offered by the environment:*
failures of, 231–233
and space travel, 422
stages of, 237
in working women, 23

Adolescence, anger in, 151
cliques in, 155–157
conformity in, 153
emotional control in, 152
fear in, 149
groups in, 155
interests in, 157–159
maturity in, 147
pleasant emotions in, 152
problems in, 146
social perception in, 154
worry in, 149
Advertising, 392
perceptual factors in, 61–63
spot, 62
Age, and creativity, 185
and performance, 183
and women workers, 23
Aggression—*A response to frustration by attacking the source of the frustration or some substitute:*
displaced, 31
elementary, 30
organized, 31
Aging, compensation in, 186
differences in, 184–185
Air circulation and work, 324
Ambition, differences in, 21
Ambivalence—*Behaving in opposite ways, as in both loving and hating the same person, or both liking and disliking a job.*
Ambivalent personality, 331–332
Amnesia—*Loss of memory, especially of personal experiences,* 87
Anger, adolescent, 151
in children, 125
Anxiety—*The emotion of dread or uneasiness. A feeling that some-*

459

Pseudophone—*A headset in which sounds from the left side enter the right ear and vice versa. Used in experiments on perception to reverse the reception of sound by the two ears:*
original study of, 52
Psychological climate (*see* Climate)
Psychological distance—*The closeness of feelings and understanding between people. Great distance means failure to understand the other person and his problems,* 4
Psychological fatigue—*Tiredness resulting from frustration and conflict rather than from physical effort,* 296
Psychological group, 193
Psychological warfare, 436–439
Psychology, applied, definition of, 4
clinical, 406
and common sense, 10–11
engineering, 395–398
in law, 410–415
in medicine, 406–410
Psychomotor abilities—*Abilities which require good perception, muscular coordination, and dexterity,* 423–424
Psychosis—*A serious mental disorder, commonly requiring hospitalization,* 235–236
Public health, psychologists in, 407
Public relations, 394
Punishment in learning, 80
Purchase behavior, 394

Quackery, 9

Rank and tension, 409
Rapport—*The feeling of mutual understanding between people:*
in counseling, 250
Rationalization—*The process of justifying one's conduct or opinions by inventing socially acceptable reasons; a wishful-thinking defensive reaction:*
example of, 33
in propaganda, 438

Reaction formation—*Doing or saying the opposite of what one really feels. Sometimes we are unaware of the behavior,* 37
Reading, fixation pauses in, 108
speed of, 108–109
in study, 108–109
tests of, 242–243
Recall, and overlearning, 86
and recognition, 90
Recitation in learning, 101
Recognition, feelings of, 38
and recall, 90
Recruit, military, 429
Recruiting interview, 281
Recruitment, employee, 257–258
Reinforcement—*Strengthening. Satisfaction of a drive by reward, e.g., getting a good grade for efficient study:*
in brainwashing, 435
and habit, 69
lack of, 68
in learning, 67–69
in programmed learning, 403–404
Reinforcers, negative, 404
positive, 404
Remembering, details, 89
and learning, 82
unfinished tasks, 88
Repression—*An inhibition of the recall of some event because of its unpleasantness or shamefulness,* 87
Resistance to change, 376
Responsibility, lines of, 326
and stress, 237
and tension, 409
Rest pauses, 297–299
Retention—*The probability of future recall or recognition of a past event, literally "remembering":*
measuring, 90–91
and overlearning, 85–86
and sleep, 83
tests of, 84
Retina—*The layer of nerve cells of the eye which contains rods and cones for night and day vision,* 45
Retirement, criteria for, 187
and personality, 189–190